Sam
We hope you enjoy
this book and please
don't forget us when you
are famous.
love
Nicky & Steve
xo

Making a Masterpiece

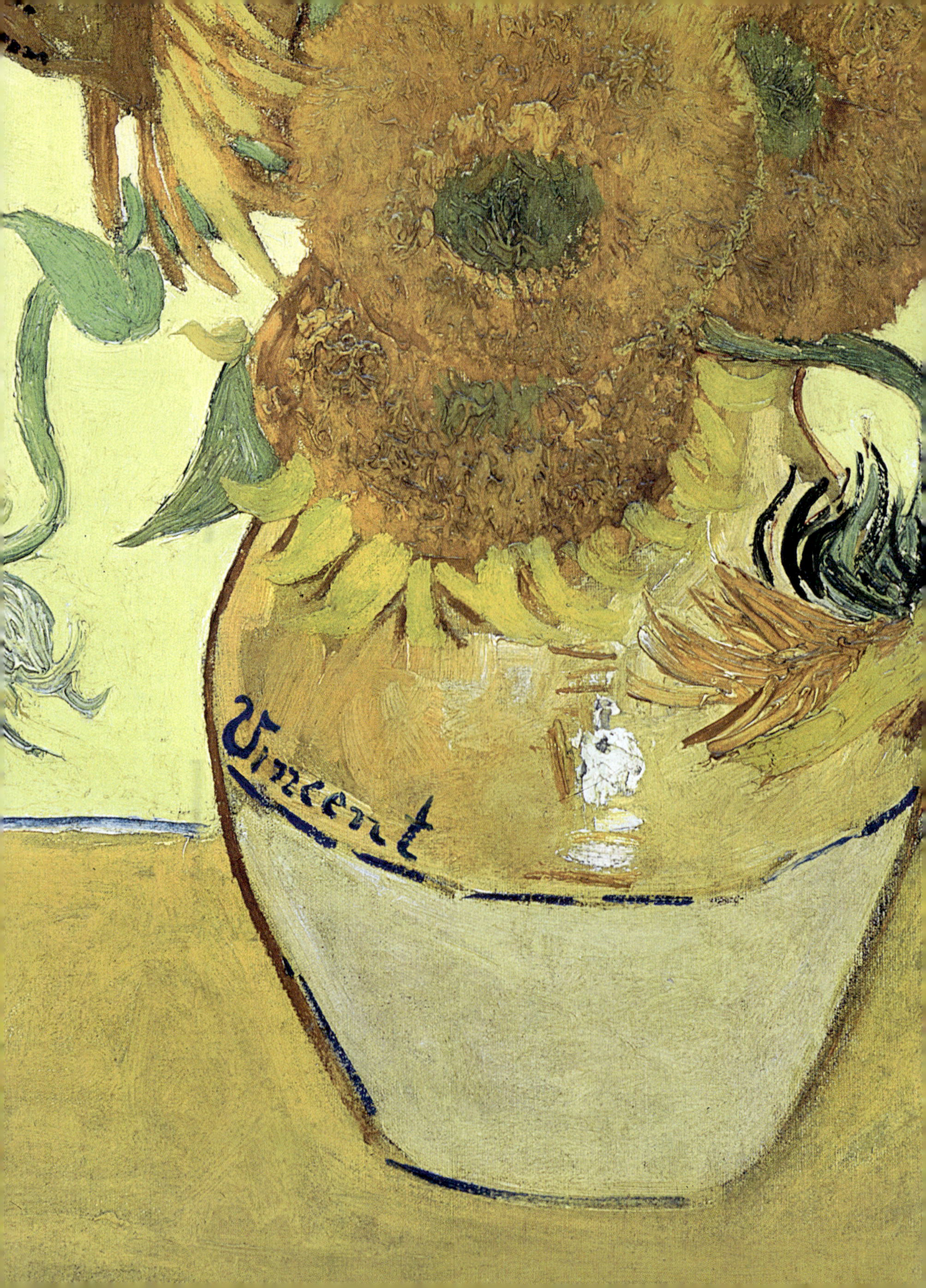
Vincent

MAKING A MASTERPIECE

The stories behind iconic artworks

Debra N. Mancoff

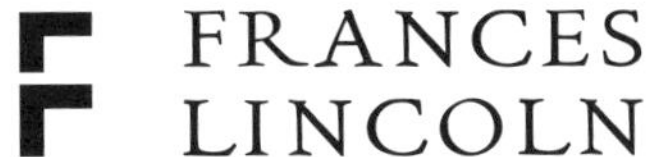

FRANCES LINCOLN

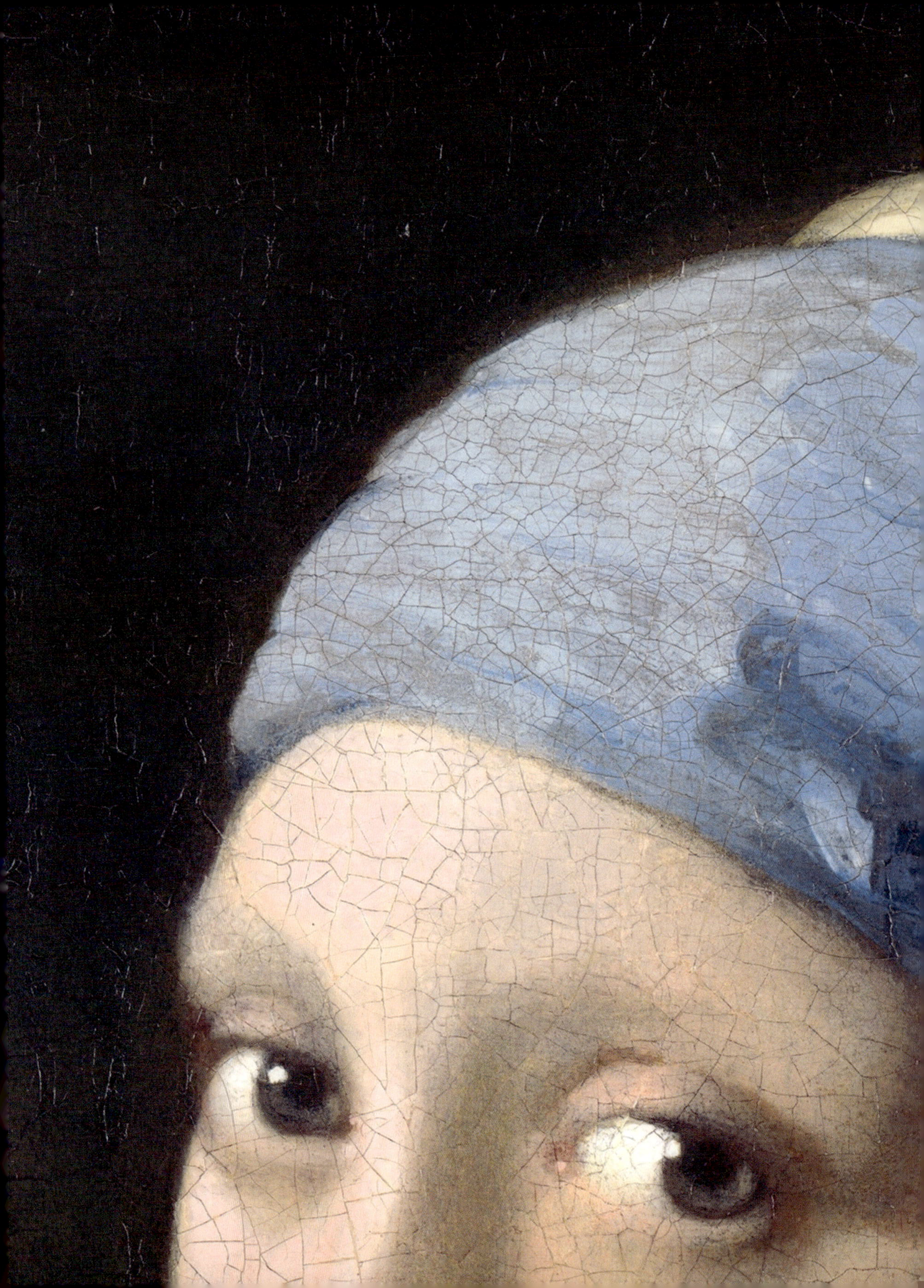

Contents

Introduction

What makes a masterpiece?

What makes a work of art a masterpiece? The label is a mark of prestige, asserting that the work is the finest of its kind. As a material object, a masterpiece is seen to embody the spirit of an era and to exemplify the unique vision of an individual artist. It is also assumed to possess an intrinsic excellence that transcends time as well as national and cultural boundaries. A masterpiece wields an iconic authority; even if we have not seen the work, it lives in our visual imagination through reproduction, influence and imitation. To call a work a masterpiece is to declare that it manifests a universal and enduring power, and we accept this judgement, often without questioning the time, the taste and the circumstances that led to such high regard. But our admiration of a work's greatness gives us no insight as to why it is considered great. Every work of art has a story, and the stories of the most renowned masterpieces reveal that making a masterpiece often involves much more than a demonstration of consummate artistic skill.

The use of the word 'masterpiece' to indicate a standard of achievement has origins in the artisanal guild system of late medieval Europe. In those days, rather than marking a superlative achievement – the best of its kind – the production of a masterpiece proved that an aspiring craftsman had attained the body of knowledge and the necessary skills to present himself as a qualified practitioner in his chosen field. If members of the guild judged that the work demonstrated the requisite proficiency, the craftsman – almost invariably a man – would be awarded the status of master craftsman, and he would secure the right to open his own workshop, hire and train apprentices and to become a member of the guild. By the end of the fifteenth century, as the categories of fine art – painting, architecture, sculpture – began to be regarded as separate and superior to categories of craft – building, metalwork, textiles – the word 'master' acquired the gloss of virtuosity. Within two centuries, art academies replaced the guilds as the preferred training ground for painters and sculptors, and although the practice of producing a work that marked the transition from trainee to professional endured, the work itself was more commonly called a 'diploma' or 'reception piece'. And, as the arts rose in cultural value, the term 'masterpiece' came to define the highest possible standard of achievement: a designation of rare excellence above and beyond fundamental mastery.

As a term with a long history, the concept of a masterpiece also carries the burden of problematic presumptions. The exclusivity at its core is at odds with today's pluralistic art world. We no longer believe that works of art should conform to a singular standard or that they embody some inscrutable quality or intrinsic value that is timeless and universal in their appeal. We now celebrate how artists express the human experience in diverse ways, and we seek to broaden the ideas that inform the interpretation and evaluation of works of art. The word 'masterpiece' contains troubling associations. It is an inherently gendered term inferring an established hierarchy, and it stirs up references to dominance and control: master and servant, or, even more unsettling, master and slave. And yet, the word still has relevance, for when a particular work of art is described as a masterpiece, it draws the public's attention. We want to observe and experience for ourselves those qualities that make it great.

How then to reconcile our contemporary questioning of the concept of a masterpiece with our fascination with works of art that seem to have timeless and worldwide appeal? The pages that follow offer a fresh approach to the understanding and appreciation of a selection of some of the most admired works of art through their origin stories – stories that revisit the circumstances of creation and the rise of reputation. The featured works are all familiar; they enjoy wide popularity and critical acclaim. They each represent a turning point in the artist's creative development and have come to be instantly recognized as his or her signature work. But these works also share a more intriguing common thread: their path to fame is only fully disclosed by looking beyond what the eye can see. Using primary documents to probe into each picture's past we can uncover the rich and often unexpected story behind their iconic imagery. Theft, scandal, legal disputes, politics and even defiance of the art world's conventions have all played a part in shaping the perception of works that we now regard to be masterpieces. Rather than trying to discern and describe the elements of greatness, *Making a Masterpiece* takes account of the circumstances outside the frame that contribute to the perception of greatness and reveals that the journey from the easel to popular acclaim can be as compelling as the masterpiece itself.

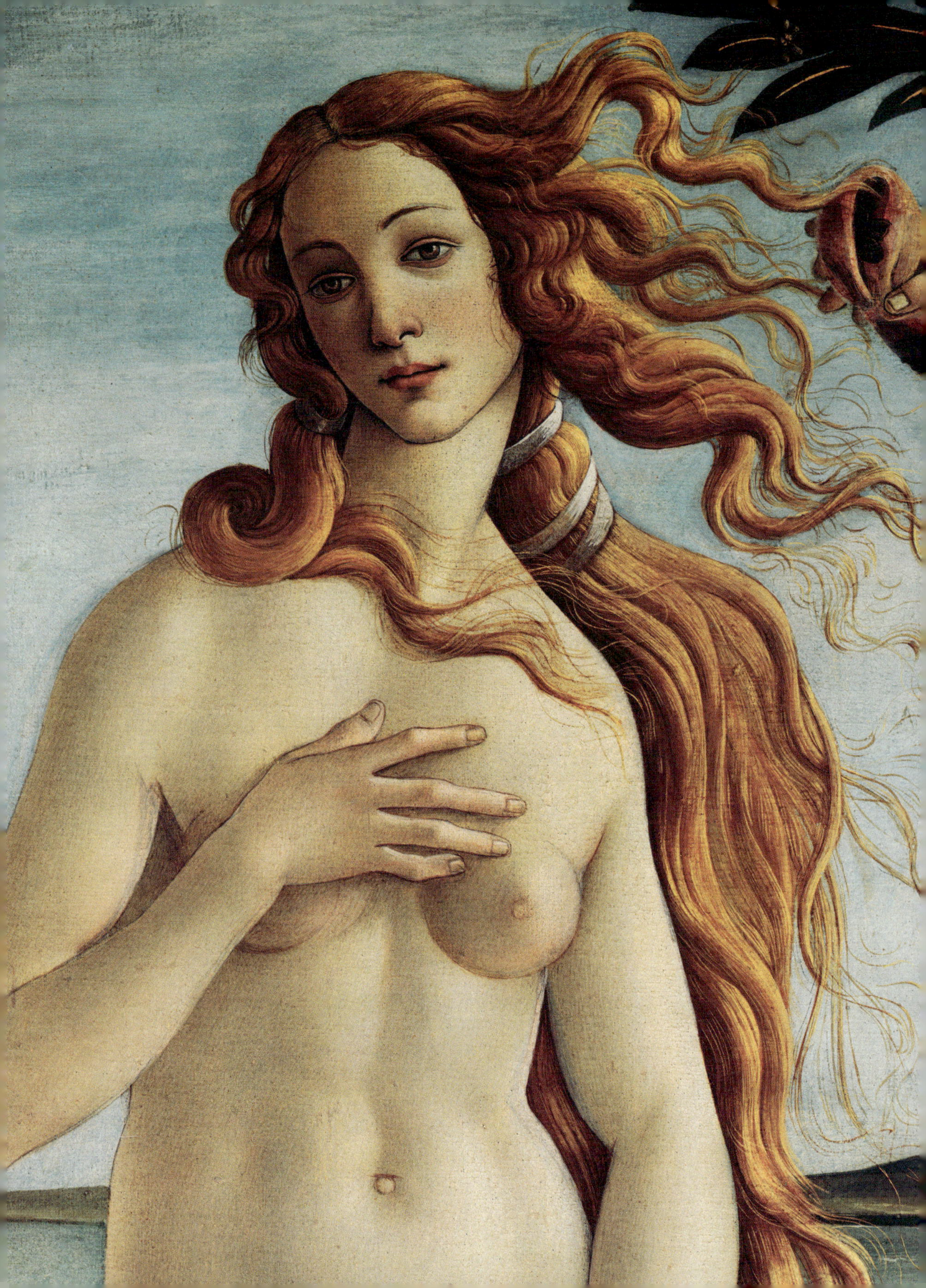

Birth of Venus
Sandro Botticelli

And borne there in gently pleasant movements,
A girl of divine face,
Shore-ward driven by unbound winds,
Drifting upon a shell, delighting the very heavens

Agnolo Poliziano, *Stanze per la Giostra*, 1475–78

On 1 January 1930, a memorable exhibition opened to London audiences at Burlington House. Organized by the Italian government, Italian Art 1200–1900 offered an unprecedented view of the nation's treasures, including paintings, sculptures and jewellery, as proof of its enduring leadership in European culture. More than a desire to celebrate Italy's rich artistic heritage, the enterprise was rooted in pride and conceived as propaganda to promote the public profile of the dictator Benito Mussolini as a man of refinement and taste. The location played a role in advancing Italy's imperial ambitions for, as the head curator Ettore Modigliani explained, it was the intent of 'il Duce' to mount an exhibition 'worthy of Fascist Italy in the capital of the British Empire'.[1] No matter the motivation, the critically acclaimed exhibition attracted more than half a million visitors before it closed on 22 March. Among the works that captivated the casual viewer and critic alike was one that had never been seen outside of Tuscany: *Birth of Venus* by Sandro Botticelli.

It is possible that more people saw *Birth of Venus* during its brief stay in London than over the previous four and half centuries. Seventy years passed between the presumed date of creation and the first known written record of the work, but its subject, style and subsequent history of ownership places it at the height of Botticelli's career. Newly returned from a prestigious commission in the Sistine Chapel in Rome, Botticelli enjoyed the patronage of the Medici family, the leading and most generous art patrons in Florence. During the middle years of the 1480s, Botticelli's work reflected the innovative philosophy of an intellectual circle also under Medici auspice. These were private pictures, endowed with esoteric meaning intended for an exclusive audience. Even after the work went on public display in the early nineteenth century it drew only limited attention. But with its debut in London, *Birth of Venus* captured the public's imagination and, as a result, it is now one of the most recognized and relatable paintings in the history of Western art. Looking back at its surprising journey from an elite viewership to almost universal popularity offers insight into what made the work a masterpiece.

According to the 'Theogony', the poet Hesiod's genealogy of the Greek pantheon (c. 700 BCE), an act of violence incarnated the goddess of love. Seeking vengeance for his mother and power for himself, Kronos (Saturn) castrated his father Ouranos (Uranus) and flung the severed genitals into the sea. A woman then rose amid the foaming waves – 'an awesome, beautiful divinity' – and she gently drifted to the isle of Cythera (Cyprus), where she reigned over 'lovers' smiles … And all the gentle pleasures of sex.'[2] Hesiod's evocation of a comely woman emerging from the waves and drifting to the shore is the oldest known source for the motif *Venus Anadyomene* or 'Venus Rising from the Sea', and this basic framework of the tale was retold and embellished over the centuries.

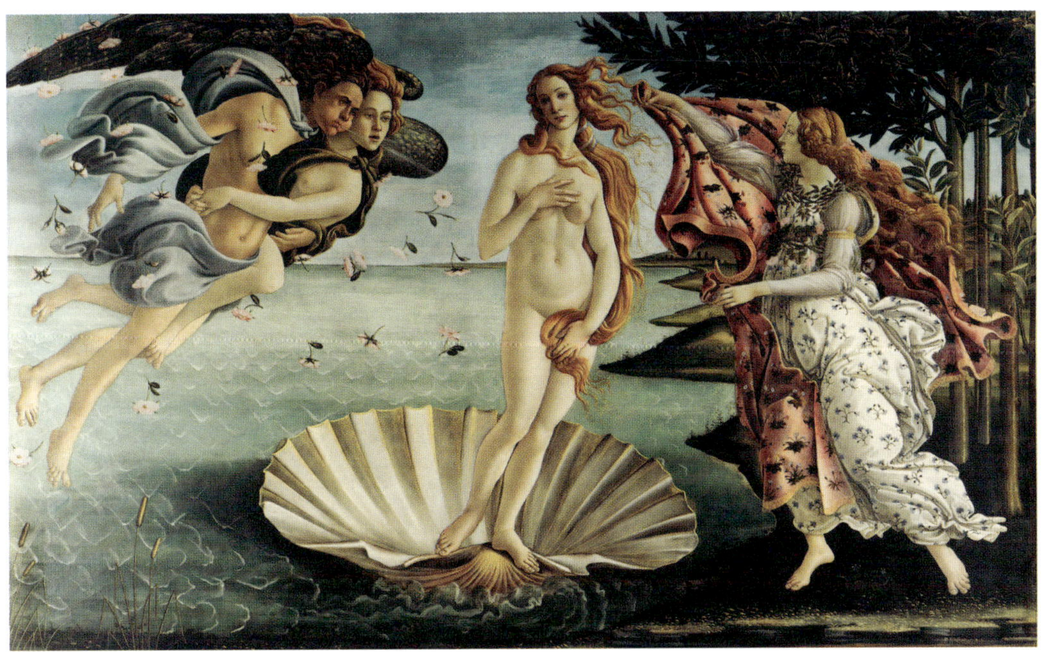

Birth of Venus c. 1485
Sandro Botticelli (1445–1510)
Tempera on canvas
172.5 x 278.5 cm (68 x 110 in)
Gallerie degli Uffizi, Florence

Botticelli most likely drew upon a contemporary source, the *Stanze per la Giostra*, written by Agnolo Poliziano to honour Giuliano de' Medici's triumph in a tournament held in Florence in 1475. The grandson of Cosimo de' Medici, founder of the banking dynasty that became the de facto ruling family of the Florentine Republic, Giuliano was known for his good looks, his sporting prowess and his infatuation with Simonetta Vespucci, a beautiful woman married to a member of the Medici court. Poliziano, a poet and humanist scholar, enjoyed the patronage of Guiliano's brother Lorenzo, who was celebrated as 'Il Magnifico' for his open-handed support of philosophy, the arts and classical studies. *La Giostra* drew upon classical sources to transfigure the love between 'Julio' and Simonetta as an embodiment of the humanist ideal of beauty that spanned the gulf between ancient

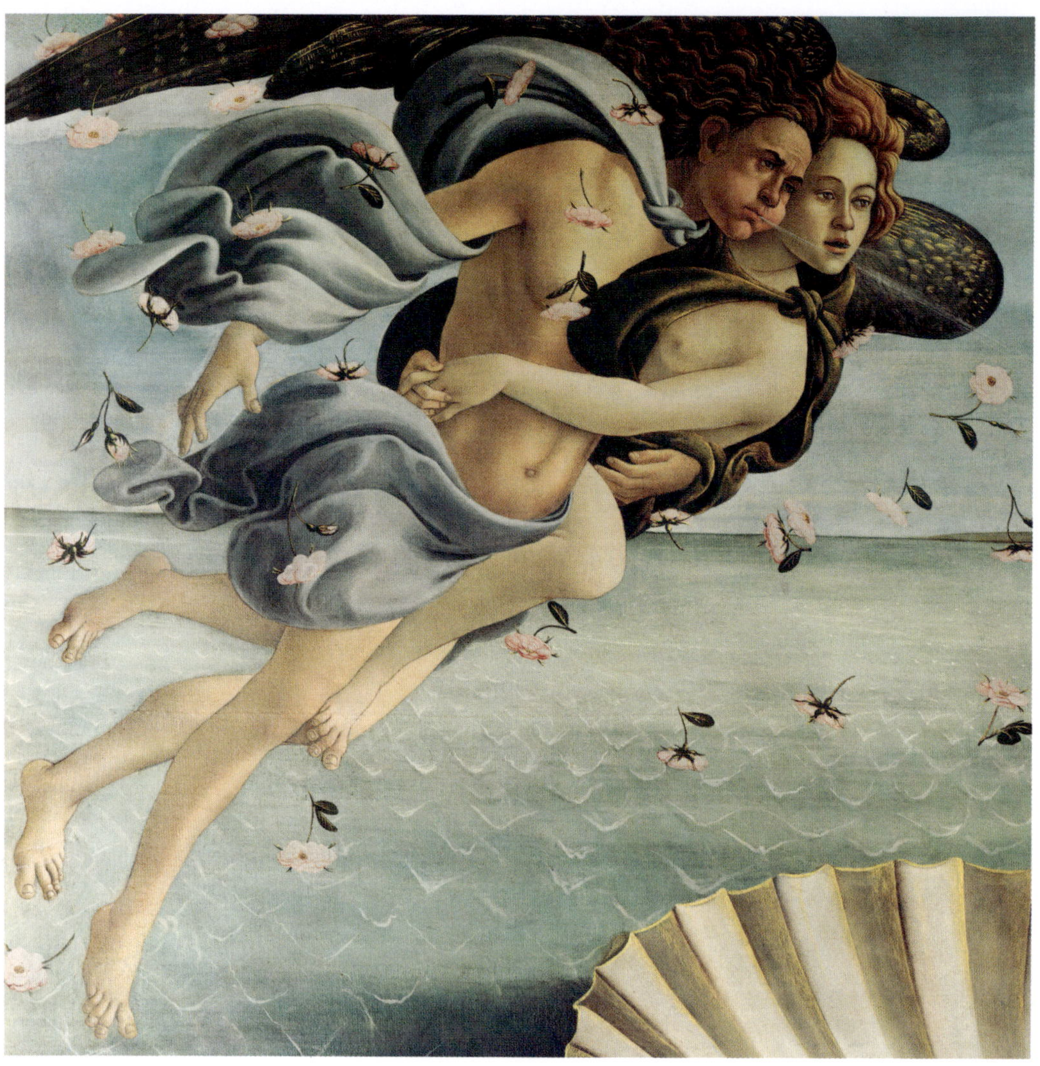

Birth of Venus, detail

ABOVE Botticelli's sinuous technique evokes a sense of movement throughout his composition. A taut line emphasizes Zephyrus's lithe, arcing body, lifted upwards by swirling draperies and his beating wings. Botticelli even paints the wind that streams from his mouth in fine, glinting lines.

OPPOSITE Spring symbols greet Venus as she arrives in Cythera. The delicate blooms on the Hora's gown, as well as the cornflowers on the robe she holds, proclaim seasonal regeneration. Tiny golden buds sparkle on the branches of the orange trees in the dense grove behind her. As the goddess of fertility, Venus will coax the buds into flower as spring transforms into summer.

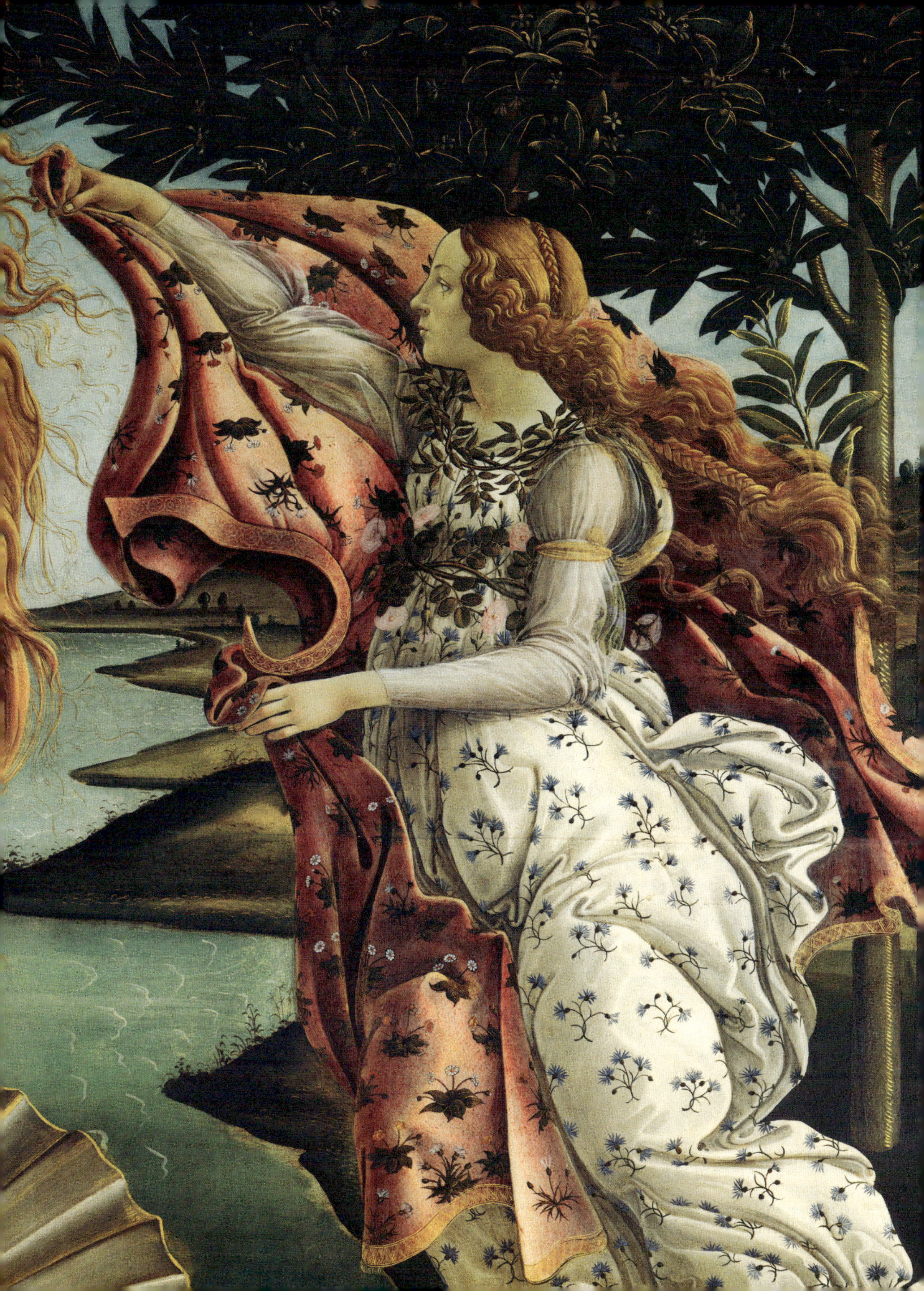

and modern times. The poem offers a graceful retelling of *Venus Anadyomene*, describing how the newly born goddess, 'A girl of divine face', was 'driven by the unbound winds' to drift shoreward on a shell 'delighting the very heavens'.[3] Botticelli also contributed to the tournament's festivities; for his first Medici commission, he painted a standard that served as the champion's prize. Although long lost, it is believed that the standard featured a portrait of Simonetta.

Painted a decade after the tournament, Botticelli's *Birth of Venus* combines the enduring myth, details of Poliziano's narrative and the painter's own pictorial invention. The figures on the left embody the 'unbound winds'. Rising on mighty wings, Zephyrus, the West Wind, hovers above the waves; the nymph Chloris clings to his side. Their breath – rendered in diaphanous streams of silvery white – stirs up ripples in the water and spreads roses through the air. The figure on the right catches the breeze in a billowing pink robe adorned with cornflowers. Her own white gown is spangled with spring flowers, and she represents the three Horae (Hours), the goddesses of the seasons who welcomed Venus to her new domain. The Hora's collar of myrtle and the branches of rose leaf twined around her waist signify that she is Venus's handmaid; myrtle was a long-standing symbol of love, and tradition held that the first rosebush bloomed when Venus arrived in Cythera. The grove of orange trees behind her echoes the theme of spring; they are just about to bud. As well as love, Venus embodies fertility, and her presence quickens the regeneration of spring into the abundance of summer. There is a single, subtle reference to the goddess's grisly origin. Bulrushes rise out of the waters in the lower left corner; they were commonly known as *fusto* (stem) *genitale*.

At the centre of the composition, Venus stands on an enormous scallop shell in a pose that seems to reflect Poliziano's poetic vision: 'Clutching her tresses with her right hand/her left conceals her lovely breasts.'[4] Rather than just following Poliziano's description, it is likely that both the poet and the painter adopted the sculptural motif of the *Venus pudica* (modest Venus), in which the goddess covers her nudity with a graceful arcing gesture of her arms. The stance derives from a cult statue of Aphrodite (Venus) created for the Temple of Knidos by the famed Greek sculptor Praxiteles in the early fourth century BCE. Long lost, but known through Roman replicas, it portrays Venus reaching for a towel with her right hand and covering her genitals with her left as she prepares for a ritual bath. The double-armed gesture is a variant and may depict the goddess's initial modesty as she rose out of the sea. Although the Medici family owned a version of the statue

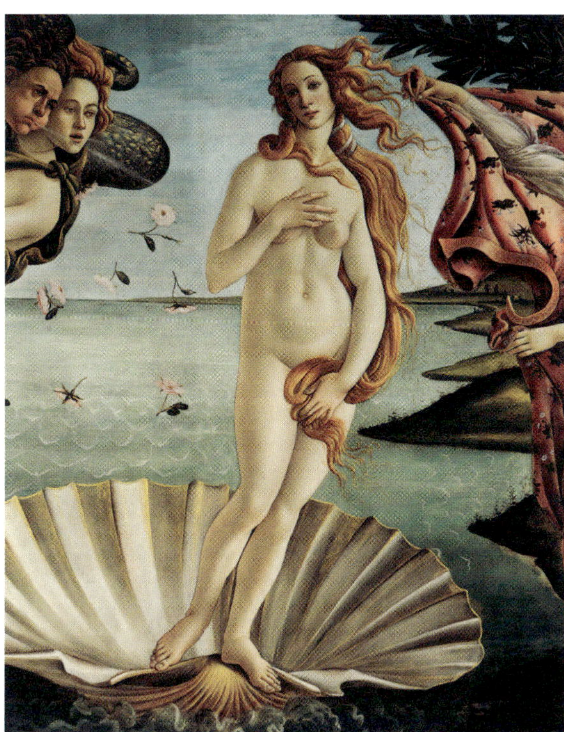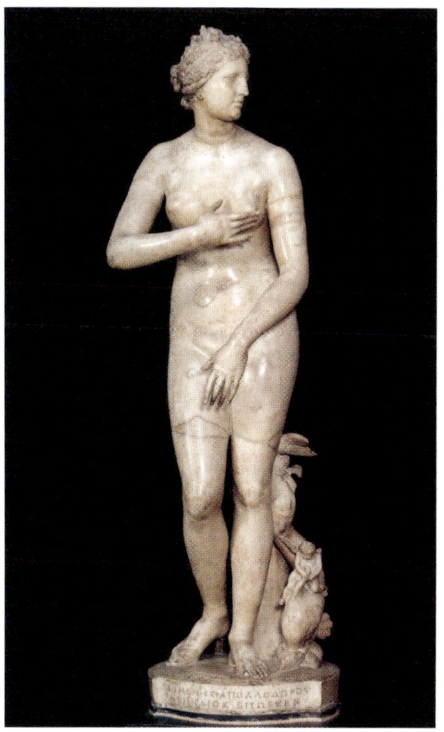

ABOVE LEFT *Birth of Venus*, detail
ABOVE RIGHT *Medici Venus* c. late 2nd and early 1st century BCE
Parian marble
153 cm (60 in)
Tribuna, Gallerie degli Uffizi, Florence

The presence of a dolphin on the base links this statue of Venus with the myth of her origins. It is uncertain if Botticelli saw this particular work – the earliest documentation is in a 1638 inventory of the Villa Medici in Rome – but the motif of *Venus Pudica* was well known. Botticelli subtly revised the stance to turn the goddess's face to the viewer and loosened her hair to be blown in the winds.

OVERLEAF *Primavera* c. 1480
Tempera on wood panel
207 x 319 cm (81½ x 125½ in)
Gallerie degli Uffizi, Florence

Arrayed in a white gown with a scarlet mantel, Venus reigns in Cythera. To her left, Zephyrus's warming breath transforms Chloris into Flora, the goddess of spring. At her right, the Three Graces dance while Mercury dispels a threatening cloud with his caduceus. Cupid hovers above her. The subject links *Primavera* to *Birth of Venus*, but it is painted on panel rather than canvas, revealing that they were not made as a pair.

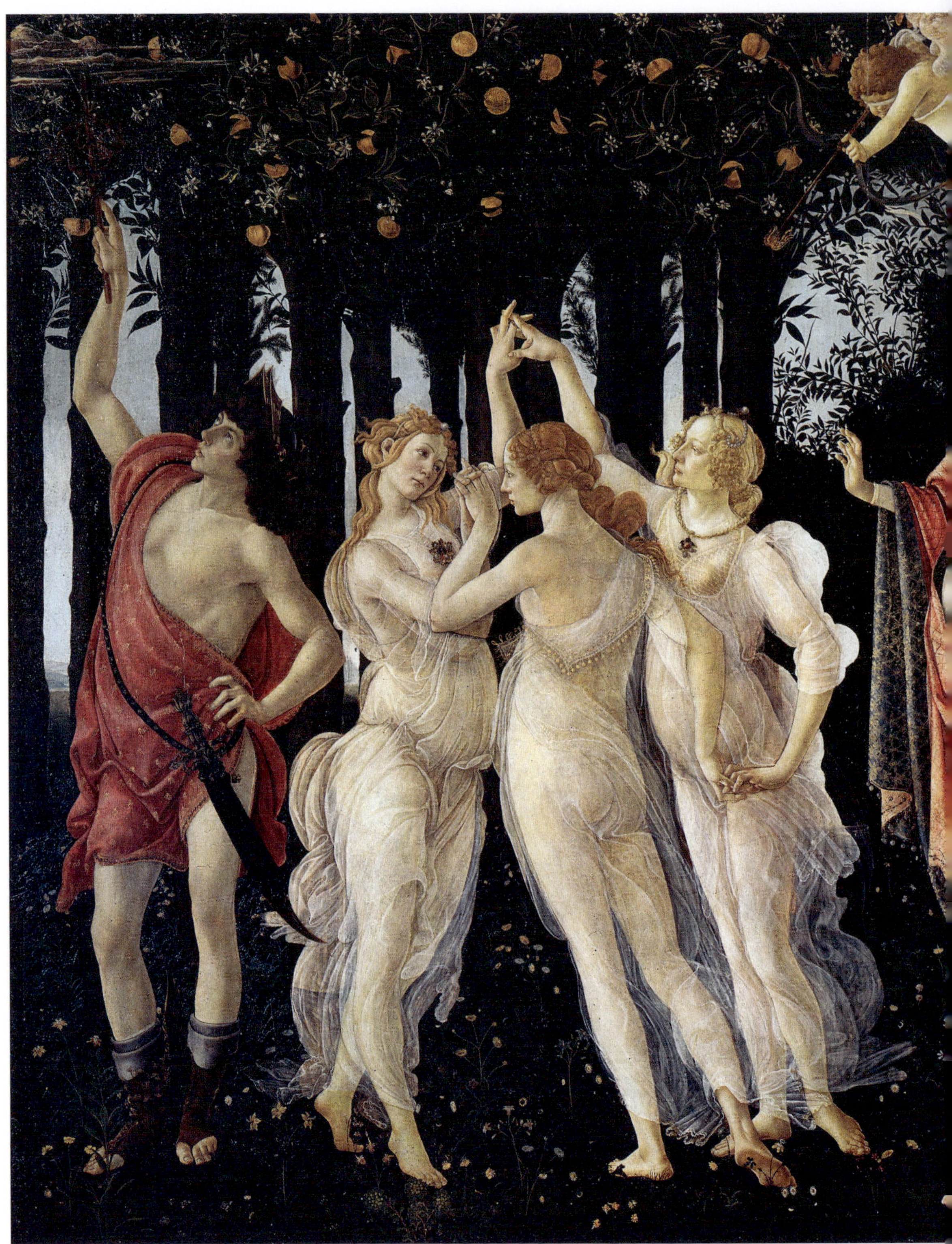

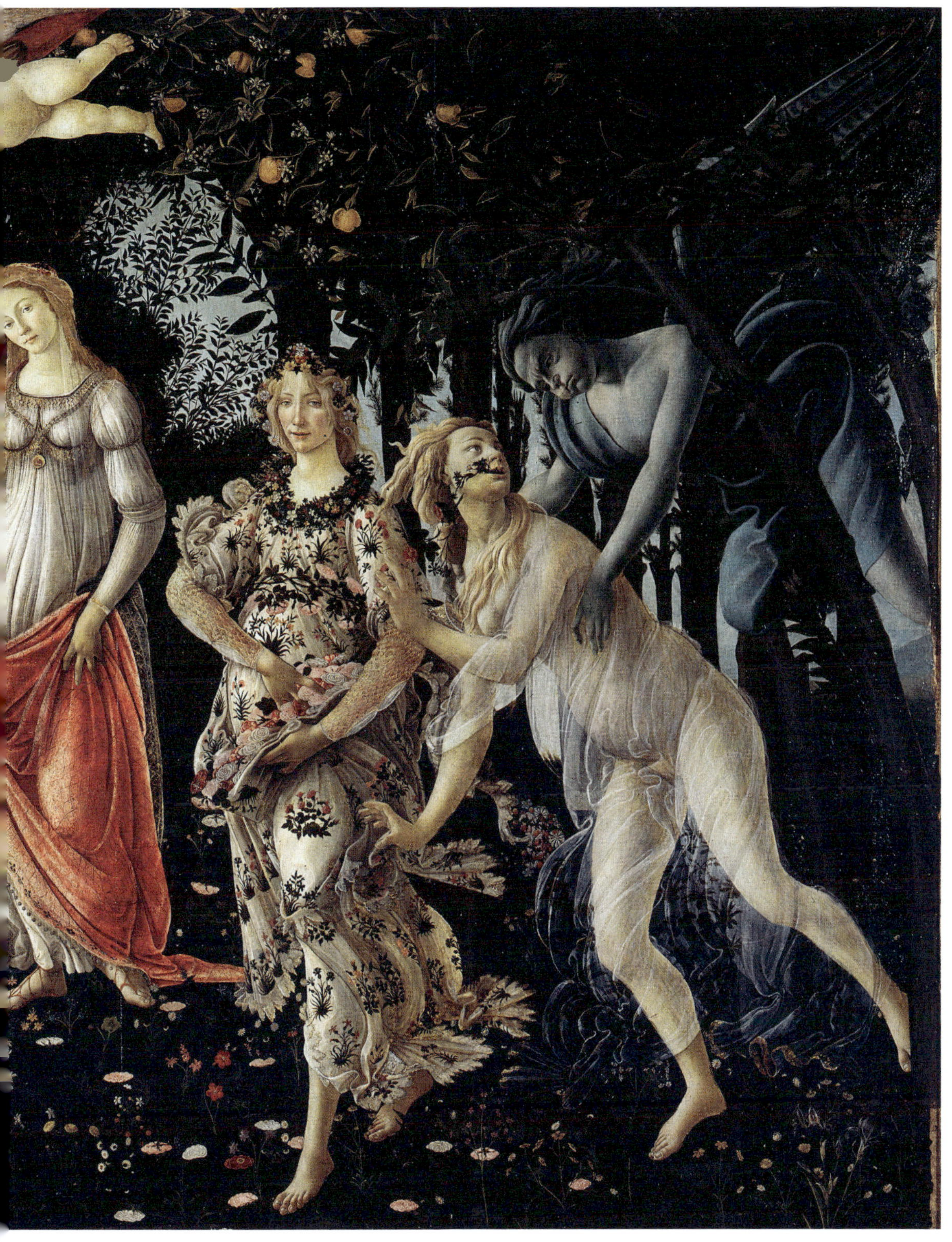

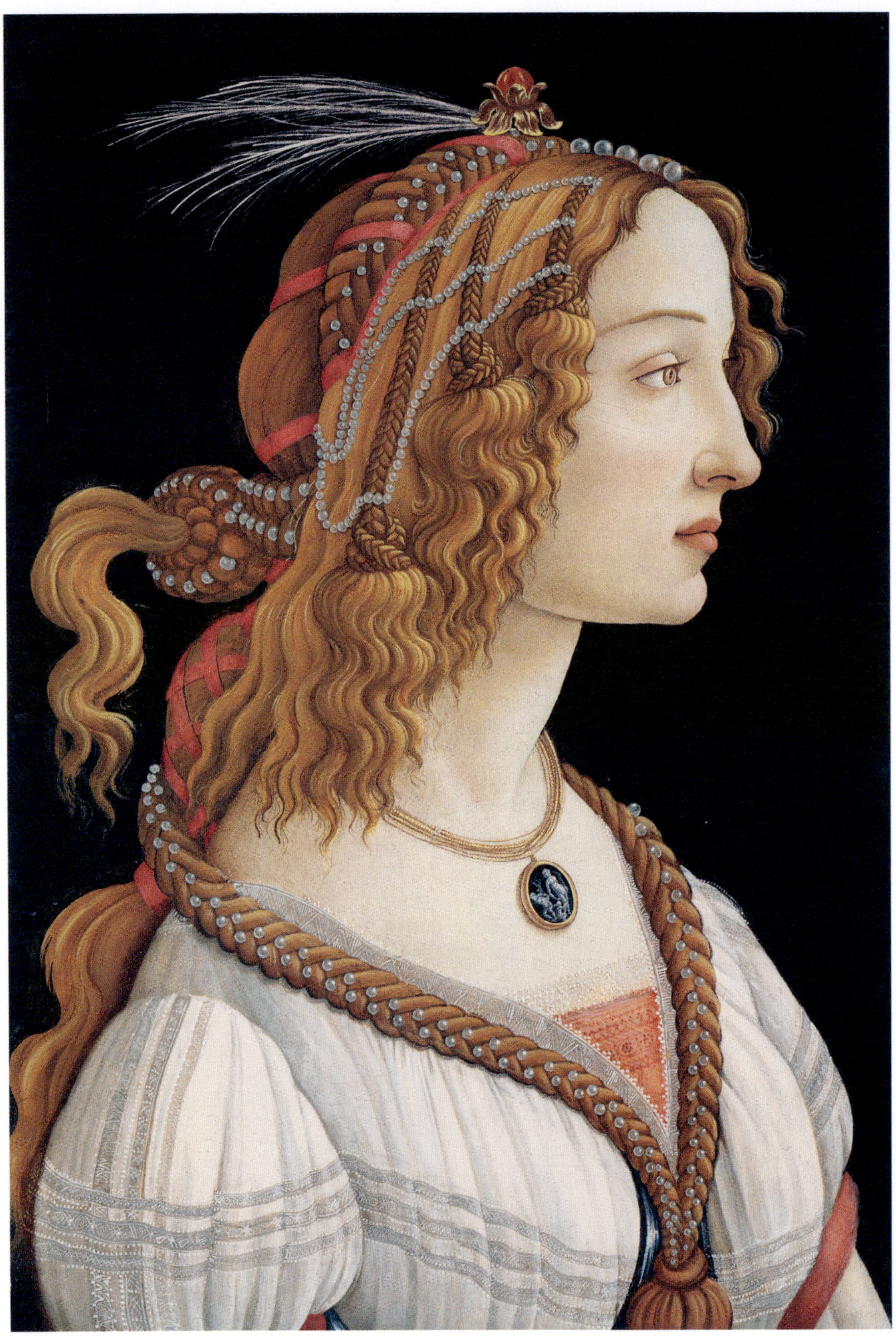

in the variant pose, the date they acquired it is not known. Whether based on an actual sculpture or a description of the motif, Poliziano and Botticelli would have been aware of the pose and its meanings.

In both stance and proportion, Botticelli followed the classical prototype of the *Venus Pudica*. The figure is long-limbed, high-waisted and athletic. With a slight bend of the right knee, the weight of the figure shifts – lowering the left shoulder and lifting the left hip – in a posture known as *contrapposto*, conceived to simulate natural movement. The placement of the figure's right hand only partially covers her breasts in an ambiguous gesture that reveals as much as it conceals. Botticelli's inventive interpretation, as well as a nod to Poliziano's poem, may be seen in the way the figure uses her left hand to cover herself with a lock of her own golden hair. Classical Venus figures have their hair bound, but this goddess's thick blonde waves are loose, blown free from white bindings by the same winds that convey her to the shore. Here, the painter reflects the taste of his own times. Blonde hair was fashionable in Florence, and the goddess's hair, as well as her facial features, resembles the tumbling blonde tresses that Botticelli depicted in two idealized female portraits painted just a few years earlier. These have long been regarded as a tribute to Simonetta Vespucci – she died in 1476 at the age of twenty-two – connecting *Birth of Venus* not only with a contemporary concept of beauty, but with the Medici family. A further link can be seen in the grove of orange trees; when the flowers turn to fruit, the colour and shape resemble golden balls, the Medici family emblem.

The earliest known record of Medici ownership of *Birth of Venus* appears in the first edition of Giorgio Vasari's *The Lives of the Most Excellent Painters, Sculptors, and Architects* (c. 1550). In his biography

Ideal Portrait of a Lady (Simonetta Vespucci) c. 1475–80
Tempera on poplar
82 x 54 cm (32 x 21 in)
Städel Museum, Frankfurt am Main

Fair, blonde and even-featured, Simonetta Vespucci (1453–76) embodied the type of beauty most admired in Quattrocento Florence. It is believed that Botticelli painted her once during her brief life for the lost champion's standard awarded to Giuliano de' Medici in a tournament held in 1475. Her comely image inspired several idealized portraits, as well as Botticelli's vision of Venus.

of Botticelli, Vasari recalls a visit to the Castello di Medici in the Tuscan hills, where he noted a representation of 'the birth of Venus, with those Winds and Zephyrs that bring her to earth'. He also described another depiction of the goddess of love – easily identified as *Primavera* – 'whom the Graces are covering with flowers'.[5] But fifty years earlier, according to a 1499 inventory discovered in 1975, *Primavera* was in the family's city palace, installed in the anteroom of Lorenzo di Pierfrancesco de' Medici's bedchamber. Born into a junior branch of the family, Lorenzo di Pierfrancesco was orphaned at thirteen and became the ward of Lorenzo Il Magnifico. To tutor his young cousin, Il Magnifico turned to the circle of humanist scholars under his aegis, including the poet Poliziano, the scribe and translator Giorgio Antonio Vespucci and the philosopher Marsilio Ficino. It is highly possible that *Primavera* was commissioned by the Medici family to celebrate the young man's marriage in July 1482. That year also marked the height of Botticelli's prestige; he was one of a select group of Florentine artists called to Rome by Pope Sixtus IV to paint frescos on the walls of the newly built Sistine Chapel. It is thought that he painted *Primavera*, as well as several other mythological subjects, for the Medici family upon his return.

Similar in size and subject matter, it was long assumed that *Birth of Venus* and *Primavera* were made as a pair. But *Birth of Venus* is not mentioned in the 1499 inventory, and there is no record of the painting's whereabouts until Vasari mentioned it in *The Lives*. And although the subjects appear to tell a sequential tale – Venus rising from the sea to reign in Cythera – a material difference sets them apart. *Primavera* was painted on a wooden panel, while *Birth of Venus* was painted on linen canvas. Lightweight yet durable, canvas was a relatively new mode of support, and at the time it was more commonly used for such informal settings as country villas. It is therefore likely that *Birth of Venus* was never intended for the city palace and might even have been commissioned for the family's hillside retreat. Without documentation, the details of the commission remain conjecture, but the visual evidence forges an indisputable bond between the two depictions of Venus. Sharing the same elegant proportions, fluid grace and serene charm, the image of Venus is conceived not just as an incarnation of physical beauty, but as an embodiment of the humanist ideal in which the body gives form to the virtue of the heart, the soul and the mind.

Over the centuries after Vasari's visit, Botticelli's fame diminished and the Medici fortunes waned; the last remaining heir, Anna Maria Luisa de' Medici, bequeathed the family's art collection to the city

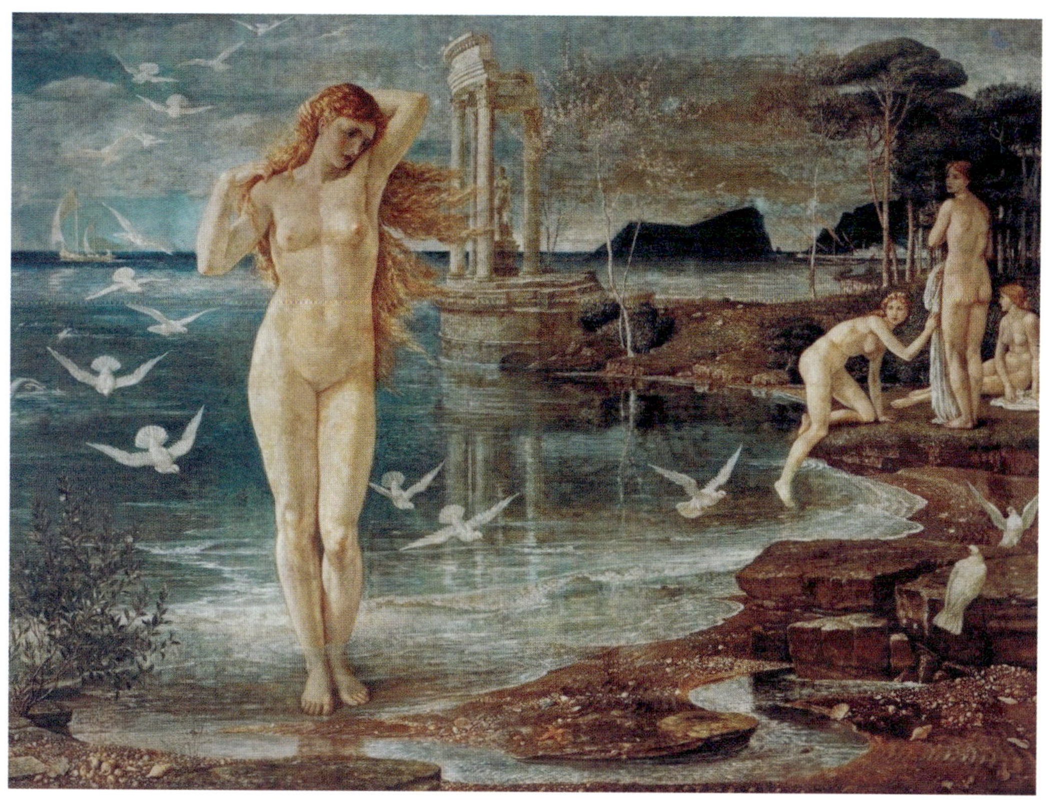

The Renaissance of Venus 1877
Walter Crane (1845–1915)
Oil and tempera on canvas
138.5 x 184 cm (54½ x 72½ in)
Tate Britain, London

The slow revival of Botticelli's reputation in the late nineteenth century introduced the subject of *Venus Anadyomene* into European artists' repertoire. Walter Crane visited Florence during an extended honeymoon (1871–72) and the charm of *Birth of Venus* made a lasting impression. His own version reflects Botticelli's influence.

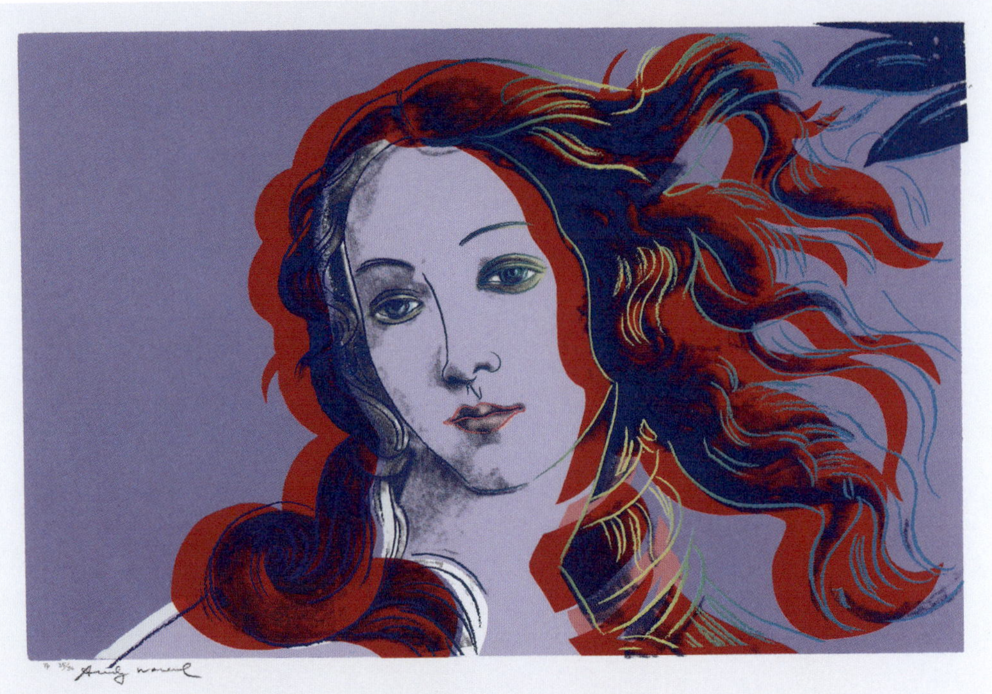

ABOVE *Details of Renaissance Paintings (Sandro Botticelli, Birth of Venus, 1482) 1984*
Andy Warhol (1928–87)
Acrylic and silkscreen ink on linen
122 x 182 cm (48 x 71½ in)
The Andy Warhol Museum, Pittsburgh

With her familiar features and wind-whipped hair, the face of Botticelli's goddess
is as instantly recognizable as that of any contemporary celebrity. Andy Warhol
gave her image his trademark treatment, using vivid, vibrating colours and
reductive stylization. His approach underscores the iconic power of Botticelli's
image in the late twentieth century.

OPPOSITE *Hilton Head Island, S.C., USA, 24 June 1992* from Beach Portraits 1992–96
Rineke Dijkstra (born 1959)
Chromogenic print
167 x 140 cm (65¾ x 55 in)
Art Institute of Chicago

In the 1990s, Rineke Dijkstra photographed adolescent bathers on various
beaches in the United States and Western and Eastern Europe. Formally, her
comparative series resemble classical portraits – figures posed frontally isolated
against minimal backgrounds. In her portraits, Dijkstra looks for glimpses of
individuality between equal types by capturing a subtle gesture or expression.
The portraits document people in a transition phase; her photos are always
between one moment and the next. A few portraits bear a striking resemblance
to the stance of Botticelli's Venus. However, these poses arose unconsciously.

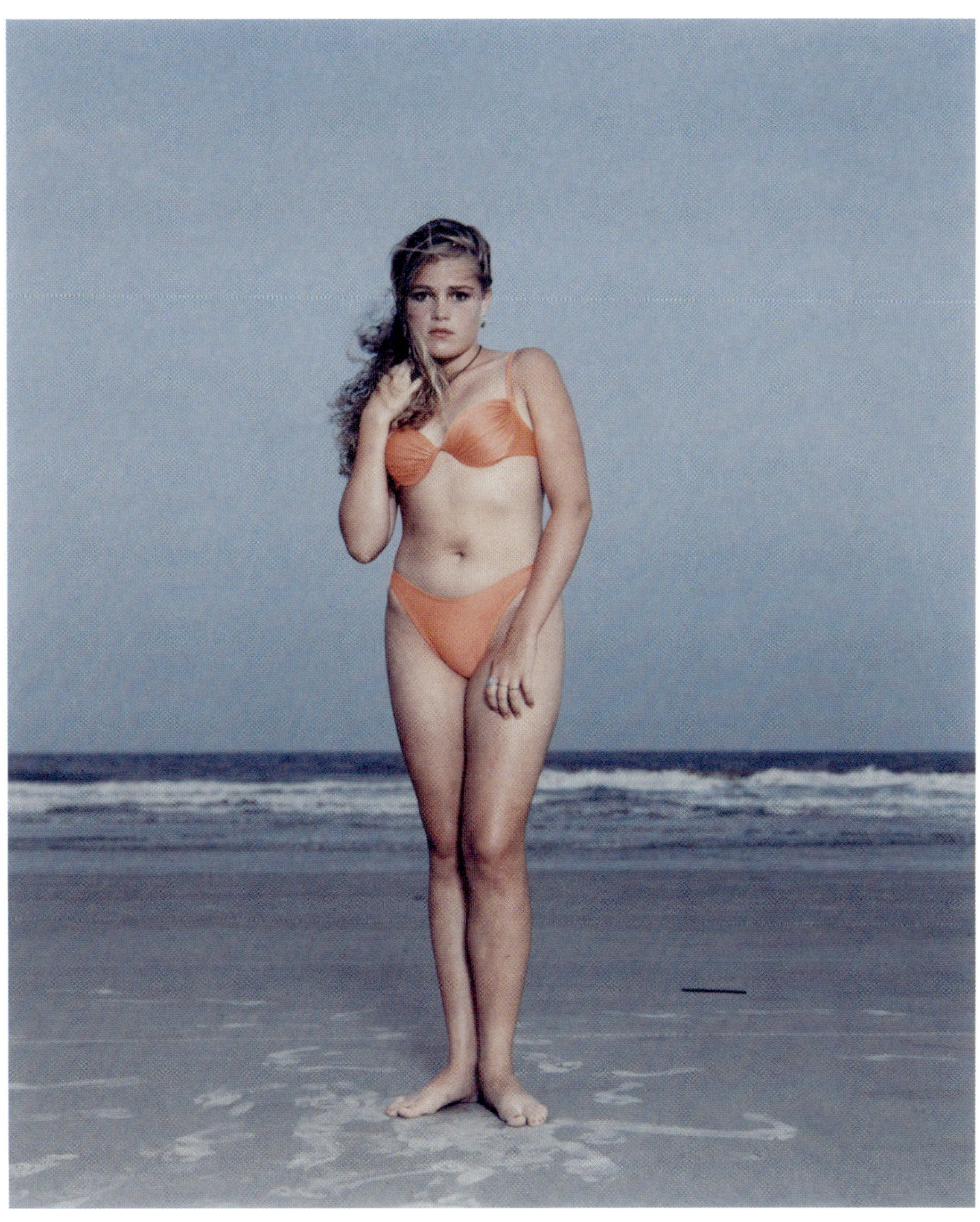

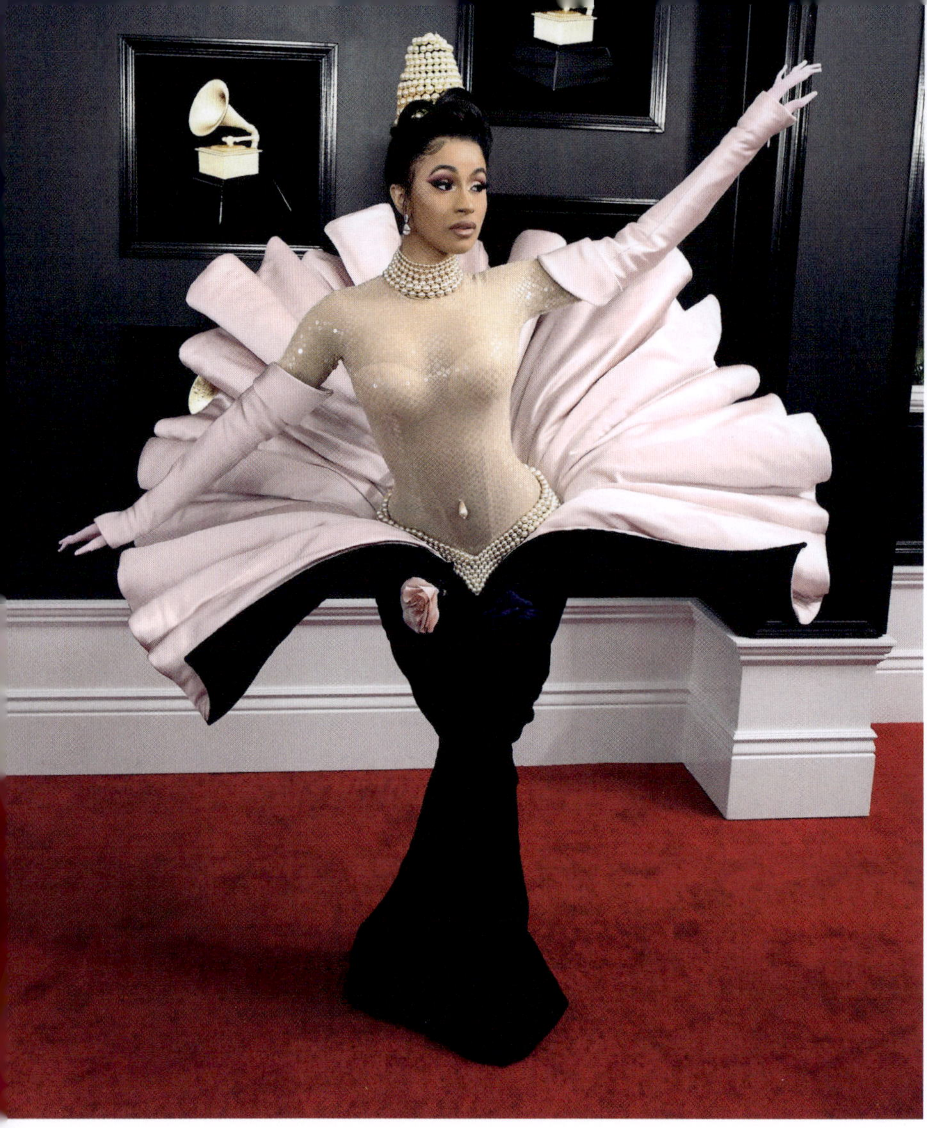

Venus Dress Spring/Summer 1995
Thierry Mugler (1948–2022)

Botticelli's paintings of women in diaphanous, flower-strewn gowns have inspired fashion designers from Elsa Schiaparelli to Alexander McQueen. Few have been as explicit as Mugler in his 1995 Venus dress: a transparent corsetry bodysuit springing out of a black velvet fishtail skirt that opens around the hips in a pink, satin-lined shell. Twenty-five years later, musical artist Cardi B revived the dress in a sensational appearance on the red carpet at the 2019 Grammy Awards.

upon her death in 1743. In 1815, *Birth of Venus* appeared on public view in the Gallerie degli Uffizi, but went unnoticed for decades. The location might have been a problem. In 1862, writer Léon Lagrange lamented that 'the Florentines themselves have abandoned Botticelli in a corridor'.[6] By this time, a few influential writers began to take an interest in the artist and his elegant rendering of the female figure. On their Italian travels in 1855–56, Edmond de Goncourt and his brother Jules praised the statuesque, blonde Venus as a vision from the legend of Faust, presiding over the Walpurgis night ritual. Walter Pater, in his influential book *Studies in the History of the Renaissance* (1873), deemed the painting 'quaint' but proposed that it presented 'a more direct inlet into the Greek temper than the words of the Greeks themselves'.[7] The composition, as well as the figure, became known through copies made by such artists as Gustave Moreau and Edgar Degas, as well as the rising popularity of reproductions. But as the image circulated without its complex context of Medici connections and humanist ideas, its message diminished into a singular but seductive symbol: the timeless ideal of white, European beauty.

The resounding success of the art treasures displayed at Burlington House prompted the Italian government to organize similar loan exhibitions, including L'Art Italien (1935) at the Petit Palais in Paris and Italian Masters (1939–40), a multivenue tour of the United States. Botticelli's *Birth of Venus* featured as the centrepiece of each exhibition and was hailed as an example of beauty that spanned the centuries. And although the painting and its history – and perhaps even its subject – were unfamiliar to most of the public and many of the critics, it presented an immediate point of recognition in the tall, blonde, beautiful woman at the centre of the composition who possessed the same physical qualities as popular actresses of stage and screen and willowy models featured in fashion magazines. The Second World War put an end to the art tours, but the image of Botticelli's Venus had made an indelible impression. Over the decades the format of the painting has been reprised as a showcase for female beauty in fine art, film and fashion, from a popular confirmation of the conventional European ideal as seen in such vignettes as the bikini-clad actress Ursula Andress striding out of the sea in the James Bond film, *Dr. No* (1962), to the appropriation and revision of the motif to celebrate non-white, non-Western and non-binary beauty. And knowingly or not, each iteration – whether tribute, critique or spoof – extends Botticelli's masterful fusion of the antique and the modern to promote contemporary ideas in the guise of eternal truth.

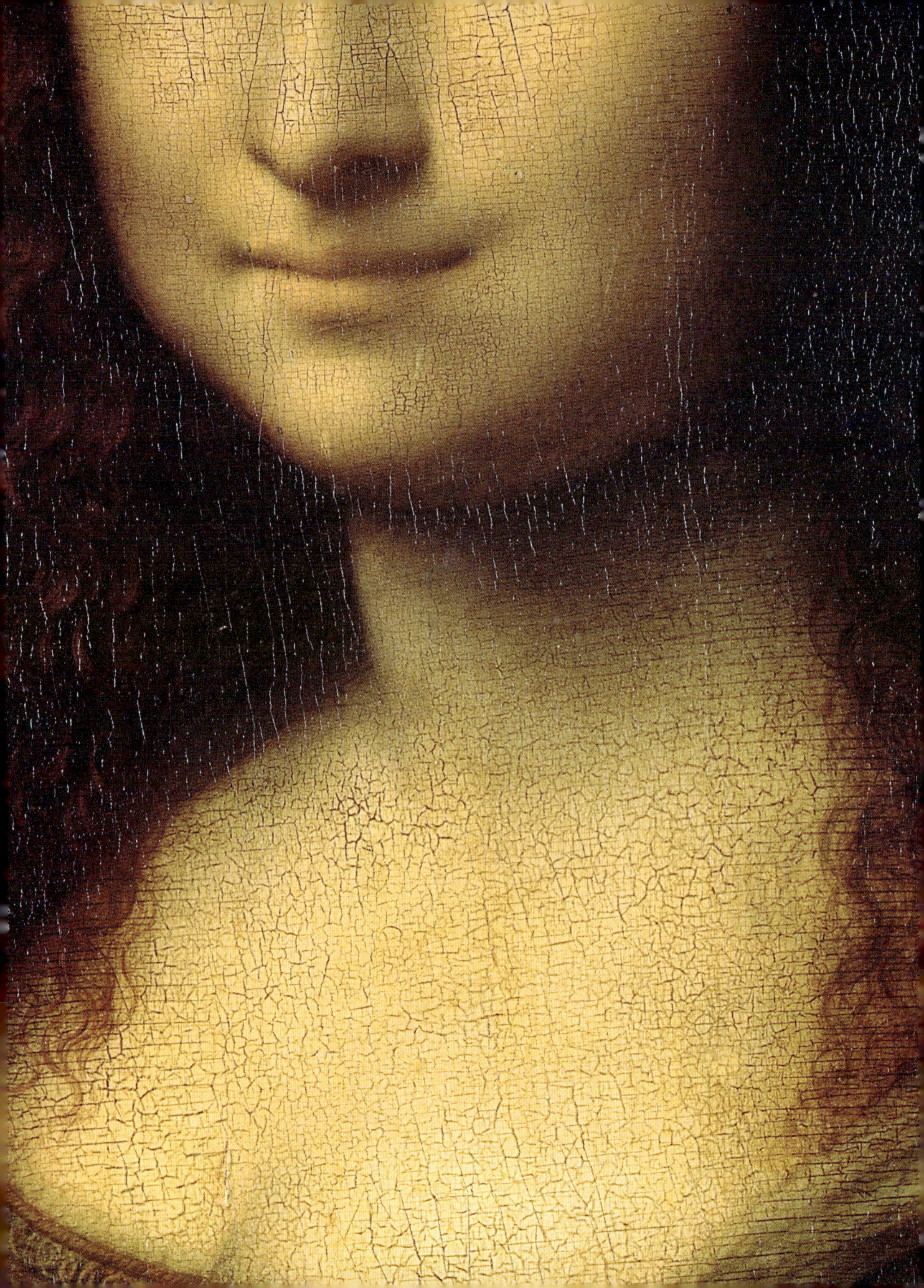

Mona Lisa

Leonardo da Vinci

Whenever I pass into the cool galleries of the Palace of the Louvre, and stand before that strange figure … I murmur to myself 'She is older than the rocks among which she sits'.

Oscar Wilde, 'The Critic as Artist' (1890)

In his account of Leonardo da Vinci's life, Giorgio Vasari declares that 'whoever wished to see how closely art could imitate nature' should study the artist's portrait of a woman named Mona Lisa. He marvels at Leonardo's ability to credibly reproduce the inherent vitality of her facial features: the eyes with a lifelike 'watery sheen' surrounded by delicate skin painted in tints of rose and pearl; eyelashes and eyebrows that appear to 'spring from the flesh'; 'a smile so pleasing, that it was a thing more divine than human to behold'.[1] Vasari claims that, to coax that smile from his sitter, Leonardo employed jesters and musicians to amuse her. And he identifies her as the wife of Francesco del Giocondo, who, he says commissioned the portrait while Leonardo lived in Florence. Vasari further explains that, after four years' work, Leonardo left the portrait unfinished, and it currently resides in Fontainbleau in the possession of the king of France. What Vasari does not reveal is that he had not seen the painting. He wrote his *Lives of the Artists* around 1550; thirty-five years earlier, Leonardo had left Italy and had taken the painting with him.

It is hardly hyperbole to state that Leonardo da Vinci's *Mona Lisa* is the world's most famous painting. In recent years, as many as 30,000 people a day have passed through the Salle des États in the Musée du Louvre, with the sole intention of doing what Vasari could not: actually look at the small, dark painting, now enclosed in a box-like frame and covered with a sheet of bullet-proof glass. Unlike Oscar Wilde, who recorded his reflections nearly a century and a half ago, present-day visitors are deprived of calm contemplation. Kept at a distance of at least 4 m (12 ft), the crowds jostle as they hold their cameras aloft to capture an image to prove that they saw it. And yet, their experience shares an important element with that of Wilde in the way it is shaped by those who had seen the painting before them.[2] From the earliest known admirers, who likely saw it in Leonardo's studio, to the contemporary viewers, who flock to the Louvre for a personal glimpse, no matter how brief, this portrait of a pleasant-looking Florentine matron has unquestionably captivated the public, raising the question as to whether the excellence of the painting itself or centuries of praise and speculation makes it a masterpiece.

Whether viewed in the gallery or seen in a high-resolution reproduction, it is hard to fully experience Vasari's rich description of the *Mona Lisa*. Over the centuries the pigments have darkened into a brownish monochrome and the thick layers of varnish have yellowed, dulling the action of light on the surface and blurring the details. But close inspection – both visual and scientific – affirms Vasari's assessment of Leonardo's mastery of his medium, in a work that would 'make every valiant craftsman' who aspires to match his standard 'tremble and lose heart'.[3] Although hardly the first Italian artist to use the relatively new medium of oil paint – in which pigments are mixed with oil rather than water (fresco) or egg white (tempera) – Leonardo's technique took full

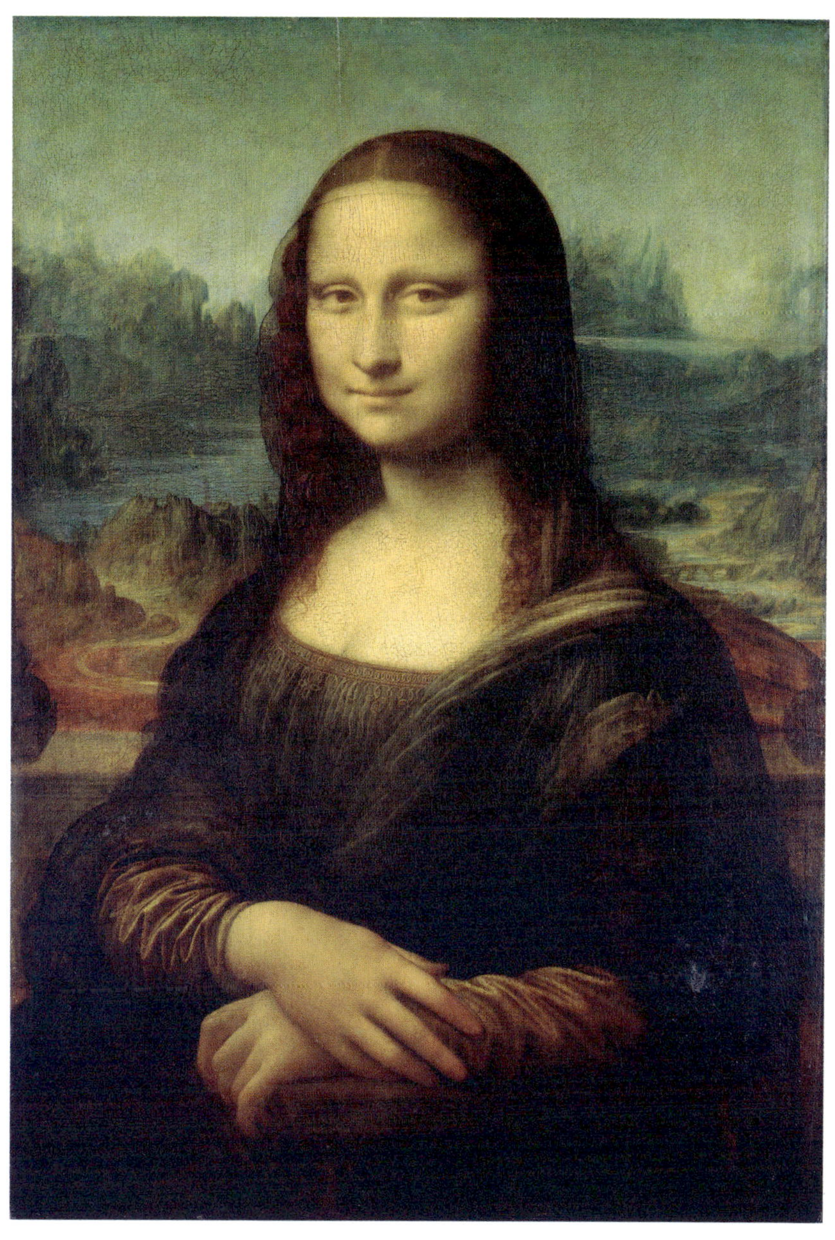

*Mona Lisa – Portrait of Lisa Gherardini, Wife of
Francesco del Giocondo* c. 1503
Leonardo da Vinci (1452–1519)
Oil on poplar
77 x 53 cm (30 x 21 in)
Musée du Louvre, Paris

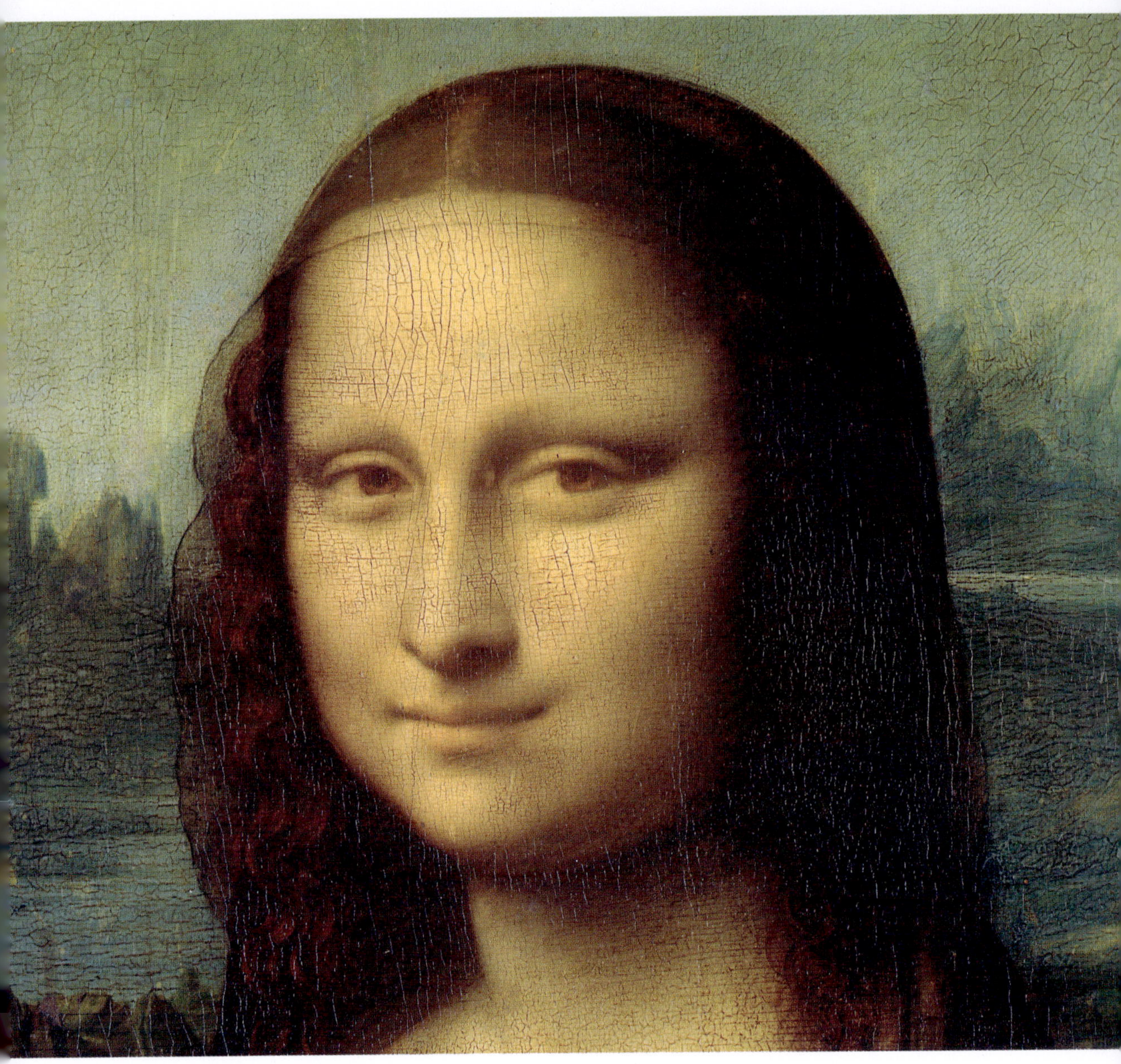

Mona Lisa, detail

No description of the historical Lisa Gherardini has been discovered, so it is impossible to tell if the portrait is a good likeness. But Leonardo achieved an unprecedented illusion of natural vitality through light and shadow. With soft, seamless brushstrokes, he conveys the potential of expressive mobility, from the side-long glance of the eyes to the pressure at the corners of the lips that creates the famous smile.

advantage of oil's inherent qualities. Its translucent properties allow light to pass through layers of the medium, and Leonardo employed very thin, colour-saturated layers that simulated atmospheric effects in a technique he called *sfumato* (smoky). Oil dries slowly, allowing the artist to modulate tone on a wet, malleable surface into a seamless gradation known as *chiaroscuro* (light/dark). Without a defining outline, the resulting illusion of three-dimensionality simulates the weight, plasticity and presence of forms as perceived in nature. And even through the layers of dirt and darkened colours, Leonardo's observant dexterity is on full display: from the subtle flush on the skin of her hands to the softness of the flesh around her eyes and the mobile delineation of her mouth, Leonardo captures his sitter's vitality as well as her likeness.

Over the years, provocative stories have circulated about the sitter and her amused expression: she was Leonardo's mistress; she had a secret; she was a contented, new mother. While her smile remains unexplained, there is no uncertainty about her identity, despite ongoing speculation. Vasari names her and her husband, and documents verify their identity and their life in early-sixteenth-century Florence. Francesco del Giocondo was a third-generation silk merchant, who oversaw his family's highly successful enterprise and owned several properties in and around Florence. The earliest known document that links him to the painting also establishes when Leonardo began to work on it. A handwritten annotation, dated '1503. October', in a 1477 edition of *Cicero's Letters to his Friends*, owned by the chancery official Agostino Matteo Vespucci, compares Leonardo's talent to that of the ancient Greek artist Apelles, as evidenced in 'the head of Lisa Giocondo'.[4] Lisa Gherardini married Francesco del Giocondo in 1495 (hence, La Gioconda). She was his second wife, and they had six children together, five of which were born before she sat for Leonardo. While the timeline of his progress on the portrait appears to be undocumented, it can be assumed that the painting remained in Leonardo's studio until sometime in 1507 or 1508, when he relocated to Milan. Tradition holds that the painting was not finished, although, even in its current state, it is hard to fathom what was left undone. What is known is that rather than handing the painting over to his patron, Leonardo transported it to Milan – and then to his subsequent residences – along with his other possessions.

The annotation dating 'the head of Lisa Giocondo' also mentions other works in progress by Leonardo, suggesting that Vespucci, the presumed author of the annotation, visited his studio. The younger artist Raphael Sanzio, newly arrived in Florence in 1504, appeared to have made several visits, and the influence of the portrait is immediately evident in a drawing featuring a different woman in the exact same pose dressed with a similar coiffure, headdress and garments. Raphael repeated the distinctive pose – a half-length *contrapposto* with the torso and shoulders tilted to the left and the head turned forward – in such later works as *Portrait of Maddalena Doni* (1506) and *Portrait of Baldassare Castiglione* (1514–15). By the time Raphael was at work on the later portrait, both artists were in Rome enjoying papal patronage, but Leonardo left in 1516 at the invitation of Francis I to join the royal court of France. He lived in the Château du Clos Lucé in Amboise, a residence in the Loire Valley provided by the king, until his death in 1519. A post-death inventory (1524) of the possessions of his long-time assistant, Gian Giacomo Caprotti da Oreno – known as Salaí – lists a portrait of 'la Ioconda', but this may well have been a replica; copying works of the master by assistants was a common studio practice in the day. Whether purchased from Salaí's descendants or bequeathed directly to the king, by 1530, the portrait of Mona Lisa had entered the French royal collection. Vasari's claim that it was in Fontainbleau is confirmed more than a half century later, in a 1625 inventory that describes it as a portrait of a 'virtuous Italian woman' known as 'La Joconde'.[5] After the revolution of 1789, when the Louvre Palace opened to the public as an art museum (1797), the *Mona Lisa* was among the requisitioned royal works that formed the core collection. With the exception of a brief period when it was removed to Napoleon Bonaparte's apartments in the Tuileries Palace (1800–04), the *Mona Lisa* remained in the Musée du Louvre.

From Vasari's time forward, writers have embellished their descriptions of the portrait with narrative inventions that give the seemingly simple painting of a sixteenth-century Florentine woman an aura of mystery. Vasari may have thought up his explanation of

Mona Lisa, detail

Brown tonality and yellowed varnish obscure the once vibrant contrasts of Leonardo's palette. Documents suggest that darkening was apparent as early as the eighteenth century; fortunately, restorers have hesitated to thoroughly clean and possibly damage the surface. But we can still observe Leonardo's masterful handling of paint, most notably in the transparent layers of the headdress, the uninterrupted gradation of tone from light to dark, and the delicate atmospheric mist cloaking the background.

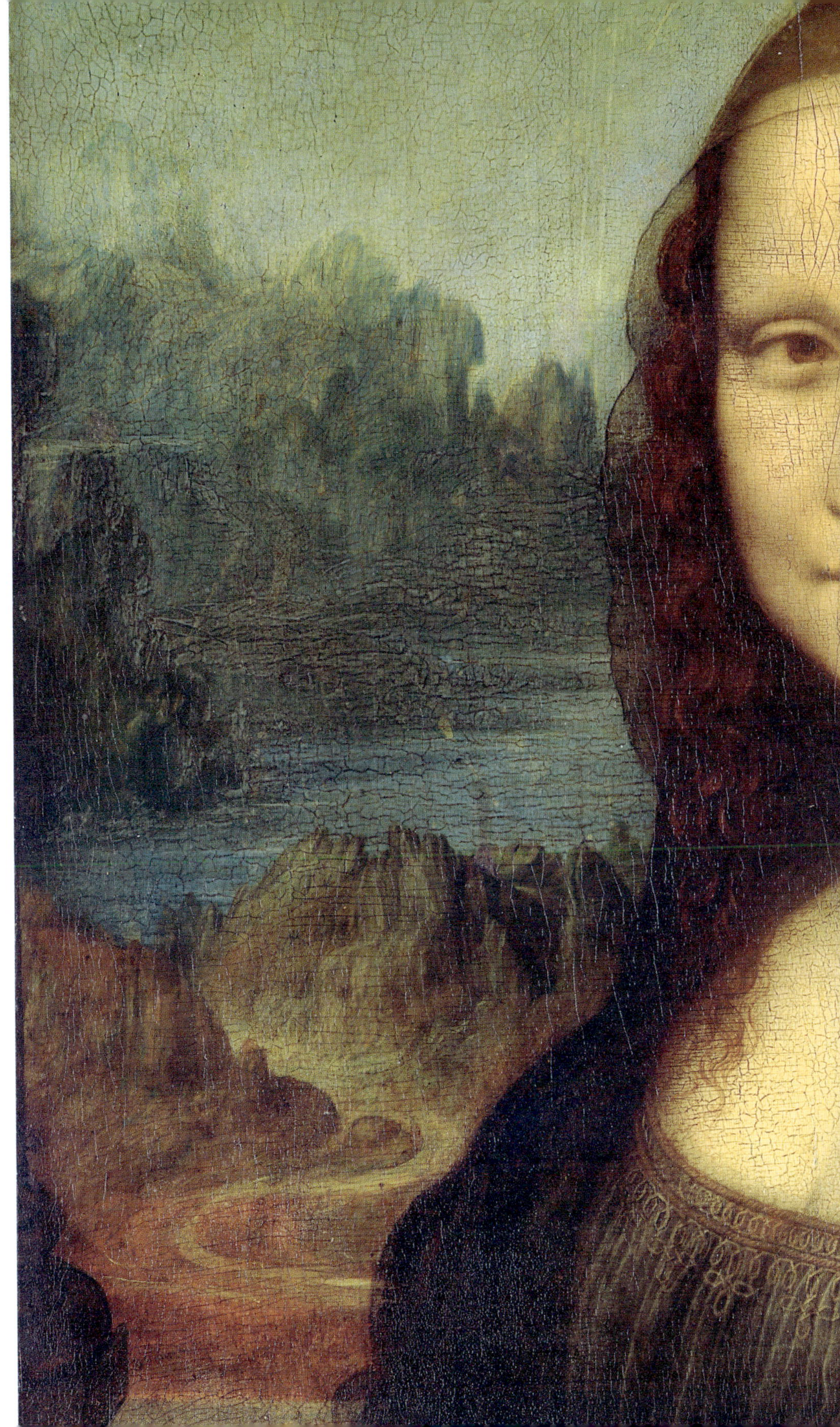

the sitter's smile – that Leonardo hired entertainers so that she would 'remain merry' – or it may have been a long-standing anecdote.[6] The 1625 Fontainbleau inventory that cites the sitter's virtue further notes that she was 'not a courtesan (as some believe)'.[7] Joseph Lavalée, the author of the *Catalogue Galerie de Musée Napoleon* (1804–15; the name of the Musée du Louvre during Napoleon's reign as emperor), was clearly beguiled by the sitter: 'If only this seductive woman could speak'.[8] The tendency to celebrate the sitter's inscrutable allure escalated through the nineteenth century, fuelled by romantic sensibilities and the desire to frame the image as more than a portrait. Rather than relating the history of the painting, such prominent French writers as Théophile Gautier, Charles Clément, Charles Baudelaire and the Goncourt brothers penned poetic descriptions that hailed the sitter as sphinx-like, a vision of all that is feminine and a true embodiment of the femme fatale.[9] Many of these writers refer to the painting with the pronoun 'she' – replacing the neutral 'it' – transforming the work from an inanimate object into an entity with her own power to think, feel and guard her secrets.

The most imaginative – and influential – evocation of Mona Lisa's mystery was written by the young Oxford don Walter Pater. After travelling through Italy in 1865, he wrote a series of essays on Italian artists. His account of Leonardo's life first appeared in the *Fortnightly Review* in 1867 and was then included in his career-making collection *Studies in the History of the Renaissance* (1873). Pater begins his discussion of the portrait by acknowledging that 'La Gioconda is, in the truest sense, Leonardo's masterpiece, the revealing instance of his mode of thought and work'. But what follows concentrates on the sitter, not the artist, presenting her as the embodiment of the eternal feminine, 'expressive of what in the ways of a thousand years men

Young Woman on a Balcony c. 1504
Raphael Sanzio (1483–1520)
Pen and ink
22 x 16 cm (8½ x 6¼ in)
Musée du Louvre, Paris

This drawing suggests that Raphael saw the *Mona Lisa* while Leonardo worked on it in his studio. The pose of the sitter is the same as in the canvas. The gowns are similar and the coiffure and headdress almost identical. But the soft, full features of Raphael's sitter – seemingly a younger woman – marks it as a response to Leonardo's work rather than a replica.

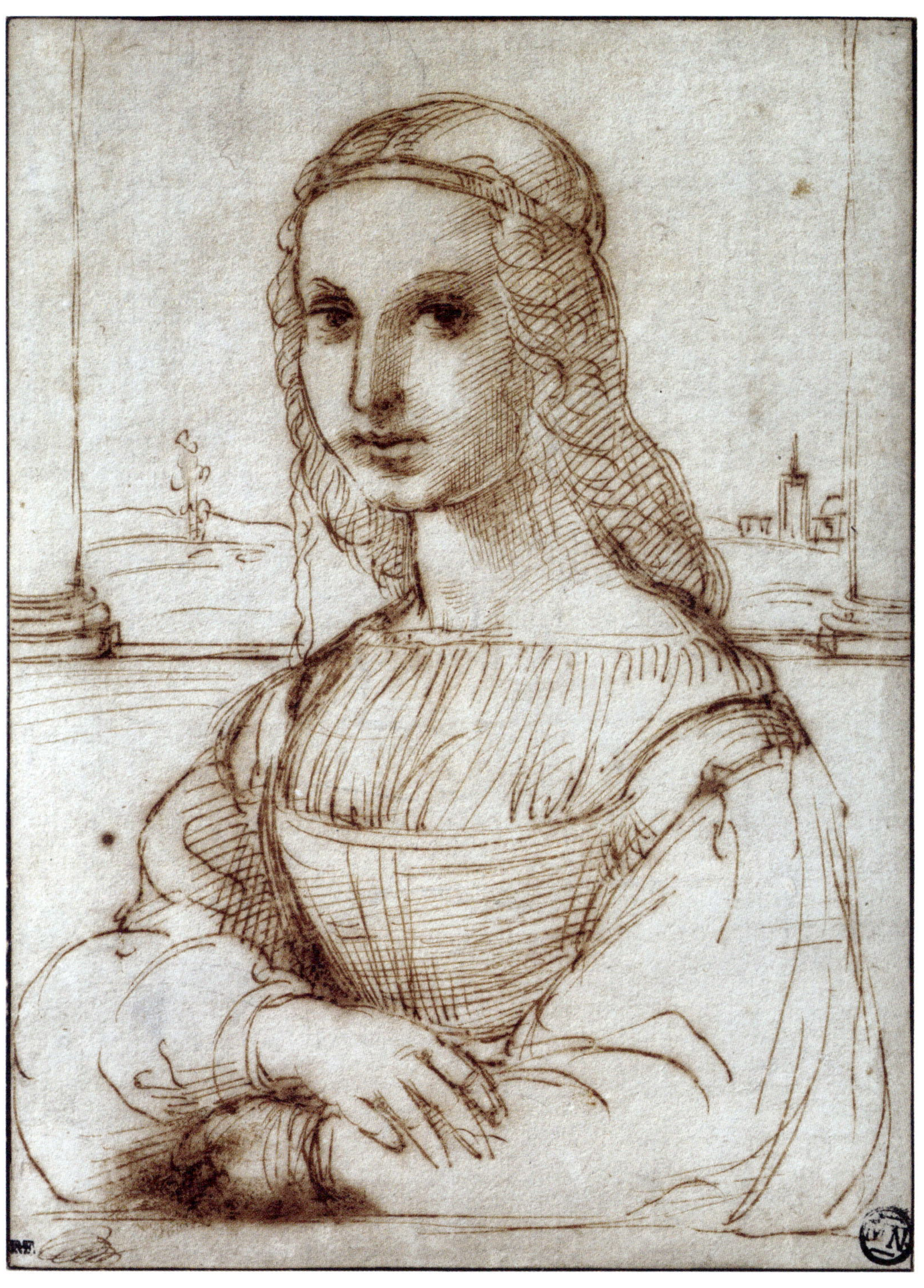

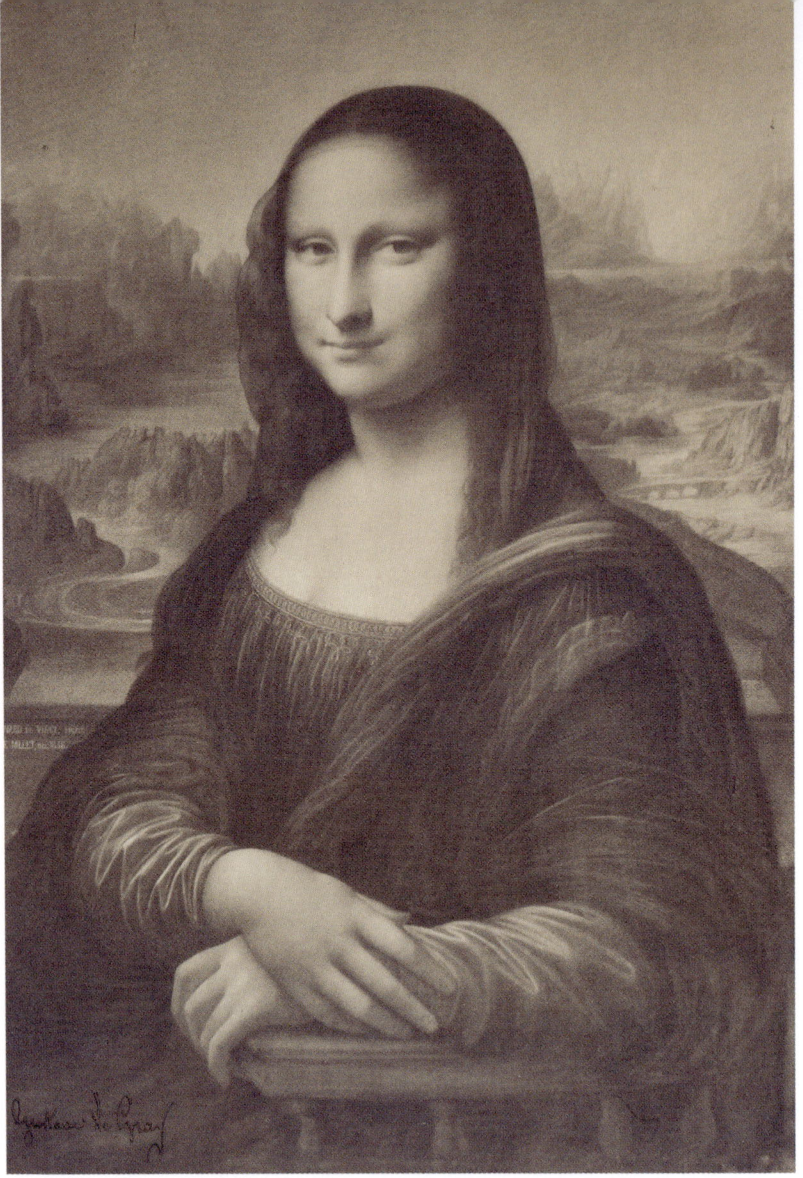

Millet's Drawing of the Mona Lisa 1854–55
Gustave Le Gray (1820–84)
Albumen silver print
29 x 19 cm (11½ x 7½ in)
J. Paul Getty Museum, Malibu, CA

Photographic reproduction played an enormous role in the painting's popularity. At the time that Le Gray created this image, the painting had darkened to the point that he could not fully capture its quality, so he photographed a carefully rendered drawing. Today, through high-resolution photography, we get a much closer and more telling view than if we saw the portrait first-hand in the gallery.

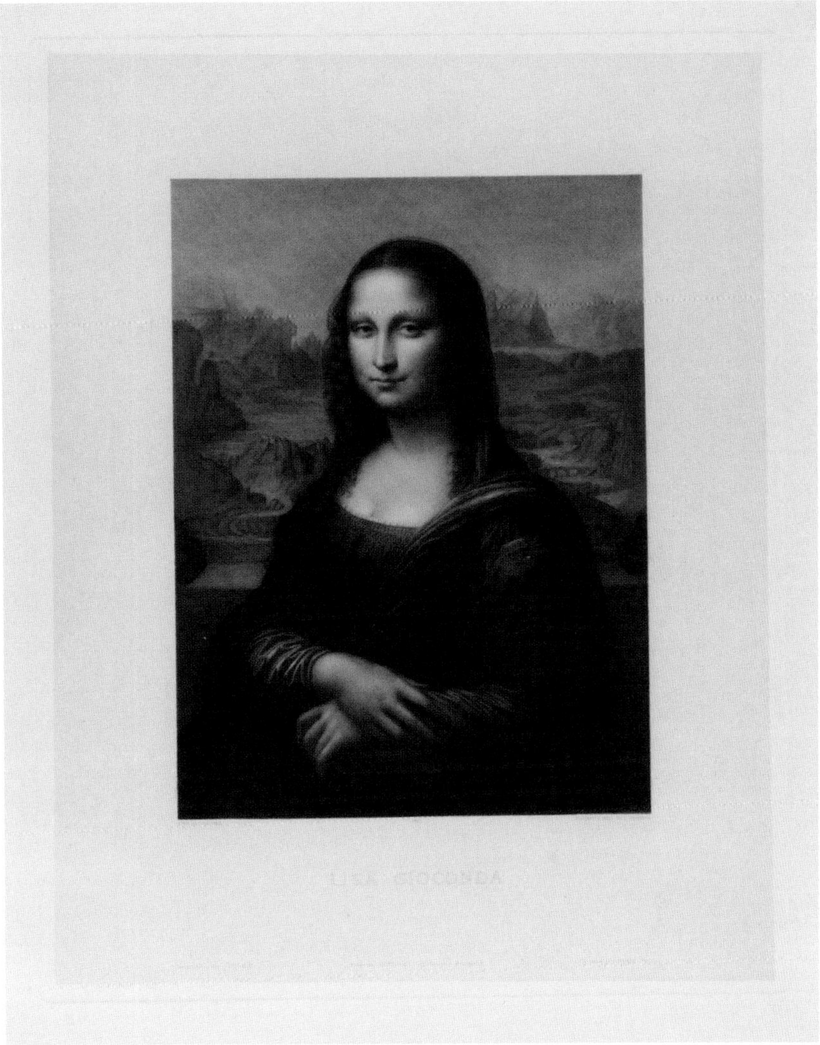

Mona Lisa (after Leonardo da Vinci) 1857
Luigi Calamatta (1802–69)
Etching and engraving with masked plate tone
56.5 x 43.5 cm (22¼ x 17 in)
Philadelphia Museum of Art, Philadelphia, PA

Early engravings and etchings flattened and hardened the subtlety of
Leonardo's artistry. Working from a meticulous drawing that he made directly
from the painting (1825–27), Calamatta carved his copper plate with a variety
of strokes – cross-hatching, lines, dots, all in different depths – to translate
Leonardo's sophisticated tonal gradation of colour into a faithful monochrome
reproduction.

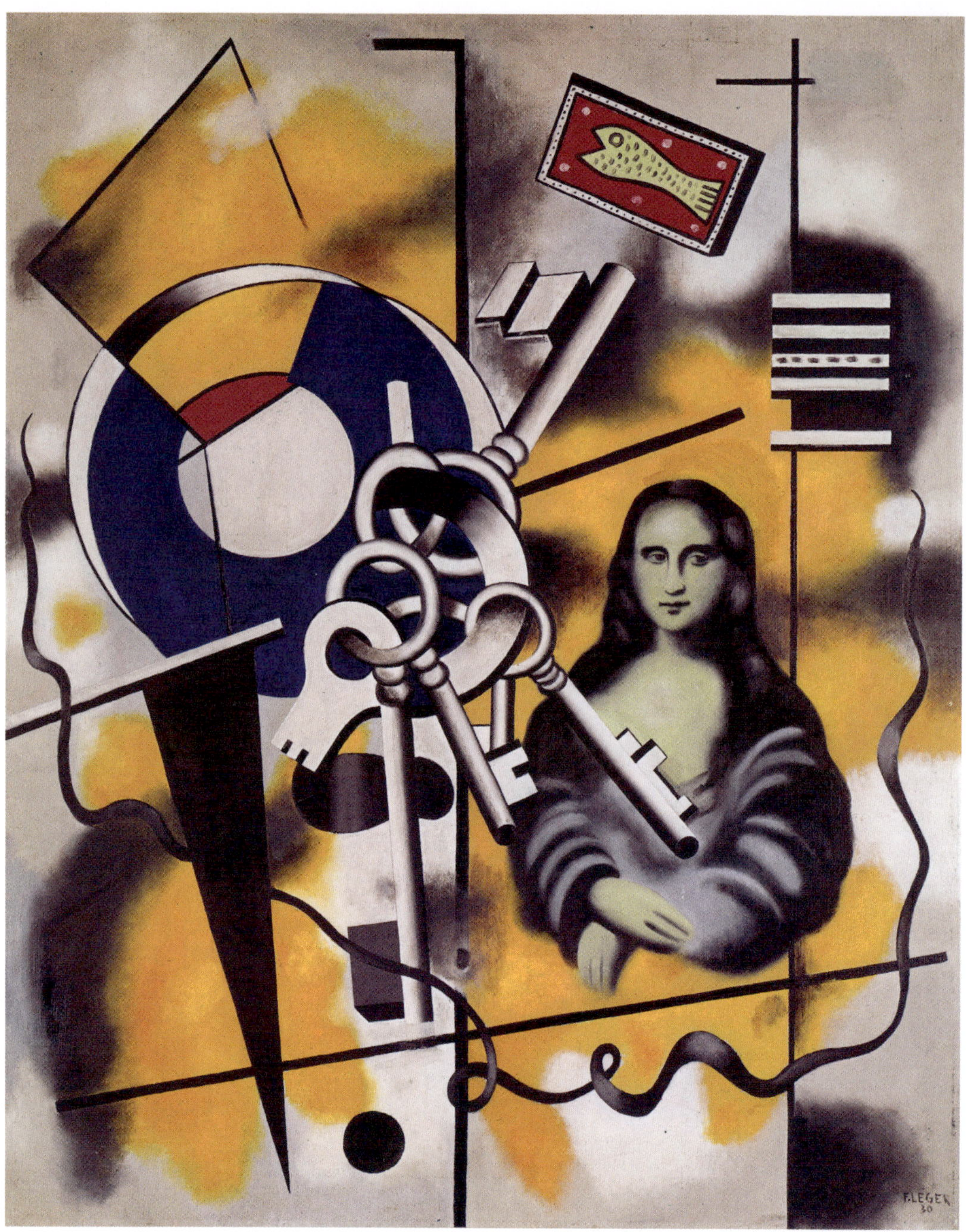

had come to desire'. Pater declares that 'She is older than the rocks among which she sits', that she is like a 'vampire' defying death, with a beauty forged through a soul possessed of 'strange thoughts and fantastic reveries and exquisite passions'.[10] When Oscar Wilde claimed that he could not see the painting without reciting Pater's evocative prose, he was drawing attention to the writer's audacious imagination: 'Who, again cares whether Mr Pater put into the portrait of Mona Lisa something that Leonardo never dreamed of?'[11]

By the end of the nineteenth century, the general public shared the vision of the *Mona Lisa* crafted by her elite, literary admirers. And many more knew the image as advances in printing and photography produced high-quality reproductions that now captured the subtlety of Leonardo's technique. Along with fine art prints and illustrated journals, the newly popular postcard widened and diversified the audience of admirers. Also, museum attendance among the middle and working classes rose significantly in the last quarter of the century, as more people enjoyed the luxury of leisure time. Most importantly, tourism was on the rise, and when visiting Paris, a stop at the Louvre was deemed essential. Travel guides served to heighten interest in the painting using language that enforced the sitter's aura of mystery; according to the 1900 edition of *Baedeker's Paris and its Environs*, even the canvas's 'darkened condition' could not diminish the fascinating power of 'the sphinx-like smile … which had exercised the wits of generations of poets and artists'.[12]

But it was the painting's absence from the Louvre that sealed its international fame. Early in the morning on 21 August 1911, Vincenzo Peruggia, a workman who had been temporarily hired by the museum as a glazier, removed the *Mona Lisa* from the wall, slipped it under his smock, and made off with the painting. When, later in the day, the theft

La Joconde aux clés 1930
Fernand Léger (1881–1955)
Oil on canvas
91 x 72 cm (36 x 28½ in)
Musée National Fernand Léger, Biot

Upon seeing a postcard of the *Mona Lisa* in a shop window, Léger concluded that the image was no more than an object, just like the keys in his pocket. Both Salvador Dalí and Marcel Duchamp also drew attention to the commodification of the painting by drawing moustaches on inexpensive reproductions.

was discovered, the museum conducted an inspection of the premises, but the only clue was the empty frame found in a stairwell. As the Louvre remained closed to the public for a week, rumours circulated, fuelled by sensational press coverage: an American millionaire had arranged the theft to add a new treasure to his collection; a madman had fallen in love with the painting and had to have her. When the museum reopened, the public thronged in to pay sombre tribute to the empty space on the wall. The police mounted an extensive investigation, but after months of false leads the effort to find the painting dwindled and the public lost interest. All the while, Peruggia had the canvas in his apartment in Paris. He would later claim that his motive was patriotism, not greed; he falsely believed that Leonardo's famous portrait had been taken by Napoleon's troops as spoils during the occupation of Italy. On 29 November 1913, Peruggia contacted Alfredo Geri, an antique dealer based in Florence, in hopes of repatriating the painting for the sum of 500,000 lire. Geri, in turn, brought in Giovanni Poggi, curator of the Uffizi Galleries, to authenticate the painting. Once the men were certain that the painting was genuine, they called the police. On 19 December, in a ceremony held in Rome, the *Mona Lisa* was handed over to the French ambassador, and by the end of the year, the painting, now more famous than ever before, was back in Paris.

During the Second World War, while rumours circulated that Hitler had stolen the painting, the *Mona Lisa* was quietly taken out of occupied Paris and stored for safekeeping in various locations in France. Two decades later, through the efforts of the American First Lady Jacqueline Kennedy, working with the French Minister of Cultural Affairs André Malraux, the painting was briefly loaned to the National Gallery of Art in Washington, DC, and then to the Metropolitan Museum of Art in New York in 1963. In 1974, it travelled to the Tokyo National Museum, and then to the Pushkin Museum in Moscow. Since then, it has not left the Louvre. And the desire to see the work has only risen: in a poll taken by the Louvre, eighty per cent of those questioned cited seeing the *Mona Lisa* as the reason for their visit. But, as the public's urge to see the painting has soared, the quality of that experience has diminished. By 2019, an average of 30,000 people a day crowded through the gallery, moving through a line that art critic Jason Farago has compared to 'a T.S.A.-style snake of retractable barriers', just to stand for less than a minute near the work and snap a picture on their phones.[13] But the disappointing reality of trying to see the work has done nothing to detract from either the masterful achievement of Leonardo or the legends surrounding the painting. The painting, in its fame, has come to define the very concept of a masterpiece.

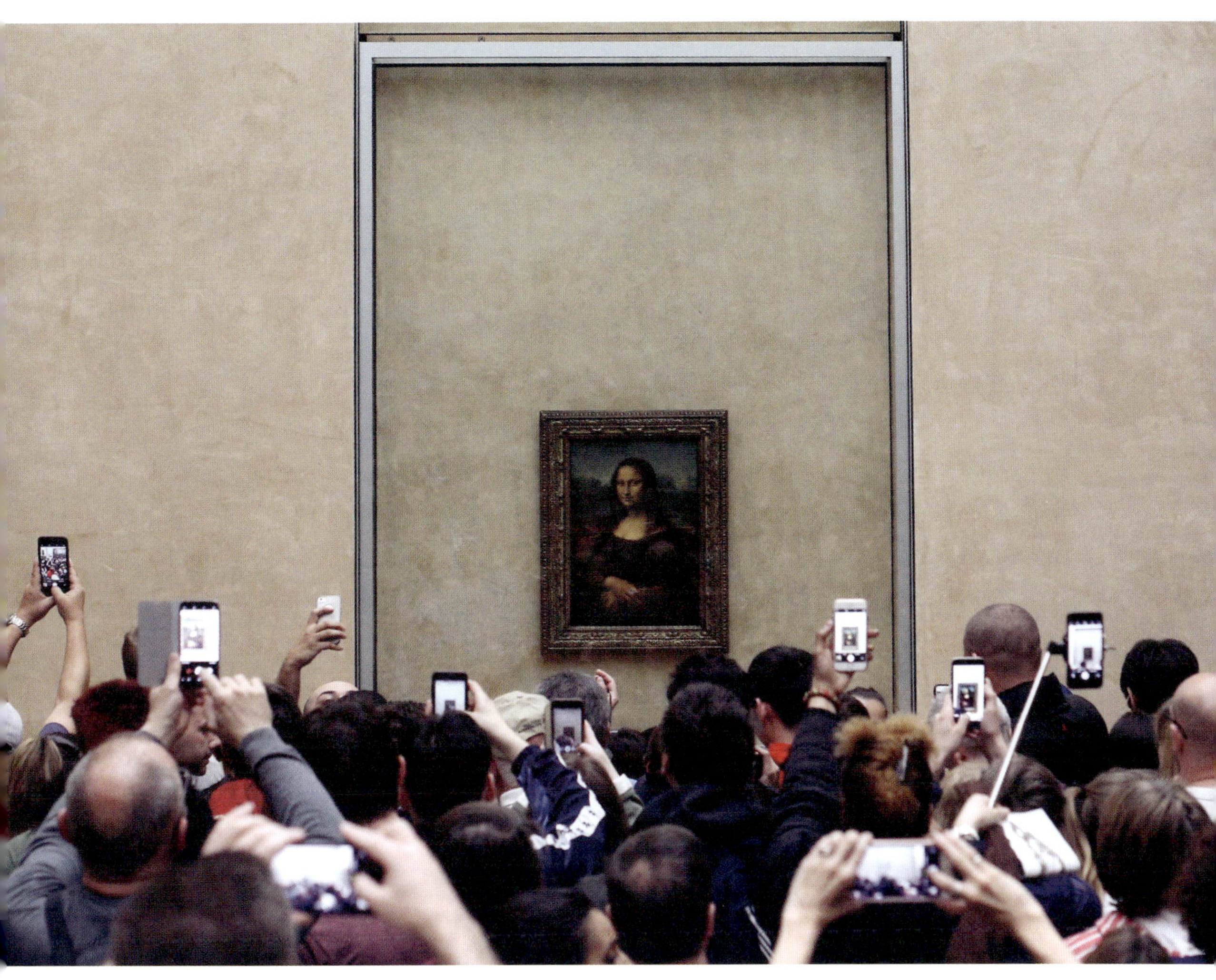

Crowds at the Louvre

ABOVE AND OVERLEAF The pressing crowds eager to see the *Mona Lisa* make it impossible to appreciate its true qualities as an intimate portrait. Many visitors come to the Louvre solely to stand – however briefly – in the gallery and point their phone at the painting. This has prompted the museum staff to post a sign reading: 'The Mona Lisa is surrounded by other masterpieces – take a look around the room'.

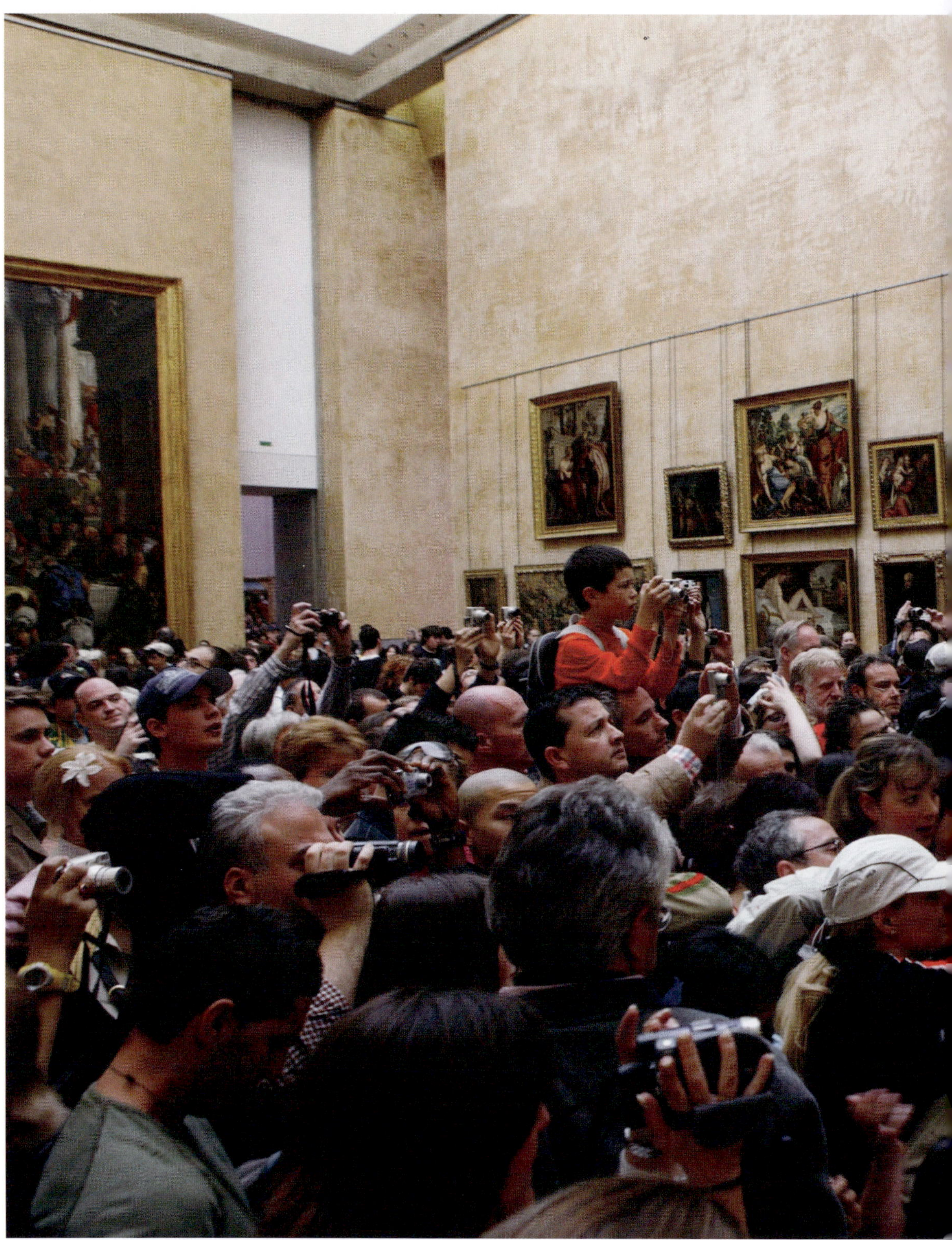

    Making a Masterpiece

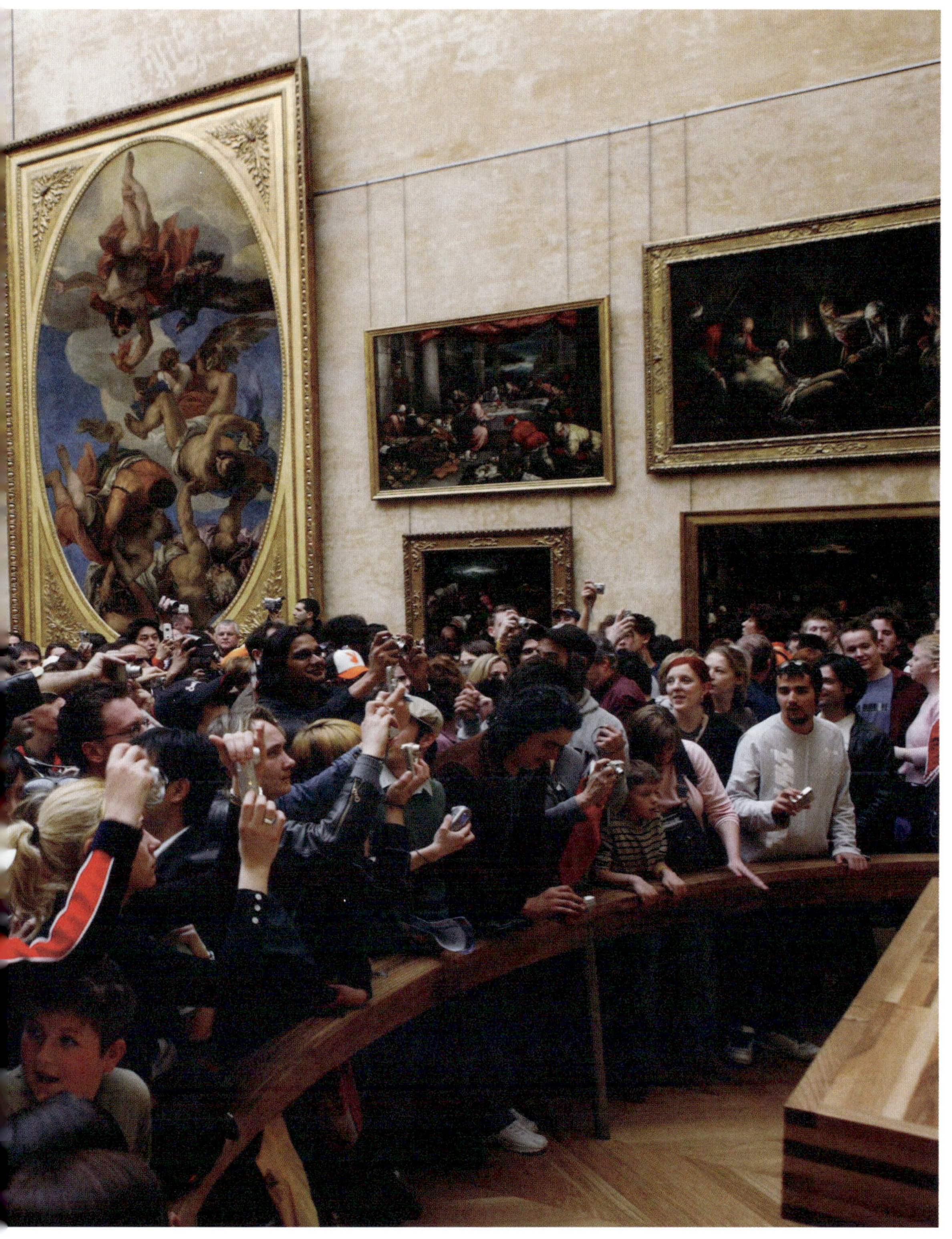

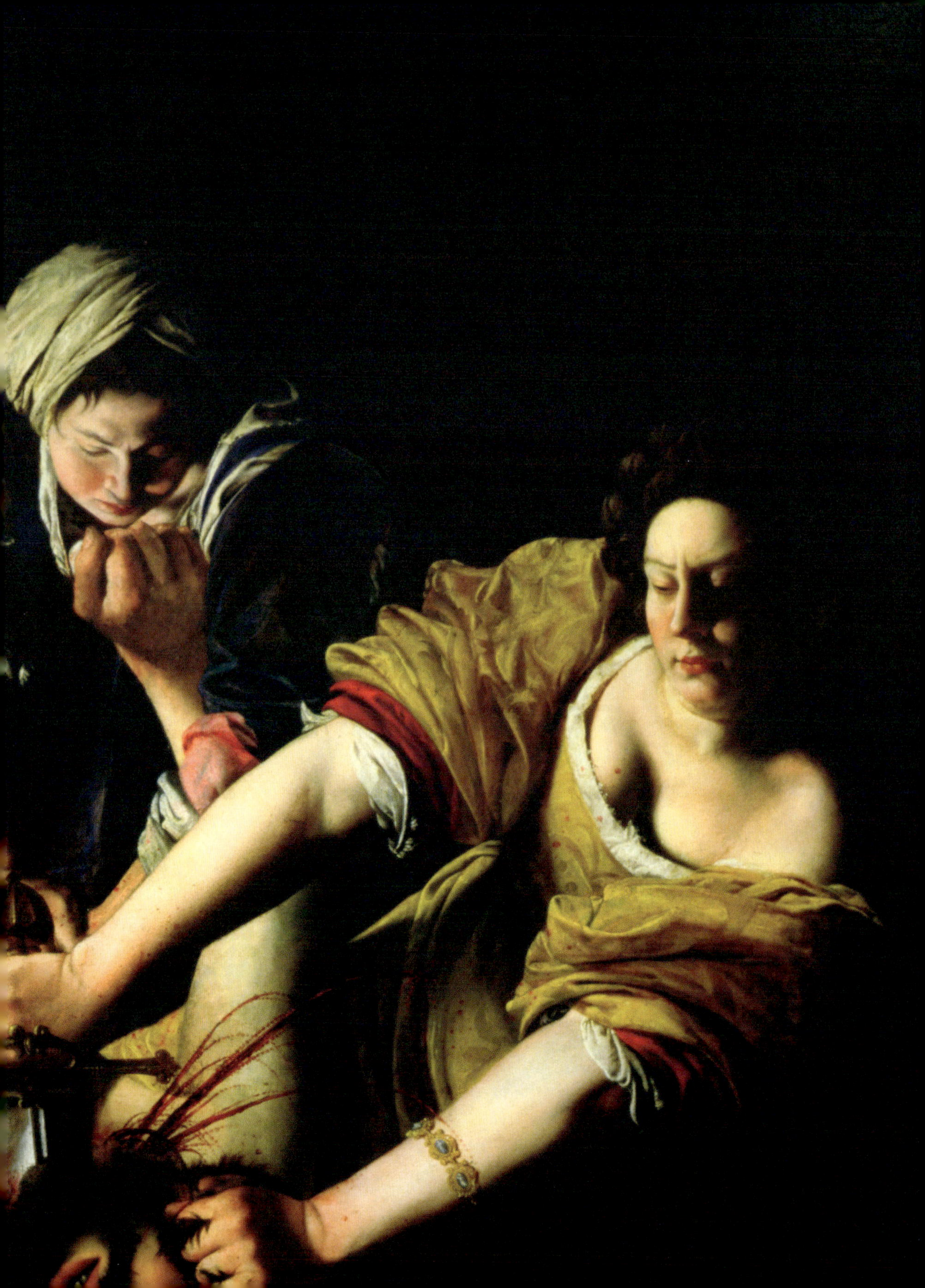

Judith Beheading Holofernes

Artemisia Gentileschi

I will show Your Illustrious Lordship
what a woman can do!

Artemisia Gentileschi to Antonio Ruffo, 7 August 1649

On the eve of the Assyrian siege of the city of Bethulia, a Jewish widow named Judith donned her finest gown to dine with Holofernes, the commander of the invading army. He drank heavily throughout the evening, eventually drifting into an inebriated slumber. Then, with the help of her handmaiden, Abra, Judith swiftly decapitated him with his own sword. The two women slipped unnoticed from the enemy camp carrying off the head as gruesome evidence that Judith had saved her city from seemingly inevitable destruction. This story of a woman's heroism was included in the Septuagint, the Greek translation of Jewish scriptures (c. third to second centuries BCE), and although Jewish scholars came to regard its contents as apocryphal, many of the early Christian Church scholars consulted it to shed light on older texts and provide moral examples. It was as such an example that Judith's legend survived, gaining even greater currency among the Catholic faithful during the Counter-Reformation. But, in the twenty-first century, her story is better known through the paintings of Artemisia Gentileschi than through the annals of biblical scholarship.

As a woman raised in a seventeenth-century Roman household, much of Artemisia's life was defined by her gender.[1] Her social interactions and movements through the city were highly restricted, and her mother's death imposed womanly responsibilities upon her when she was still a child. Her position in society, as well as her family's social standing, depended upon her future marital status. But, unlike most women of her era, Artemisia had access to a man's world through her father's profession. As a prominent Roman painter, Orazio Gentileschi welcomed artists and patrons into the studio housed in his family's home. He took early notice of his daughter's potential, giving her the same training that he would give to his sons. Her talent instilled confidence, and even the gruelling experience of a sexual assault, which resulted in a protracted trial to reclaim her reputation, did not diminish her ambitions. Years later, Artemisia wrote that, in the arts, 'a woman's name raises doubts until the work is seen'.[2] Determined that her work be seen in the context of her artistic capacity rather than her gender, she turned to the saga of the heroine Judith to make her first masterpiece.

In a letter written in 1612 to Christina of Lorraine, the Dowager Grand Duchess of Tuscany, Orazio Gentileschi asserted that his nineteen-year-old daughter Artemisia, having been painting for three years, had 'no equal'.[3] This evidence situates the beginning of Artemisia's career around 1609, but her training in her father's studio must have begun earlier. It is not known when her tuition began, but it can be assumed that, before she was allowed to paint, Artemisia took on the traditional tasks of apprenticeship: grinding paint, cleaning the premises and lending any type of needed assistance, all while watching the master at work. Orazio had established his reputation with a graceful, naturalistic style, but by the time of Artemisia's training, he had adopted a more realistic and emotive manner, influenced by the dramatic innovations of his friend and

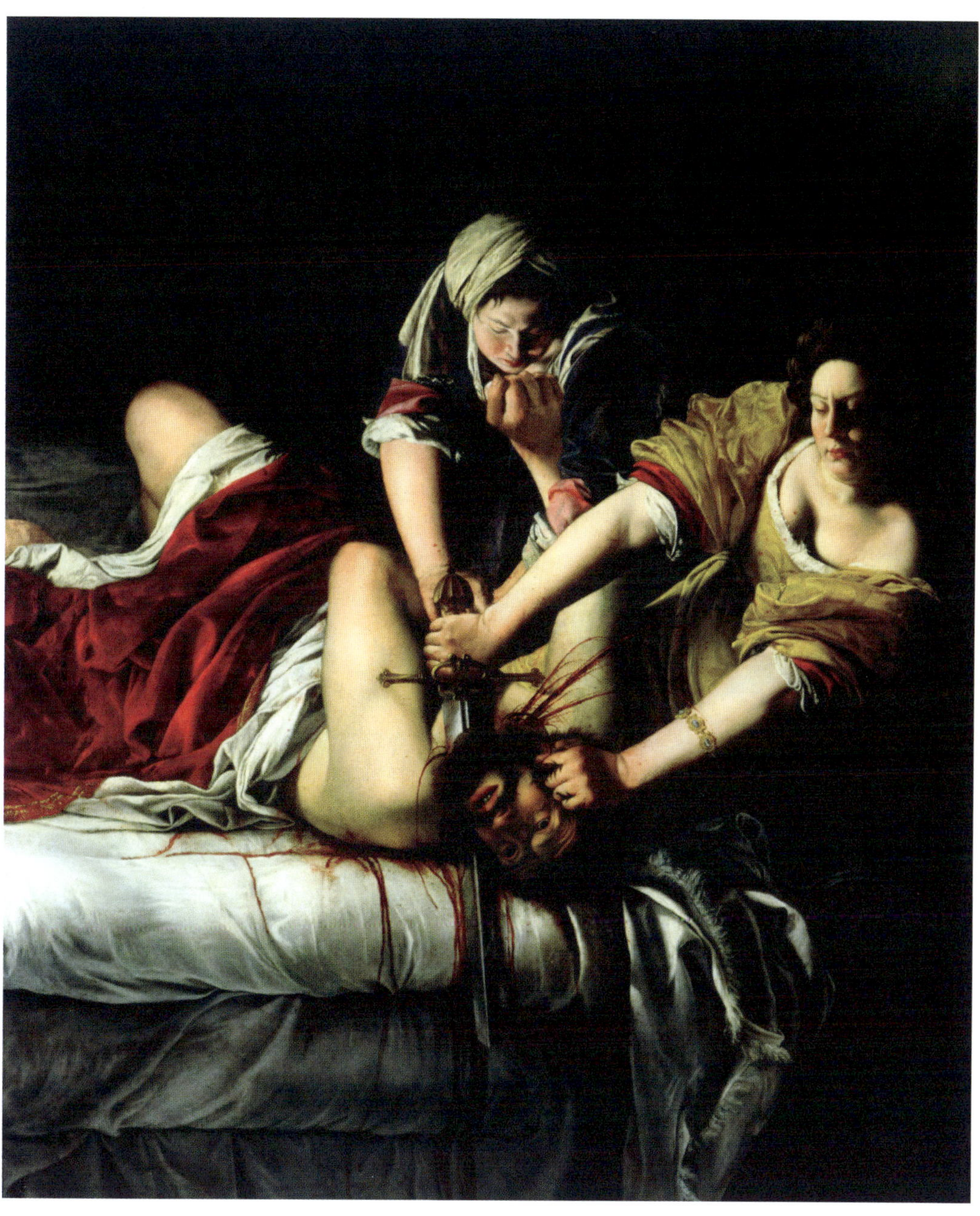

Judith Beheading Holofernes c. 1613–14
Artemisia Gentileschi (1593–c. 1654)
Oil on canvas
146.5 x 108 cm (57¾ x 42½ in)
Gallerie degli Uffizi, Florence

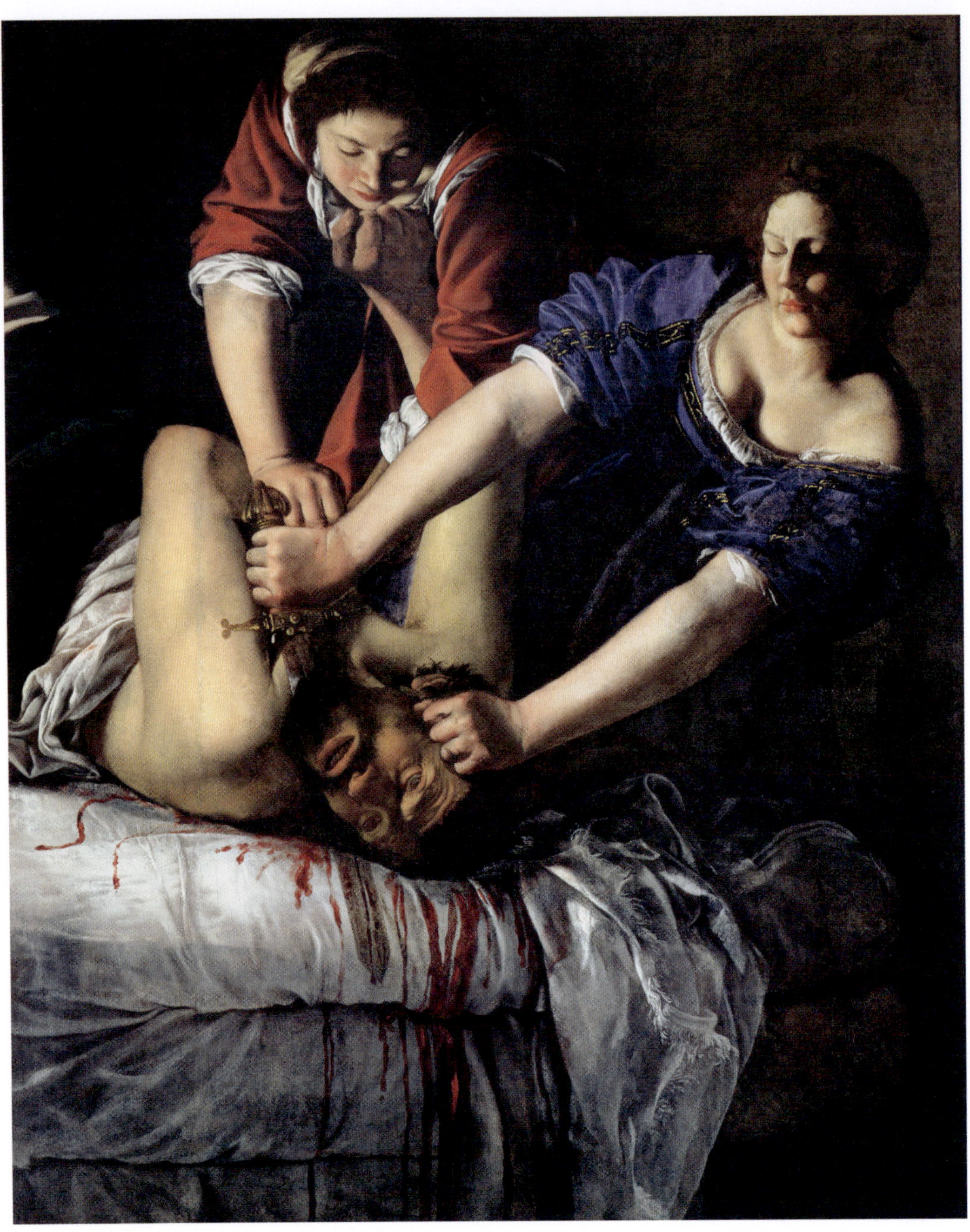

fellow painter Caravaggio. Like Caravaggio, Orazio painted directly from live models without the refining preliminary studies used in conventional practice. Artemisia soon demonstrated her own ability to create powerfully expressive, lifelike figures in her first signed and dated painting, *Susannah and the Elders* (1610); several of her father's colleagues refuted the signature, insisting that *Susannah* had to be Orazio's work.

In many ways, Artemisia's youth resembled that of other women of her generation and circumstance. The scope of her world would have been restricted by her household and domestic duties, which, after her mother's death in 1605, included caring for her three younger brothers. She could not traverse the city on her own, and her habit of gazing at the street from her window was seen as indecorous. She was meant to stay out of sight when Orazio's friends and patrons visited, but it was inevitable that she encountered men – apprentices, fellow artists, models – outside her family circle while working in her father's studio. Despite all the customary precautions, Artemisia was raped by a close colleague of her father's in 1611. In the following March, Orazio pressed charges of *stupre et lenonoinii* (deflowering and procuring) against Agostino Tassi, claiming that after violating his daughter, Tassi failed to fulfil his promise to marry her.[4] To prove the truth of her testimony, Artemisia endured the *sibille*, an ordeal in which her fingers were bound with strong cords that were tightened as she was made to profess her innocence. On 27 November, Tassi was judged guilty and given the choice of exile from Rome or hard labour; he chose exile although it was never enforced. Two days later, Artemisia married Pierantonio di Vincenzo Stiattesi – the brother of her father's legal adviser – and by the early days of 1613, the newlyweds had moved to Florence.

Judith Beheading Holofernes 1612–13
Oil on canvas
159 x 125.5 cm (62½ x 49½ in)
Museo e Real Bosco di Capodimonte, Naples

Painted in the wake of legal action against Agostino Tassi, Artemisia's decision to portray Judith beheading Holofernes has often been read in terms of personal retaliation. But her choice was more likely professional. By depicting a woman whose heroic motivation – rather than a desire for vengeance – enables her to overcome a male adversary, Artemisia invites comparison to renowned examples of the story by older artists, all of whom were men.

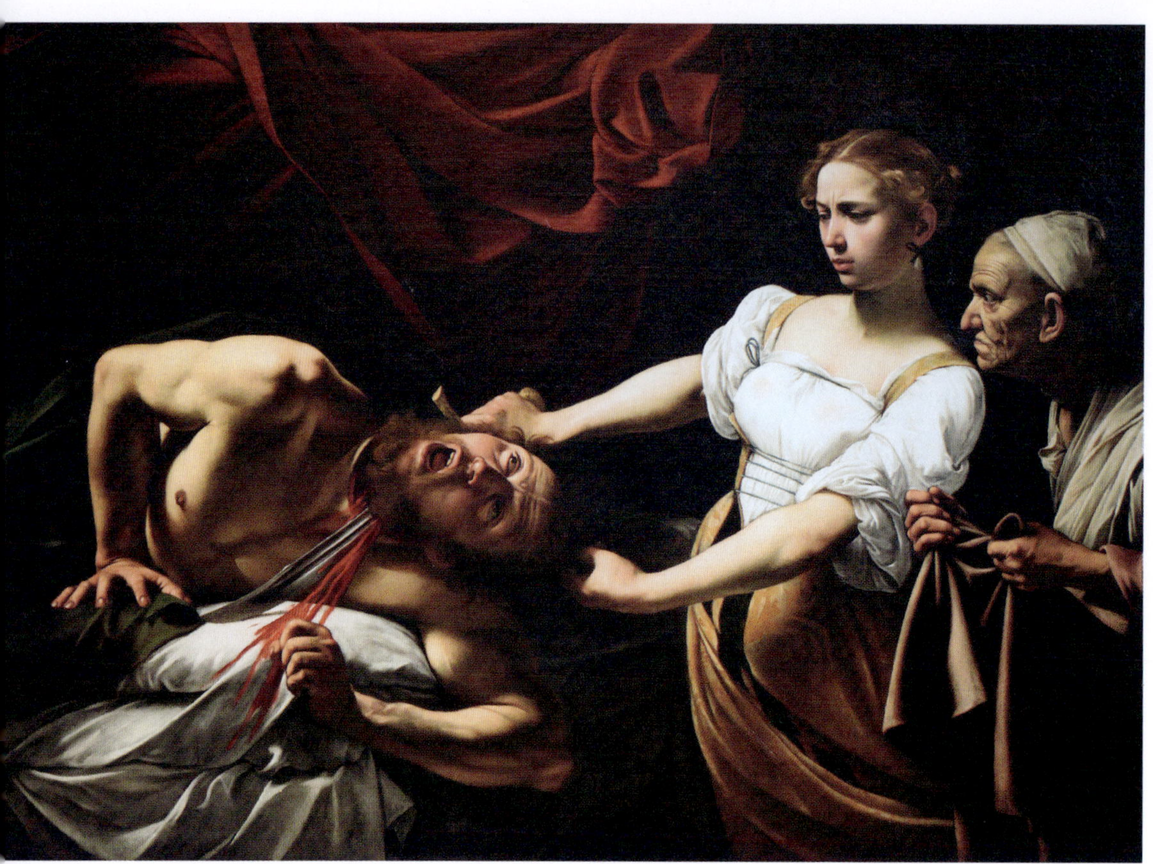

Judith Beheading Holofernes c. 1599
Caravaggio (1571–1610)
Oil on canvas
145 x 195 cm (57 x 76¾ in)
Galleria Nazionale d'Arte Antica Palazzo Barberini, Rome

Scholars disagree as to whether Artemisia saw this painting. It was in a private
collection, owned by the banker Ottavia Costa. Her decision to depict the
beheading, as well as her portrayal of a muscular Holofernes writhing in pain,
may be linked to knowledge of Caravaggio's example. But her strong, physical
depiction of Judith is in stark contrast to Caravaggio's pristinely garbed heroine
who unconvincingly subdues her victim at an arm's length.

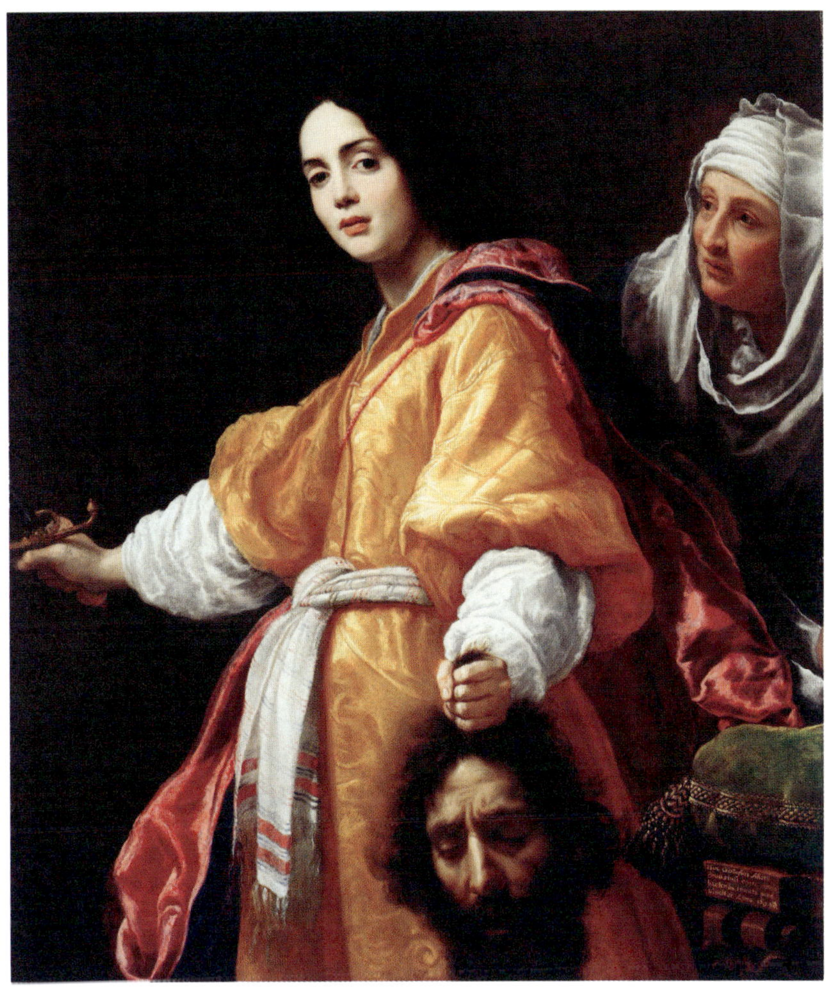

Judith with the Head of Holofernes 1610–12
Cristofano Allori (1577–1621)
Oil on canvas
139 x 116 cm (54¾ x 45½ in)
Palazzo Pitti, Florence

Allori's interpretation of Judith conforms to the conventions of the subject
from the fifteenth through to the seventeenth centuries: as a richly dressed
and beautiful woman bearing Holofernes' head. But, according to his
biographer Filippo Baldinucci, Allori gave the saga a personal twist by using
the likeness of his mistress, La Mazzafirra, for Judith and that of his mother
for the maidservant.

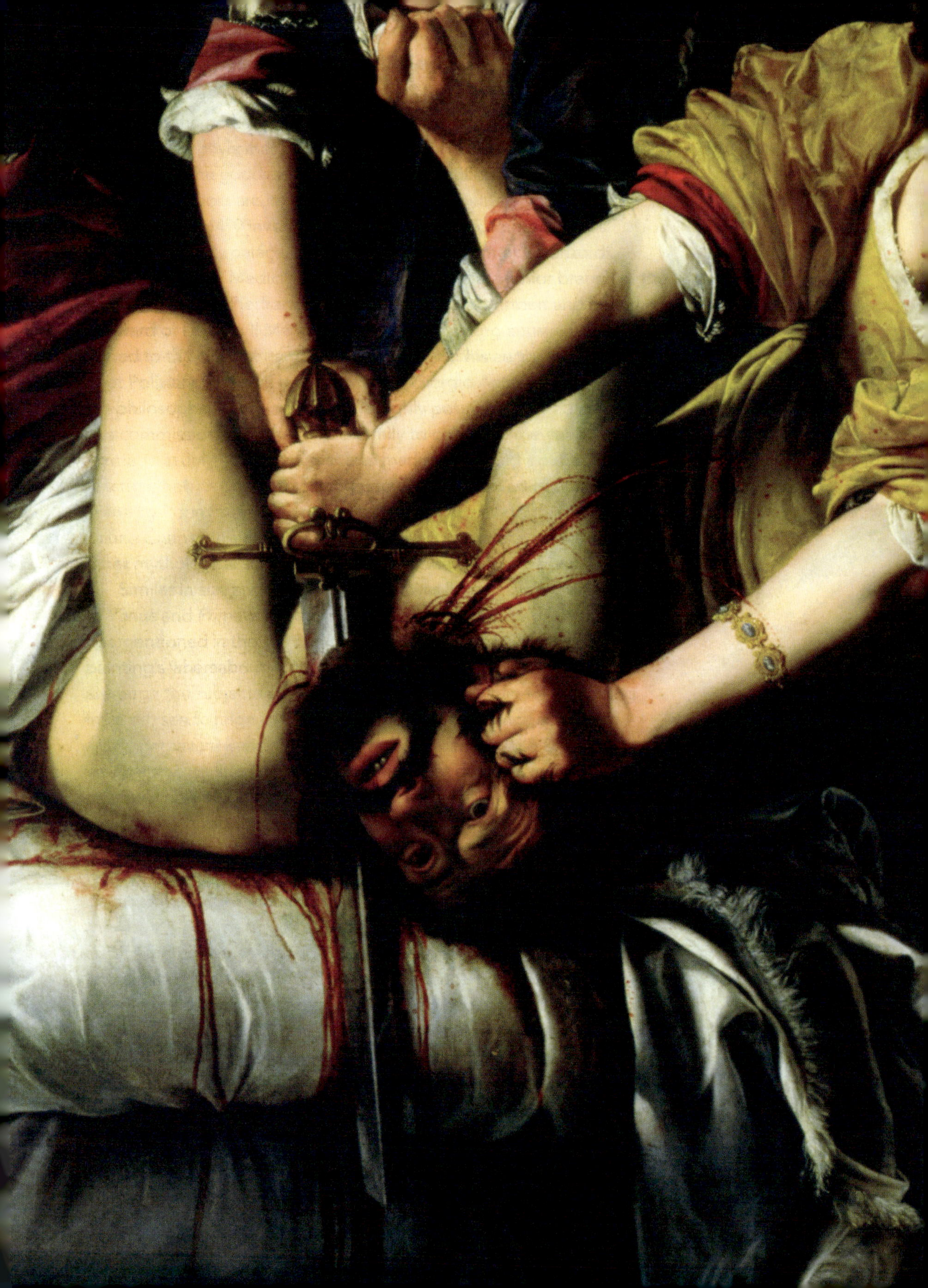

Artemisia began her first known interpretation of the story of Judith either in the midst or the aftermath of the trial. From our current perspective, it is hard to separate the trauma she endured from her portrayal of female heroism, and while the events of an artist's life undoubtedly have an influence on their work, to better understand Artemisia's engagement with this subject, other contexts must be explored. The popularity of the subject had been rising in Italian art since the fifteenth century, with notable examples by Botticelli, Andrea Mantegna, Giorgione and Titian, as one that allowed the artist to portray nobility, bravery and feminine beauty in a single character. While Artemisia may not have seen any of those examples, she could not have overlooked Donatello's magnificent interpretation in Florence. The towering, gilded-bronze statue of Judith grasping Holofernes' hair as she brandishes the sword to deliver the fatal blow represented the triumph of righteous strength over brute aggression; it was installed as a symbol of civic virtue in the Piazza della Signoria, the large public square in front of Florence town hall, the Palazzo Vecchio. Artemisia would have already been familiar with Judith's saga before she left Rome. In 1608, her father Orazio painted Judith and her handmaiden, Abra, with their grisly trophy, while a decade earlier, Caravaggio portrayed the climactic scene of the slaying.

Artemisia chose to represent the moment when Judith beheaded Holofernes. While it is not known whether she saw Caravaggio's painting – it was in a private collection – his reputation was such that she had likely heard about it. And rising to the challenge of painting a subject chosen by Donatello for his civic masterpiece might have been a confident – and even audacious – way to establish her reputation in Florence. But her bold, blunt and yet intimate interpretation owes nothing to these precedents. She painted two versions of *Judith Beheading Holofernes* between 1612 and 1614, and both feature the same scenario: Abra pins down the struggling

Judith Beheading Holofernes, detail

OPPOSITE AND OVERLEAF Judith's firm grasp on the sword hilt acts as a linchpin in the complex crossing of the three figures' arms. The steady downward thrust of her right fist and forearm draws power from the full force of her body. Notice the gold-draped form framed by the sword, her forearm and Holofernes' upper right arm; Judith kneels on the bed for better leverage.

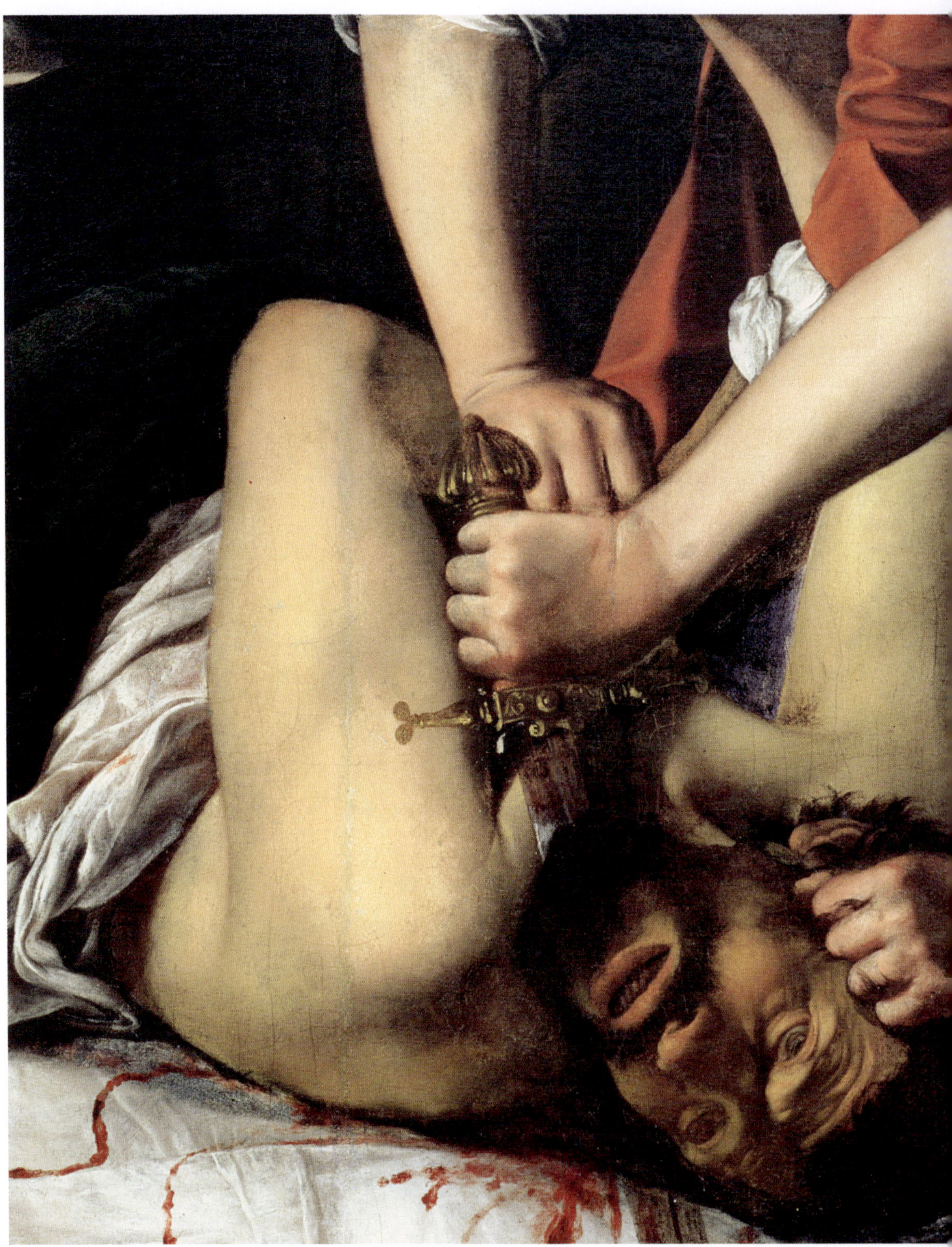

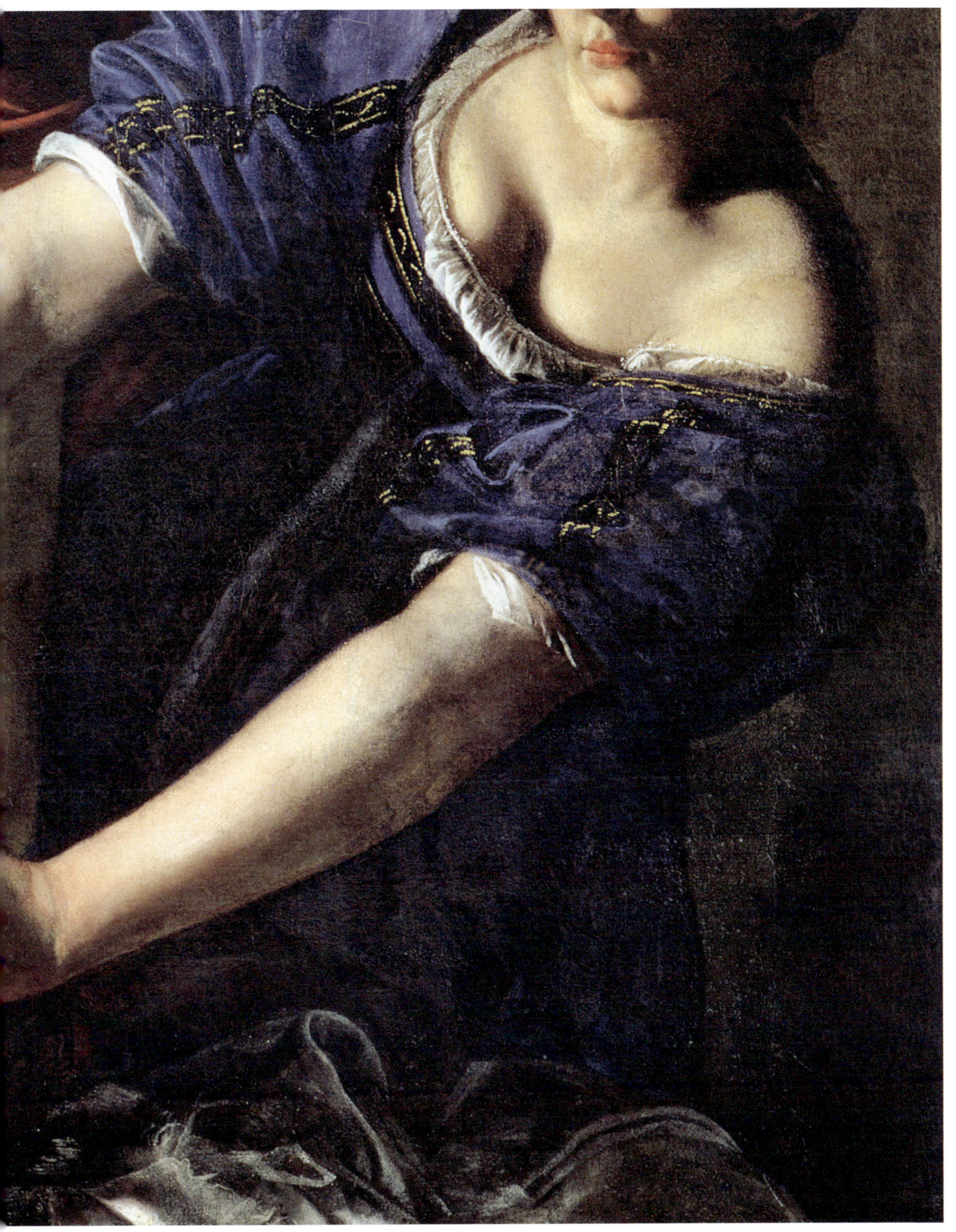

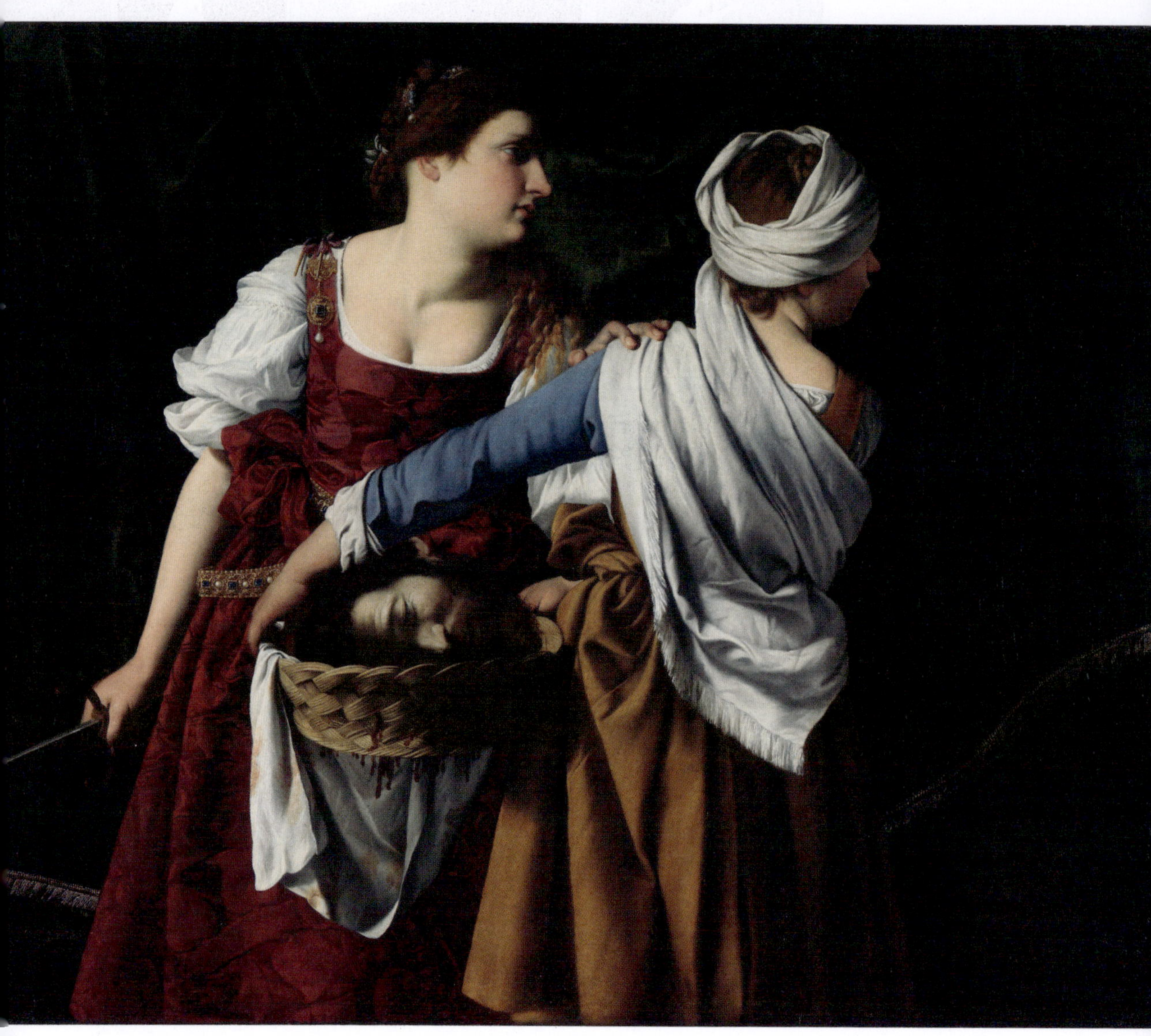

Judith and Her Maidservant with the Head of Holofernes c. 1608
Orazio Gentileschi (1562–1639)
Oil on canvas
136 x 160 cm (53½ x 63 in)
Nasjonalmuseet, Oslo

Most artists chose to portray the incident after the beheading. The women, having completed their daring mission, must flee the enemy camp. Orazio heightens the tension with dramatic lighting and a simple gesture; by lightly touching her handmaid's shoulder, Judith keeps Abra still until it is safe to leave.

Holofernes while Judith drags the sword through his neck. The raw honesty of Artemisia's depiction is unparalleled. Holofernes strikes out at his attackers, pushing back at Abra with his enormous fist while he writhes and grimaces in pain. Blood spurts from his wound and stains the bedclothes. But Judith does not recoil. Artemisia presents her as composed and determined, using the full weight of her body to counter the superior power of her adversary.

No known written record confirms either version – one in the Museo e Real Bosco di Capodimonte, Naples, and the other in the Gallerie degli Uffizi, Florence – as the first. At some point in time, the Naples version was cut down, altering the full scope of the composition. But the precisely structured figure placement is intact, and the similarities between the two paintings suggest that Artemisia traced one to make the other. This was a common practice in her day. In 1983, X-radiographic analysis of the Naples version revealed *pentimenti* (subsurface changes), reflecting Artemisia's method of making changes to her composition as she worked directly on her canvas. This physical evidence has led to the assumption that Artemisia resolved the configuration in the Naples version before she painted the Uffizi version.

Despite the compositional similarities, there are subtle, but significant, differences between the two paintings, differences that may be indicative of Artemisia's ambition and her ability to tailor her work to a specific audience. The most obvious change is in Judith's costume. In the Uffizi version, Artemisia replaces the sumptuous blue gown with one of gold. Both colours indicated wealth – the dyes required were expensive – but, in Florence, gold was the more fashionable. The folds of the sleeves, pushed clear of Judith's forearms, are characteristic of different fabrics; the heavier roll of the blue gown evokes velvet, while the more crumpled gold simulates a more delicate silk brocade of a type preferred by the Tuscan aristocracy. In the Uffizi version, Judith wears a gold and jewelled bracelet; in the Naples version, her arms are bare. These enrichments suggest that the second version was painted with regard to refined Florentine taste. The painting's provenance establishes that it was long in the possession of the Medici family – the most prominent family in Florence – and it is widely believed that Artemisia either painted it to attract the attention of the Grand Duke Cosimo II de' Medici or that he might have commissioned the work.

The dramatic physicality of both versions sets Artemisia's interpretation of Judith's heroism apart from earlier examples. Prior artists had preferred the scene of escape, emphasizing Judith's calm stealth as she completed her mission. In Caravaggio's depiction of the beheading, Judith appears repulsed by her own actions; she leans away from her victim, even as she severs his neck. In contrast, Artemisia's Judith leans in. Anchoring her knee on Holofernes' bed for leverage, she subdues her opponent with the full weight of her body. Her outstretched arms draw power from the forward thrust of her shoulders and back. Artemisia takes into account the discrepancy of size and strength and what it would take for Judith to overwhelm such a large and robust man. In the Uffizi version, a slight shift in Judith's position intensifies her actions. She torques her body and raises her right shoulder, adding more force to her sword arm. Her grip on Holofernes' hair tightens; she seems to dig into his scalp. Her face – almost impassive in the Naples version – hints at her straining efforts. She narrows her eyes and furrows her brow; her lips are taut with concentration. And, along with this heightened reality, the Uffizi version is far more brutal. Blood sprays out of the gash in Holofernes' neck, spattering Judith's golden gown and the flushed skin of her breast. In the late seventeenth century, Filippo Baldinucci used ironic understatement to describe the painting's effect as *non poco terrore* (not a little terror), and some time in the eighteenth century, after the Grand Duchess Maria Luisa declared it *ribrezzo* (horrifying; disgusting), the painting was moved out of sight to a darkened staircase in the palace.[5]

Artemisia would return to Judith's saga to paint two separate interpretations of the more common subject: Judith and her handmaiden with Holofernes' head. In the earlier painting (1614–15, Gallerie degli Uffizi, Florence), Judith rests the sword on her shoulder and Abra balances the basket holding the head on her hip as they both look warily into the darkness. In the later painting (1623–25, Detroit Institute of Arts), they are still in Holofernes' tent: Abra kneels as she

Judith and her Maidservant with the Head of Holofernes c. 1623–25
Oil on canvas
187 x 142 cm (74 x 56 in)
Detroit Institute of Arts, Detroit, MI

When Artemisia portrayed the same subject that her father painted – Judith and Abra preparing to leave Holofernes' tent – she elevated the sense of menace. As in Orazio's version, Judith cautions Abra with a gesture, but here, her raised hand is active, illuminated by the light of a candle. In her other hand, she holds the sword ready for defence, while Abra is caught in the motion of shoving the head into a sack.

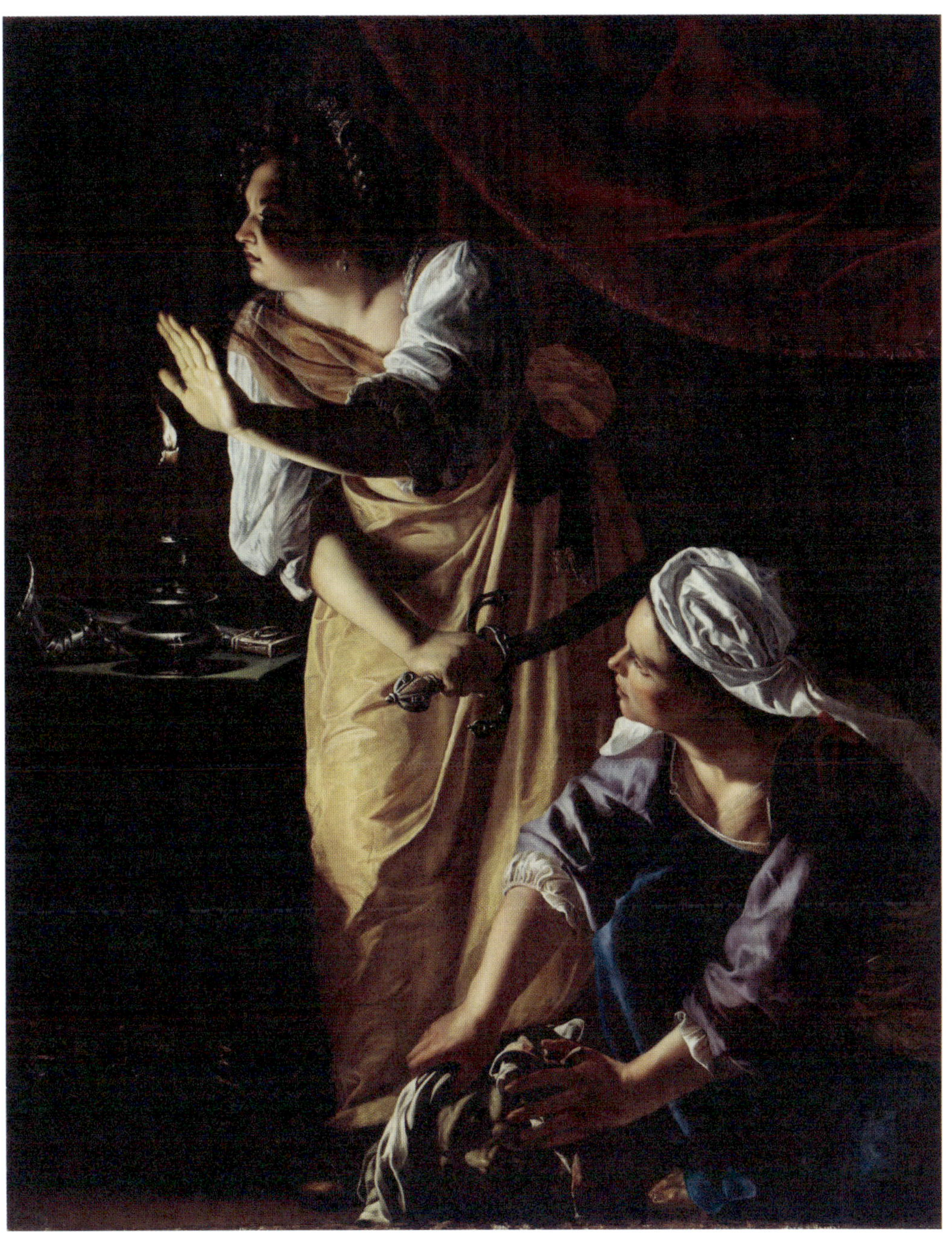

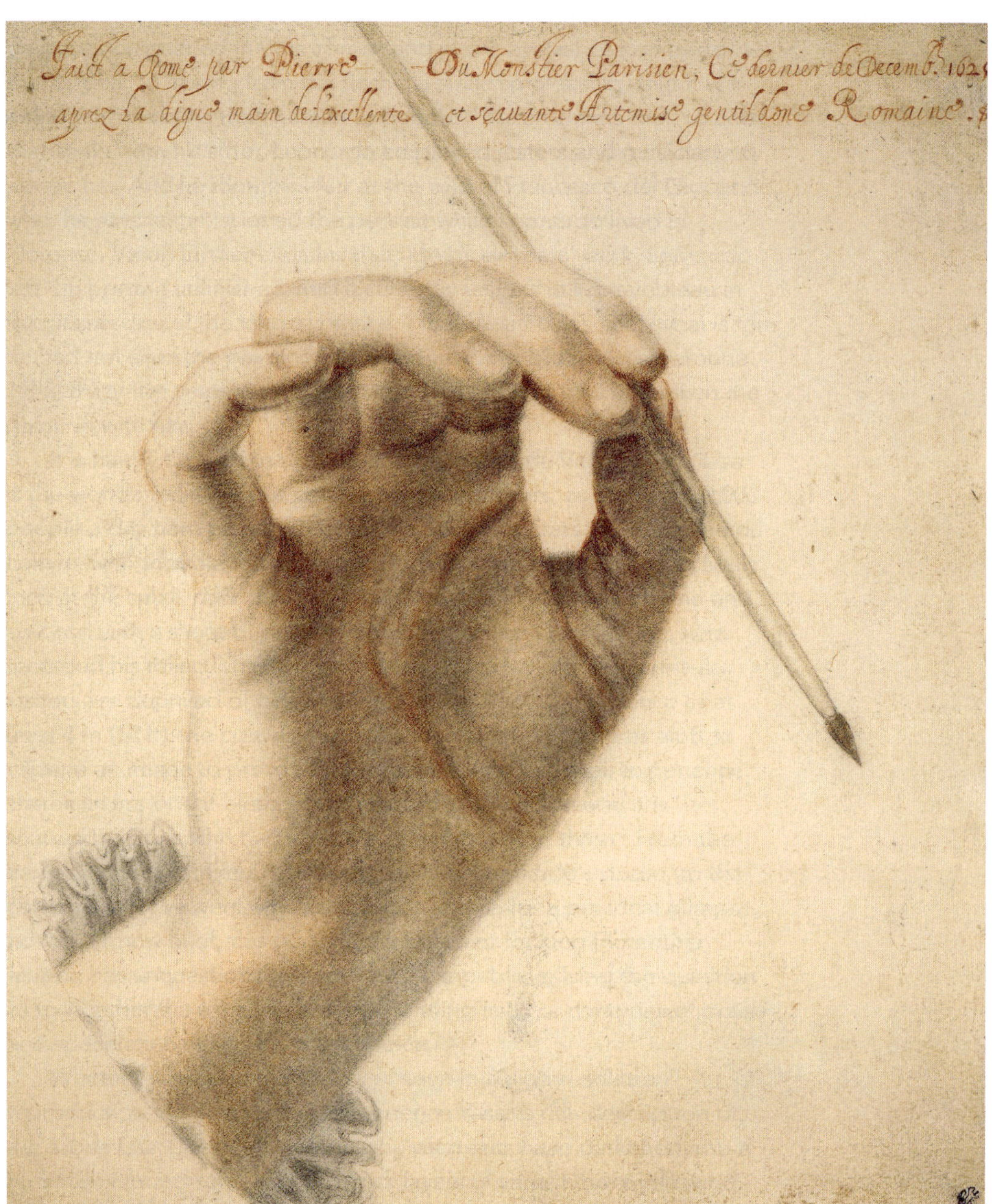

Faict a Rome par Pierre — Du Monstier Parisien, Ce dernier de Decemb. 1625
aprez la digne main de l'excellente et scauante Artemise gentildone Romaine.

hides the head in a sack while Judith, holding the sword at the ready in front of her body, cautions her to be still with her left hand. In both, Artemisia displays a full mastery of the new Roman realism pioneered by Caravaggio and practised by her father in the strongly built naturalistic figures, expressive gestures, dramatic lighting and emotional storytelling. By the time she painted the second picture, Artemisia had laid the foundation of a stellar career, being the first woman to be admitted to the prestigious Accademia delle Arti del Disegno (1616), and, in the decades that followed, she gained pan-European fame, working in Rome, Venice, Naples and even London. But after her death, her reputation slowly faded, and in the centuries that followed many of her works were misattributed to her father. Interest in her career revived in the twentieth century, as feminist scholars sought to recover and re-evaluate the lives and careers of women artists.

In the current wave of appreciation, Artemisia's name is so well known that it can stand alone – without her surname – as the title of the most important survey exhibition of her work to date.[6] But even in the arc of her long and wide-ranging career, her youthful masterpiece, *Judith Beheading Holofernes*, defines her as an artist. As young as she was, she refused to be limited by her gender, her elders or her personal experience. She portrayed Judith, not just as an exemplar of righteous action, but as a woman with courage and resolve, the type of woman with whom she could identify, and one more than able to make good on the claim that Artemisia made to a patron decades later: 'I will show Your Illustrious Lordship what a woman can do!'[7]

Right Hand of Artemisia Gentileschi Holding a Brush 1625
Pierre Dumonstier II (1585–1656)
Black and red chalk on paper
22 x 18 cm (8½ x 6¼ in)
British Museum, London

The inscription in French at the top of the drawing reads: 'Made in Rome by Pierre Dumonstier, Parisian, the last day of December 1625, after the worthy hand of the excellent and learned Artemisia, gentlewoman of Rome'. Another inscription in the same hand on the verso of the drawing, compares the beauty of the hand to that of the goddess Aurora, but deems it 'a thousand times more worthy for knowing how to make marvels'.

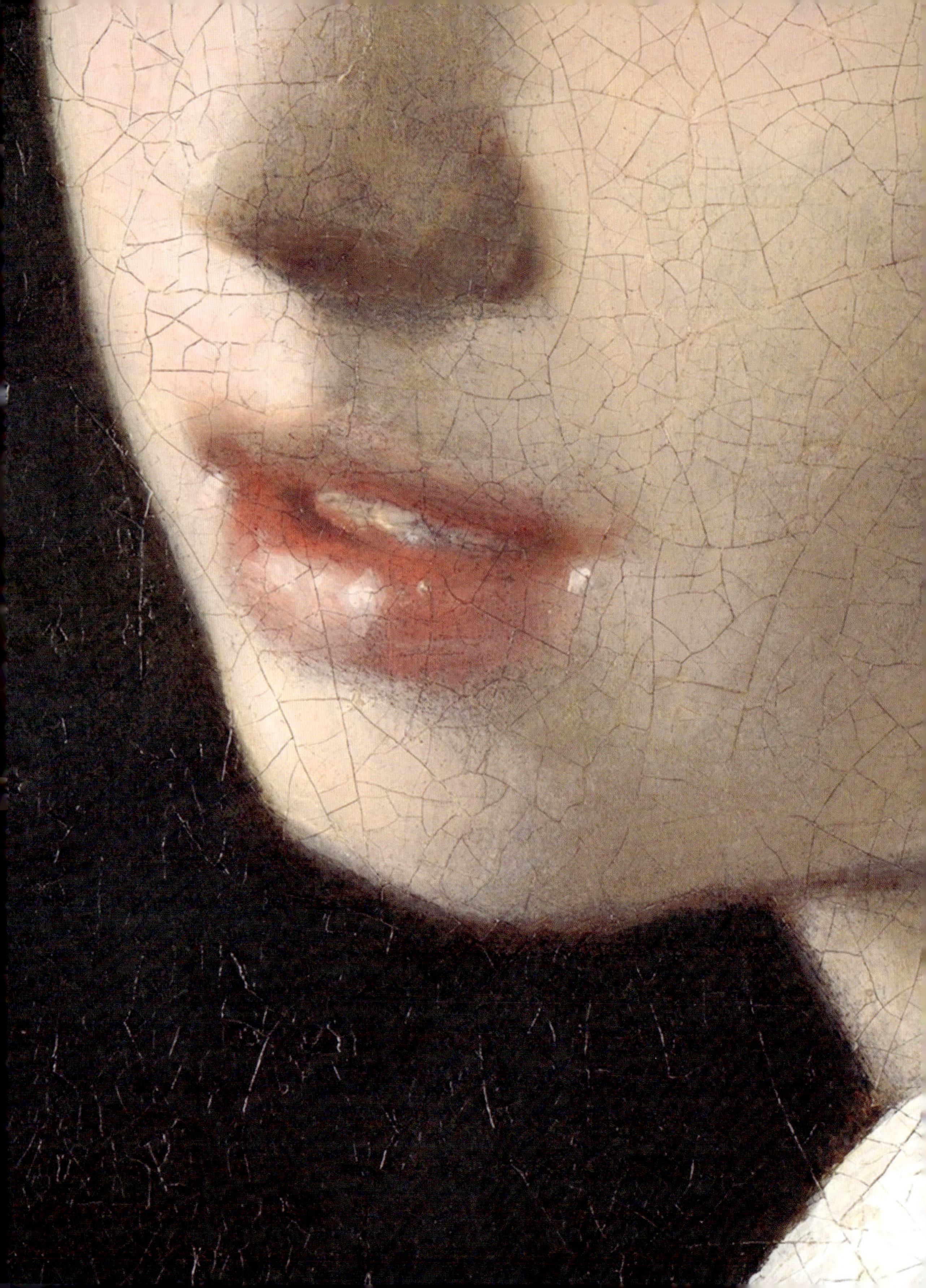

Girl with a Pearl Earring

Johannes Vermeer

A head study …, uncommonly artful.

Dissius Sale list, 1696

At an auction in The Hague, in 1881, Arnoldus des Tombe bid on a small, soiled painting of uncertain origins by an unidentified artist. It was an odd choice for the distinguished collector, but his friend, the art historian Victor de Stuers, had noticed the work in the catalogue and urged des Tombe to acquire it. With little competition, des Tombe secured the painting for only two guilders and a buyer's premium of a few cents (roughly £28). De Stuers sent the work to a restorer he knew in Antwerp who stabilized the fragile painting with a supplemental lining. He then removed layers of dust and dirt to reveal an image of extraordinary beauty: a young woman with wide eyes and parted lips adorned in a blue and yellow headdress and a large pearl earring. Although not dated, the painting was signed 'IVMeer'.

Whether acting upon prior knowledge or pure instinct, de Stuers had uncovered a rare and important work by a long-neglected artist. Today it is hard to conceive that the work of Johannes Vermeer would ever have to be rediscovered, but given his small output – only thirty-six works have been authenticated – within a few decades of his death his name had faded into obscurity. It took more than a century to reignite his reputation, and at the time of des Tombe's purchase, the full power and extent of Vermeer's work had yet to be charted. Des Tombe and de Stuers next turned to Abraham Bredius, an expert on Dutch Golden Age art. The subtle handling of paint and the glowing tonality convinced Bredius that the work was genuine, prompting him to declare: 'Vermeer slays them all'.[1] Upon his death in 1902, des Tombe bequeathed the work to The Hague's Mauritshuis. The public and critics alike hailed the newly titled *Girl with a Pearl Earring* as a Dutch treasure, while the press lauded its rise in value from its paltry purchase price to 40,000 guilders.[2] But even in the light of this newfound fame, the work, like the man who painted it, remained shrouded in mystery, raising an intriguing question: Does what was not known, as well as what is known about the painting, play a role in making the *Girl with a Pearl Earring* a masterpiece?

Johannes Vermeer lived the whole of his life in the prosperous trading city of Delft. Although his father's name appears once on the annual rolls of the Academy of Saint Luke (the painting guild), there is no evidence that he worked as an artist. Nothing is known of Vermeer's own training, but by 1653, the year of his marriage to Catharina Bolnes, he was a member of the academy and served as its dean twice. Vermeer and his wife lived with Catharina's mother, Maria Thins, a wealthy widow who dealt in paintings. His career differed from that of his contemporaries in that he neither marketed his work nor sought fame in a specific subject matter. Perhaps his mother-in-law's financial support allowed him to work as slowly and sporadically as he desired, without concern for productivity. His reputation, however, attracted attention beyond Delft, and over the years such connoisseurs as the French diplomat Balthasar de Monconys and Pieter Teding van

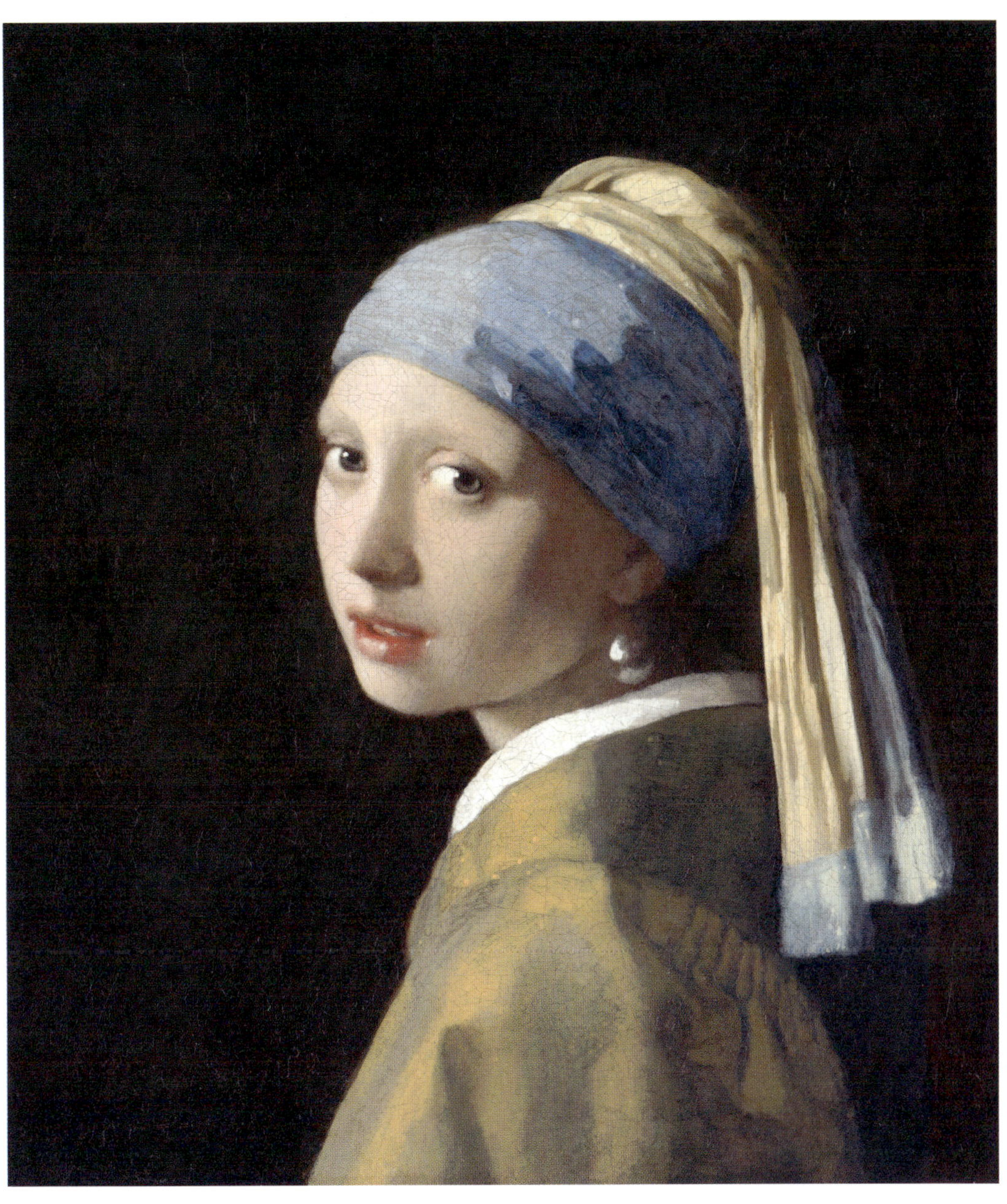

Girl with a Pearl Earring c. 1665
Johannes Vermeer (1632–75)
Oil on canvas
44.5 x 39 cm (17¾ x 15½ in)
Mauritshuis, The Hague

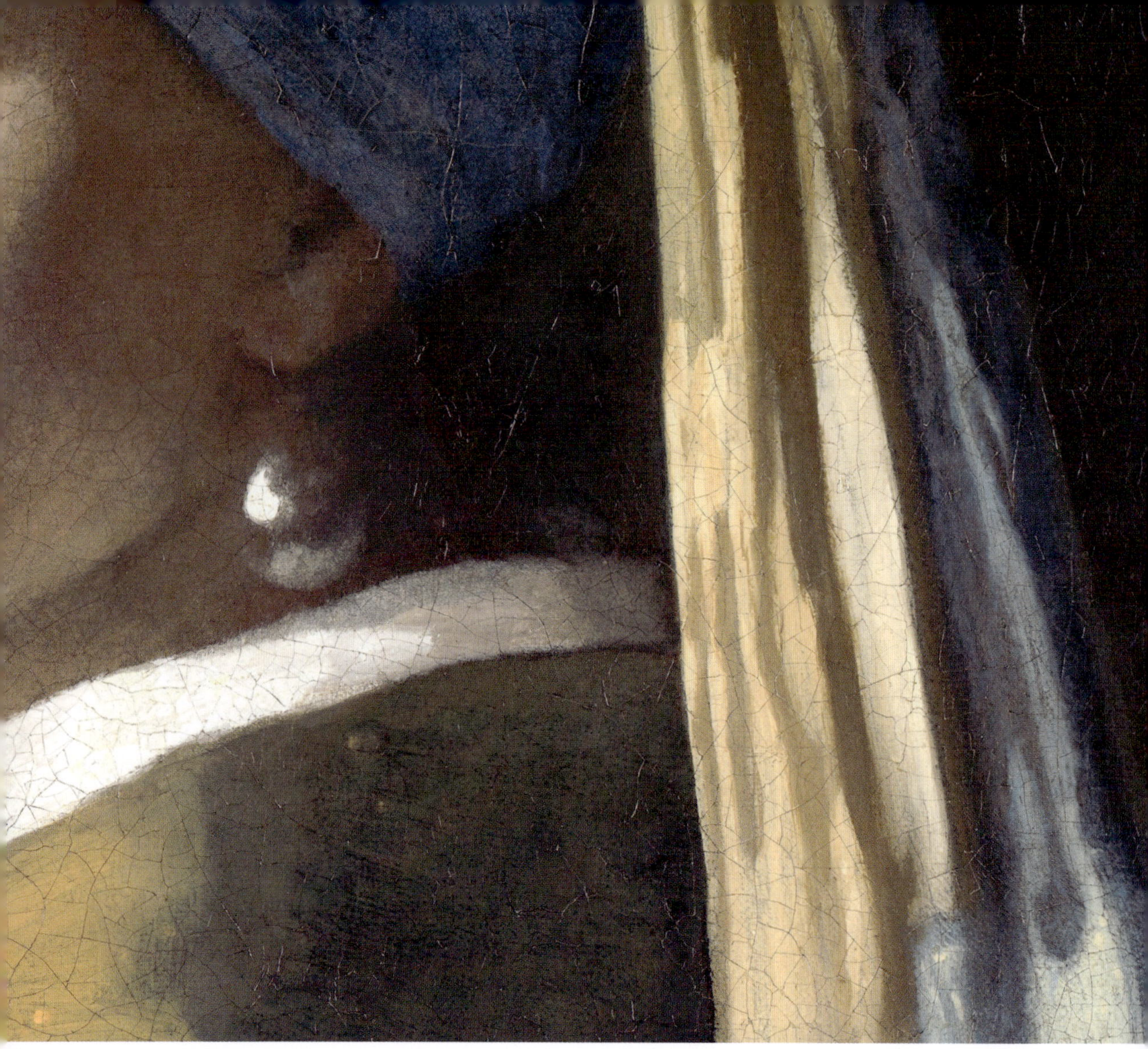

Girl with a Pearl Earring, detail

A matched pair of large, lustrous pearls for earrings – *unions d'excellence* – would have been extremely rare, but high-quality, glass drops filled with a glistening substance such as white wax or *ablette* (fish scales) were widely available. To portray the pearl's nacreous surface, Vermeer used just two strokes of white on a tear-shaped grey volume.

Berkhout, a regent from The Hague, visited him. Both recorded their disappointment in that there was nothing available to buy. Vermeer appeared to have only one devoted patron, Pieter van Ruijven, who had inherited his wealth and increased it through investments.

Vermeer died young, leaving his wife and their eleven children burdened by debt. It is not entirely clear how many of his own paintings were left in his studio, but it is documented that Catharina appeared in court on 22 July 1677 in an attempt to protect her mother's ownership of Vermeer's *The Art of Painting* (1666–67) from seizure by creditors. In 1696, van Ruijven's collection – by then acquired through inheritance by his son-in-law, Jacob Dissius – was auctioned. The catalogue for the sale listed twenty-one works by Vermeer. Over the following century, with the untraced dispersal of these paintings, Vermeer's reputation dimmed. His name never completely disappeared, but his work resided out of public sight in private collections or appeared under other painters' names through misattribution. When John Smith compiled his *Catalogue Raisonné of the Works of the Most Eminent Dutch, Flemish, and French Painters*, in 1833, he praised Vermeer, based on the few examples he had seen at the Mauritshuis in The Hague. This aroused the interest of scholars and specialists; here was a unique and masterful painter who could not be linked to a prominent teacher, a notable patron or an important school. Three decades later, erudite regard turned into popular curiosity when the French critic Théophile Thoré, writing under the Dutch-sounding pseudonym Willem Bürger, published an article about Vermeer in the widely circulated journal, *Gazette des Beaux-Arts* (1866). Thoré told a lively tale of his pursuit of this mysterious master's work in private and public collections. Thoré manipulated the absence of information into myth, falsely claiming that the 'Sphinx of Delft' had gone unnoticed even in his own day.

Throughout his brief career, Vermeer experimented with subject matter: religious narrative, modern-life scenarios, allegory and even two meticulously observed views of Delft. But today he is best known for domestic scenes depicting women carrying out such ordinary actions as reading a letter, opening a shutter, pouring milk or fastening a necklace. Many artists of the era, including Gerard ter Borch, Pieter de Hooch and Nicolaes Maes, also painted captivating and naturalistic imagery featuring women in their homes at work and at leisure, but Vermeer's approach differs in that his domestic scenes resist narrative interpretation beyond the depicted action. There are no knowing glances exchanged with the viewer, and if there is a hint of an underlying story, the tale itself remains unresolved. This is

notably evident in his portrayal of solitary figures, in which the woman's
deep focus on the task at hand lends gravity and grace to mundane
activity. The viewer is kept at a respectful distance, making the act of
observation feel intimate and even covert. The skilfully painted objects
in these works are as artfully arranged as in a still life; one shift in the
placement of a chair or a pitcher would upset the tranquil balance.
And while the objects themselves can be linked to the language of
Dutch pictorial symbolism – the pearl necklace, a balance scale, a
letter, a map – their presence does not always align with conventional
iconographic readings. In a time when so many painters mastered the
art of true-to-life representation, Vermeer's naturalism attains an almost
abstract beauty. His colours glow in a wash of natural illumination, and
his handling of his paint ranges from broadly modulated patches of a
singular tone to deftly rendered details.

In the absence of a date on the canvas, or in an associated
document, art scholars have turned to Vermeer's handling of paint
to situate *Girl with a Pearl Earring* in his career. By the mid-1660s,
Vermeer had developed his own interpretation of the conventional oil
painting practice of laying coloured glazes over a rough underpainted
image in a neutral tone. To create additional depth and modelling,
Vermeer varied his base colours and worked his image in thin,
alternating layers of opaque paint and translucent glazes. This
approach is masterfully demonstrated in the way he painted the
sitter's face in *Girl with a Pearl Earring*. The high-lit, rounded contours
of her brow, her cheeks and her chin are worked over a cream-toned
base; the shadowed areas that define the structure of her cheekbones,
the hollows of her eyes and her jawline are underpainted in tones of

Woman with a Pearl Necklace 1664
Oil on canvas
55 x 45 cm (21½ x 17¾ in)
Gemäldegalerie, Berlin

Vermeer's domestic scenes feature women absorbed in their daily routines.
Here, the yellow *mantelje* (house jacket) identifies the woman as affluent,
likely the lady of the household. The string of pearls she fastens were a
popular bride's gift in seventeenth-century Netherlands; they represented
an orderly home. The *mantelje* and necklace, like the pearl earrings, appear
repeatedly in Vermeer's paintings suggesting that they belonged to a
family member.

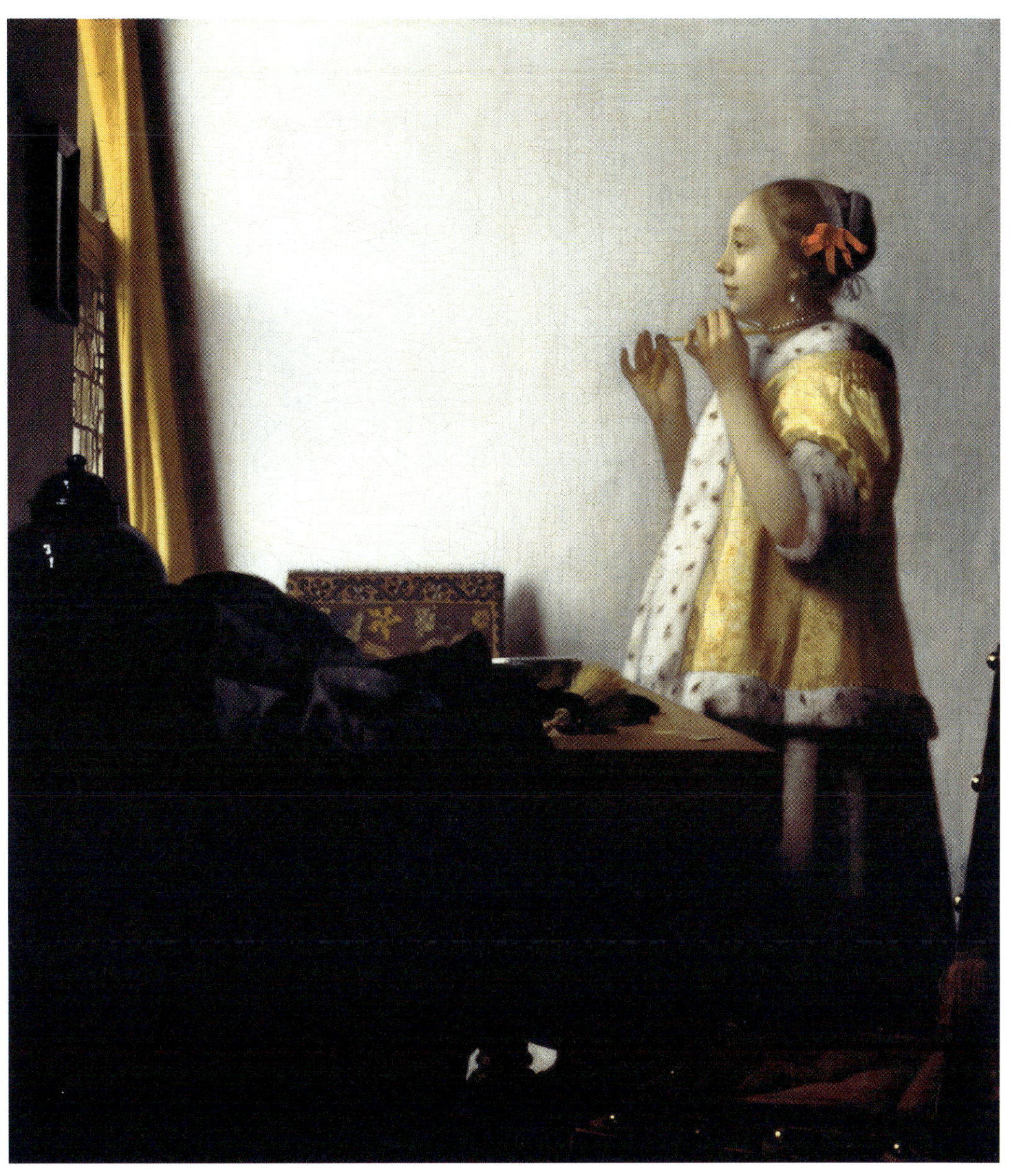

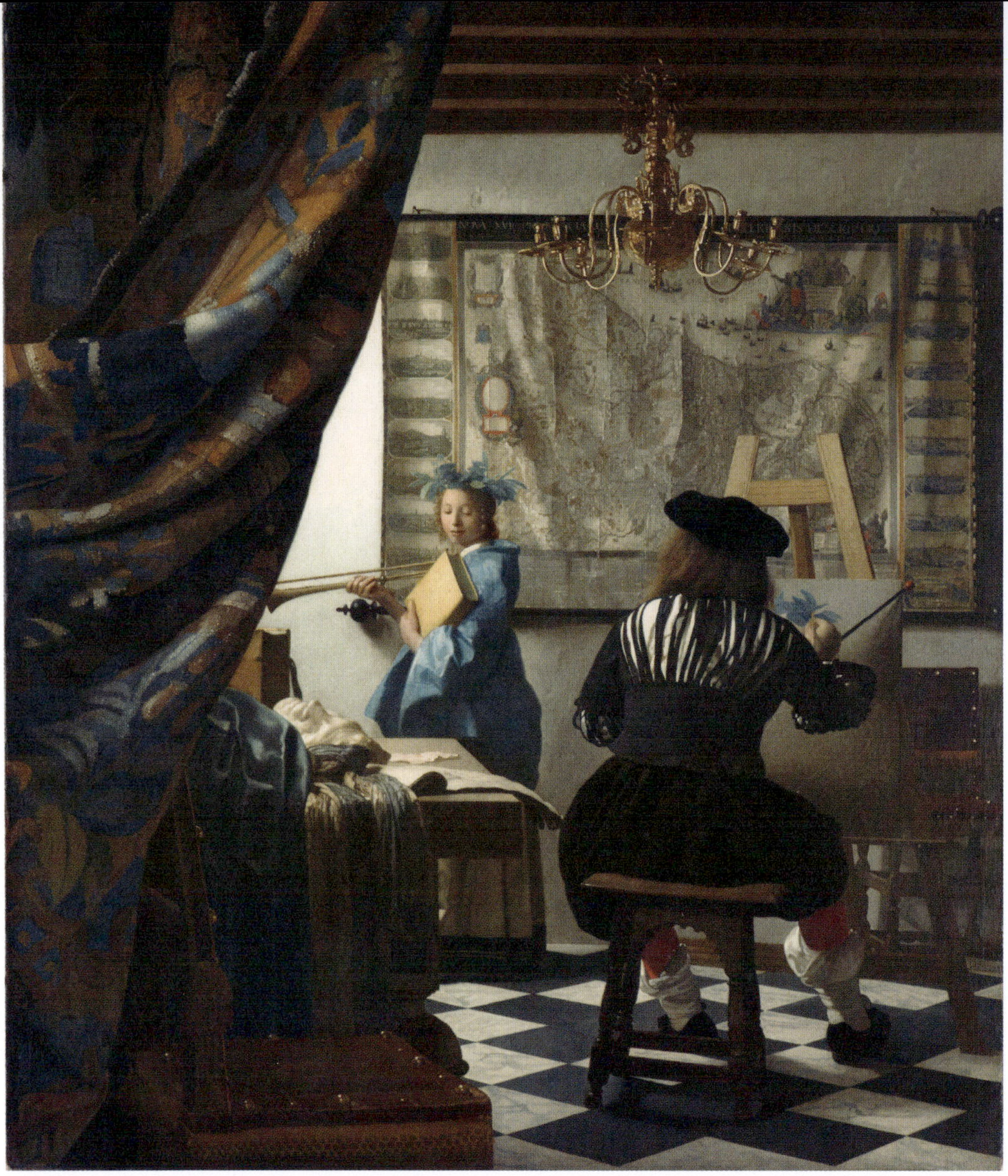

The Art of Painting 1666–68
Oil on canvas
120 x 100 cm (47 x 39 in)
Kunsthistorische Museum, Vienna

In *The Art of Painting*, the woman displays attributes – a crown of laurel, a book, a trumpet – that symbolize fame and history. Her presence as a personification is meant to be read as part of an allegory about painting. In contrast, the *tronie* in her turban and pearl is a flight of artistic fancy.

reddish brown. The result is an illusion of an inner glow, as if she is illuminated by the radiance of her own youth. Vermeer selected other base tones, as well as other modes of handling, for different areas of his composition. The ochre of the jacket is broadly brushed over a black underlayer. He employed a wet-in-wet method – mixing strokes of colour into layers of paint that have not yet dried – to evoke a silk-like sheen on the folds of the lapis blue and pale-yellow headdress. New conservation studies, undertaken at the Mauritshuis in 2016–18, have revealed that the deeply shadowed background features a dark green curtain, thinly painted over a black ground.

From the time of the painting's rediscovery, the prominent placement of the sitter, bathed in warm, lifelike light, has raised the question of who the girl might be. The format of the composition suggests that it is a portrait, with the sitter the sole object of attention, filling the darkened space and positioned at the edge of the picture plane. The features of her face are remarkable, not just for youth and beauty, but for their individuality. Her striking looks call for an identity. As she turns to the viewer her eyes appear to widen in recognition and her lips part as if to speak. Vermeer was not known to have painted portraits, but over the years scholars have sought to link this sitter to someone with a name and a history. In 1921, the art critic Jean-Louis Vaudoyer referred to the model in Vermeer's *Art of Painting* as the painter's daughter.[3] The general resemblance between the sitters – in the size and shape of the eyes, the high set of the eyebrows and the breadth of the forehead and cheekbones – is the likely origin of the persistent assertion that the painter's eldest daughter Maria posed for the *Girl*. But, if the presumed date in the mid-1660s is correct, Maria would have been no more than eleven years old, hardly an adolescent on the brink of womanhood. And her sisters would have been even younger. While clothing often provides information about a sitter, the *Girl's* garments are hard to read. Her bodice is a common, informal house jacket, worn by Dutch women and girls no matter their age or status. But her head wrap, made of two lengths of fabric in a turban-like twist, does not resemble any type favoured by women of the era. And that massive, tear-shaped pearl, painted in a few deft strokes of white and grey, is less an emblem of wealth than a visual highlight that echoes the shape and the contour of the *Girl's* extraordinary face.

This odd attire leads to a more plausible interpretation: that *Girl with a Pearl Earring* is not a portrait but a *tronie* (head study). In Vermeer's day, the term – a generic word for face derived from the French slang *trogne* or 'mug' – described a character study featuring a

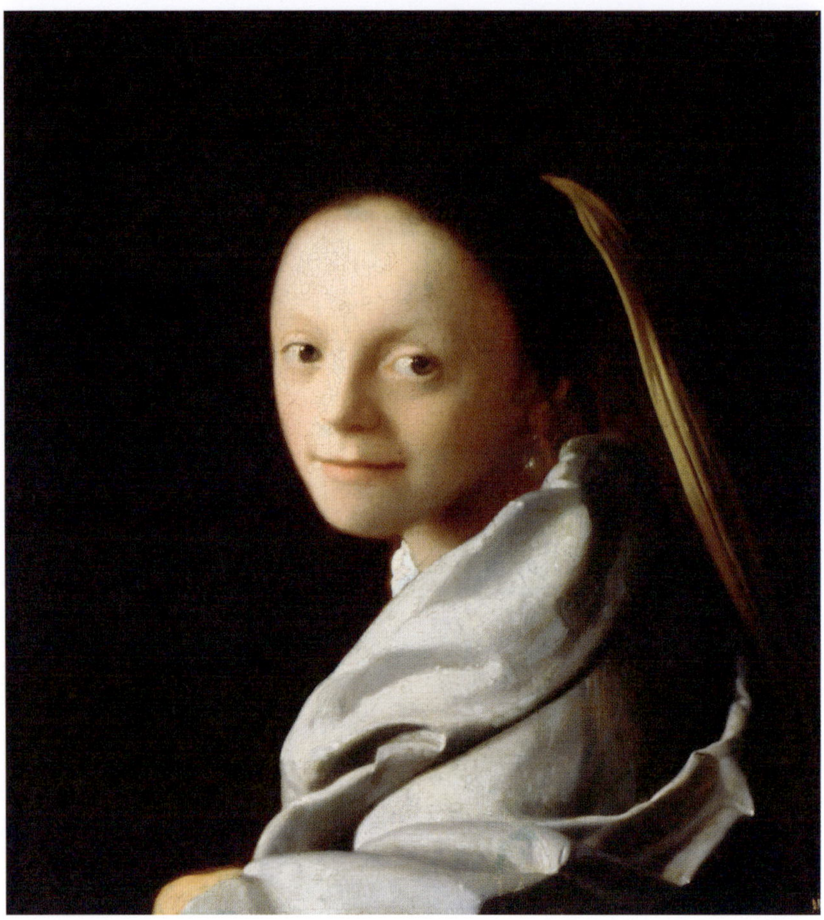

ABOVE *Study of a Young Woman* c. 1665–67
Oil on canvas
44.5 x 40 cm (17½ x 15¾ in)
Metropolitan Museum of Art, New York

Two *tronies* in the 'Turkish fashion' appear in Vermeer's estate list. Here, as with the description 'antique dress' in the Dissius sale, the reference is to fanciful, rather than historical, dress. This image of a young woman in a pale gold head wrap is believed to be one of the 'Turkish' *tronies*; *Girl with a Pearl Earring* may be the other, suggesting that Van Ruijven acquired it after the painter's death.

OPPOSITE *Girl with a Pearl Earring*, detail

Vermeer used deft dabs of white to simulate the shine of the *Girl's* large eyes and the suppleness of her rose-tinted lips. The soft modelling evokes the expressive mobility of a young face and is a poignant reminder of the evanescence of youthful beauty.

72   Making a Masterpiece

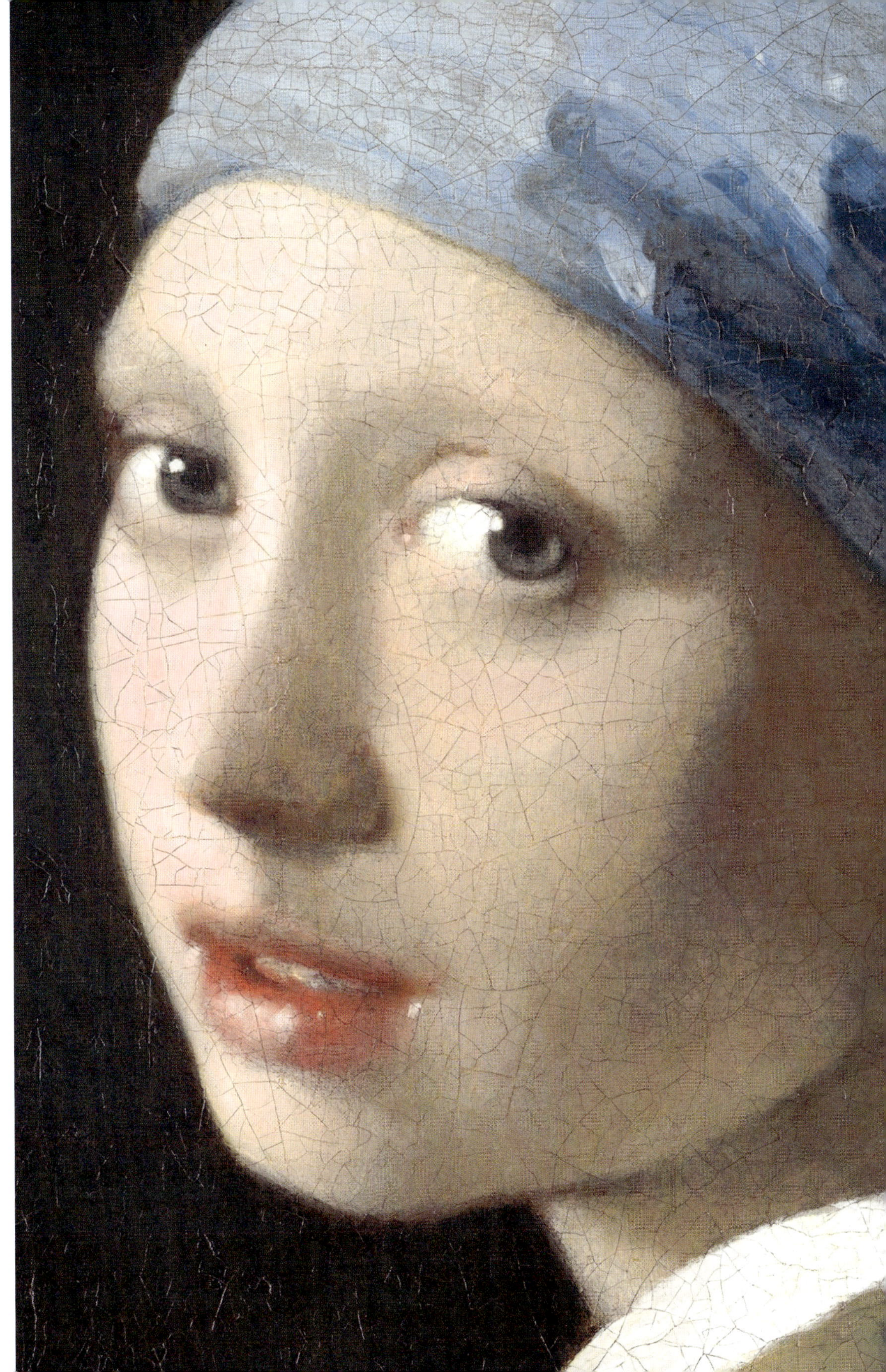

bust-length figure, generally in fanciful dress. Painters created them to demonstrate their skill at costume, ornaments and facial expressions. The identity of the model didn't matter; Rembrandt van Rijn, for example, based his *tronies* on family members and professional models, as well as his own appearance. They were intended as display pieces to promote an artist's ability and collected as decorative works to add an exotic or playful touch to a domestic interior. Vermeer painted a number of *tronies* during his brief career. An inventory of his estate made shortly after his death lists two *tronies*, and the catalogue for the Dissius sale (which included the collection of Pieter van Ruijven) lists three, including one described as 'in antique dress, uncommonly artful'.[4] Of the four *tronies* authenticated as the work of Vermeer – the other three being *Girl in a Red Hat* and *Girl with a Flute* (both c. 1665–70; National Gallery of Art, Washington, DC) and *Study of a Young Woman* (1665–74; Metropolitan Museum of Art, New York) – it is *Girl with a Pearl Earring* that best fits the superlative description.

If, in fact, the 'uncommonly artful' *tronie* referred to the painting we now call *Girl with a Pearl Earring*, the catalogue author was undoubtedly citing Vermeer's painterly skill and the sitter's beauty. But it is also the positioning of the figure that has given the work its enduring allure. In contrast to the self-absorbed women in his domestic scenes, those in Vermeer's four known *tronies* face the viewer with a direct gaze. Three of the four turn to look over their shoulder, but only *Girl with a Pearl Earring* has evoked the level of expressive engagement that critics and scholars have recorded since the painting's re-emergence. As one of the first experts to view the work, Abraham Bredius saw an unparalleled vitality in the work; he claimed that it made him forget that he was looking at a painting. Nearly a century later, the writer John Updike, after seeing the work in

Girl with a Bamboo Earring 2009
Awol Erizku (born 1988)
Chromogenic print

In his brilliantly coloured photographs, Awol Erizku confronts the paucity of Black figures in traditional works of art. Both tribute and critique, he re-envisions *Girl with a Pearl Earring* with a woman of colour, who wears the iconic head wrap, but replaces the pearl with a bamboo heart. Born in Ethiopia, the artist works in Los Angeles.

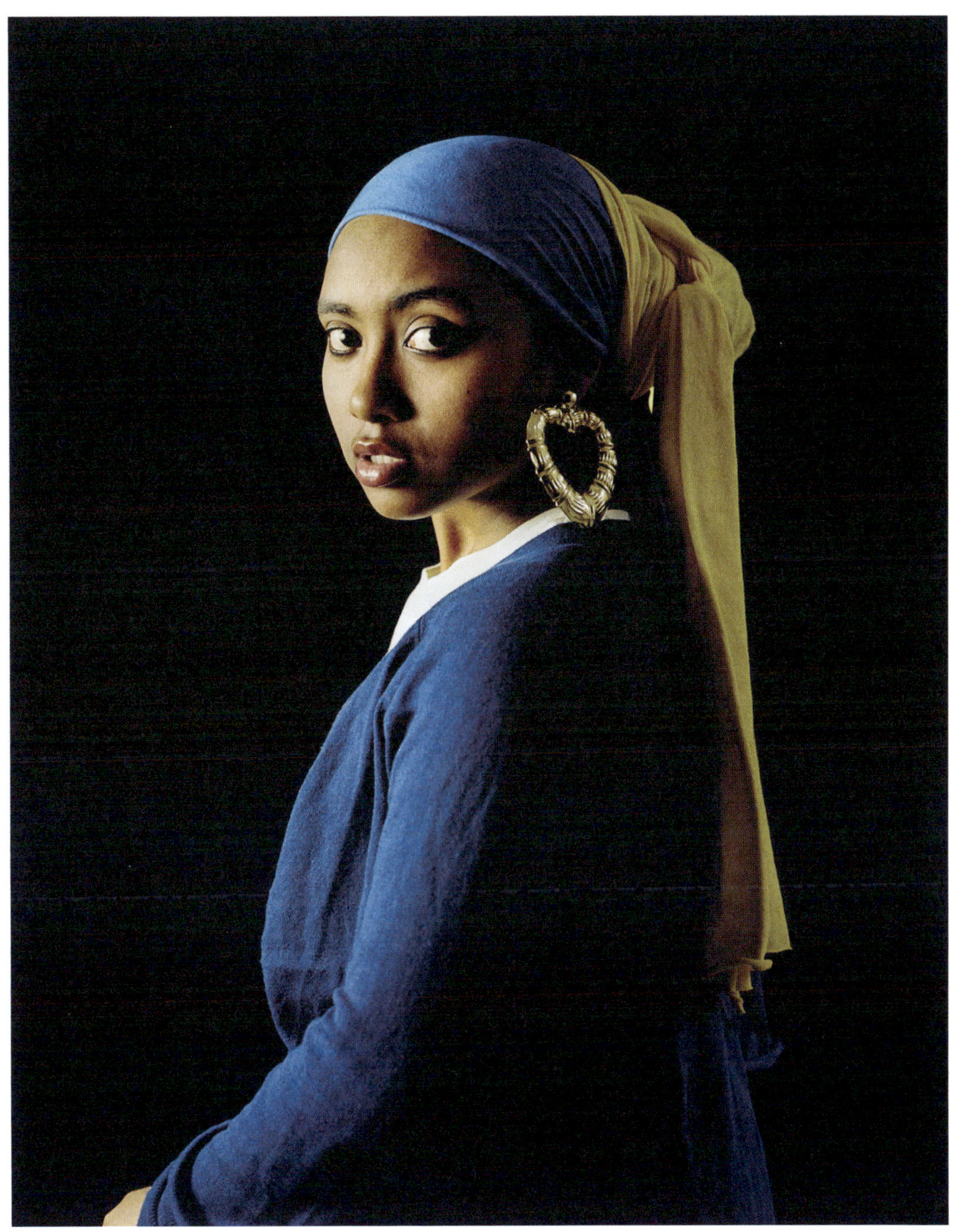

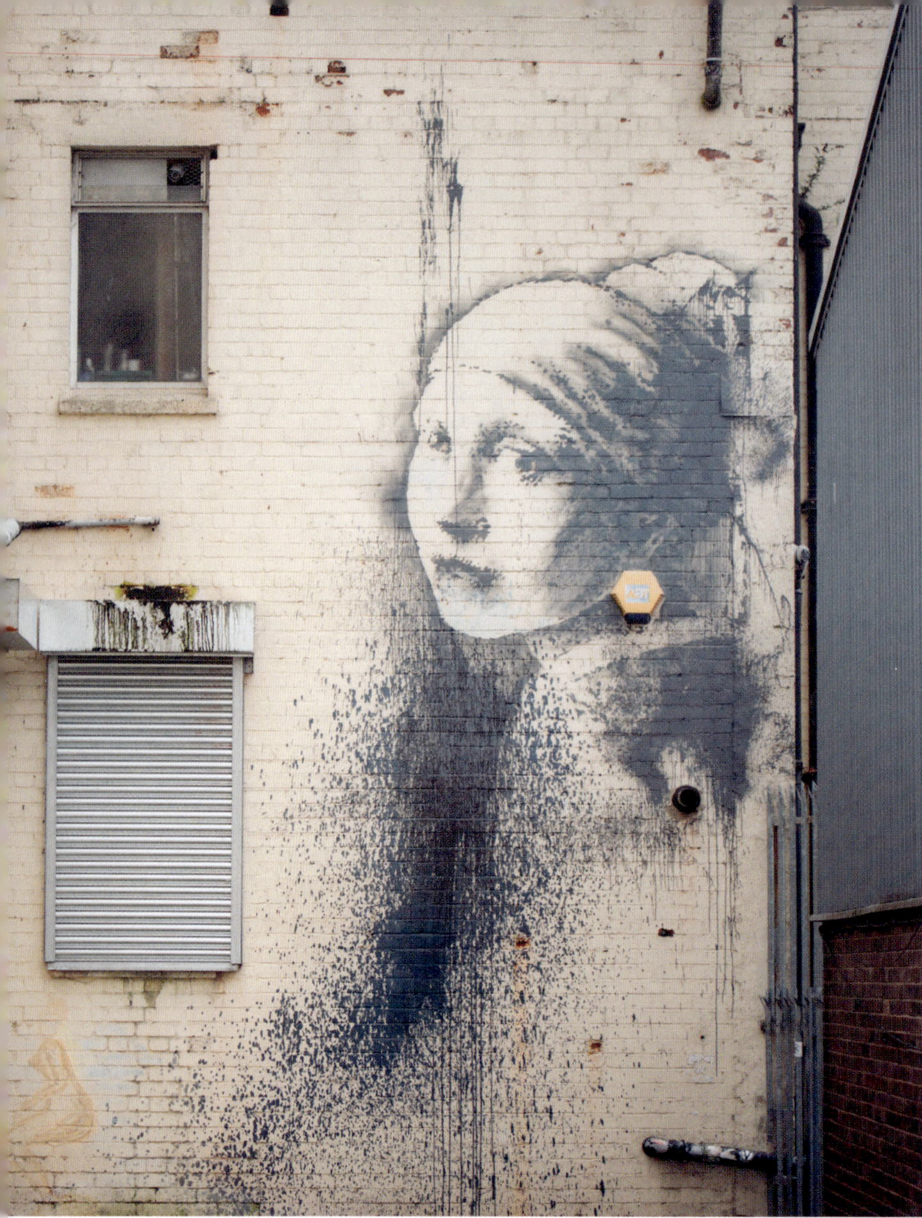

Girl with a Pierced Eardrum 2014
Banksy (born c. 1974)
Hanover Place, Bristol

With her unmistakable pose and attire, *Girl with a Pearl Earring* has been
impersonated, replicated and parodied. Celebrities have been photographed
in her head wrap and pearls. Websites offer tutorials on the scarf-twist and
make-up. Replacing her trademark pearl with a security alarm, street artist
Banksy painted her on a harbour-side wall in Bristol; in April 2020, during the
COVID-19 pandemic, someone added a face mask.

an exhibition at the Metropolitan Museum of Art in New York, mused upon his experience in the poem 'Head of a Girl, at the Met' (1985). He presents the encounter as a reunion; he had seen the girl in her 'turban and pearl', years earlier at the Mauritshuis in The Hague. Updike wonders at her undiminished youth – unlike his own aging body and care-worn heart – and he celebrates the timelessness of her existence – 'You will outlive me, artful girl' – and he envisions her 'with averted head' giving new admirers the gift of a 'moment's glance' in the coming centuries.[5]

The power of that fleeting, yet mesmerizing, glance also inspired author Tracy Chevalier, who imagined that it rested not on a random viewer but on Vermeer, prompting her to surmise: 'She knows him, she's close to him.'[6] In her novel, *Girl with a Pearl Earring* (1999), Chevalier gives the sitter a name and an identity; she becomes Griet (short for Margriet, deriving from the Latin *margarita* or pearl), a young maid in the Vermeer household. Written as a first-person narrative, readers come to know Griet through her own thoughts and observations, and her experiences go well beyond posing for her employer's painting. Film director Peter Webber translated Chevalier's story to the screen in his film *Girl with a Pearl Earring* (2003) starring Scarlet Johansson as Griet. In both the novel and the film, the 'real' Griet seems far from the ethereal figure on the canvas; she endures harsh treatment and hard work with stoic substance and grows into a young woman of intelligence and independent purpose. In the novel, Griet never sees the finished painting, but the film captures the moment when Griet, wearing the blue and yellow head wrap and the weighty pearl, assumes the exact pose. The camera first captures the gleam of light on the pearl and then pulls back to reveal the transformation of the housemaid – and the actor portraying her – into an iconic image, luminous on a darkened screen.

Perhaps it is transcendence rather than substance that draws us to *Girl with a Pearl Earring*. With her yielding pose and yearning glance, she rivets our attention by seeming to return our gaze, but, in fact, she cedes nothing. Her clothing, her presence – even the pearl dangling from her ear – are all an illusion, a masterful manipulation of colour and light on canvas. The harder we press to engage with her as an actual entity with a name, a history and a purpose, the more elusive her image becomes. The painting fascinates us because it is an artful enigma, ready to receive and reflect whatever we project upon her. We will likely never know who the sitter was or why Vermeer chose her. But would *Girl with a Pearl Earring* be more compelling if we knew her name?

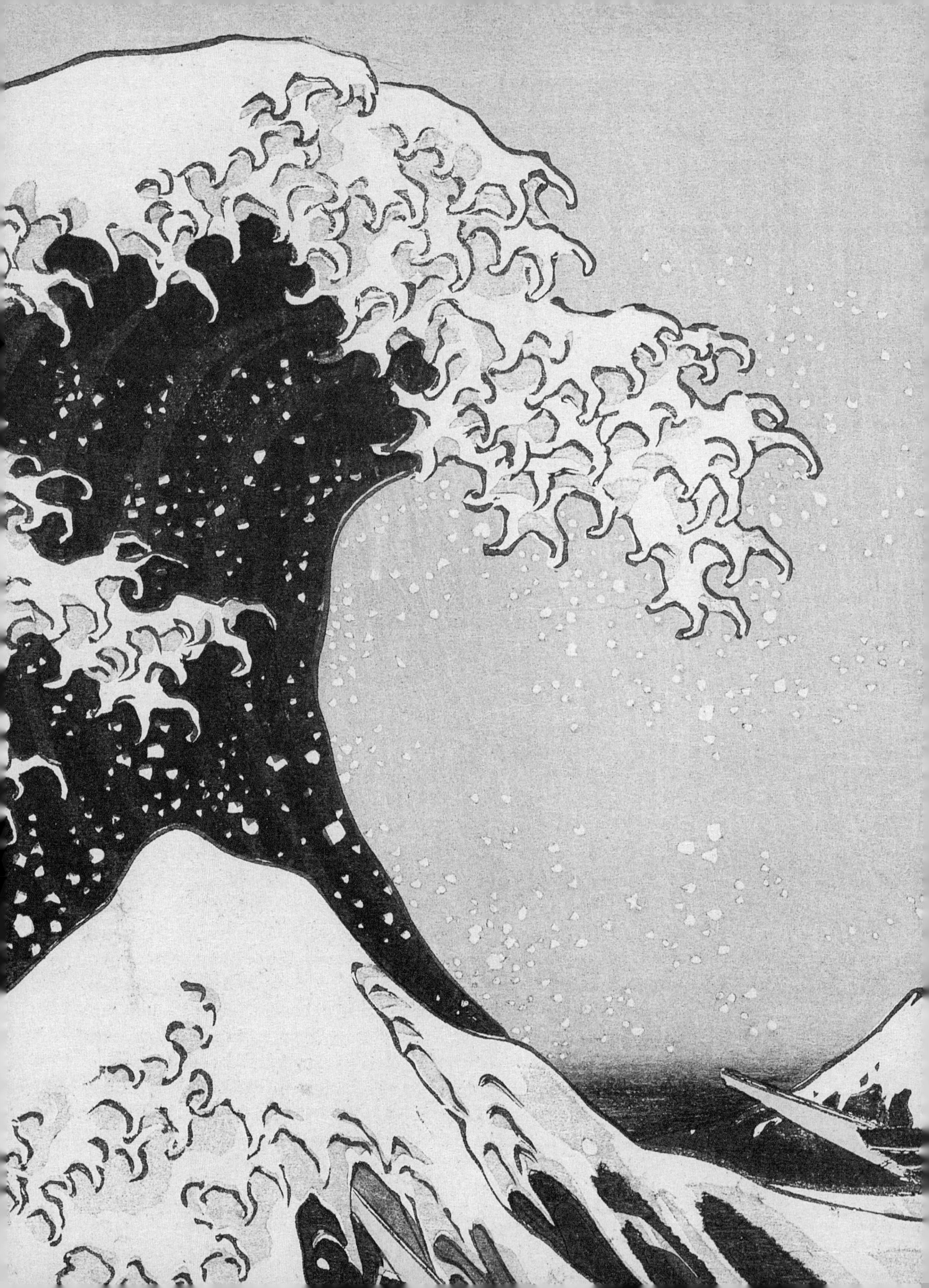

The Great Wave Katsushika Hokusai

Drawn by Old-man Iitsu, the former Hokusai, printed in blue.

Advertisement for Thirty-Six Views of Mount Fuji, 1831

In the advertising section of the latest installation of a popular serial novel, the publisher Nishimuraya Yohachi announced an ambitious new venture. Thirty-Six Views of Mount Fuji, a colour woodblock print series, had all the hallmarks of a best seller. Although landscape was a relatively new subject for the type of print known as *ukiyo-e*, the focus on the towering volcanic peak that loomed over Edo (present-day Tokyo) guaranteed interest for its long-standing association with spiritual beliefs and regional identity. Katsushika Hokusai – at seventy years of age, one of Japan's most beloved and respected artists – would design the images to be printed on large-scale sheets in the colour of the moment, Prussian blue. Luxurious but affordable, the Thirty-Six Views were to be issued sheet by sheet for individual purchase and if demand warranted, the number of views were 'not limited to thirty-six'.[1] The series proved extraordinarily successful – both in its day and to the present – with one work far surpassing all the others in its captivating popularity: *Under the Wave off Kanagawa*, now known as *The Great Wave*.

With its vibrant palette and graphic evocation of raw natural power, *The Great Wave* transcends the boundaries of geography, time and culture in terms of fame. There is no other work in the history of Asian art as universally recognized or as enduringly influential. It is believed that over the years as many as 8,000 impressions of the print were pulled; around 200 have been identified. The finest of these are preserved in museum collections and revered by connoisseurs, while the image itself has been almost infinitely reproduced, replicated and commodified. Few works have gained the same level of acclaim as both a treasured work of art and as a popular image. Looking back to the commission of the print and its commercial context reveals that, from its conception, Hokusai sought to strike that difficult balance and in doing so he made *The Great Wave* a global masterpiece.

The Buddhist precept *ukiyo* (floating world) cautions that yearning for transitory pleasures is the root of human suffering. The spirit that shaped Hokusai's world took the same name, only the premise was reversed. Seventeenth-century writer Asai Ryōi likened the sensations of 'living for the moment', in thrall to such ephemeral charms as moonlight or fresh-fallen snow or cherry blossoms, to that of a 'gourd floating along with the river'. Buoyant but brief, the experience was enriched by its evanescence: 'this is what we call *ukiyo*'.[2] But more than mere indulgence, the pleasures of the floating world provided a release for men of wealth and position during the prosperous, but rigidly ordered reign of the Tokugawa shogunate (1603–1868). The major cities – most notably, the capital Edo – hosted so-called pleasure districts where a man of means could escape his political obligations and social restrictions and live for the moment, enjoying entertainments that ranged from literary circles, the visual arts and staged performances to sporting events and hired female companionship. This mix of high and popular culture – both sophisticated and sensuous – is the

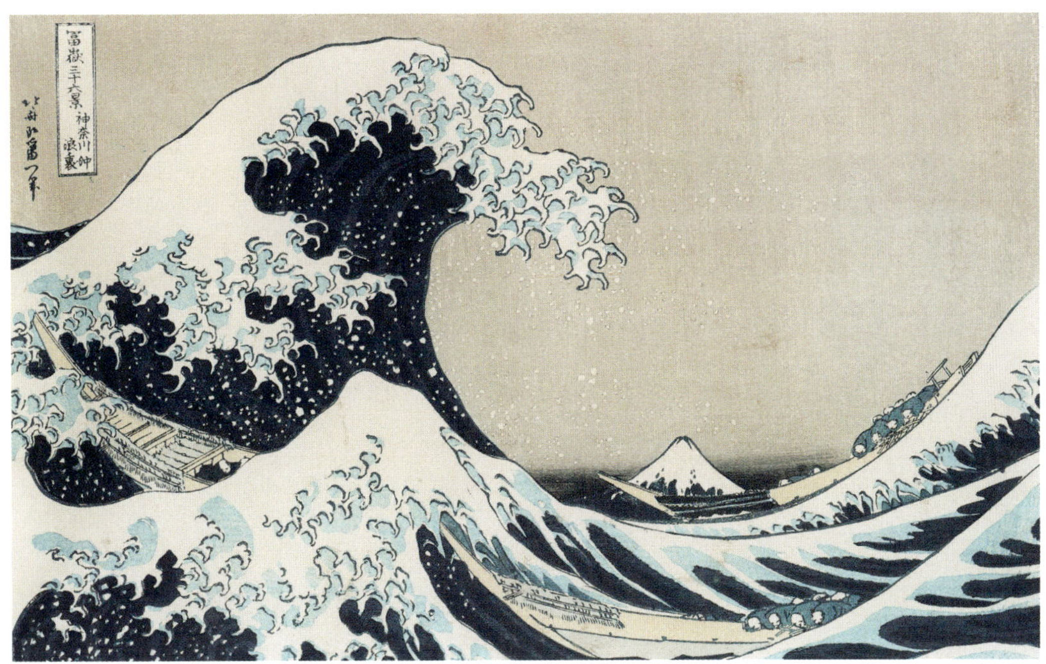

Under the Wave off Kanagawa
From Thirty-Six Views of Mount Fuji c. 1830–32
Katsushika Hokusai (1760–1849)
Woodblock print, ink and colour on paper
26 x 38 cm (10¼ x 15 in)
British Museum, London

essence of the *ukiyo* ethos. Urbane, entertaining and ever-changing, *ukiyo* diversions appealed to both physical and intellectual desires in a delicate balance of artistry and playfulness, as well as refined taste and constant innovation.

With his prodigious talent and restless spirit, Hokusai rose to fame at the height of the *ukiyo* milieu. During a career that lasted more than seventy years, he painted, he drew and he designed prints. Noted for his eccentricities, Hokusai became a celebrity in the *ukiyo* world, and he changed his name at least thirty times to reflect the current state of his mind, as well as the stages of his career.[3] The full title of his best-known work, *Manga* (published in fifteen volumes from 1814–78; the late volumes published posthumously), *Denshinkaishu: Hokusai Manga*

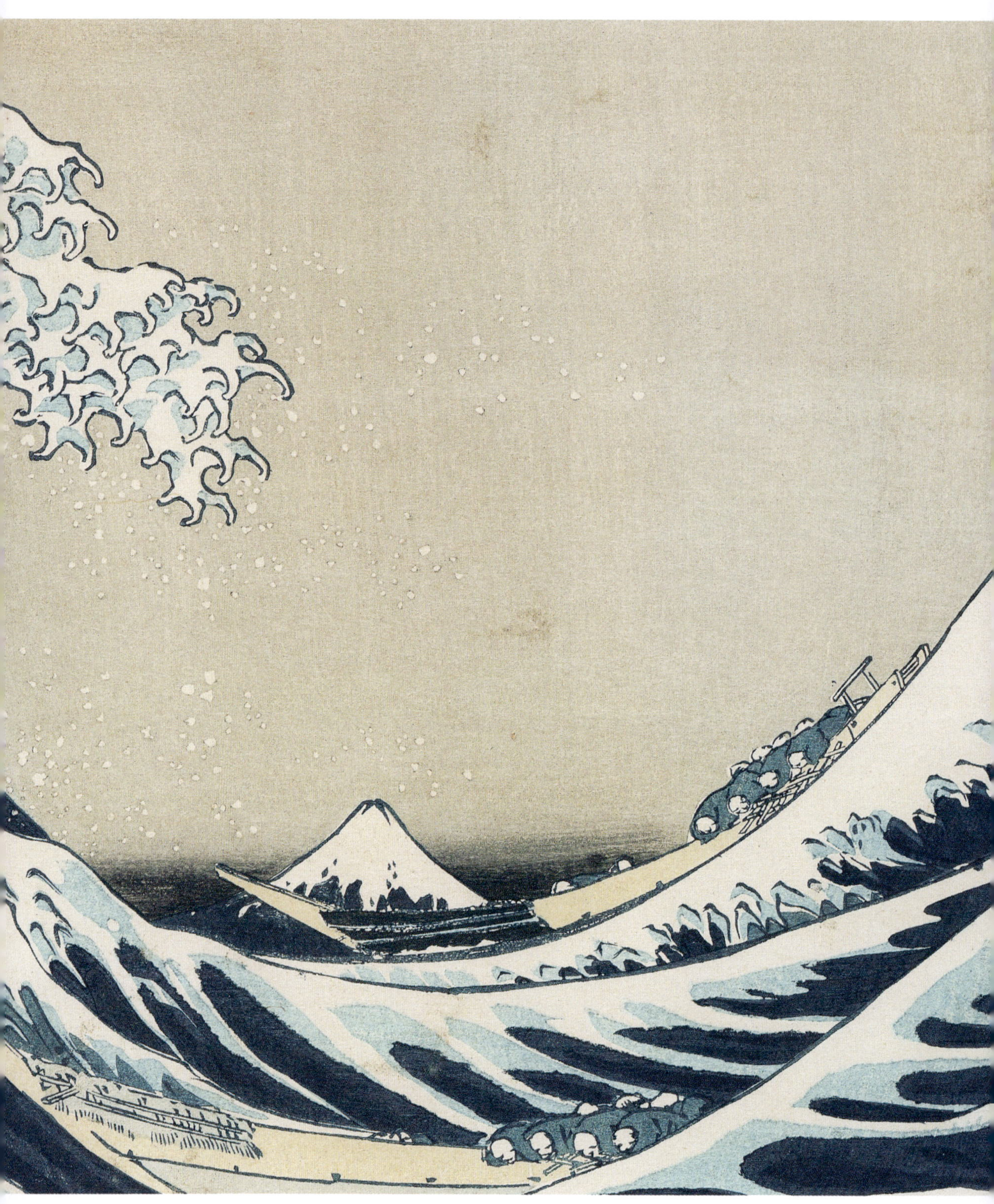

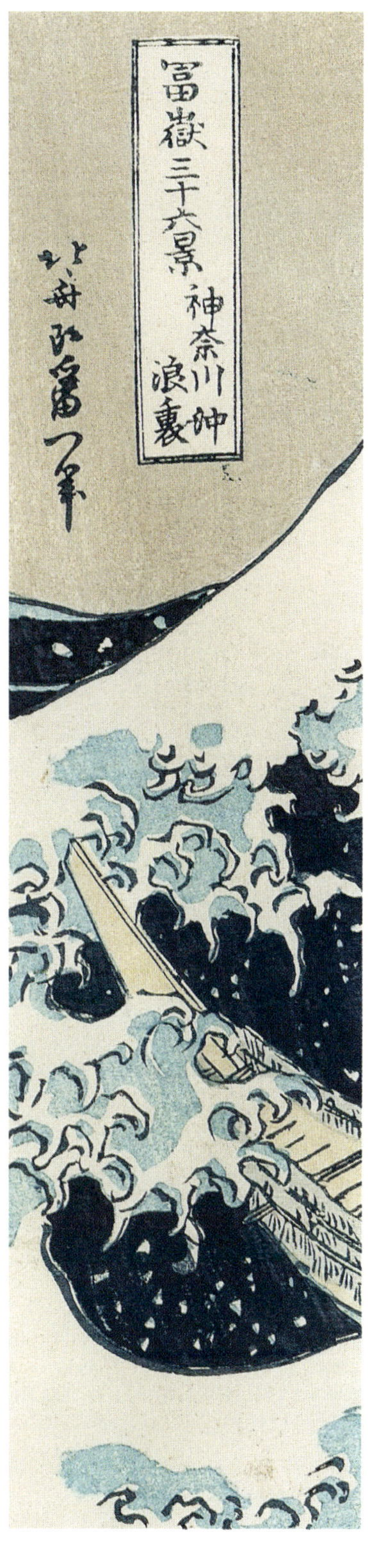

Under the Wave off Kanagawa, detail

OPPOSITE Contrasting themes of transience and endurance unify the print series, presenting human activity in the foreground with Mount Fuji as a steady, monumental presence in the distance. Here the swelling waves highlight the gap between human endeavour and nature's power, as the oarsmen struggle to steer their *oshiokuri*, the narrow skiffs that ferry freshly caught fish from the Edo Bay fleets to the shore.

RIGHT The inscription in the signature cartouche states: 'Brush of Iitsu, changed from Hokusai'. Hokusai adopted the name Iitsu (become one with creation) in 1820, to mark what he hoped would be his second sixty-year cycle of life. The reference to his brush identifies Hokusai as the designer; other craftsmen carved the blocks and printed the image.

(*Beginner's Manual for transmitting the true image as Hokusai pleases*) suggests that it was an instruction manual, but it was created as more than that.[4] In page after page of lively line drawings of men and women engaged in an infinite number of activities, of facial expressions, flora and fauna, and scenes from the natural and built environment, it is a testament to the scope of an extraordinarily capacious mind.

Throughout his working life, Hokusai was involved with the production of the colour woodblock print known as *ukiyo-e* (floating world prints). From the mid-eighteenth century onwards, highly skilled printers collaborated with artists to create multicolour prints featuring every aspect of popular culture, including portraits of actors, courtesans and other celebrities, fashionable attire and activities, myths and moral tales, as well as erotica. The artist provided a detailed line drawing to guide the craftsman, who carved the needed number of blocks to print the individual colours. The printer generally consulted with the artist about the colours, but not in every case, and a publisher oversaw the whole collaborative endeavour. The prints were produced at all price points, and they were widely circulated and eagerly collected. Suites of prints were often released in sequence, with new images as highly anticipated as the latest installation of a serialized novel. Even the most deluxe prints were non-editioned; publishers ran impressions until demand waned or the blocks wore out. Over the years, Hokusai was involved in every aspect of *ukiyo-e*. In his teens, he spent a four-year apprenticeship cutting blocks before he became the pupil of the *ukiyo-e* master, Katsukawa Shunshō. It is estimated that he produced designs for as many as 3,000 prints.

Rough Waves c. 1704–09
Ogata Kōrin (1658–1716)
Two-panel folding screen; ink, colour and gold leaf on paper
150.5 x 169 cm (59¼ x 66½ in)
Metropolitan Museum of Art, New York, NY

Hokusai was not the first to portray the dynamic force of cresting waves. Japanese artists embraced the challenge of depicting nature's fleeting effects – light, snow, water – and the variable appearance of the sea no doubt appealed to inhabitants of an island nation. As in Hokusai's design of more than a century later, Kōrin's waves crest and break into dissolving foam and claw-like cascades.

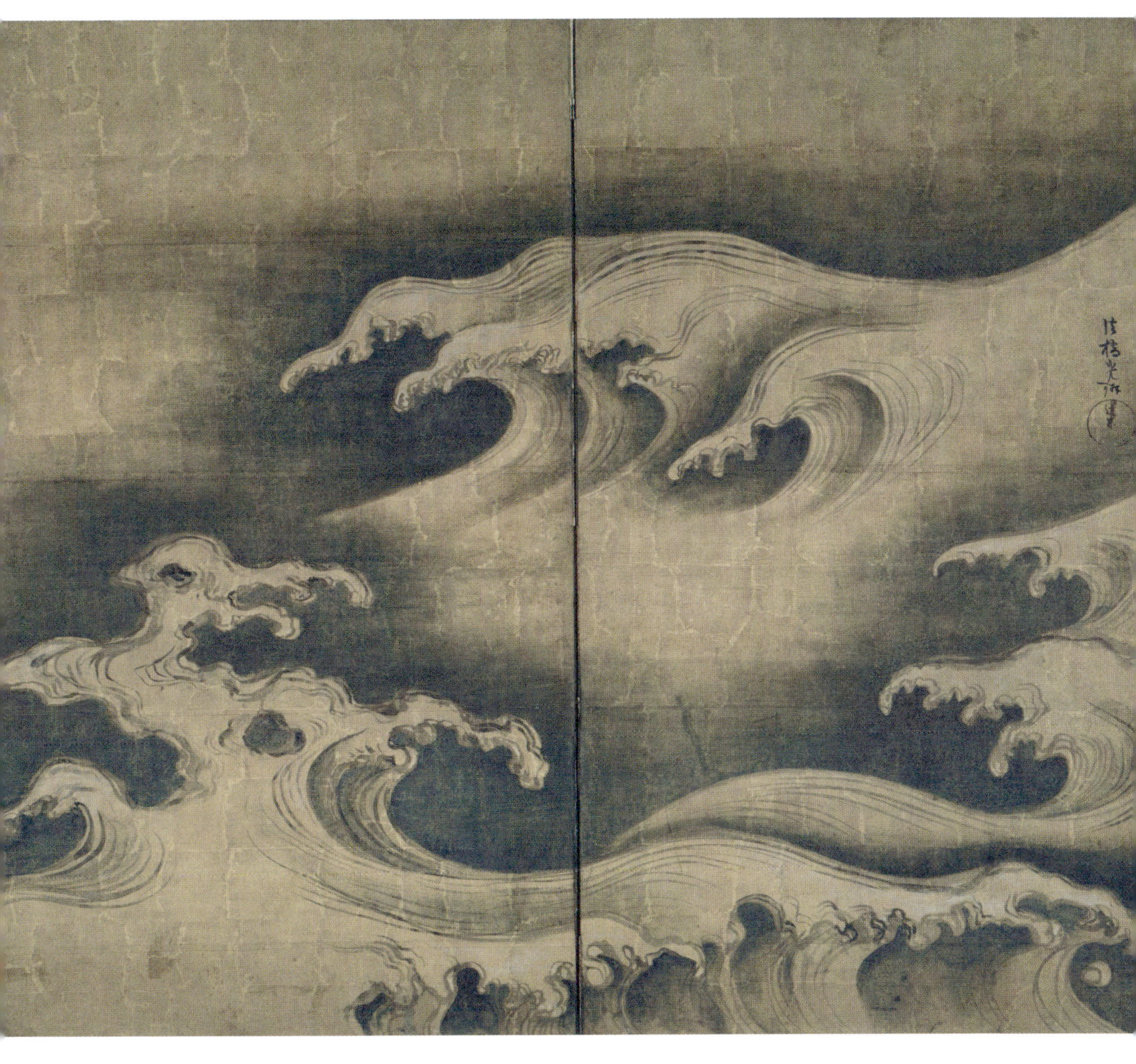

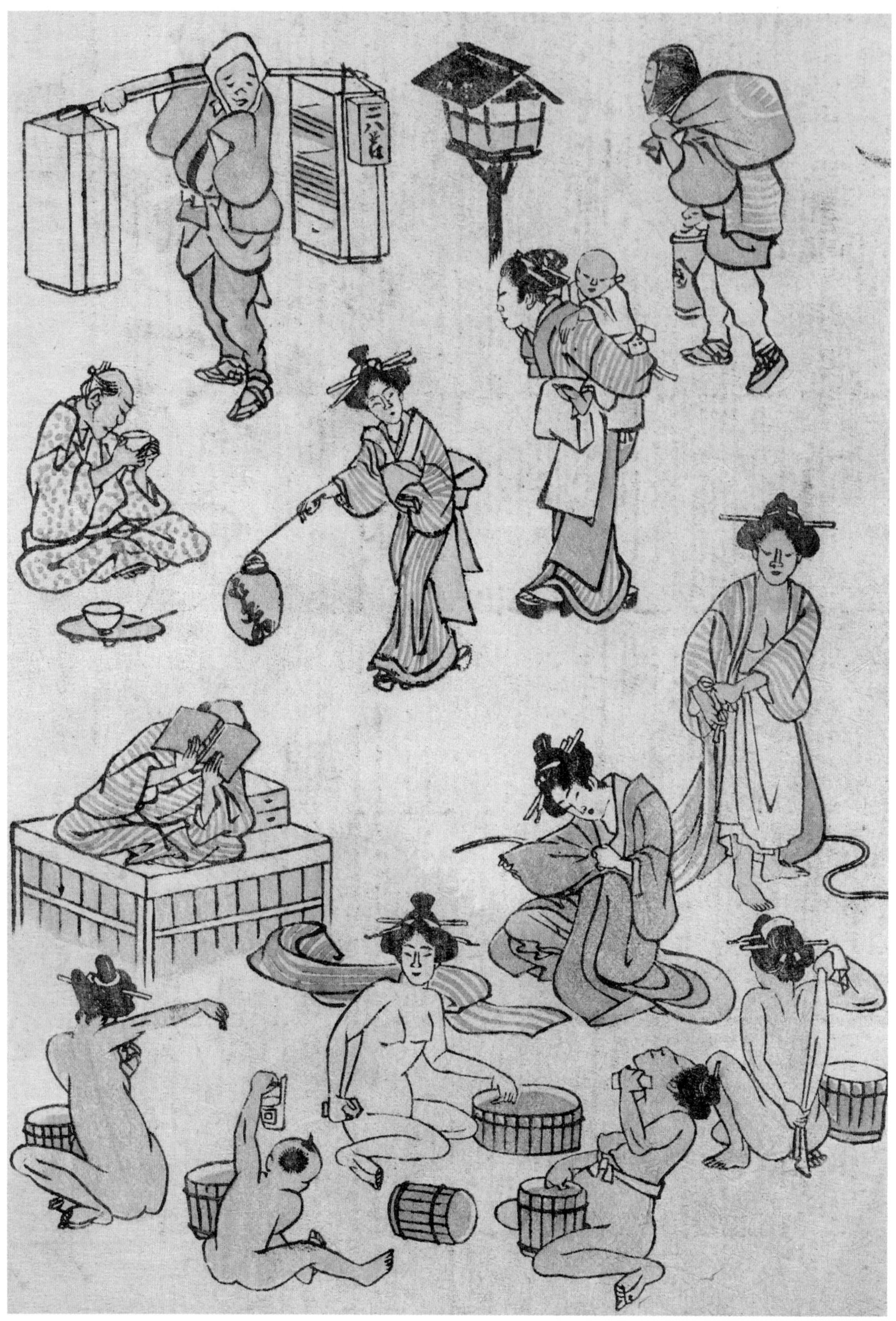

    Making a Masterpiece

Traditionally, a publishing house formulated ideas for *ukiyo-e* and hired an artist to create the designs. It is possible that Hokusai suggested views of Mount Fuji to Nishimuraya Yohachi – he had depicted it several times – but it is more likely the publisher offered the eminent artist what was sure to be a well-received, highly marketable and personally significant commission. Rising more than 3,600 m (12,000 ft) and roughly 100 km (62 miles) southwest of the city centre, the majestic form of Mount Fuji could be seen from almost anywhere in Edo. It was the landmark of the capital and had long been a venerated site as home to the spirits of immortality. Over the centuries, pilgrims journeyed to Edo to climb Mount Fuji, but by the nineteenth century, as domestic travel became a more common diversion, tourists sought their own first-hand experience of the towering, snowcapped peak. As a successful publisher, Nishimuraya knew what would please his audience, even though landscape was not an established *ukiyo-e* subject. The number of views specified in the title evoked the thirty-six immortals, and the views themselves would offer a vista from every possible angle. Hokusai's imaginative artistry and reputation further guaranteed that the series would appeal to an audience that valued innovation as much as artistic interpretation.

OPPOSITE *Daily Life Gestures from Manga*
Woodblock print
Musée Marmottan Monet, Paris

Hokusai's fifteen-volume *Manga* (1814–78; the last three volumes published posthumously) compiles lively renderings that depict daily activities; costume and facial expressions; plants, animals and insects; and supernatural and mythic figures. With its clarity of line and array of subjects, the *Manga* provided an invaluable training tool, but even more, the volumes reveal the acuity of Hokusai's observation as well as his sharp wit and unbounded imagination.

OVERLEAF *Clear Day with a Southern Breeze (Red Fuji)*
From Thirty-Six Views of Mount Fuji 1831
Colour woodblock
26 x 38 cm (10¼ x 15 in)
British Museum, London

This eastern-facing view captures the first light of morning rising behind the mountain. The rich variety of colours – russet red, forest green, pale pink, Prussian blue – accentuates the majestic form of the venerated mountain against a cloud-streaked, mackerel sky.

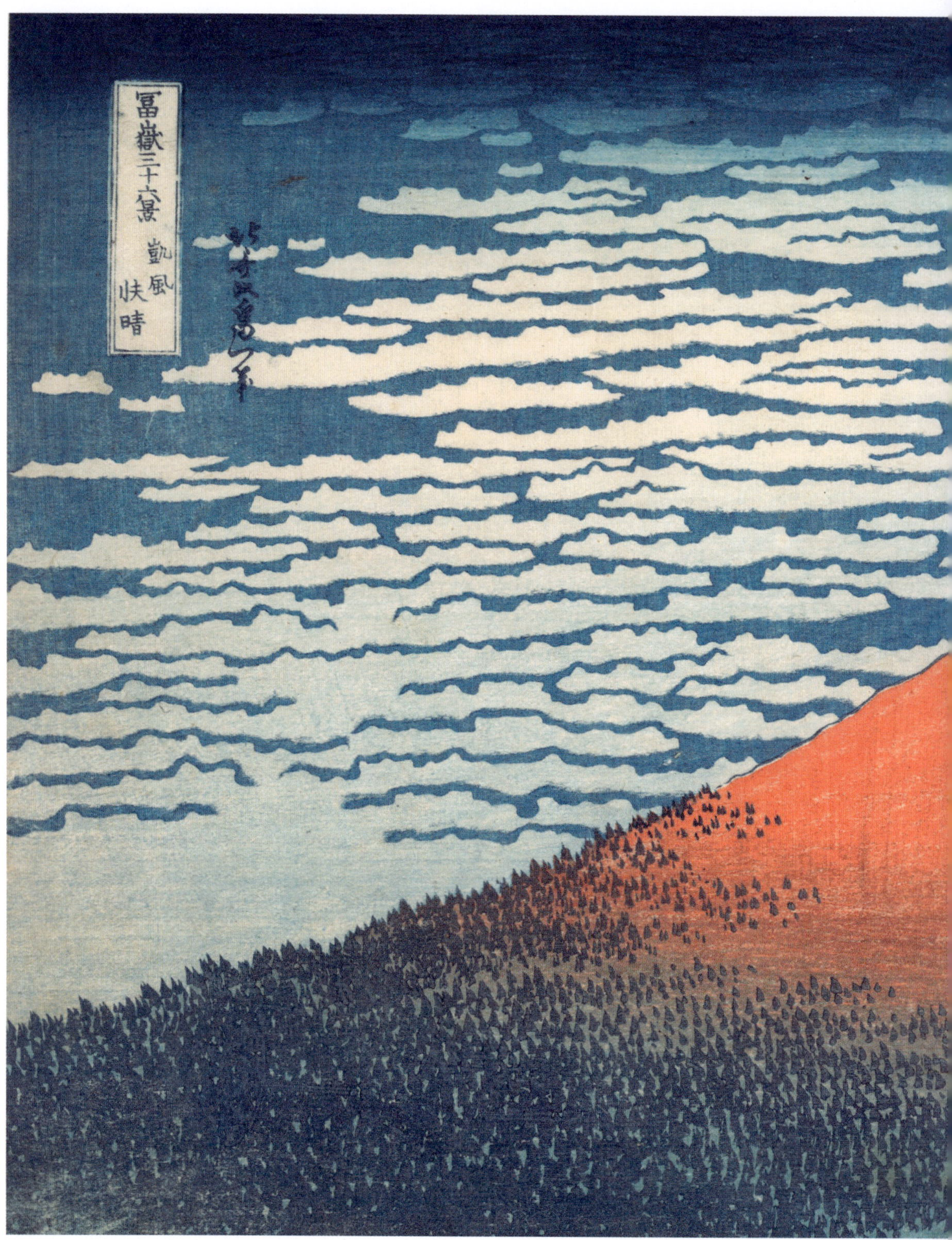

冨嶽三十六景　凱風快晴

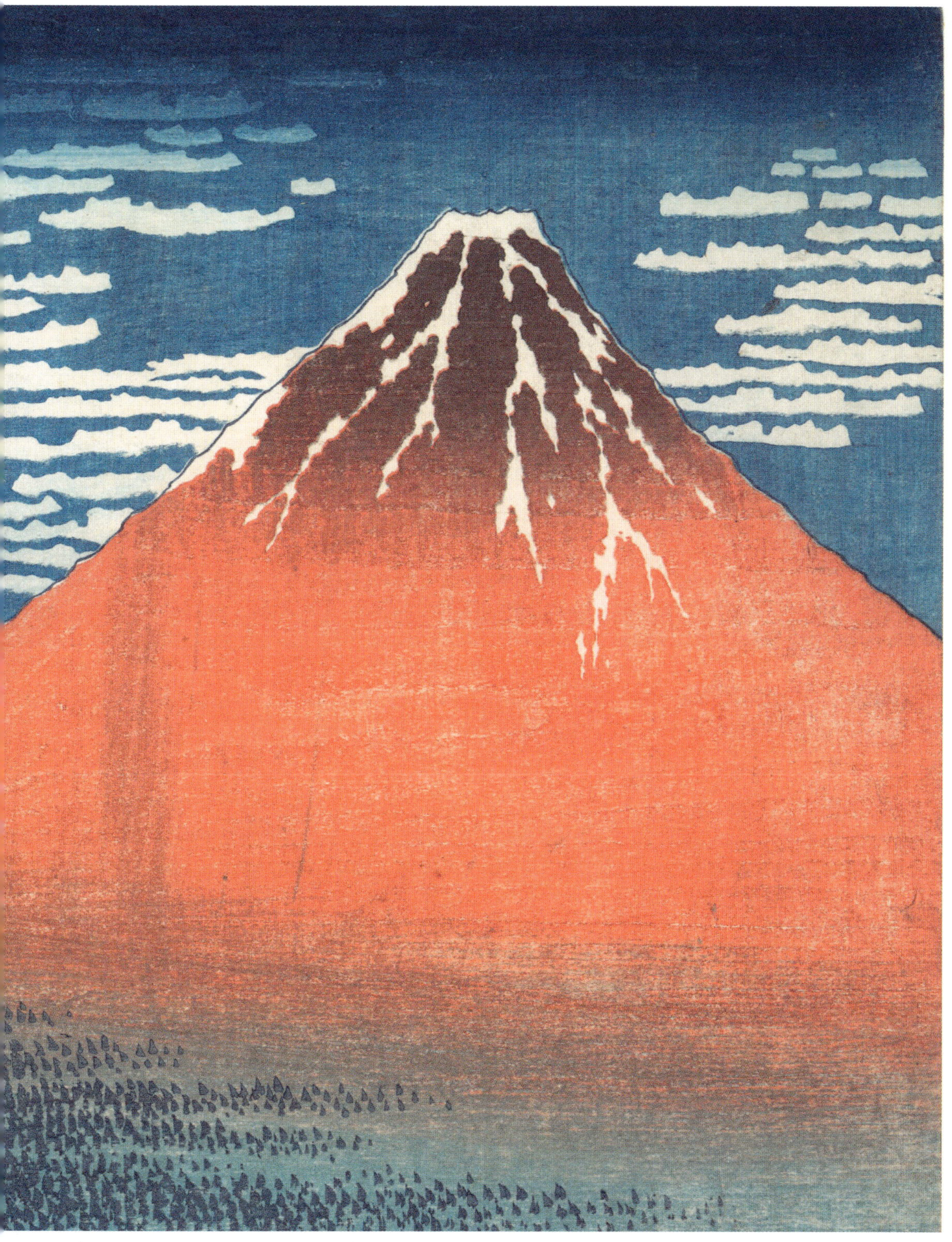

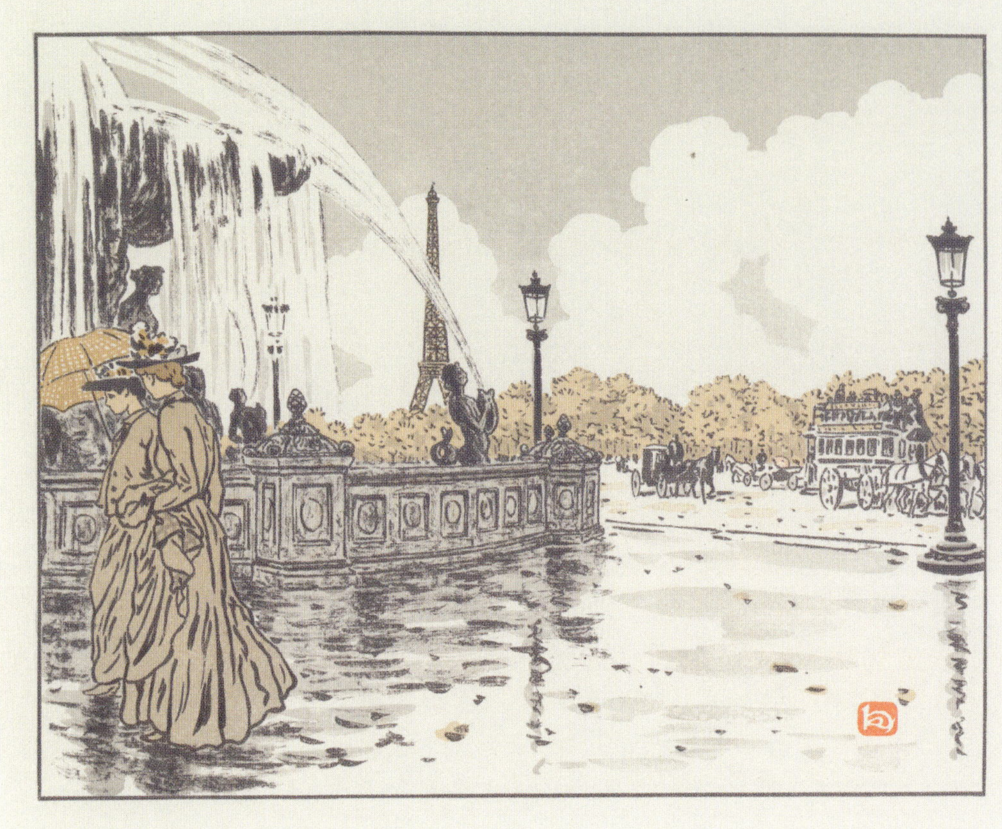

Place de la Concorde
From the series Thirty-six Views of the Eiffel Tower 1888–1902
Henri Rivière (1864–1951)
Colour lithograph
17 x 20 cm (6¾ x 8 in)
Musée d'Orsay, Paris

In his own suite of views, Rivière cleverly referenced Hokusai's compositions
to showcase the sites of modern Paris. In place of the towering breaker of *The
Great Wave,* Rivière positions a pair of elegant strollers and the lower basin
of one of the grand fountains on the square. A graceful arc of water, spouting
from the mouth of a fish held by a sculpted Nereid, offers a playful alternative
to the threatening wave.

As the unifying subject of the series, Mount Fuji embodies permanence and stability, but in Hokusai's print, *Under the Wave off Kanagawa*, the waters of Edo Bay roil with dynamic power. The momentum builds from the right as the waters dip and surge, culminating in a titanic wave that crests and breaks into a foam-covered summit, edged with claw-like cascades. Three slender boats toss in the turbulence. These are the swift, oar-powered *oshiokuri* that rush the catch from the fishing fleets to the shore to supply Edo's markets. While the boats seem imperiled, the oarsmen are determined, pitting whatever strength they can against the driving force of nature. Deep in the centre distance, Mount Fuji appears low on the horizon. It is the single stationary element in the maelstrom, representing manifest endurance as well as anchoring Hokusai's tumultuous composition.

Under the Wave off Kanagawa reveals Hokusai's mastery of balance. The troubling fate of the delicate boats navigating the raging sea is countered by Mount Fuji's reassuring presence. The vortex of water, dominated by the towering wave, encircles the space where the mountain stands as it has always stood. The lives of the oarsmen are transitory, but Mount Fuji is immutable and immortal. Just as Hokusai finds the balance between chaos and calm in his composition and his narrative, he incorporates traditional ideas in his work in innovative ways. The distinctive form of the wave, with its cascading edges can be found in eighteenth-century Japanese painting; precedents in Chinese painting date centuries earlier. From the early 1800s, Hokusai experimented with the form in painting and print design, but here he pushes it to an unparalleled extreme to represent the vast power of nature in a palpably powerful graphic expression.

The depth of the composition, established by the low horizon, reveals Hokusai's grasp of Western perspective. Since the 1630s, to maintain spiritual and cultural purity, Japan had been a *sakoku* (closed country). But it was not completely closed; limited trade with Dutch and Chinese merchants was allowed through a single port. During the eighteenth-century, European books in Chinese translation introduced so-called 'Dutch studies', featuring many forms of Western technology, including perspective, which, in turn, gave rise to a vogue for 'perspective prints'. It is not spatial illusion that marks Hokusai's innovation, however, but his choice to use it to position Mount Fuji. Similarly, the vivid blue mentioned in the advertisement also enjoyed a vogue in *ukiyo-e.* Traditional organic blue inks – made from indigo or dayflower – faded, but a synthetic blue invented in Berlin around 1707 was not only stable but had the depth and vibrancy of lapis lazuli.

Prussian blue (ferric ferrocyanide) first appeared in Japan as a luxury pigment in the late eighteenth century. A drop in manufacturing costs in the late 1820s set off a brief fascination with 'blue prints' that featured only Prussian blue, or *bero*. Hokusai incorporates the hue into his palette in a more nuanced way, having the key block (which establishes the outline of the design) inked in muted indigo and using the *bero* in three shades to portray his wave. Here, again, Hokusai deploys innovation in counterpoint to a more traditional application of the ink, as seen in the masterful grey *bokashi* (gradation of tone) that surrounds Mount Fuji.

The enthusiastic reception for Thirty-Six Views of Mount Fuji, prompted Nishimuraya Yohachi to fulfil his teasing promise of an extended series in the 1831 advertisement; the suite ended in 1833 with forty-six different prints. Hokusai immediately returned to the theme with One Hundred Views of Mount Fuji (1834), and once again changed his name – this time to Manji, meaning ten thousand things or everything – to commemorate the important turn in his life. He also incorporated a stylized image of Mount Fuji on his seal. Although the series itself closed, the publishing house continued to run impressions long after the artist died. In the 1880s, when the blocks were too worn to produce a saleable image, replicas were carved. Prints pulled from these blocks are known as 'facsimile prints'. Through the end of the century, the most admired and valued print of the series was a sweeping and majestic view of the red-brown face of the immortal mountain titled *Clear Day with a Southern Breeze (Red Fuji)*, but the dynamic imagery in *Under the Wave off Kanagawa* proved far more influential. Hokusai's explicit portrayal of nature's formidable power – in the towering wave, cresting into claw-like cascades – forged a new graphic convention for the depiction of storm-tossed seas.

In 1853, Commodore Matthew Calbraith Perry sailed his three 'black ships' into Edo Bay, and the gunboat diplomacy of the United States Navy forced the closed country of Japan to open to trade. By the end of the decade, Japan established generous trade agreements with several Western nations, including Great Britain and France, as well as the United States, and a wide array of Japanese goods entered the global market. Conceived to be popular and created for easy circulation, *ukiyo-e* played a central role in the rise of Japonisme, an artistic response in Western fine arts as well as popular culture. But Hokusai's fame had already taken root in Europe when the German botanist Philipp von Seibold, who had journeyed to Japan (1823–29), reproduced images from the *Manga* in his seven-volume study *Nippon*. No one is sure as to when impressions from Thirty-Six Views of Mount

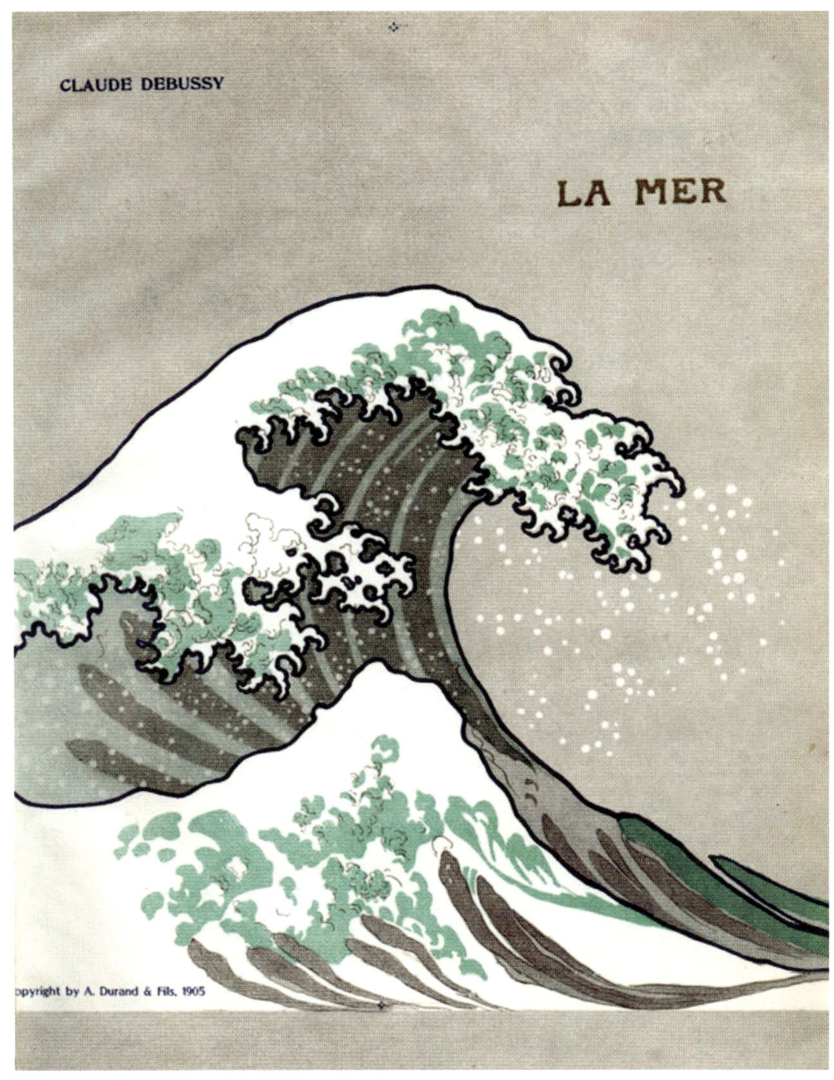

Cover, musical score of *La Mer* by Claude Debussy (1862–1918) 1905
Published by A. Durand, Paris
Bibliothèque nationale de France, Paris

Impressionist composer Claude Debussy responded to *The Great Wave* in a set of symphonic sketches that he titled *La Mer* (1903–05). Hokusai's distinct wave appears in shades of green on the cover of the first publication of the suite, and a 1911 photograph of Debussy in his home reveals that he owned a copy of the print.

Fuji first reached a European audience; the earliest known record of the series was in Louis Gonse's *L'art japonaise* (1883). In 1890, the art dealer Siegfried Bing, who specialized in works imported from Japan, listed *La Vague* (*The Wave*) as part of the series in the catalogue of an exhibition of Japanese prints held at the École des Beaux-Arts in Paris. Once introduced to the Western public, *Under the Wave off Kanagawa* acquired its common name, *The Great Wave*, and became a global icon with a force that remains undiminished to this day.

The variety and ubiquity of *The Great Wave*'s influence in the recent century is too vast to trace here. From Claude Debussy's symphonic sketch suite *Le Mer* (1903–07) to John Galliano's 'Great Wave' dress for the House of Dior's Spring/Summer haute-couture collection (2007, Paris), the enthralling image of that towering wave has been reinterpreted in every form of the arts. The wave has served as a metaphor of an unpredictable and even insurmountable force. It appears in literal form in adventure stories for young and old – for example, in Hergé's *Cigars of the Pharaoh* (1936), featuring the enduring boy hero Tintin – as well as in films, video games and advertising. It has been replicated in every medium from ceramics and textiles to postage stamps and Lego, and there is even *Water Wave*, an emoji approved by Unicode in 2015. In Japan, the image is now known as *Guereito ueibu* (*The Great Wave*) rather than its original title.[5] But this widespread popularity has not detracted from the value of a superb impression; in March 2021, a print of *Under the Wave off Kanagawa* sold at auction for a record-breaking 1.6 million dollars.[6] More than any other work of art, *The Great Wave* maintains a dual identity as an object of connoisseurship and as a commercial commodity. But that should not be surprising, given Hokusai's deep understanding of how to make a popular masterpiece.

'Great Wave' Dress 2007
John Galliano (born 1960)
Haute couture for Christian Dior, Paris

To celebrate the fiftieth anniversary of the House of Dior, designer in chief Galliano blended the aesthetics of Japonisme with founder Christian Dior's most notable silhouettes. The 'Great Wave' dress uses pleating for the bodice and a face-framing collar to evoke the foaming crest of the breaker, while Hokusai's brilliant blue waves swirl around the hem.

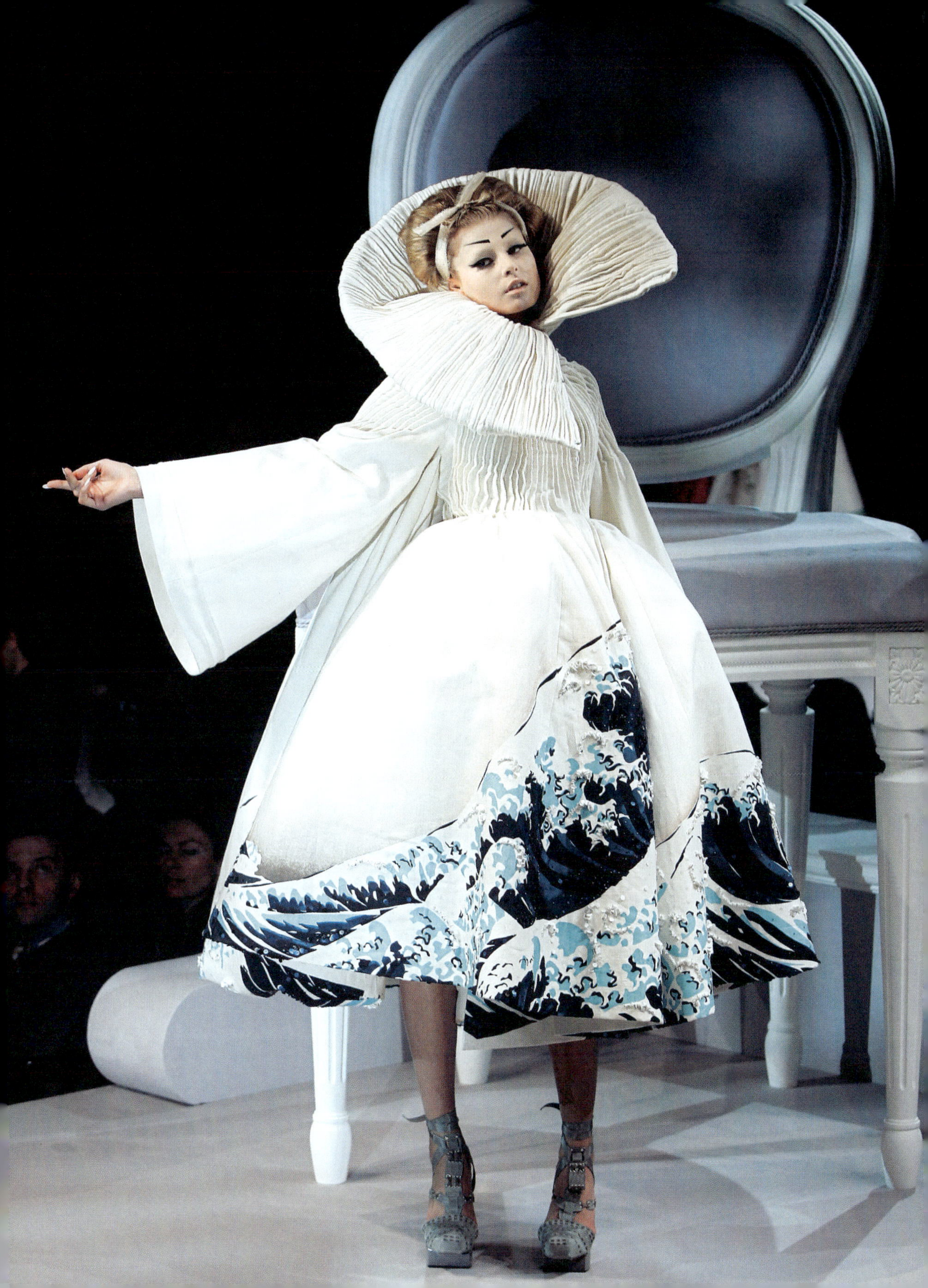

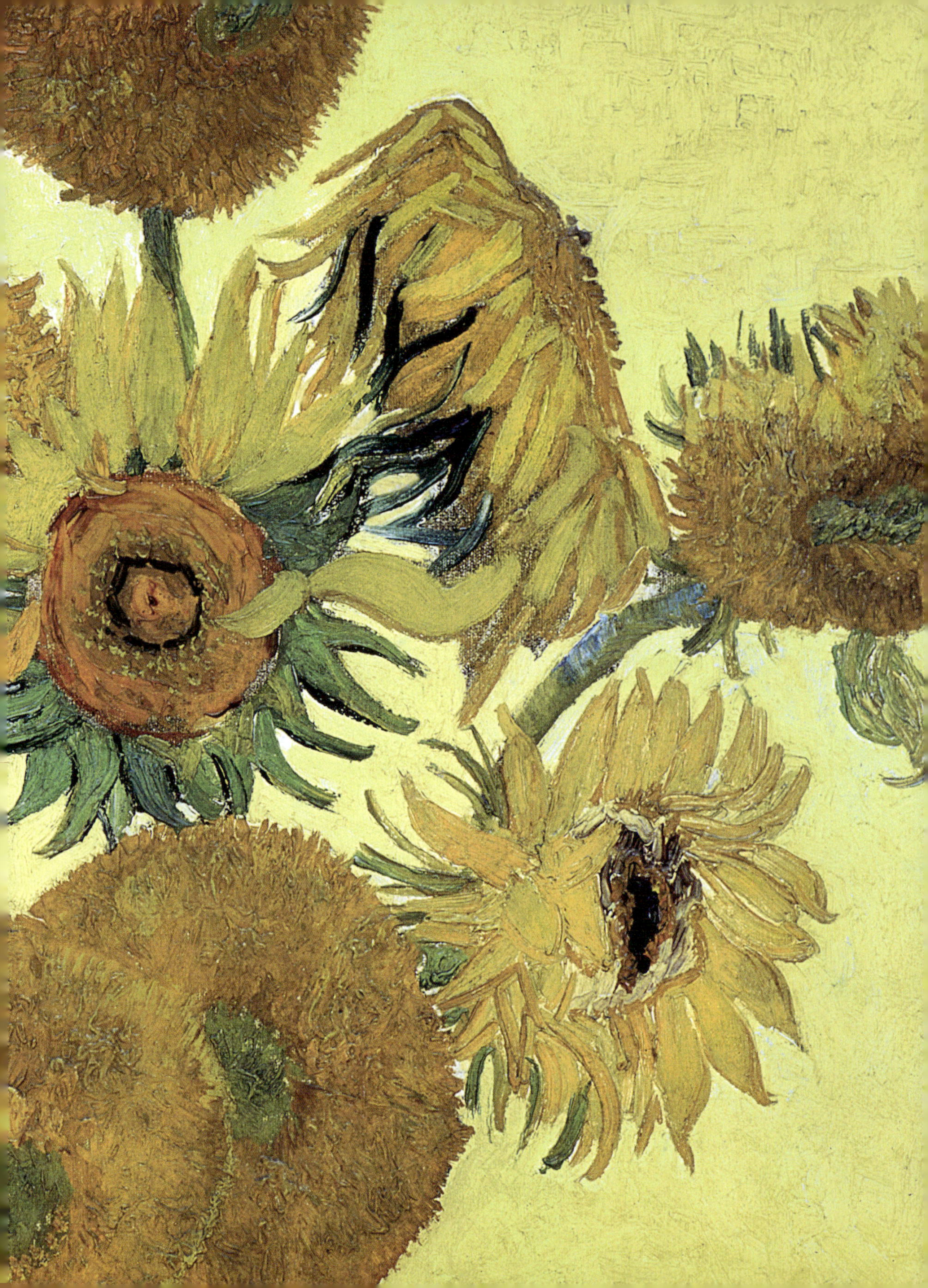

Fifteen Sunflowers

Vincent van Gogh

My paintings are, however, almost a cry of anguish while symbolizing gratitude in the rustic sunflower.

Vincent van Gogh to his sister Wil, 19 February 1890

On 30 July 1890, a small group assembled in a room at the Auberge Ravoux in Auvers-sur-Oise to pay their last respects to Vincent van Gogh. Vincent (who preferred to be known by his first name) had lodged at the inn since 20 May, and he died in his room on 29 July from a self-inflicted gunshot. For the gathering, Vincent's last paintings were hung on the walls. His easel, his folding stool and his brushes were laid out, as if ready to use, before a simple coffin covered by a plain white cloth. In describing this tribute to a friend in Paris, the painter Émile Bernard took comfort in the array of yellow flowers covering the coffin. The warm and radiant hue had been Vincent's favourite colour, for, as Bernard explained, it embodied the light that 'Vincent dreamed of as being in people's hearts as well as in works of art'. And standing out among the profusion of loose blooms and bouquets were sunflowers, the vivid yet short-lived flowers that Vincent 'loved so much'.[1]

The story of Vincent van Gogh's brief but spectacular life as a painter is frequently framed solely as struggle and failure. The lack of recognition in his lifetime – as well as his self-mutilation, his emotional crises and his suicide – prevails as a sensational myth in the popular imagination. His letters to his family and friends record a truer and fuller view, and when seen within the context of his sensitive and self-aware observations, even a work as familiar and well-loved as *Fifteen Sunflowers* gains new meaning. Rather than a single burst of joy in a calamitous existence, the subject itself was expressive of Vincent's ongoing engagement with what he loved the most: colour, nature and connection. Read in this way, his well-known statement 'the sunflower is mine', can be understood as a testament to the power of art rather than as the declaration of a personal emblem. Vincent defined his artistic ideals and aspirations in this exuberant subject, and, in doing so, made it his masterpiece.

Vincent van Gogh (1853–90) left home at the age of sixteen to take a position as a junior clerk in The Hague branch of Goupil et Cie, Paris-based art dealer and publisher. In 1873, the company transferred him to their London branch, but his interests began to shift to a desire to serve the poor. Restlessness accompanied his new sense of vocation, and when the firm dismissed him in 1876, he returned to The Netherlands to study theology and follow in his father's path as a minister in the Dutch Reformed Church. Unable to concentrate on his preparations for the entrance examinations, Vincent abandoned his hopes of a university degree and entered training to become an evangelical minister. After three months, when he was denied a post, he set off on his own to preach to the disadvantaged mining community in the Borinage in Belgium. By the end of 1879, he informed his younger brother Theo, who was working at the Goupil headquarters in Paris, that his mission had changed. He had resolved to become an artist.

As a child, Vincent did not display a particular inclination towards the arts over his other studies, but now he embraced his new ambition

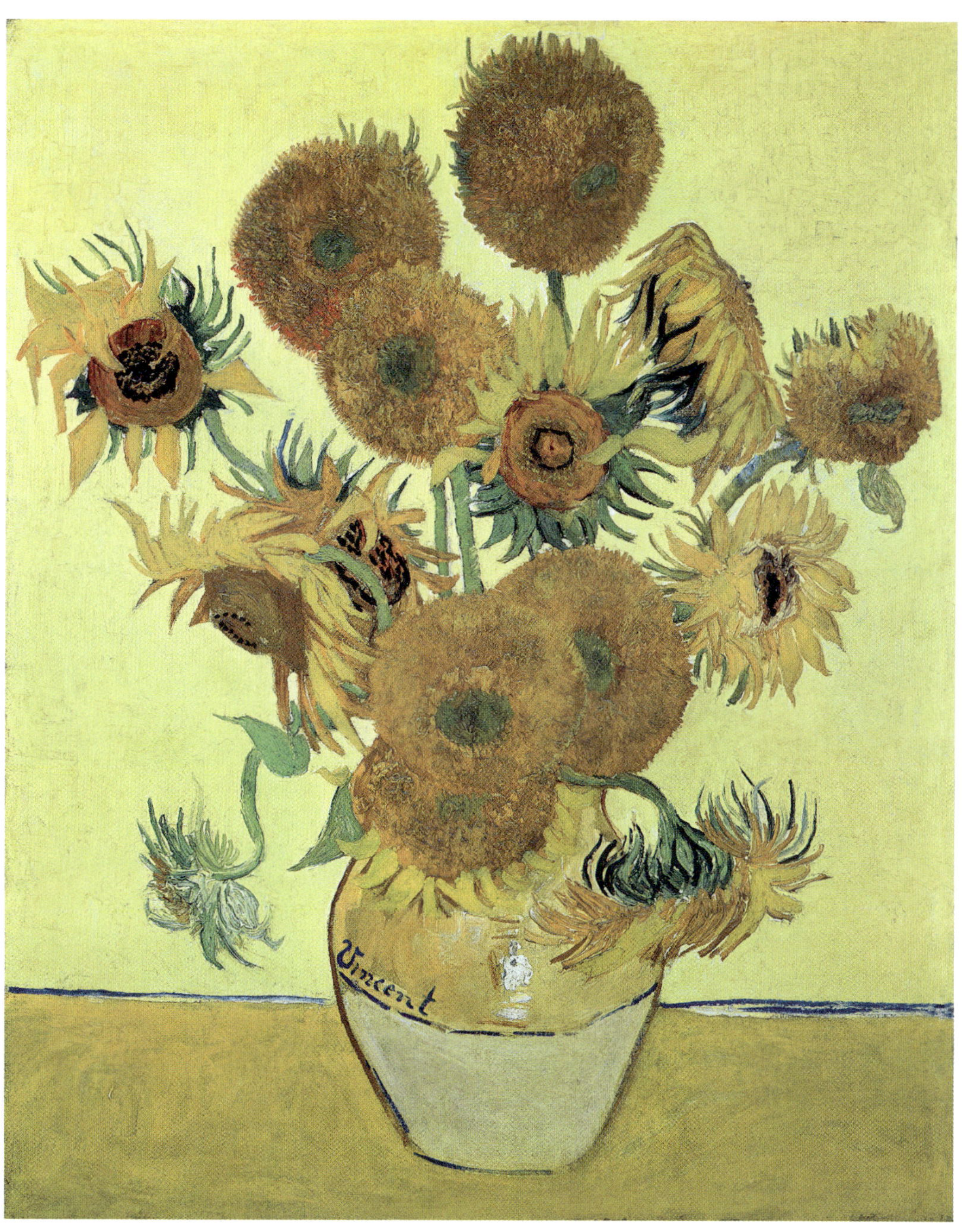

Fifteen Sunflowers August 1888
Vincent van Gogh (1853–90)
Oil on canvas
92 x 73 cm (36¼ x 28¾ in)
National Gallery, London

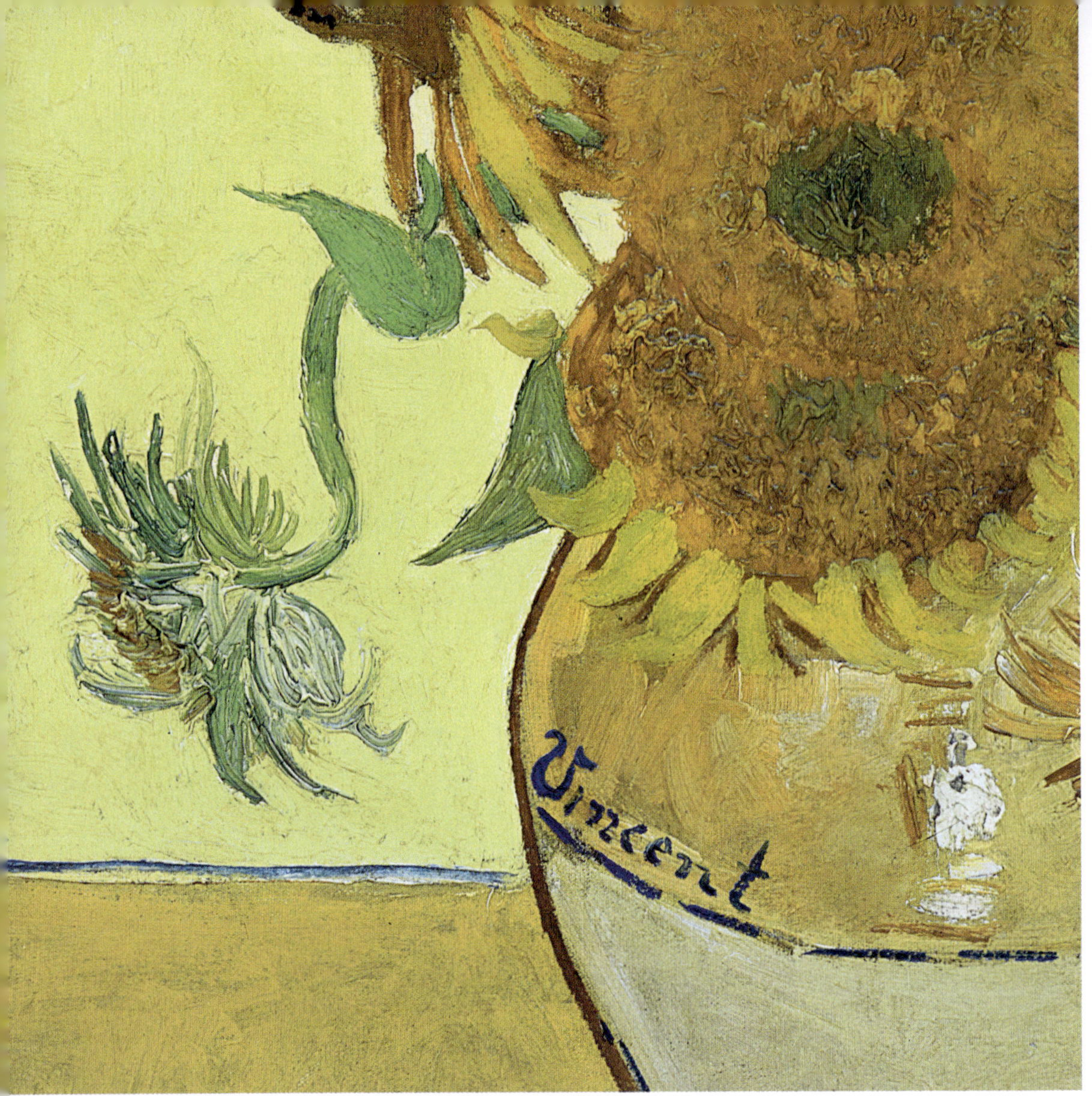

Fifteen Sunflowers, detail

Vincent once explained to his brother that he signed his paintings with his first name because their surname was too difficult to pronounce. In another letter he mentioned that he no longer felt like a Van Gogh. After all, Rembrandt and the Renaissance masters were known solely by their given names. Whatever his reason, his signature strikes the intimate tone he yearned to express in his painting.

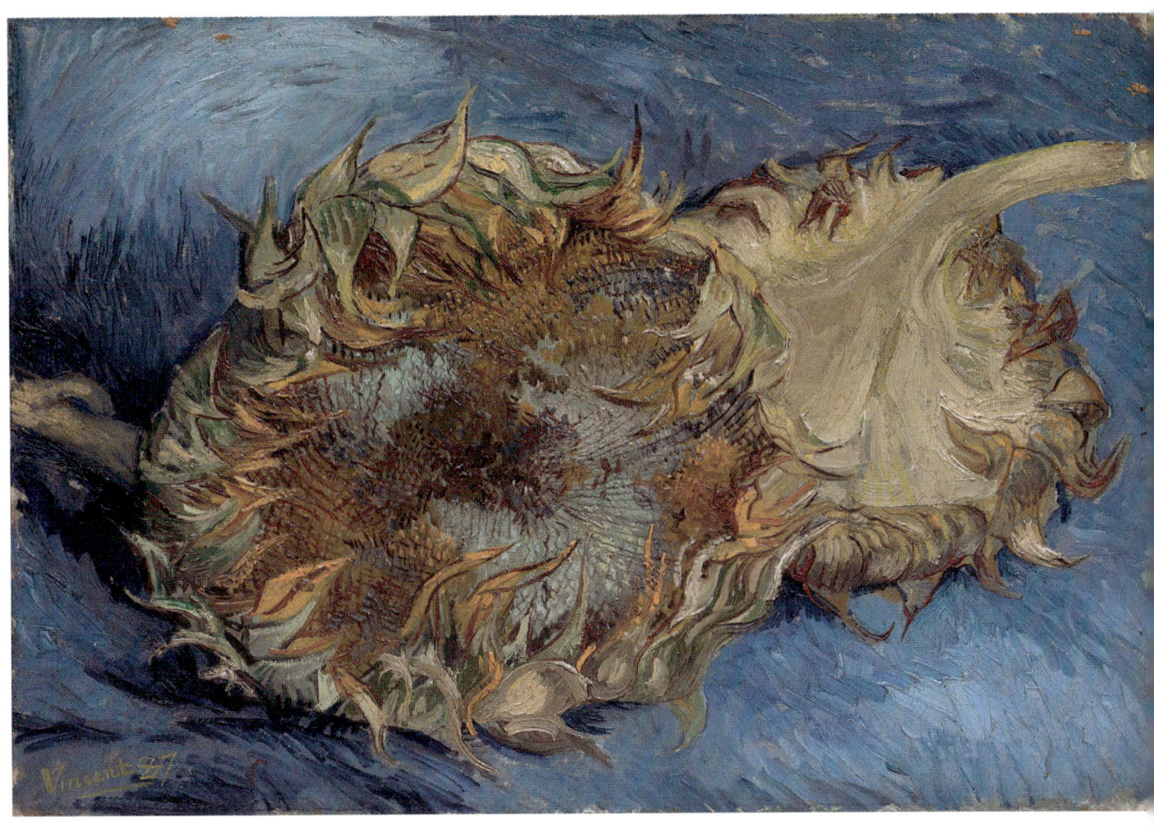

Two Sunflowers 1887
43 x 61 cm (17 x 24 in)
Oil on canvas
Metropolitan Museum of Art, New York

The enduring tradition of Netherlandish flower painting emphasized naturalistic
illusion and encoded floral iconography. Although Vincent admired the work
of his predecessors, he painted flowers to better understand line, colour and
brushstroke. These wilted flower heads may be read as an expression of decay,
but Vincent sought to capture the compelling rhythm of the twisted petals and
the vital energy of contrasting colour.

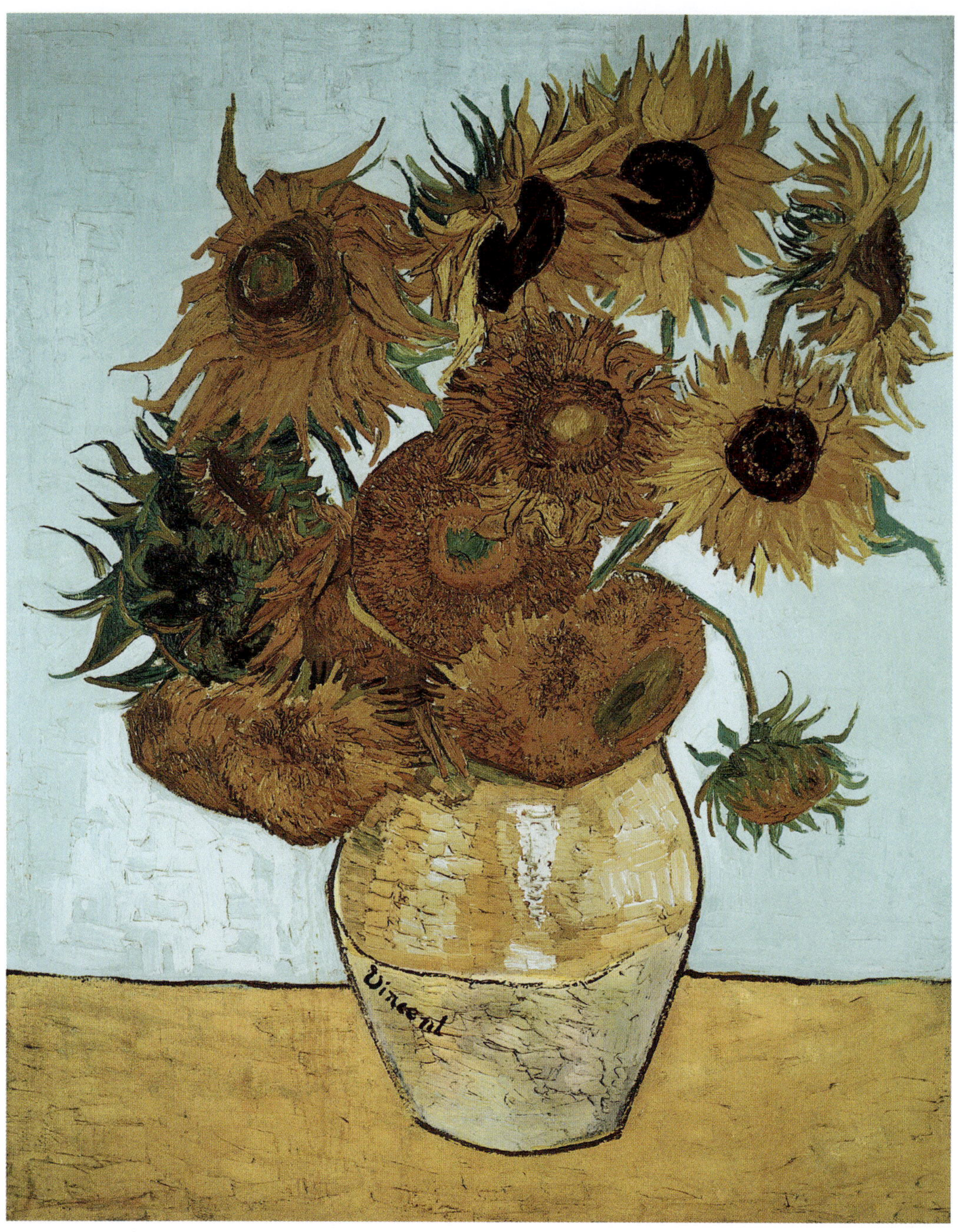

with the intensity of a religious calling. He asked his brother to send him art supplies, prints to copy and drawing manuals. Seeking experience and inspiration, he moved back and forth between the countryside and several cities across The Netherlands and Belgium. He studied colour theory in The Hague, he drew farm workers in Nuenen and, in November 1885, he moved to Antwerp to enroll in classes at the École des Beaux-Arts in the coming year. But his stay there was brief; late in February, he arrived in Paris and moved into his brother's apartment in Montmartre.

Paris was the centre of advanced ideas in the arts, and Theo now managed a gallery that showcased rising artists. Vincent briefly attended classes in Fernand Cormon's studio, where he met Henri de Toulouse-Lautrec, Paul Signac and Émile Bernard. He attended the final Impressionist exhibition, and he became a passionate *plein-air* (open-air) painter, setting up his easel in the further reaches of Montmartre, where the city gave way to cottage gardens. But more than anything, colour fascinated him. To break away from the grey and brown palette that he had adopted for his rural subjects, he began to paint bouquets. He described his project to the English painter Horace Livens, a friend from the Antwerp academy, in a letter written in early autumn, 1886: 'I have made a series of colour studies in painting simply flowers.'[2] Vincent purchased his bouquets from the local flower market, and when Theo's friends saw his floral studies, they started sending bouquets as gifts. Vincent chose his flowers by happenstance; he painted whatever was available in the season. His letters reveal no interest in traditional floral iconography, and in the months that followed he painted so many bouquets that he wrote to his youngest sister Wil in October 1887, 'last year I painted almost nothing but flowers'.[3]

Sunflowers 1888
Oil on canvas
92 x 73 cm (36¼ x 28¾ in)
Neue Pinakothek, Munich

Vincent based his colour theories on observations of primary and complementary colours in nature. He was particularly fascinated with contrasts, believing that pairing colours enhanced their inherent brilliance. In three of the initial four sunflower paintings, he set the vivid yellow blooms against a blue background. But he believed that the subtle 'light on light' of *Fifteen Sunflowers* attained the finest effect.

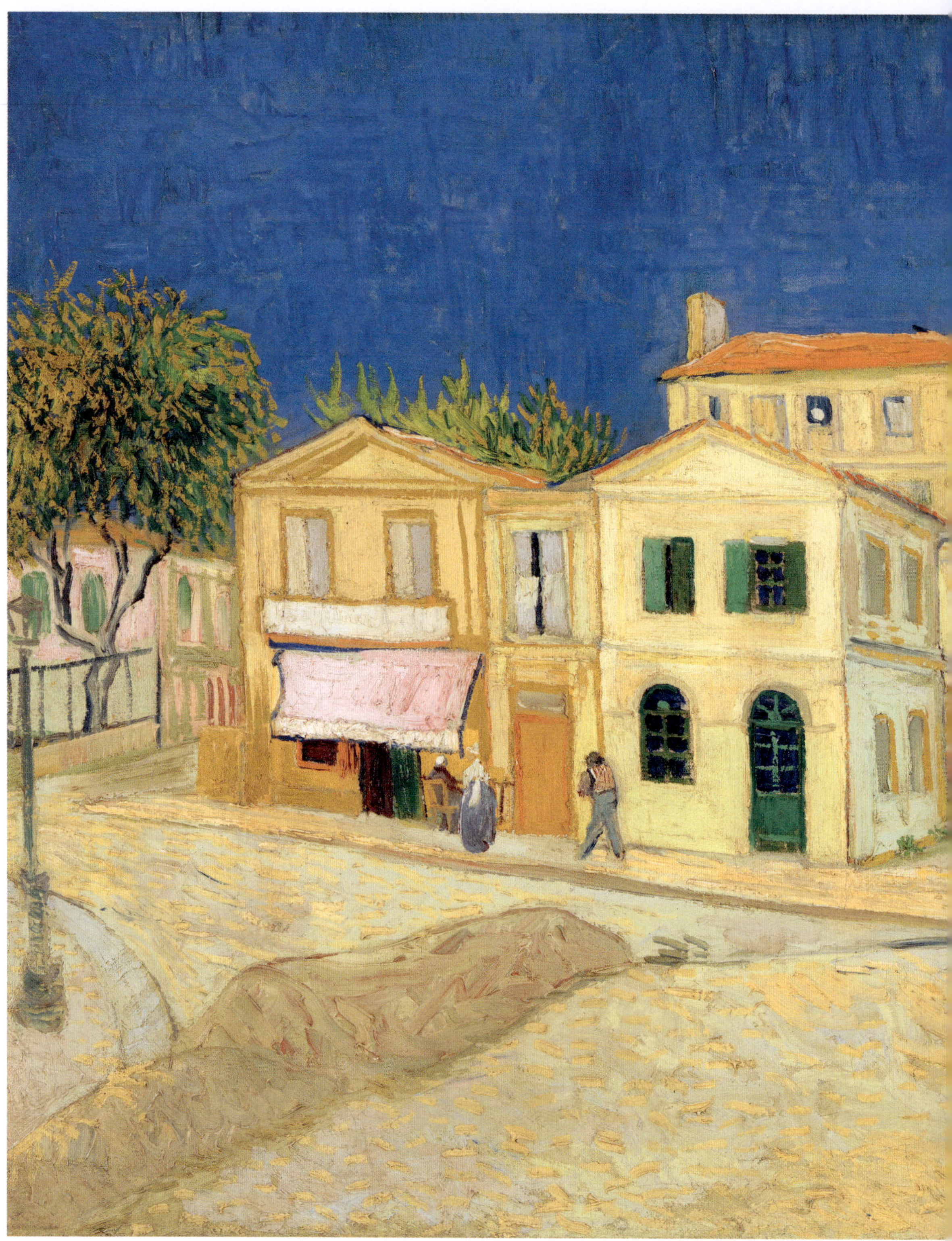

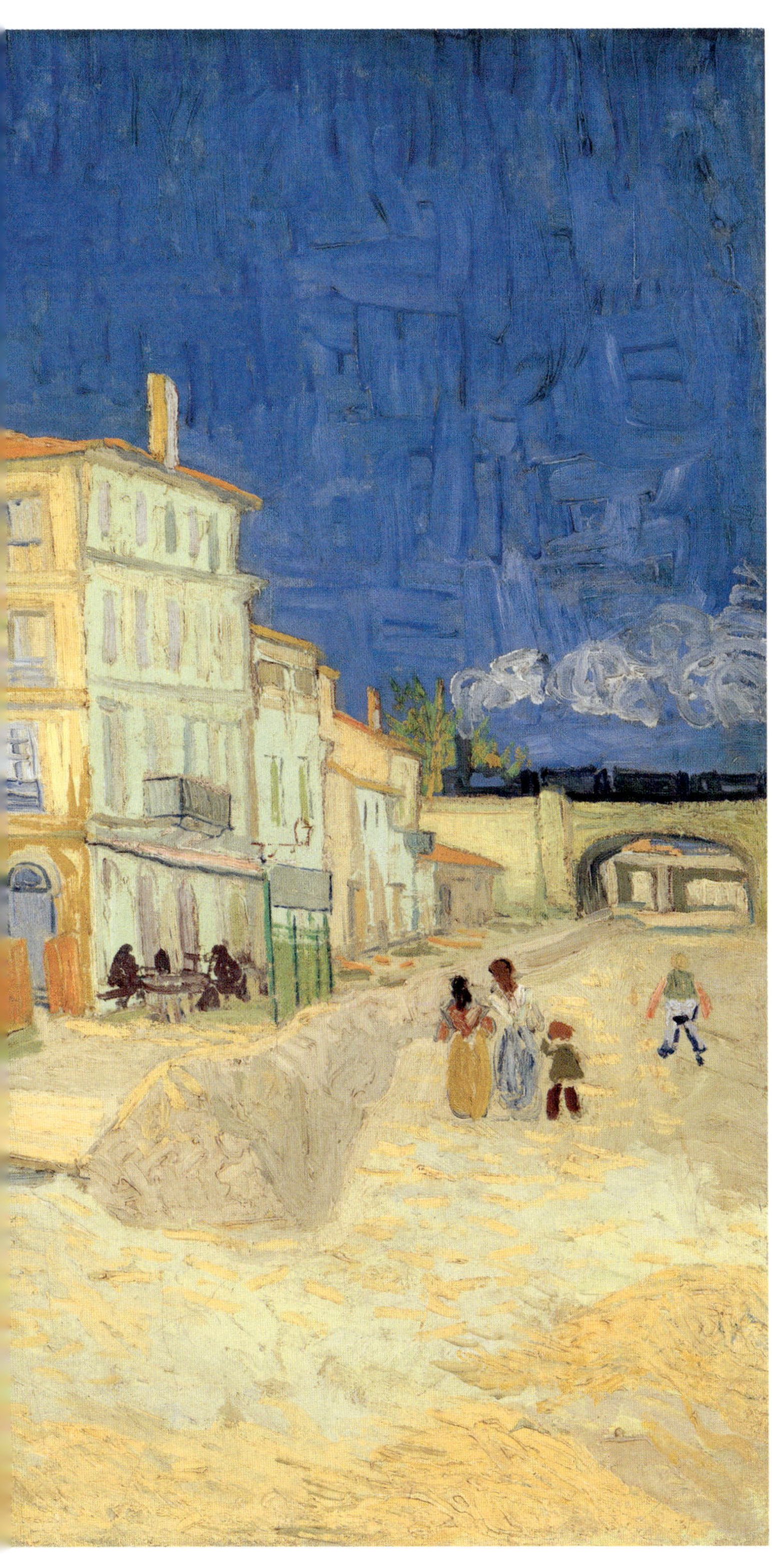

The Yellow House September 1888
Oil on canvas
72 x 91.5 cm (28¼ x 36 in)
Van Gogh Museum, Amsterdam

The radiant hue of the Yellow House
exterior aligned with Vincent's
associations with the colour: energy,
warmth and the southern sun. The
house was already painted yellow
when he rented four of its rooms,
but Vincent gave it the name.

The sunflower first appears in Vincent's work in his *plein-air* paintings and drawings of cottage gardens. Sunflowers bloom briefly from late July through early September, and often grow to towering heights, which seemed to intrigue Vincent. As for his studio flower studies, there are few sunflowers; their brief season and tendency to wilt soon after they are cut made them a poor choice for commercial bouquets. But this ephemeral quality ignited Vincent's imagination, and in the late summer of 1887 he painted four studies of cut sunflowers. In each, he carefully rendered the shrivelled ray petals, the dried disc petals and the woody, withered stems with expressive brushstrokes and bold colour contrasts. These qualities reveal that he painted the faded blooms for their visual potential rather than out of botanical interest. That November, Vincent included two of the cut sunflowers in an informal exhibition he organized in a local café. They caught the eye of Paul Gauguin, who had just returned from an extended stay in Panama and Martinique. Theo represented Gauguin in his gallery, and when Gauguin proposed an exchange of paintings – the two cut sunflowers for one of his new Caribbean seascapes – the Van Gogh brothers agreed. Vincent admired Gauguin's visual innovations and adventurous spirit and hoped to strike up a friendship, but early in the new year, Gauguin departed for Brittany. Vincent grew restless and decided to carry out a plan he had been thinking about for nearly a year: 'I may be going to the south of France, the land of the *blue* tones and gay colours.'[4] Mid-February, during an unusually harsh and dismal winter, Vincent boarded a train to Provence.

On 20 February 1888, when Vincent arrived in Arles, he was surprised to find the countryside covered with snow. But spring arrived early in the south, and as soon as the trees began to blossom, he headed into the local orchards with his easel, stool and paints. His subjects reflect the unfolding of the season; as the weeks passed, the flowering almond, apple and cherry trees gave way to fields of poppy, iris and spring wheat. At first, he resided in a hotel, but after a dispute over his bills, he began to look for a more permanent residence, and early in May, he rented four rooms in a house on the Place Lamartine. The interior was plain with whitewashed walls, but the exterior had been painted a shade of yellow that Vincent likened to 'fresh butter'.[5] Over the summer, with his brother's financial support, Vincent furnished and decorated his four rooms, creating what he hoped would be the ideal environment to merge his life and work.

Vincent's letters to Theo record his household purchases: a big table, twelve chairs, chests of drawers, bedsteads and linens.

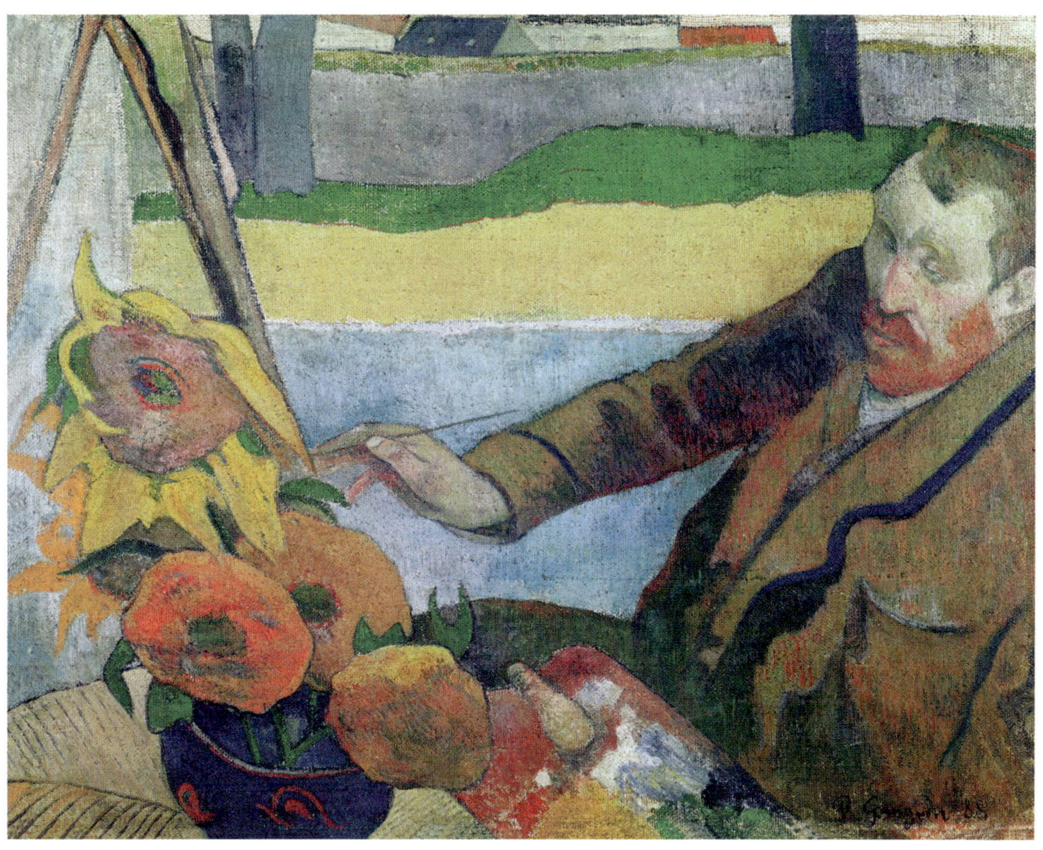

Vincent van Gogh Painting Sunflowers 1888
Paul Gauguin (1848–1903)
Oil on canvas
73 x 91 cm (28¾ x 35¾ in)
Van Gogh Museum, Amsterdam

When Gauguin portrayed Vincent as 'The Painter of Sunflowers', he was the first to assign Vincent an emblematic flower. Theo deemed this the best portrait of his brother, not in terms of physical resemblance, but as an expression of Vincent's artistic spirit.

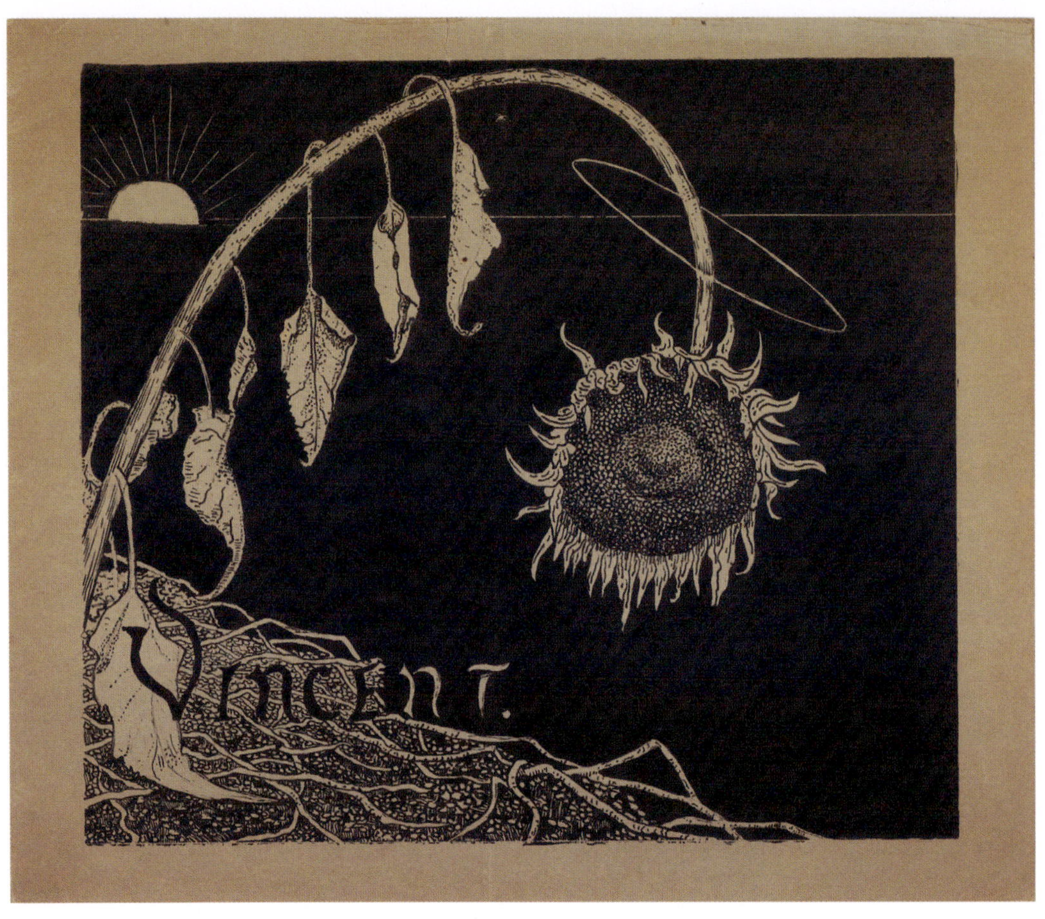

Vincent
Richard Roland Holst (1868–1938)
Cover of the catalogue of the Vincent van Gogh exhibition in the Kunstzaal
Panorama, Amsterdam, December 1892
Lithography
17 x 18.5 cm (6¾ x 7½ in)
Van Gogh Museum, Amsterdam

This elegiac illustration of a haloed sunflower fading in the light of a setting
sun was designed for the catalogue cover of a posthumous solo exhibition
at Amsterdam's Kunstzaal Panorama in December 1892, where none of the
sunflower paintings were on display.

His choices make it clear that he expected others to join him; he furnished both upstairs rooms as bedrooms, an austere one for himself and a welcoming room for a guest. As he explained to Theo, the guest room would be the 'prettiest', with walnut furniture 'and everything else elegant'. Best of all, the room would feature a *décoration* – a decorative set of paintings – featuring nothing but sunflowers on the whitewashed walls. He assured his brother: 'It won't be commonplace.'[6] In a letter written to Theo earlier in August, Vincent had connected the colour yellow with the life-enhancing light of the southern summer sun. 'Sunshine, a light which, for want of a better word I can only call yellow – pale sulphur yellow, pale lemon, gold. How beautiful yellow is!'[7] Little more than a week after that, Vincent began painting sunflower bouquets, working every morning from sunrise, 'Because the flowers wilt quickly and it's a matter of doing the whole thing in one go.'[8]

By the end of August, over a ten-day period of intensive work, Vincent completed four canvases.[9] This was the height of the flower's season, and, feeling pressured to capture their natural vitality before they faded, he worked on three paintings at once. His interest in vibrant colour contrasts can be seen in the variants within the series. Two compositions feature the flowers in a green vase, one against an aqua background and the other against a rich, royal blue. The fourteen sunflowers of the third composition were set in a yellow vase against a paler aqua-blue background. The fourth was to be 'light on light' – yellow flowers, yellow vase, yellow background – and he confided to Theo that he expected it to 'be the best'. In his enthusiasm for the project, Vincent declared that he wanted to paint as many as a dozen or more and hang them in the studio in a 'symphony of blue and yellow'.[10] But the 'light on light' canvas – *Fifteen Sunflowers* – was the last of these endeavours. By the time he shared his plan to place them in the guest room, summer had ended and the fields of sunflowers had started to wane.

Vincent welcomed his first – and a much anticipated – guest in late October. Since his return from Martinique, Gauguin had suffered financial straits and when he turned to his dealer, Theo, for help, Theo suggested that Gauguin move to Arles and live with his brother. Not only would Gauguin save on living expenses, but he would provide Vincent with the like-minded company he so desperately desired. After months of delay, Vincent greeted his guest with enthusiasm and wrote to Theo of the practical benefits of living together. He was pleased that Gauguin expressed his liking for several of his studies: 'the Sower, the Sunflowers, the Bedroom'.[11] Things went well at first. Gauguin cooked for Vincent, they painted together, and had lengthy debates about art.

But their relationship grew fractious, as Vincent tried to monopolize
the famously independent artist's time and took every disagreement
as an assault on his beliefs. Their conflicts accelerated until the night of
23 December, when Gauguin fled the Yellow House after a particularly
heated argument. He returned the next day to discover that Vincent
had maimed himself with a razor. Gauguin summoned Theo to Arles,
and as soon as Vincent's condition stabilized, they boarded a train
together to return to Paris.

On 7 January, Vincent left the hospital to recover on his own in the
Yellow House. He resumed painting as part of his convalescence, and,
in response to Gauguin's request that he send him *Fifteen Sunflowers*,
along with the possessions that he had left in Arles, Vincent revived his
sunflower series. With fresh flowers unavailable, he used his previous
compositions as models, and rather than exact replicas, Vincent copied
the works with slight variations: one of *Fourteen Sunflowers* and two
of *Fifteen Sunflowers*, leaving one of the latter unsigned without
explanation. He confessed to his brother that it was a difficult task:
'to melt those golds and those flower tones … takes an individual's
whole and entire energy and attention'. But convinced that the series
constituted his best work, the challenge was worthwhile, and he
modestly asserted, 'I have the sunflower, in a way.'[12]

In telling his own story of the sunflowers, Vincent emphasized colour,
skill and commitment to painting. He assigned them a meaning only
once, in a letter written to his sister, Wil, a year later when he was about
to leave the asylum of Saint-Rémy-de-Provence to settle in the northern
city, Auvers-sur-Oise. He acknowledged that his work was 'almost a
cry of anguish', but in 'the rustic sunflower' he had found a symbol of
'gratitude'.[13] By this time Vincent moved to Auvers, all the paintings –
the first series and the copies – were in Theo's possession, but as soon
as they began to be exhibited and sold to private collectors and public
institutions, the rustic flower became inextricably linked with Vincent's
name and reputation. Vincent could never have anticipated the attention
and the fame his sunflowers attracted over the coming century. They
reign as among the most recognizable works in the history of art and the
unsigned *Fifteen Sunflowers* broke all standing auction records when it
was purchased for £25 million by the Yasuda Museum (now the Sompo
Museum) in Tokyo in 1987. But Vincent did not judge a masterpiece by
the number of people that viewed it or by the price it could fetch in the
market. His own words reveal that the true worth of his sunflower paintings
resided in the power of colour, the beauty of nature and his deeply held
conviction that art could forge a connection between like-minded souls.

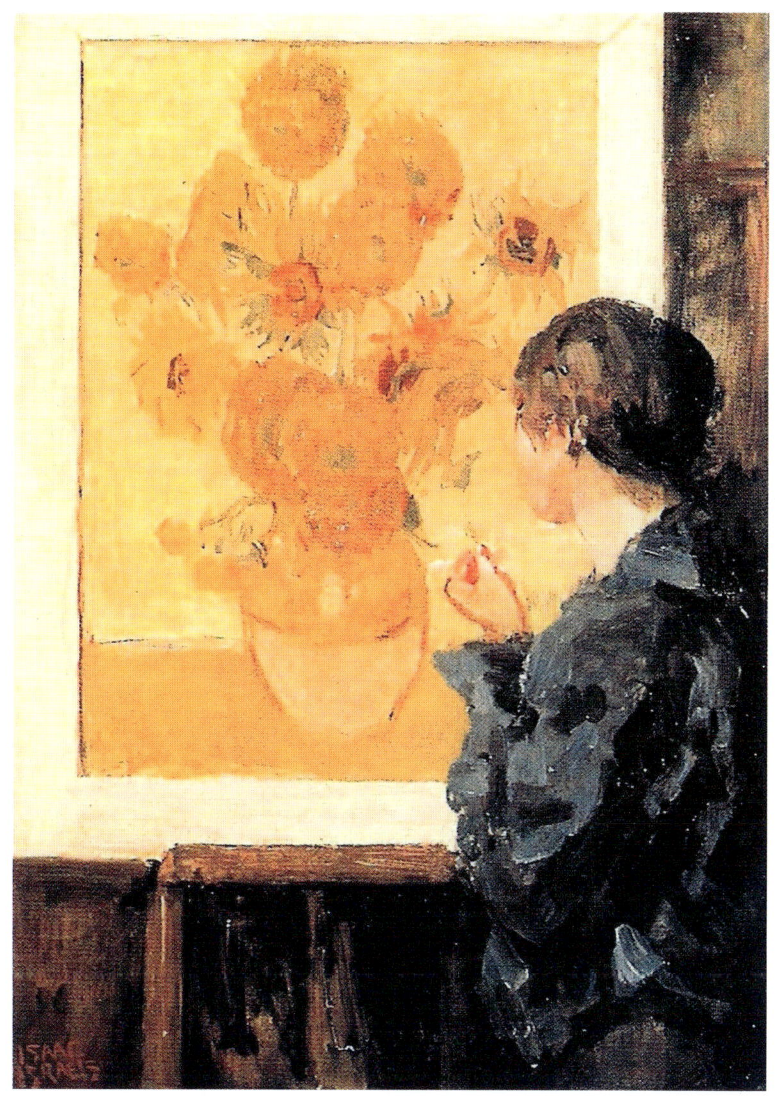

Woman Smoking next to Sunflowers c. 1920
Isaac Israëls (1865–1934)
Oil on canvas
Van Gogh Museum, Amsterdam

Fifteen Sunflowers remained in Vincent's sister-in-law's possession until 1924. Prior to selling the painting, she lent it for two years (1918–20) to Isaac Israëls, who featured it in several of his own paintings. *Three Sunflowers* is still in private hands, and *Six Sunflowers*, purchased by a Japanese collector, was destroyed during a bombing raid in the Second World War. The others are in public collections, including the unsigned copy of *Fifteen Sunflowers*, auctioned at a record-shattering price of more than £25 million in 1987.

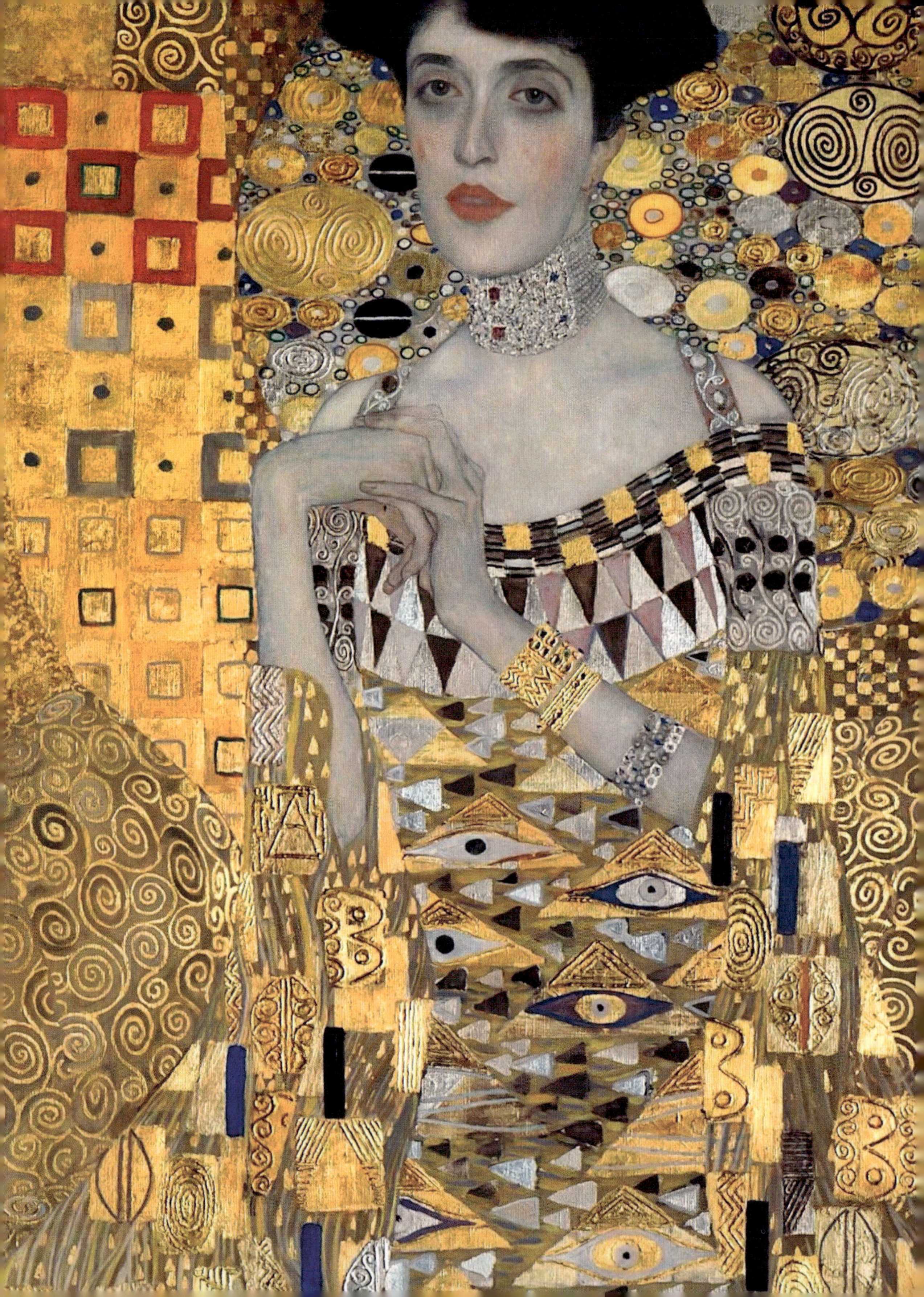

Woman in Gold Gustav Klimt

The history of stolen art is the
history of stolen lives.

Sophie Lillie and Georg Gaugusch (2007)

In 1941, the Österreichische Galerie Belvedere in Vienna acquired a magnificent painting. This portrait of a beautiful woman – with brooding eyes, a pale complexion and abundant, upswept hair – epitomized Viennese master Gustav Klimt's Gold Period. Its richly embellished, radiant surface prompted one critic to proclaim that the 'awe-inspiring' image was 'covered with a shimmering crust of gold'.[1] During the first decade of the twentieth century, Klimt had developed a distinctive aesthetic, melding the decorative exuberance of Art Nouveau design and the innovative abstract patterning of avant-garde art with influences drawn from across time and spanning the globe. He also enjoyed the patronage of an important intellectual and affluent enclave in Vienna: the cosmopolitan Jewish community known for liberal views, entrepreneurial energy and its generous cultivation of the arts. The sitter had been an admired member of that community, but at the time the painting came into the Belvedere's collection, Austria belonged to the German Reich. To sever the connection between the valued painting and a population the government sought to purge, the sitter's name was stripped from the portrait, which was then displayed to the public as *Woman in Gold*.

Few paintings illustrate the observation 'The history of stolen art is the history of stolen lives' as well as Klimt's *Portrait of Adele Bloch-Bauer I (Woman in Gold)*.[2] Painted at a time when progressive ideas and conspicuous support of the arts signified upward mobility and cultural capital, the painting gave an idealized form to the urbane ethos of turn-of-the-century Vienna. Klimt's unparalleled ability to enhance his modern artistic vision with old world material luxury conveyed the glamour of his female sitters and their refined milieu: golden images for a golden era. Adele Bloch-Bauer exemplified this distinctive spirit; she was admired as much for her intellectual curiosity and her philanthropy as for her elegant appearance and sophisticated salons. But when the German Reich annexed Austria, her family and her circle suffered loss of status and property – and many, their lives – as the Nazi regime implemented its programme of Aryanization, a quest to acquire the possessions and erase the accomplishments of the populace they deemed non-Aryan. No painting can replace broken lives and the deliberate obliteration of a community, but the journey of this painting from its commission and confiscation to its eventual return to the family, restores Adele's rightful role in making Klimt's glittering portrait a masterpiece.

When Adele Bauer married Ferdinand Bloch in 1899, they strengthened the ties between two family fortunes. Adele's paternal line had long been involved in finance; her father headed the Weiner Bankverein, one of the dominant financial institutions in Austria. Ferdinand's family members were successful entrepreneurs in the expanding sugar trade and manufacturing industry. Just a year earlier, Adele's sister Therese had married Ferdinand's brother Gustav, and in 1915, when the last Bauer descendant died without a male heir, both couples took the compound name Bloch-Bauer. Adele became

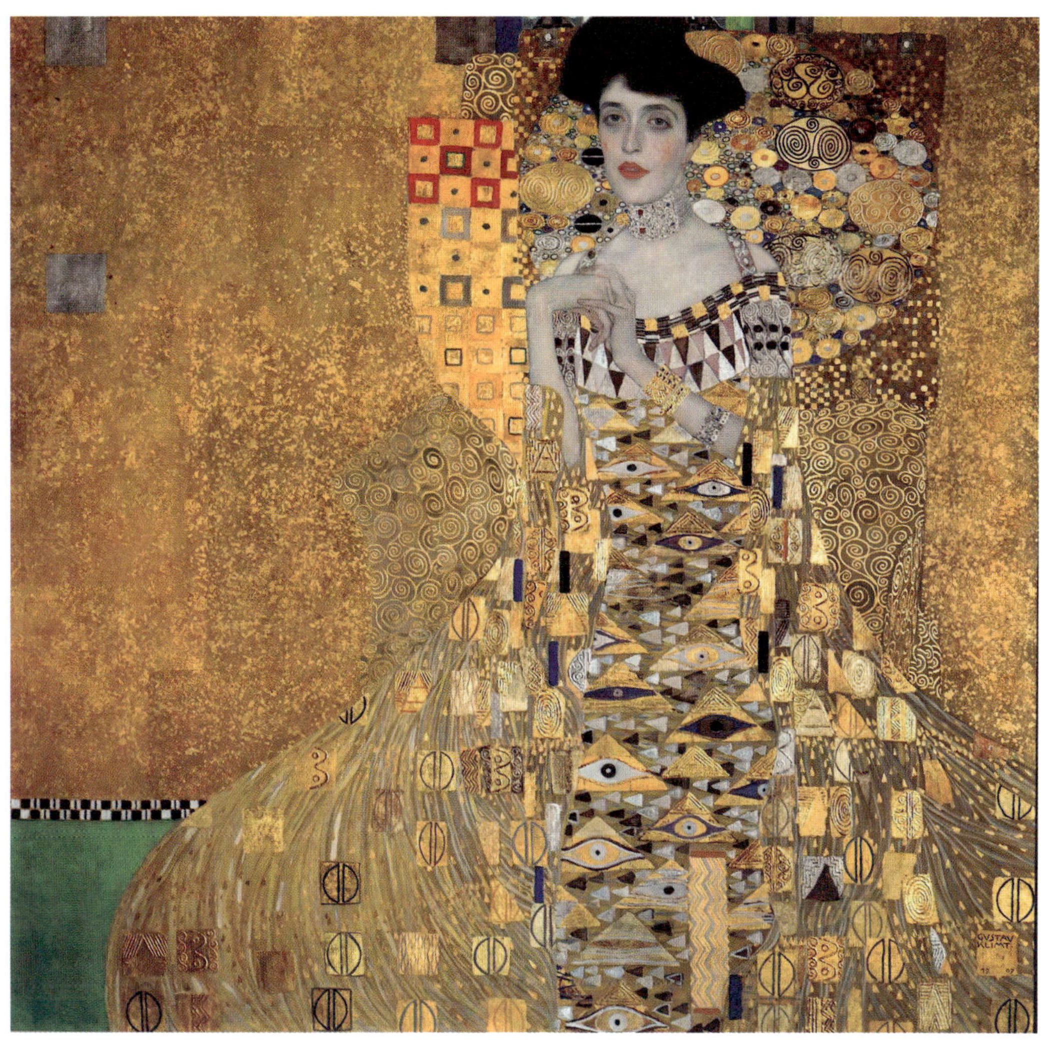

Portrait of Adele Bloch-Bauer I (Woman in Gold) 1903–07
Gustav Klimt (1862–1918)
Oil, silver and gold on canvas
138 x 138 cm (54 x 54 in)
Neue Galerie, New York, NY

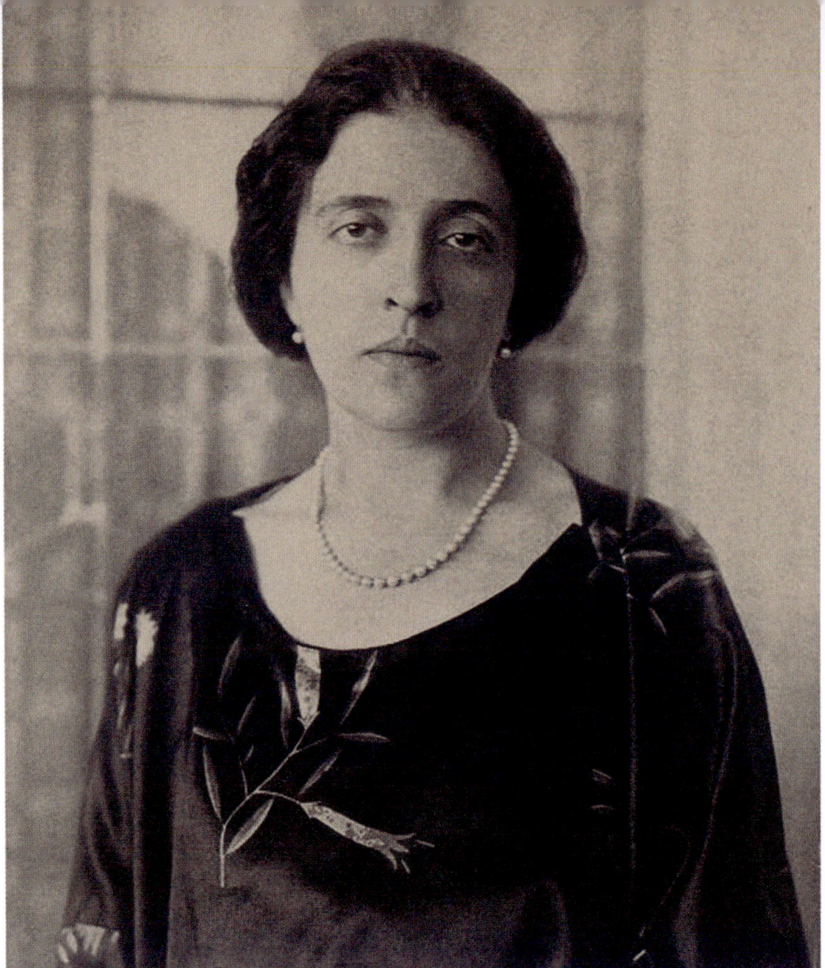

Adele, like most women of her time and social status, did not have a formal education, but from her youth she was an avid reader and interested in the arts. Her circle of friends included such progressive figures as the musician Gustav Mahler and his widow Alma Werfel, the writer Stefan Zweig, and the socialist advocate Julius Tandler. She favoured the socialist cause and generously supported children's charities and adult education.

OPPOSITE *Empress Theodora and Attendants* c. 547 BCE
Mosaic
Basilica di San Vitale, Ravenna

On a visit to Ravenna in 1903, Klimt admired the splendid Byzantine mosaics in San Vitale. He reflected their opulent aesthetic in his Gold Period paintings, working his pigments to evoke the depth and sheen of the glowing glass tesserae enhanced with marble, mother-of-pearl and gold.

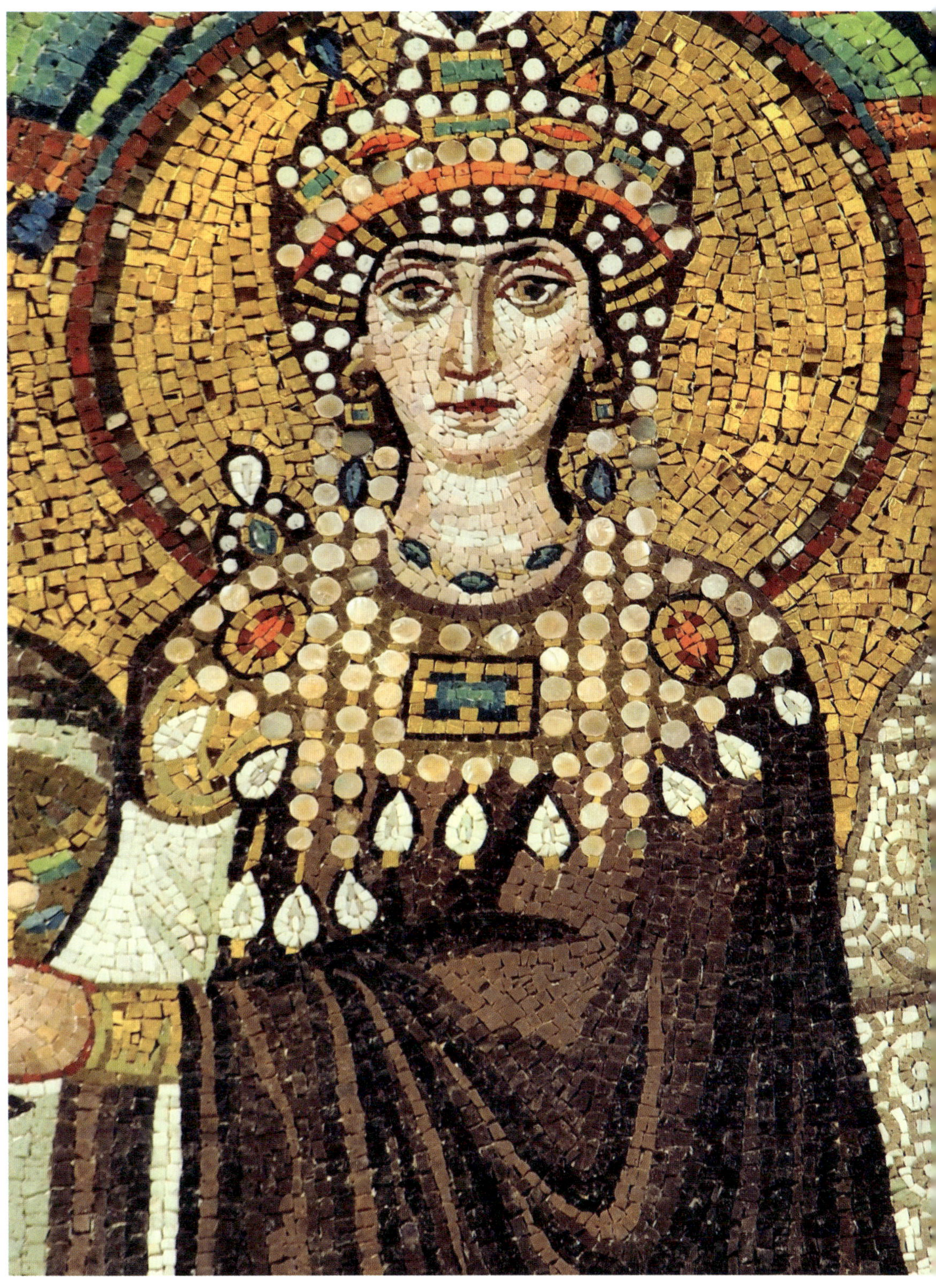

a gracious and open-minded society hostess, whose circle stretched
beyond the haute-bourgeois Jewish community, and she regularly
welcomed prominent intellectual and cultural figures into her home.
Ferdinand generously supported the arts and assembled an important
and eclectic collection that ranged from works by the Biedermeier
master Ferdinand Georg Waldmüller to Modernist sculptures by
Auguste Rodin and Georges Minne, as well as several Old Master works
and a vast collection of eighteenth-century Viennese imperial porcelain.
He also collected contemporary Viennese art, favouring above all others
the work of Gustav Klimt. In 1903, Ferdinand arranged to have Klimt
paint Adele's portrait.

Klimt, the son of a goldsmith, studied architectural painting at the
Vienna Kunstgewerbeschule (now the University of Fine and Applied
Arts) and launched his career painting murals in public buildings. He
won early recognition, including the Golden Order of Merit awarded
by Emperor Frans Josef I in 1888, but in 1897 he abandoned the
conventional path to success and became the founding president of
the Vienna Secession. As an exhibiting society and artists' association,
the Vienna Secession promoted principles rather than a single style.
Secession members sought international ties, rejected the chauvinism
of the national academy, and believed in the seamless collaboration
of fine and decorative arts practice. Building on his strong figural work
and aptitude for patterning, Klimt developed a distinctive ornamental
style that reflected wide-ranging influences from ancient Mediterranean
cultures to Japan, as well as the contemporary innovations of Art
Nouveau embellishment and the elusive – and often erotically charged
– Symbolist approach to subject matter. In the early years of the new
century, Klimt's lavish use of gold leaf defined what became known
as his Gold Period (roughly 1901–08). As he continued to secure
public commissions, he also built a practice in portraiture. His opulent
aesthetic was seen as particularly suited to female sitters, and, although
Klimt himself was not Jewish, he painted many of the prominent women
in Vienna's affluent Jewish community.

Adele mentioned the portrait in a letter to a friend written on
22 August 1903. The painting had been intended as an anniversary
gift from Adele and Ferdinand, as well as from Therese and Gustav,
to the sisters' parents, but Klimt was too busy to complete the work in
time. Ferdinand decided to commission the work on his own; Adele
wryly mused, 'So my parents must be patient'.[3] Aside from this letter
and the preparatory sketches, little else is known about the painting's
progress. In the later months of 1903, Klimt produced more than one

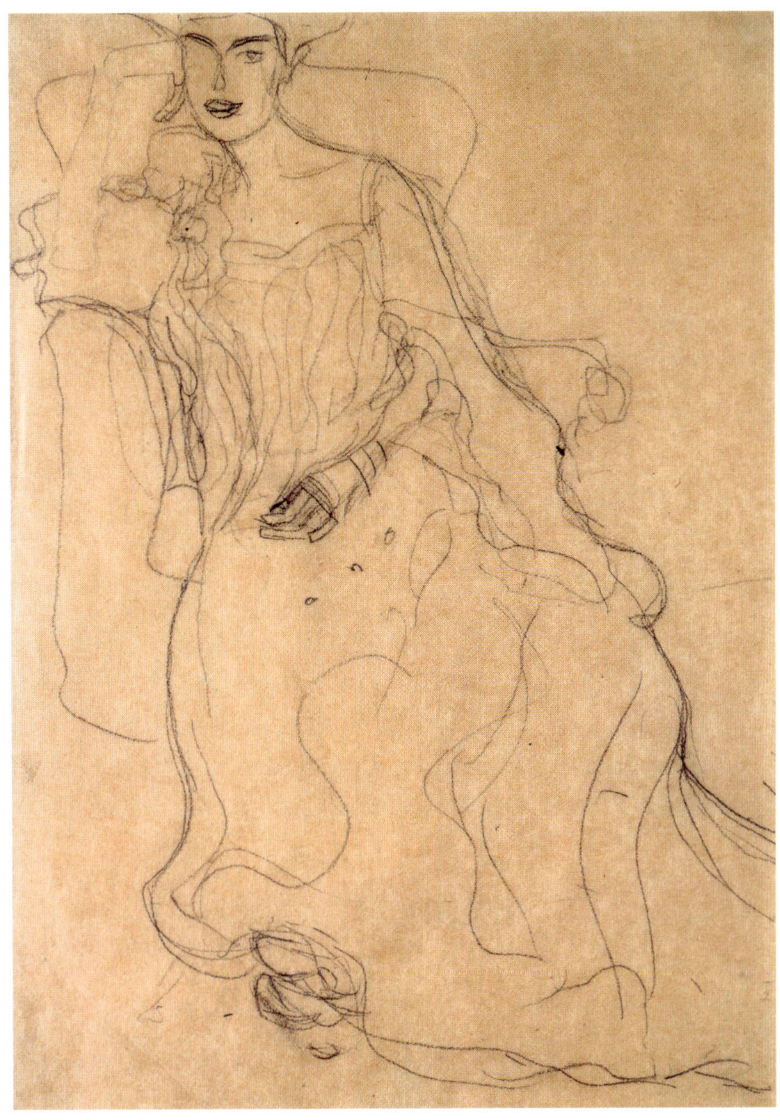

Adele Bloch-Bauer, Seated in an Armchair Facing Forward, Resting Her Temple on Her Right Hand 1903
Black chalk on paper. 45 x 32 cm (17¾ x 12½ in).
Neue Galerie, New York, NY

More than one hundred sketches made in 1903 chart Klimt's process in posing Adele. He captures her facial features in strong, confident strokes, using a lighter, more descriptive touch for her garments. He draws her hands with wiry, attenuated lines that suggest nervous movement. In the sketches the armchair grounds the figure, but in the finished painting it all but dissolves into the decorative background.

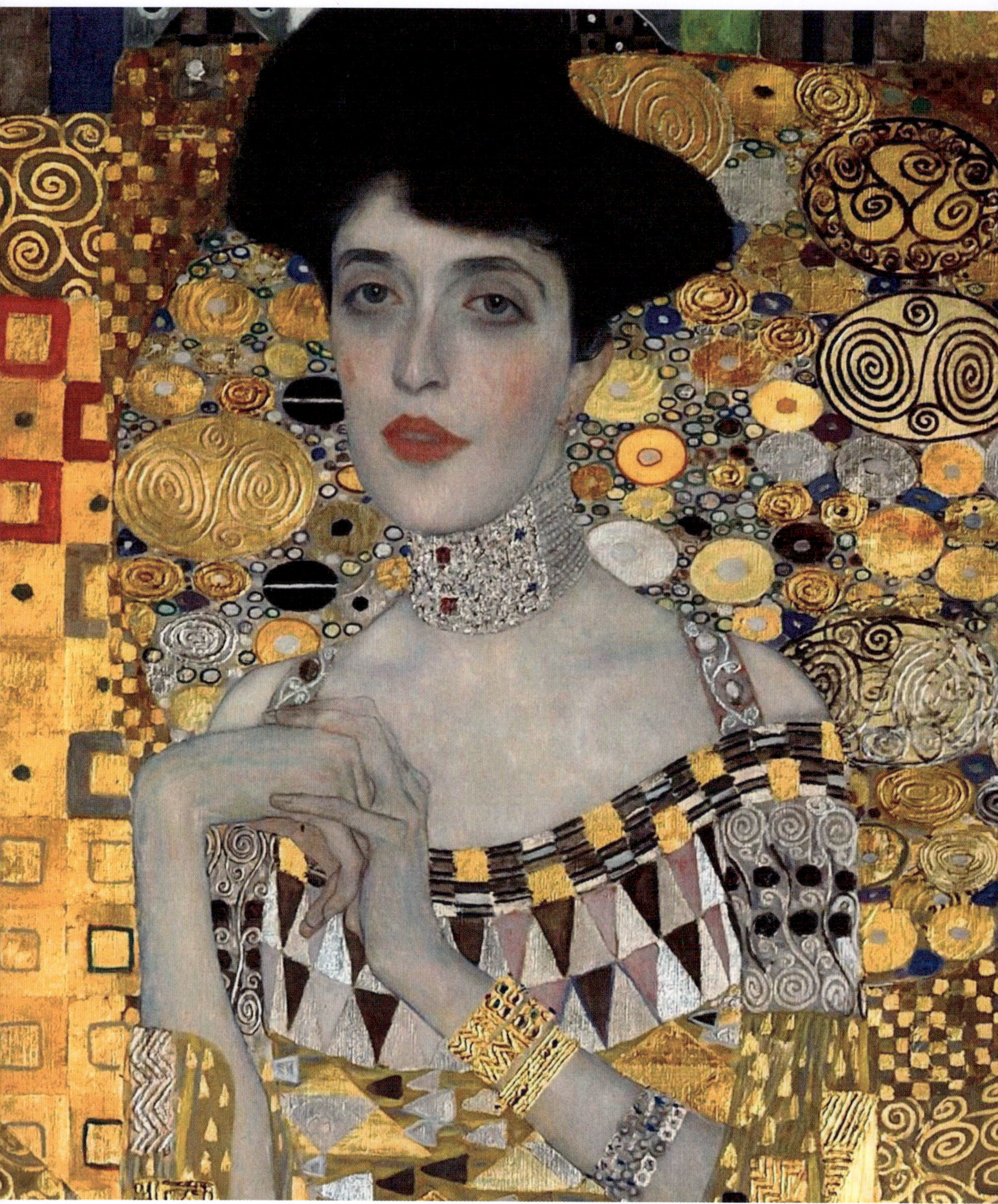

hundred sketches of Adele both sitting and standing. From the first, he posed her with an armchair and her hair arranged in her signature upswept chignon. She wears the same gown in all the sketches, readily recognized by the shoulder straps, the loose dropped sleeves, the ornamented yoke and the free-flowing, high-waisted skirt. In the early months of 1904, Klimt produced about thirty more sketches concentrating on garment detail, and then there is no further record of his work until he exhibited the finished portrait in 1907 at the International Art Exhibition in Mannheim.

Photographs of Adele reveal that Klimt captured an excellent likeness. At the same time, the contrast of porcelain pale skin with raven hair, deep brown eyes and vividly enhanced scarlet lips gives her an otherworldly, Symbolist aura, which is heightened by her enigmatic expression. She seems lost in reverie: simultaneously pleased and melancholic, as if a bittersweet memory has distracted her. Her long fingers clasp nervously together in a characteristic gesture.[4] Adele is magnificently dressed in a golden gown, with style lines that resemble the gown in the sketches. She wears gold and silver bangles on her left arm and a high, jewelled – and highly fashionable – 'dog collar' around her neck. The armchair, while barely discernable, is also included; rather than sitting on it, Adele floats in front of it. And the surface of the painting is awash in gold. This evocative metal stirs any number of possible associations and influences from religious imagery to royal portraiture, Japanese screens, Eastern Orthodox icons and the precious objects found in Egyptian tombs. In 1903, before taking on the portrait, Klimt had travelled to Venice and then to Ravenna, where he observed the glowing Byzantine mosaics in San Vitale, commissioned by Emperor Justinian in the mid-sixth century. The wealth of materials used in the depiction of the Empress Theodora – glass tesserae augmented with marble, mother-of-pearl and gold – enthralled him. In response, he gilded his own canvas and enriched the surface with built-up gold and

Portrait of Adele Bloch-Bauer I (Woman in Gold), detail

It is not known if the golden gown existed. Heavily embellished with metallic embroidery, beads and appliqué, the painted garment sheathes Adele's body like a glittering carapace in contrast to the light, floating folds in the sketches. Adele did own a multi-string, diamond-and-pearl dog collar; Ferdinand gave it to their niece Maria when she married, but it was taken from her by the Nazis.

silver leaf and jewel-bright pigments of cinnabar red and cobalt blue. When the work was displayed at the Mannheim exhibition, art critic Ludwig Hevesi described Klimt's technique as *Malmosaik* (painted mosaic) and lauded the portrait as a 'feast for the eyes' that gave the viewer the opportunity to 'rummage through gems'.[5]

After the Mannheim debut, Klimt presented the portrait again in 1908, at the newly opened Kunstschau in Vienna. Not every critic was as captivated as Hevesi; writing for the *Weiner Extrablatt*, Theo Zasche tartly complained that the portrait was '*mehr Blech als Bloch*' (more brass than Bloch).[6] But the patron was more than satisfied. Ferdinand commissioned a second portrait of Adele in 1912 and eventually acquired additional works by Klimt: four landscapes and a portrait of the family's friend Amalie Zuckerkandl. In 1919, when the family moved into a spacious mansion on the elegant Elisabethstrasse, Ferdinand created a special salon – *Das Klimt-Zimmer* – to display his favourite paintings. Adele deeply valued the paintings, and in 1923, when she wrote her last will and testament, she requested that Ferdinand bequeath the two portraits of her to the Belvedere upon his death.[7] Two years later, Adele died, the cause being either meningitis or encephalitis. She left a generous sum to the *Kinderfreunde*, a children's charity, and her library to the *Volksheim Ottakring*, a school for disadvantaged adults. Ferdinand kept the portraits in his special salon, which he renamed *Das Gedenkzimmer*, the Memory Room.

Early in March 1938, Ferdinand left Vienna and never returned. Shortly after his departure, the German Reich annexed Austria as part of the *Anschluss*, an expansionist strategy to unify German-speaking nations. The annexation was followed by a systematic programme of stripping Jewish business and property owners of their wealth and possessions. This so-called Aryanization, carried out by German administrators and assisted by complicit Austrian functionaries, sought

OPPOSITE LEFT *Portrait of Adele Bloch-Bauer I (Woman in Gold)*, **detail**

The patterning on the gown reflects a range of influences. The dominant source is Egyptian, notably the god's-eye motif, the standing oblongs in cobalt and ebony and the repeating triangles of different sizes. Klimt used these for visual richness rather than for symbolic references, linking the golden gown to the luxurious display of ancient cultures rather than their meanings in history.

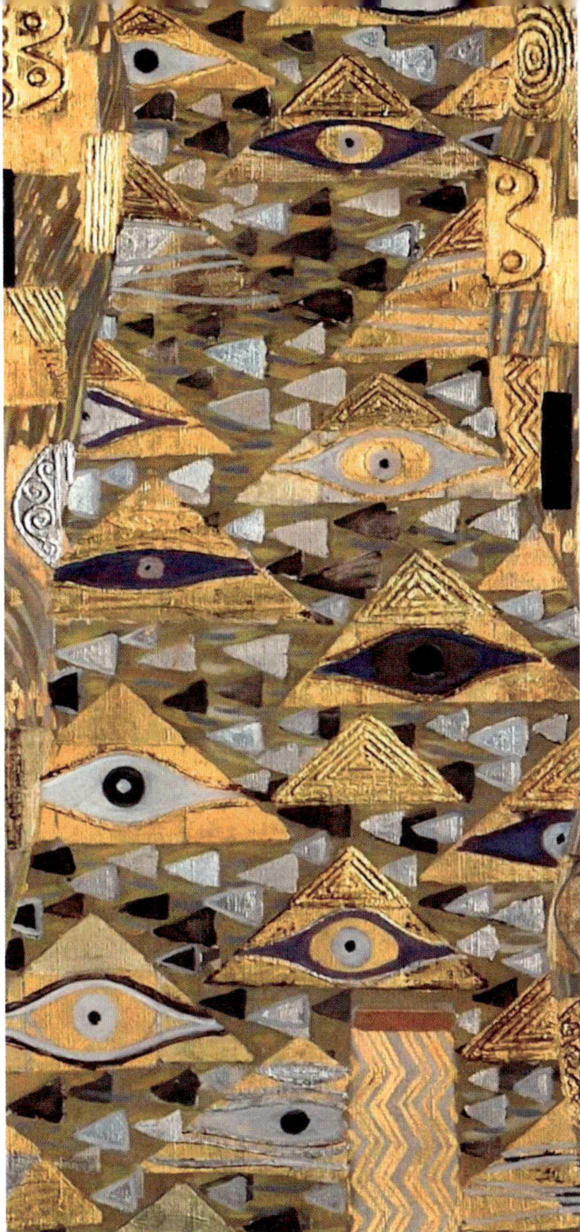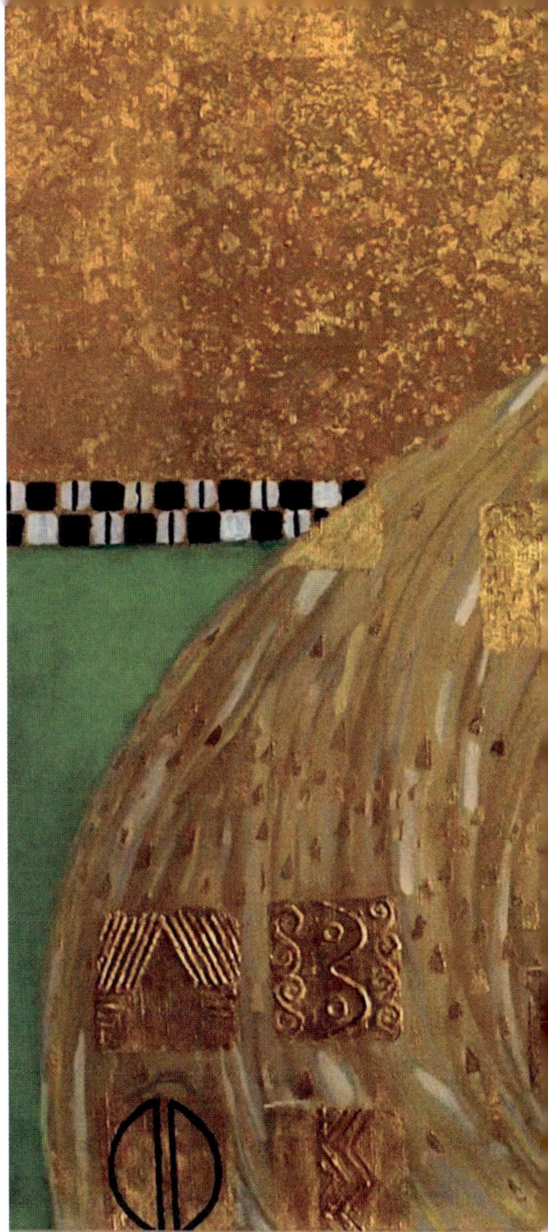

 Portrait of Adele Bloch-Bauer I (Woman in Gold), detail

The area of modulated green, set off by a band of chequered squares, is likely the dado of the wall, but in the context of Klimt's lavish palette it evokes a verdigris patina. It also sets off the curve of Adele's voluminous over gown, adding even more dimensionality to the texture of the paint. Working the surface like a goldsmith, Klimt has engraved Adele's initials 'A' and 'B' into separate squares near the hem of the garment.

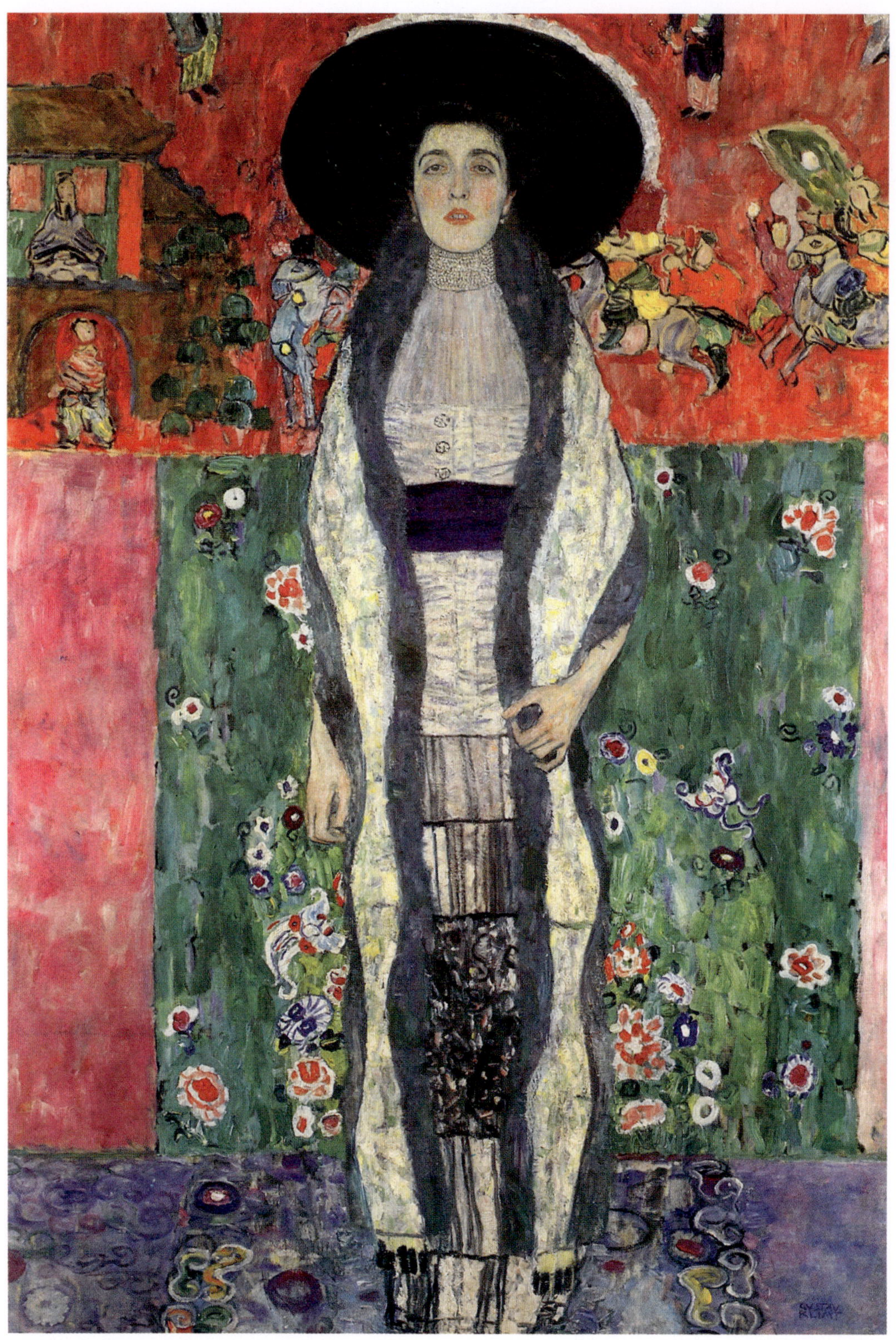

not only to enrich the Nazi regime and its high-ranking officials, but
to expunge every trace of the influential Jewish community. Criminal
charges for ten years' tax evasion were filed against Ferdinand in
his absence on 27 April, along with other false claims to follow. This
fabricated debt stripped the Bloch-Bauer family of its fortune.[8] In the
new year, a group of arts professionals, including several museum
curators and representatives of the *Zentralstelle für Denkmalschutz*
(Monuments Office) assessed the family art collection in the Palais
Bloch-Bauer and expropriated Ferdinand's valued possessions. The
works by Waldmüller and other significant German masters were
seized by high-ranking Nazi officials; the best were singled out for the
Führervorbehalt (Führer's reserve), intended for Adolf Hitler's private
collection and for the *Führermuseum* that he intended to build in
Linz, where he spent his childhood. Other objects were designated
as Austrian national treasures and barred from export. Erich Führer,
an Austrian lawyer and longtime supporter of Nazi ideology, was
appointed the family's legal counsel, and he oversaw the divestiture
of the Austrian works. The porcelain collection was sold in diverse lots
at auction, and through Führer as broker, the Belvedere acquired the
golden portrait and one of Klimt's landscapes.

From his refuge in Switzerland in 1941, Ferdinand wrote to his
friend, the artist Oskar Kokoschka, of his hesitant hopes of gaining
some restitution: 'They stripped me of everything . . . *Perhaps* I will get
the paintings of my poor wife.'[9] But the Belvedere valued the Klimt
paintings as exquisite examples of Austria's distinctive contribution
to Modernism. In 1942, the museum acquired the second portrait of
Adele, and in the following year held a retrospective of Klimt's career.
As the glittering focus of the exhibition – and a superb example of

Portrait of Adele Bloch-Bauer II 1912
Oil on canvas
190 x 120 cm (75 x 47 in)
Private Collection

The second portrait of Adele commissioned by the Bloch-Bauers is more
naturalistic, although just as decorative as the first. Here Adele is dressed in
an elegant afternoon ensemble and crowned with a broad-brimmed, feather-
trimmed hat that highlights her pale, distinctive face. The figurative wallpaper
and the floral carpet share the patterns and tones of her garments recalling the
Vienna Secessionist belief in the harmonic blend of all the arts.

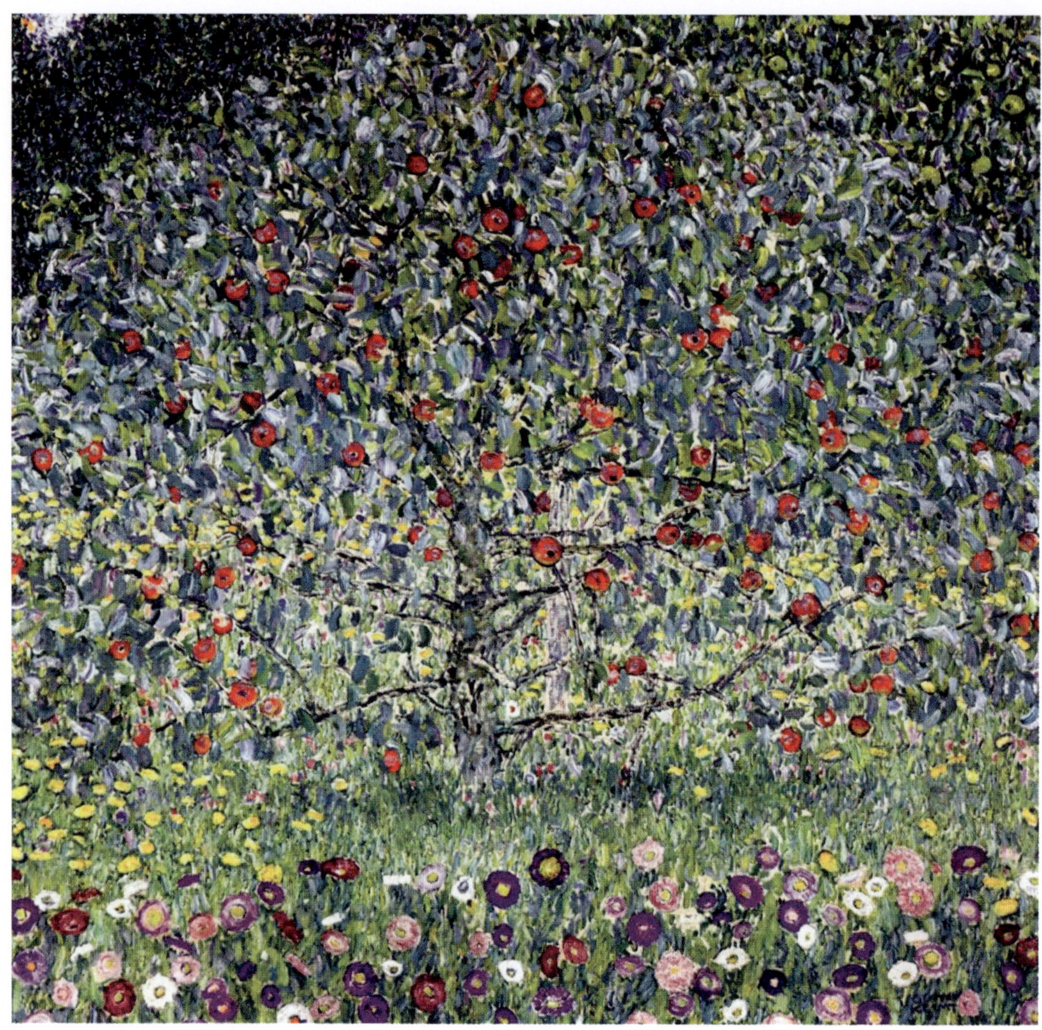

Apple Tree I c. 1912
Oil on canvas
110 x 110 cm (43¼ x 43¼ in)
Private Collection

Klimt's landscapes echo the *Malmosaik* handling of his Gold Period paintings in dabs of pure, bright pigment. The carpet of pink and purple wildflowers in the foreground and the red apples and multi-toned leaves on the tree glimmer like coloured glass in the sun. Shortly after Ferdinand's possessions were confiscated, this painting, along with the gold portrait, was acquired by the Belvedere under suspect circumstances.

the artist's Gold Period – the *Portrait of Adele Bloch-Bauer* – became the *Woman in Gold*, listed in the official catalogue as a portrait of a woman against a golden background. Ferdinand lived long enough to see the defeat of the German Reich, but not the restitution of his possessions. Over the next five decades, the surviving members of the Bloch-Bauer family mounted efforts to reclaim the properties and the paintings. In 1998, the Austrian Restitution Act which, expanded accessibility to previously classified documents, inspired the last surviving family member – Adele and Ferdinand's niece, Maria Altmann – to pursue the Belvedere paintings. Working with her lawyer, E. Randol Schoenberg, and drawing on the research of the Austrian journalist Hubertus Czernin, Altmann argued that the Belvedere held her aunt and uncle's paintings on a misreading of her aunt's will; Ferdinand was still alive at the time of the acquisition. It took Altmann almost eight years, enormous court costs, and a series of petitions that led up to a decision by the United States Supreme Court to allow her to sue the Austrian government. Ultimately, Altmann and her lawyer agreed to submit the case to arbitration and in January 2006, a panel of three Austrian judges decided in her favour.[10]

By the time Altmann obtained the painting, the identity of the sitter was widely acknowledged, but the well-loved and highly influential painting was still known as *Woman in Gold*. Altmann's efforts and persistence not only restored the painting to its rightful owner, it reconnected the golden portrait with its authentic identity as an enduring image of a woman shaped by, and active in, a community that had made such an essential contribution to Austrian culture that history's most effective programme of genocide could not fully erase it. Six months after she acquired the portrait, Altmann sold it to Ronald S. Lauder for $135 million – breaking all records for any painting previously sold – and he gave it to the Neue Galerie in New York. The gallery, founded by Lauder and Serge Sabarsky, is host to a meticulously curated collection of progressive, early twentieth-century art and design primarily from Austria and Germany. The golden portrait of Adele can once again be seen within its original cultural milieu, reminding the viewer that it takes more than gold to make a masterpiece.

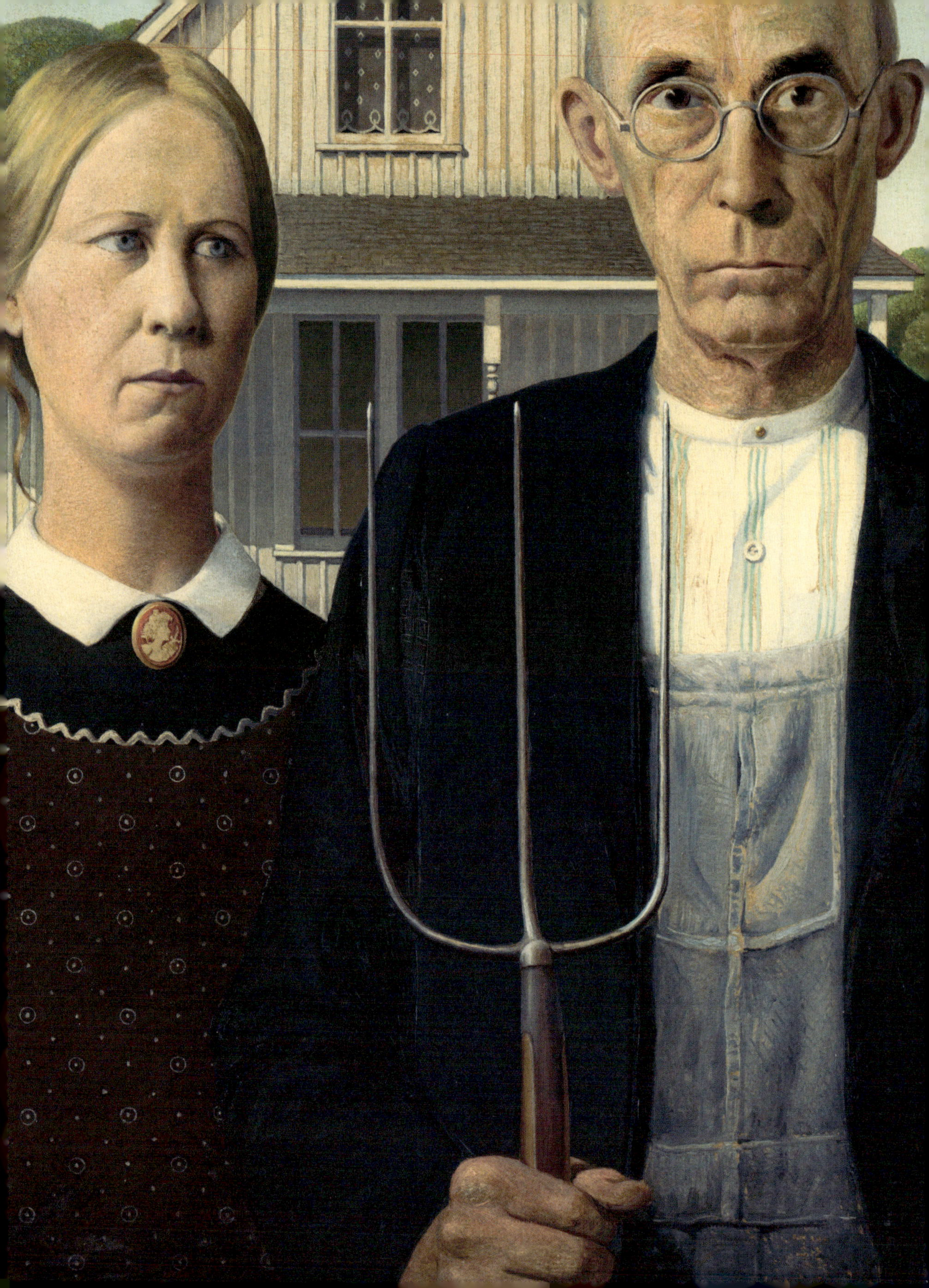

American Gothic
Grant Wood

All that I attempted to do was to paint a picture of a Gothic house and to depict the kind of people I fancied should live in that house.

Grant Wood, December, 1930

Driving through Eldon, Iowa, on an August day in 1930, Grant Wood caught sight of a white, board-and-batten house with a steeply pitched roof. He stopped the car to get a closer look, and then, using the oil paints and the back of a paperboard he had carried with him, he made a quick sketch. Wood's impressionistic image captured the hazy light, the wind stirring the leaves on the trees, and the tumble of plants in the yard, as well as the architectural details of the modest, weathered building, including a canopied porch on the ground floor and a double lancet window piercing the second storey gable. He then asked a friend to return to the house to take a photograph for future reference. But it was more than the house that intrigued him, as seen in a small pencil sketch that he subsequently made on the back of an envelope. Later explaining that he wanted to 'depict the kind of people I fancied should live in that house', Wood placed two front-facing figures in the foreground: a prim woman in a print dress trimmed with a white collar and a cameo and a stern man in overalls and a jacket holding a rake.[1] He surrounded the composition with a roughly rendered frame and inscribed the words 'American Gothic' on the lower moulding.

Just two months later, Wood submitted his finished painting to the prestigious 43rd Annual Exhibition of American Paintings and Sculpture at the Art Institute of Chicago. He was hardly a novice; he had pursued formal training at home and abroad, carried out significant local commissions and even exhibited a portrait of his mother in the previous year's exhibition. But *American Gothic* made Grant Wood an overnight sensation. The work received the Norman Wait Harris Bronze Medal for painting, and the Friends of American Art purchased it for the museum's collection.[2] More importantly, *American Gothic* ignited a lively conversation about representing national ethos at a time when the nation was facing crises of economy and identity. Did these two flinty figures, posing in front of their unpretentious house incarnate a true image of the essential American spirit, or was Wood satirizing stereotypical assumptions about Midwestern rural life? Whatever his intentions, Wood's image appealed to an unprecedentedly wide audience – popular and critical alike – as an authentic representation of salt-of-the-earth, American character. Since its debut, *American Gothic* has remained in the forefront of American imagery in the form of reproduction, recreation and parody. In making his masterpiece, Wood forged an idea of 'American' that remains potent today.

In a 1936 interview, Grant Wood explained the pull of his home state on his imagination. Over a decade earlier, during an extended sojourn in Paris, he 'realized that all the good ideas I'd ever had came to me while milking a cow. So I went back to Iowa.'[3] Although born in Iowa, Wood was being disingenuous. While he had spent his childhood on a farm outside of Anamosa, a small town in eastern Iowa, he was hardly a farm boy. By the time he was ten, his family had relocated to the state's second largest city, Cedar Rapids. After attending art schools

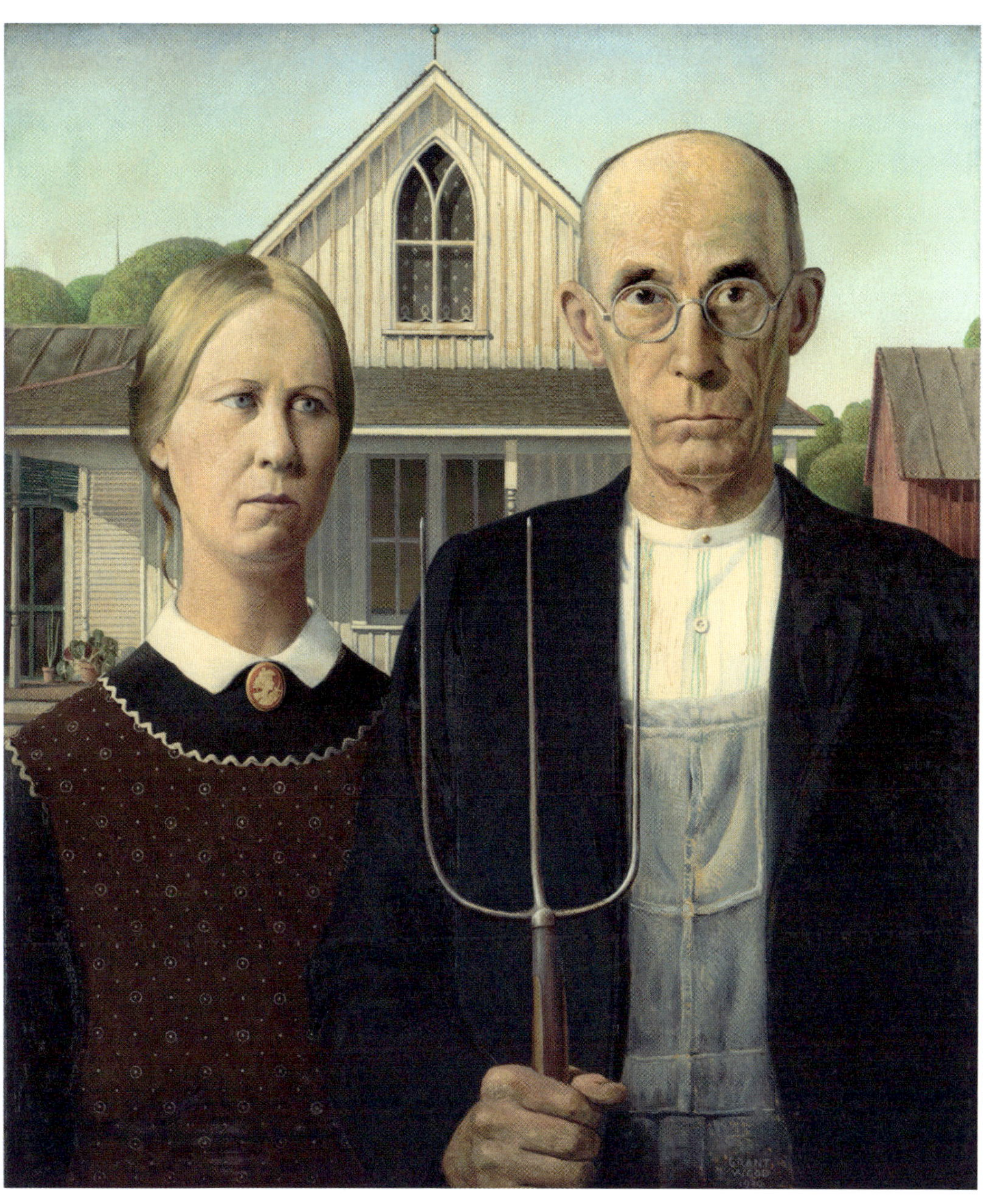

American Gothic 1930
Grant Wood (1891–1942)
Oil on beaver board
78 x 65.5 cm (30¾ x 25¾ in)
Art Institute of Chicago, Chicago, IL

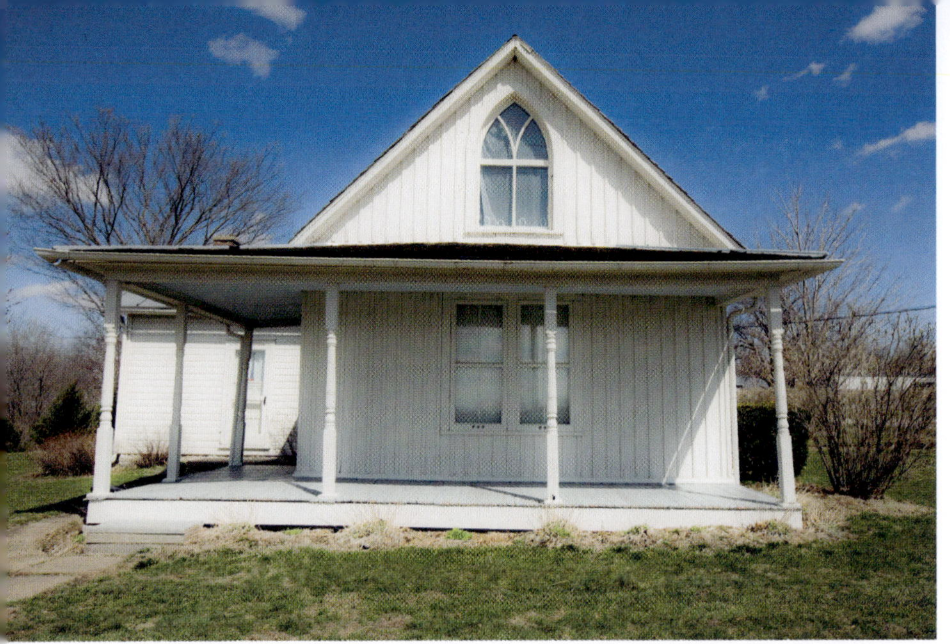

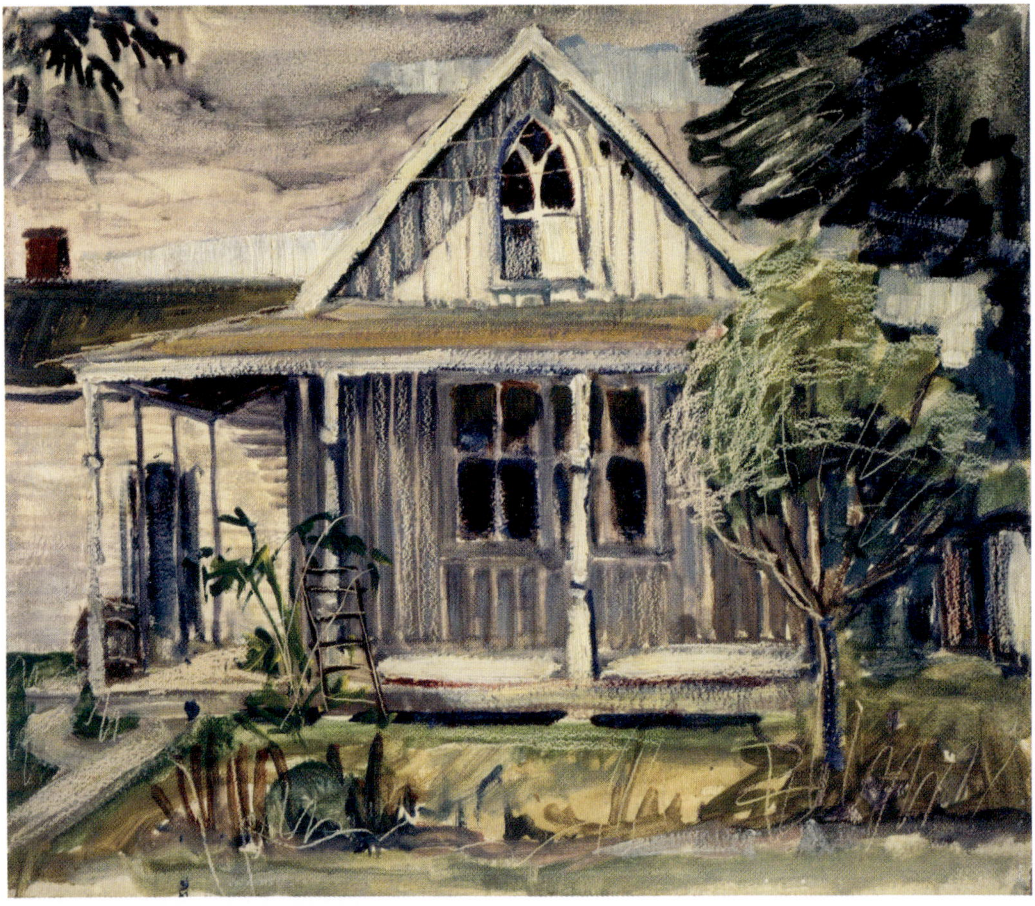

132   Making a Masterpiece

in Iowa City, Minneapolis, and Chicago without completing a degree, he settled back in Cedar Rapids, where he designed furniture and interiors and taught art in local high schools. Like so many American artists of his generation, he responded to the allure of European avant-garde developments and travelled abroad in 1920 and again in 1923–24 to study them first hand. He made his third trip to Europe in 1927, spending a few months in Munich to study stained glass in preparation for his most important commission to date: a commemorative window for the Cedar Rapids Veterans Memorial Building, honouring local soldiers who had died in the First World War. While in Munich, Wood attended an exhibition featuring paintings by Hans Memling and other Northern Renaissance artists, and in the hard-edged imagery and meticulously rendered details of their work he discerned an aesthetic anchored in truth. He returned to Iowa determined to portray the world he knew with the same unvarnished vision.

Wood's desire to turn away from European ideas and depict the stories and the spirit of his own region was part of a larger vision for the American arts that rose out of a confluence of economic hardship and national identity. After the end of the First World War,

OPPOSITE TOP **The Dibble House 1881–82**
Eldon, IA

With patterns published in builders books and materials available through mail-order catalogues, Carpenter Gothic houses were practical, affordable and easy to build. It is believed that Charles Dibble ordered the fittings for the 'Gothic' window from a mail-order catalogue. Now owned by the state and maintained by the State Historical Society of Iowa, the house is a popular tourist destination where visitors are encouraged to photograph their own version of *American Gothic*.

OPPOSITE BOTTOM **Sketch for house in *American Gothic* 1930**
Oil on paperboard
32 x 37 cm (12½ x 14½ in)
Smithsonian American Art Museum, Washington, DC.

Wood captured his first impression of the house in a loosely painted oil sketch made on the spot. He emphasized the setting and the atmosphere rather than the details and asked a friend to take a photograph as a memory aide for the studio. This sketch was painted on the back of a paperboard that he happened to have in the car; a landscape of rolling hills is on the front.

increased war effort production saddled many small farmers with an unmarketable surplus, which, in the worst cases, led to debt and foreclosure. Along with the stock market crash of 1929, the plains states were further ravaged by years of unprecedented droughts and dust storms. It seemed as if the defining advantages of American existence – abundance and opportunity – were slipping away. Throughout this time, a group of writers, including Sinclair Lewis, Willa Cather and Sherwood Anderson, turned their attention to life in the nation's small towns and rural homesteads, which they portrayed as solid and secure, as well as conservative and conformist. This forged a model of essential American character that was rooted in American soil and shaped by a commonplace, Midwestern experience. By the end of the 1920s, a parallel trend emerged in the visual arts in the depiction of small town and agrarian life as the bastion of such enduring values as hard work, thrift and resilience. The movement became known as Regionalism to distinguish it from the more cosmopolitan art world based in New York, and its most influential advocates included Thomas Hart Benton, John Steuart Curry and Grant Wood.

Wood's own interest in local culture was long-standing. He lived in his family's home in Cedar Rapids, surrounded by inherited furniture, family albums and the personal ephemera of several generations. He collected old photographs, prints and mail-order catalogues and held a subscription to *The Midland*, an Iowa-based literary magazine featuring the work of regional authors. But it was not until his trip to Munich that he embraced local subjects as central to his work; a portrait of his mother, painted in 1929, suggested that he had found the inspiration through his kindred response to the Northern Renaissance aesthetic. *Woman with Plants* is a straightforward depiction of the sixty-nine-year-old widow Hattie Weaver Wood in a black dress, covered with a faded green apron with rickrack trim, and holding a potted snake plant (*Dracaena trifasciata*). While there is no flattery in this likeness, Wood compassionately observed her care-worn expression and work-worn hands. According to his sister Nan, the 'losses and hardships' that their mother had experienced 'became part of the record etched in the face of the painting'.[4] Northern Renaissance sitters often held objects or wore garments that lent insight to their status or character, and Wood formulated localized symbols to distinguish his sitter. The snake plant, as well as the beefsteak begonia to the left, may link the houseplants to the traditional attribute of a devoted homemaker, but they are also resilient plants that thrive with little attention in harsh conditions. And Hattie grew them. As for the cameo, the image of Persephone holding

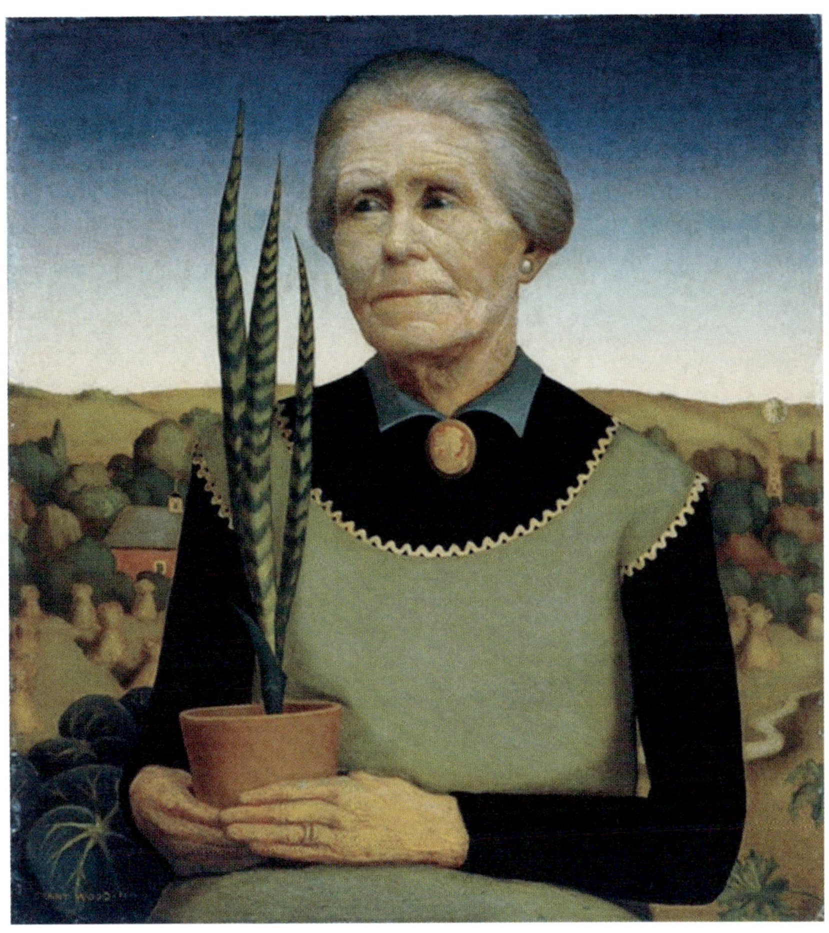

Woman with Plants 1929
Oil on upson board
50 x 45 cm (20½ x 17¾ in)
Museum of Cedar Rapids, Cedar Rapids, IA

In depicting his mother, Wood draws on the conventions of Northern Renaissance portraiture. The figure, pushed to the front of the picture plane, dominates the composition. Wood does not flatter his sitter; her features are rendered with an almost relentless clarity. Her cameo, her wedding ring and even her apron are more than accessories. They are attributes that proclaim her identity.

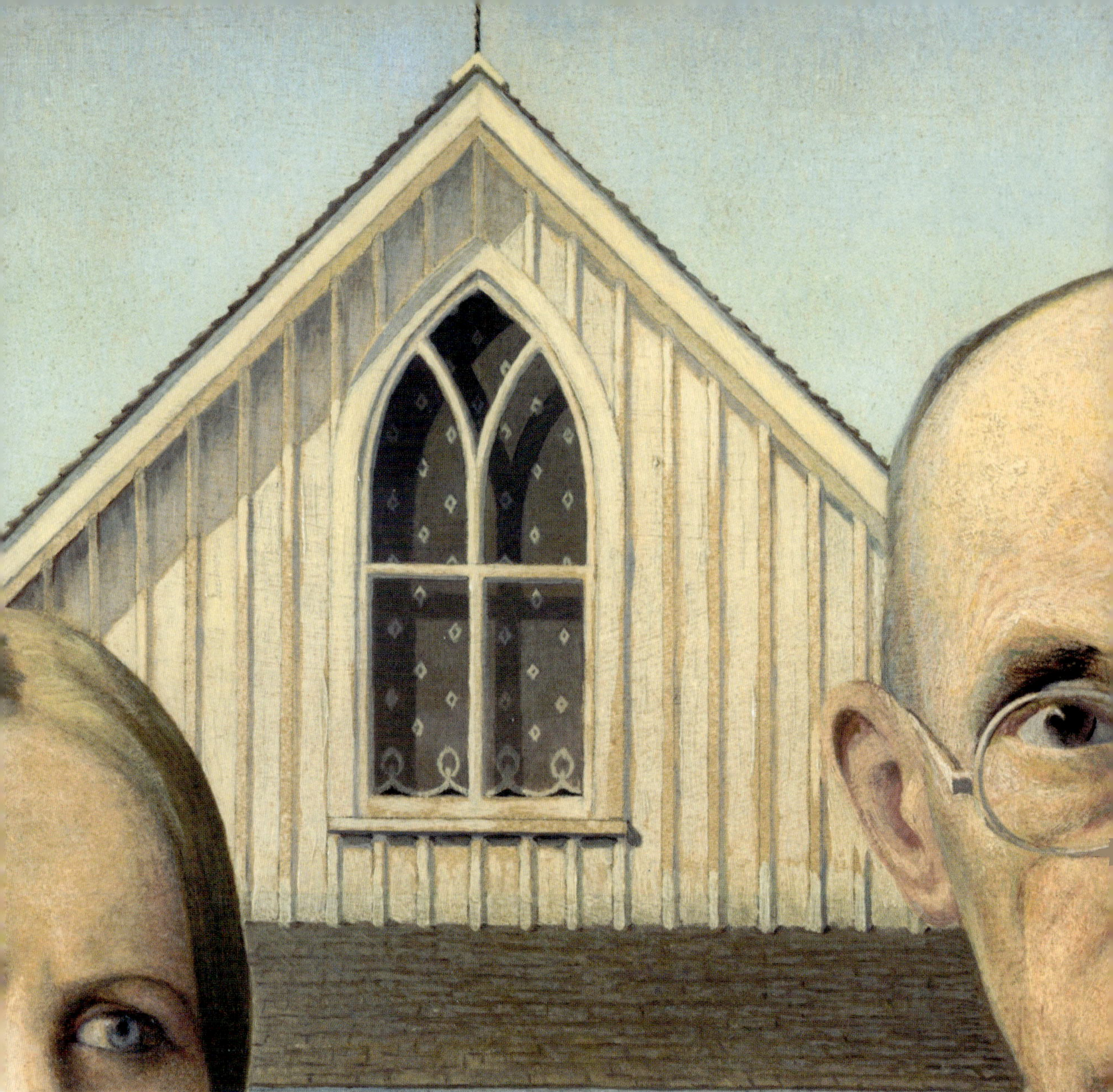

American Gothic, detail

The tall, pointed window – a distinguishing element of the Carpenter Gothic style – simulates the stone mouldings and mullions of medieval architecture in wood. Although Wood remained true to the Dibble House as his model, his rendition of the window is taller and narrower in an echo of his elongated figures. And he added a print, scalloped-edge curtain, perhaps as a sly reference to stained glass.

her pomegranate – the classical symbol of seasonal renewal – may, in fact, be incidental. Wood had bought the brooch for his mother in Europe; he believed that the face bore a striking resemblance to Nan's. Despite the meticulous rendering of his mother's form and features, in *Woman with Plants* Wood had represented an American archetype: a modest small-town housewife, dignified but down to earth, with an idealized Iowa landscape unfolding in the distance behind her.

The house that Wood saw in Eldon was as much a part of the Iowa landscape as the broad plains and the cultivated fields. This particular house, built in around 1881 for the livery stable owner Charles Dibble and his wife Catherine, is an example of 'Carpenter Gothic', an American vernacular style that spread with the westward agricultural expansion in the mid- to late nineteenth century. With its simple form and wood-frame structure, this type of house was inexpensive and could be quickly assembled with little help and rudimentary skill. Typically, the house featured two storeys, two rooms each, fronted by a covered porch and crowned by a steeply pitched roof. Finished with board-and-batten siding – invariably painted white – pre-cut wooden window treatments and moulding in the Gothic style gave the type its name. For *American Gothic*, Wood presented the Eldon house as he saw it, although he did tidy up the yard, give the siding a fresh coat of paint, and add a print curtain behind the lancet window. To complete his setting, he added the red barn on the right, a church spire in the left distance and placed the potted snake plant and beefsteak begonia from *Woman with Plants* in the corner of the porch.

Wood stated that the 'severe' lines of the house had appealed to him, and he wanted to find 'two people, who by their severely, strait-laced characters, would fit in such a house'.[5] But he chose his sitters, not for the lives that they lived, but for their personal appearance. For the man, he posed his dentist, Dr Byron McKeeby, whose spare physique and doleful demeanour conveyed the resolute integrity that Wood saw as an apt trait for the head of a small-town household. His sister Nan gamely took on the role of the grown-up daughter, washing out her Marcel waves to adopt a straight, skinned-back coiffure and pinching her soft, delicate features into a prudish expression. Wood costumed his characters to emulate those he saw in the photographs from his family's albums. And while the clothing in the painting is often described as out of date, the garments are more an example of non-fashion, practical items selected for durability and function rather than style. The man wears bib overalls over a well-washed, collarless shirt that Wood claimed to have found in a bag of old clothes given to him

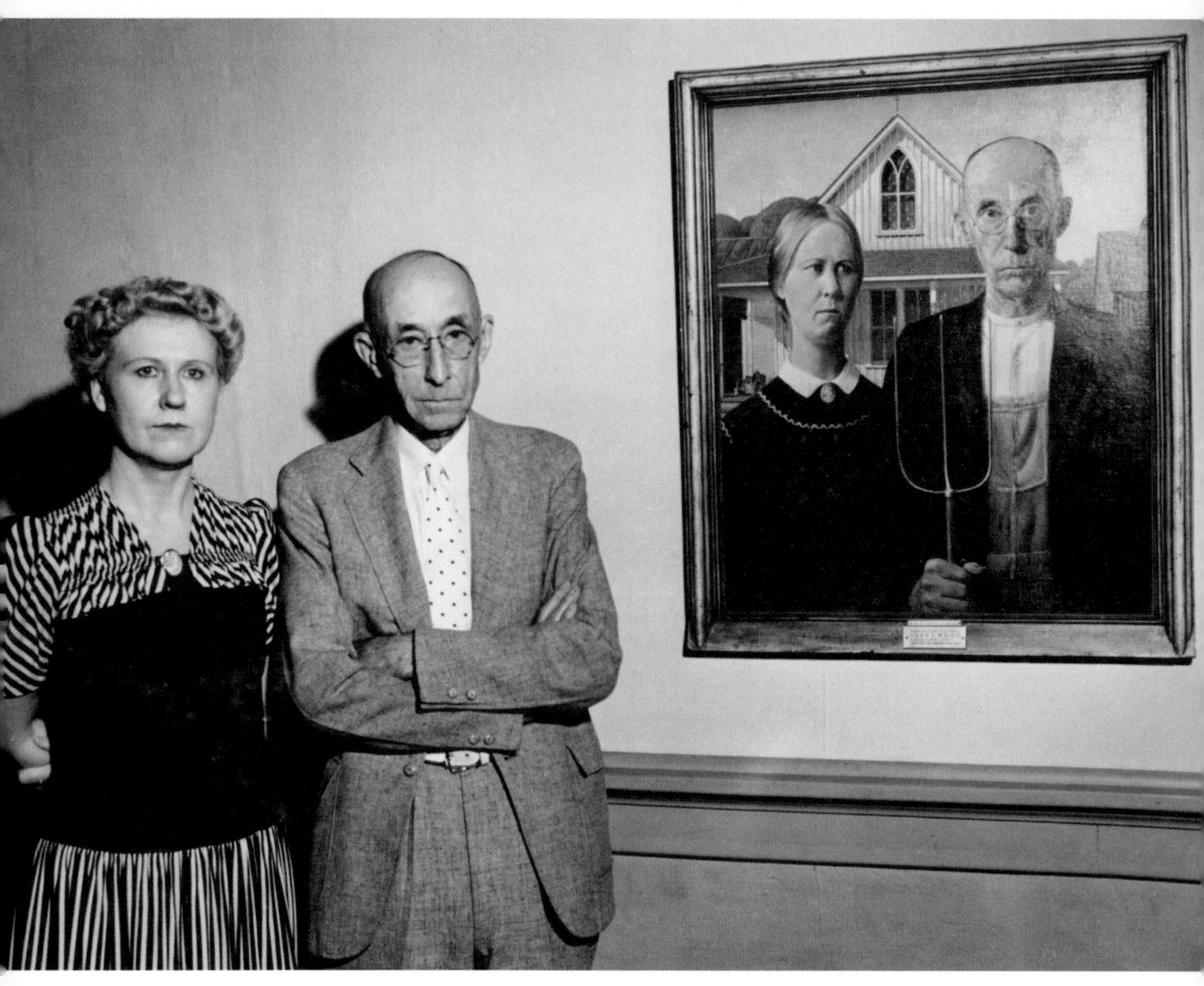

Photograph of Nan Wood Graham and Dr Byron H. McKeeby in front of
American Gothic September 1942
Unknown Photographer
Memorial Exhibition
Cedar Rapids Public Library

The first time that Dr McKeeby and Wood's sister Nan actually posed together
was at a memorial exhibition for Wood held in 1942. Wood painted them
separately, using their likenesses, but inventing their characters. He rendered
McKeeby's doleful demeanour with relentless accuracy, but he narrowed Nan's
rounded face and hardened her delicate features.

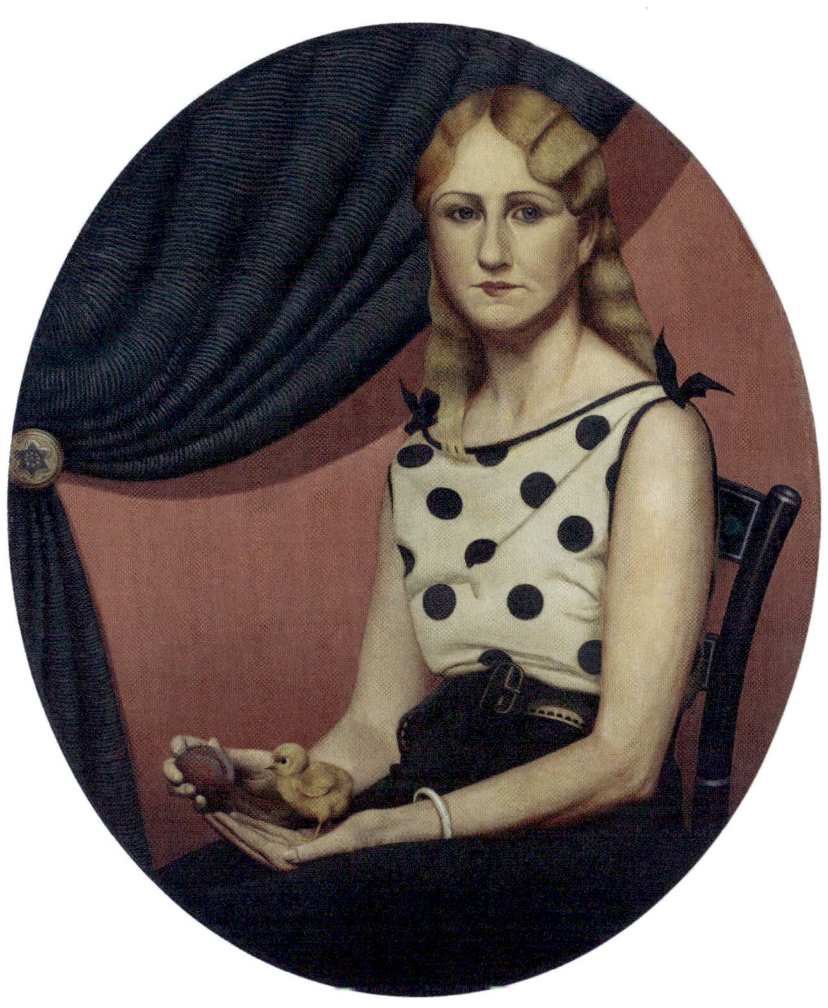

Portrait of Nan 1933
Oil on masonite
88 x 72 cm (34½ x 28½ in)
Chazen Museum of Art, Madison, WI

Wood presented a very different image of his younger sister Nan (1899–1990) in a portrait painted three years after she posed for *American Gothic*. In her memoir, Nan explains that her brother wanted her freshly waved hair worn loose, and that he suggested the stylish polka-dot bodice, improvised from an old sheet. The curious attributes that she holds – a plum and a baby chick – were chosen for their colour rather than any secret meaning.

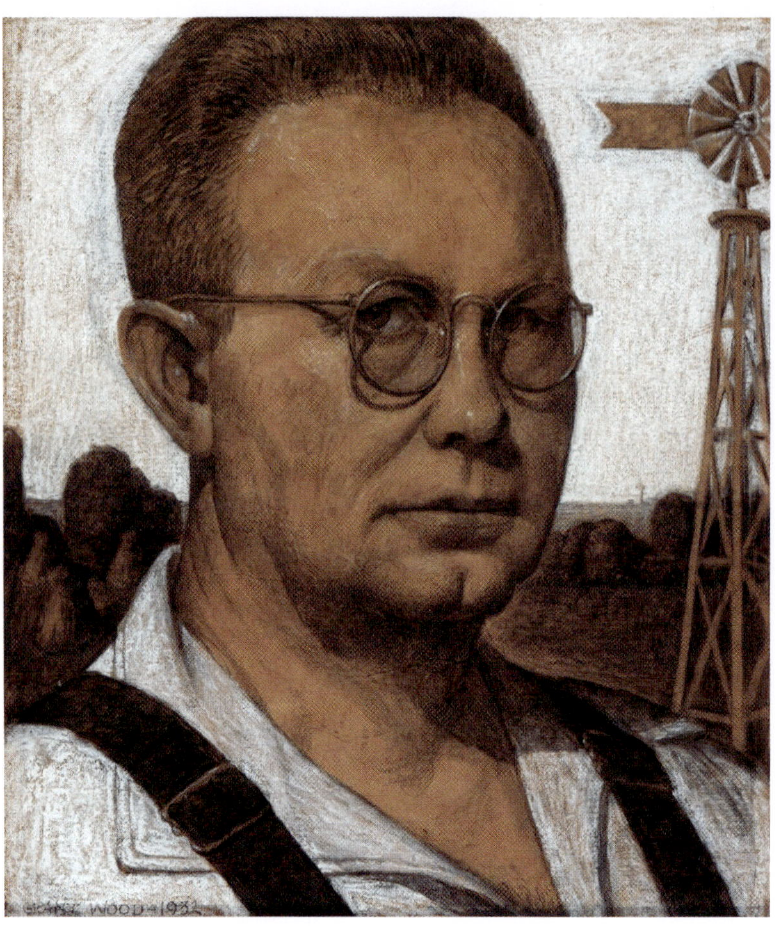

Study for Self-Portrait 1932
Charcoal and pastel on paper
Cedar Rapids Art Museum, Cedar Rapids, IA

In the years immediately after gaining fame for *American Gothic*, Wood played up his rural roots. Agricultural settings and small-town life dominated his repertoire, and he posed for a number of studio photographs in overalls. In this study for a self-portrait, Wood wears a worn-looking work shirt with the collar pressed down by tightly buckled overalls straps. He never regarded the final version as complete and, at some unknown date, he painted over his rural attire in bright teal-green but kept the background expanse of rolling fields.

by a relative to use as painting rags. The jacket would have come from a worn-out suit, rather than the man's 'Sunday best'. The daughter's costume echoes the attire worn in *Woman with Plants*: a plain dress with a contrasting collar, covered by a well-ironed apron trimmed with rickrack and enhanced with the same cameo. Nan said that she made the apron with trim removed from one of her mother's old dresses, but Wood claimed that he ordered it from the Sears Roebuck catalogue. As in the pencil sketch, the figures dominate the foreground, but the man now holds a pitchfork rather than a rake. Wood explained the change: a rake is a farmer's tool, and since many small-town residents kept horses, the pitchfork was more appropriate. But the attenuated shape also reinforced the overall linear aesthetic, repeated in the stripes on the shirt, the pockets on the overalls, the narrow lancet window, and the lean features of the sitters' faces.

Wood's initial inspiration came from the little white house, but the crowds that gathered around *American Gothic* at the Annual Exhibition of American Paintings and Sculpture at the Art Institute of Chicago in 1930 were fascinated with the characters that he invented. And not all the response was positive. The Art Institute, as well as regional newspapers throughout the Midwest, received a spate of letters from viewers complaining about the character's sour expressions, the way Wood represented Iowa farmers and the age discrepancy between the man and his presumed wife. Critics, taking for granted that the work was satire, judged Wood's humour as harsh, even cruel. But Wood responded, pointing out to the press that he had no intention to criticize or 'localize' the pair; they were a father and daughter, a 'small-town' rather than a farming family and they were not meant to be associated with Iowa but were essentially 'American'.[6] All the publicity only increased curiosity about *American Gothic*, and as the painting became widely known through news reports and reproductions, the tone of reception shifted to positive, crediting Wood with incarnating the core resiliency of the true American spirit to celebrate steadfast values in uncertain times. Christopher Morley, writing in the internationally circulated *Saturday Review of Literature*, observed that 'In those sad and fanatical faces may be read much of what is right and what is wrong with America'.[7]

The enduring popularity – and seemingly endless parody – of *American Gothic* has proved it to be a concept as resilient as the values that Wood set out to represent. Over the decades since it debuted, the composition of two front-facing figures, dominating the foreground with a small, white house behind them, has been restaged to feature political allies and rivals; punks and preppies; friends and enemies; and advocates of causes ranging from gun rights to disarmament. In each case, the pair – whoever they are – stand in front of the little house in Eldon. Even today, tourists flock to the site to photograph their own tableaux of what is now indisputably an American icon. The most powerful response to Wood's vision, however, did not need the house to evoke the composition. In 1942, Gordon Parks joined the staff of the Farm Security Administration's photographic unit. As the sole Black member of the unit, Parks was eager to contribute to the project of recording the American experience, but the level of racial prejudice that he encountered on the streets of Washington, DC, made him realize that he could use the opportunity to expose discrimination through the process of documentation. A chance conversation with Ella Watkins, a cleaning woman working the night shift at the headquarters, inspired him to take her portrait: Watkins in a worn work dress, with a broom in her right hand and a mop beside her, standing straight and dignified in front of an American flag. Parks later reflected on his idea: 'American Gothic . . . That's what I felt about America and Ella Watson's position inside America.'[8] Parks saw the flaws in Wood's 'authentic' representation but also recognized it as a template that could accommodate expansion – an iconic vision through which he could offer other perspectives and other truths about what it meant to be American.

Washington, DC, Government Charwoman (Ella Watson)
Gordon Parks (1912–2006)
1942 [printed later]
Gelatin silver print
71 x 51 cm (28 x 20 in)

Parks's photograph opens a relevant dialogue with Wood's painting. He took this portrait after a conversation with Watson, who revealed that she was a qualified stenographer but, as a Black woman in Washington, DC, she could only find employment scrubbing floors. In Watson, Parks recognized an authentic embodiment of those values that Wood celebrated – resilience and determination – in an American experience that was all too often overlooked.

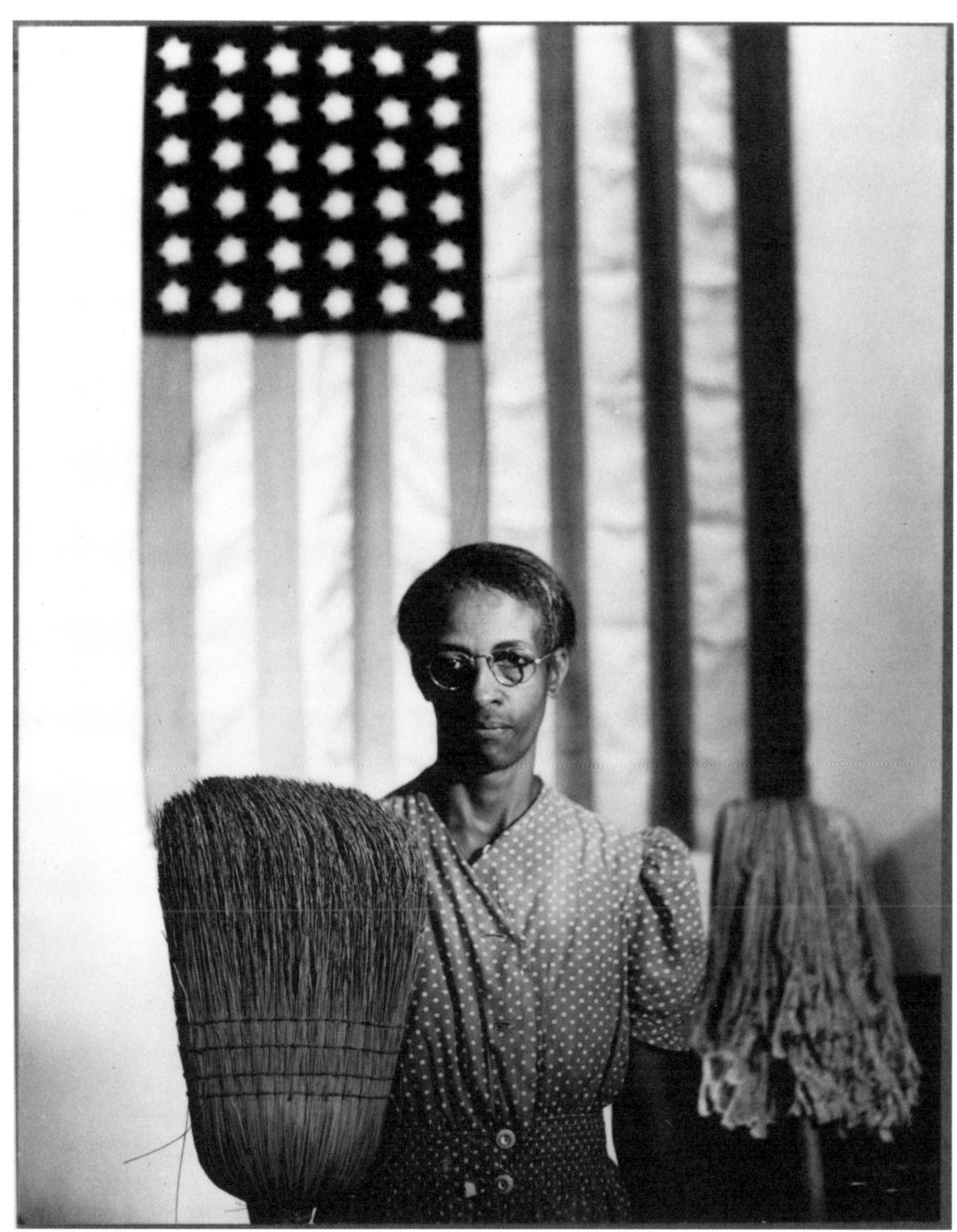

American Gothic

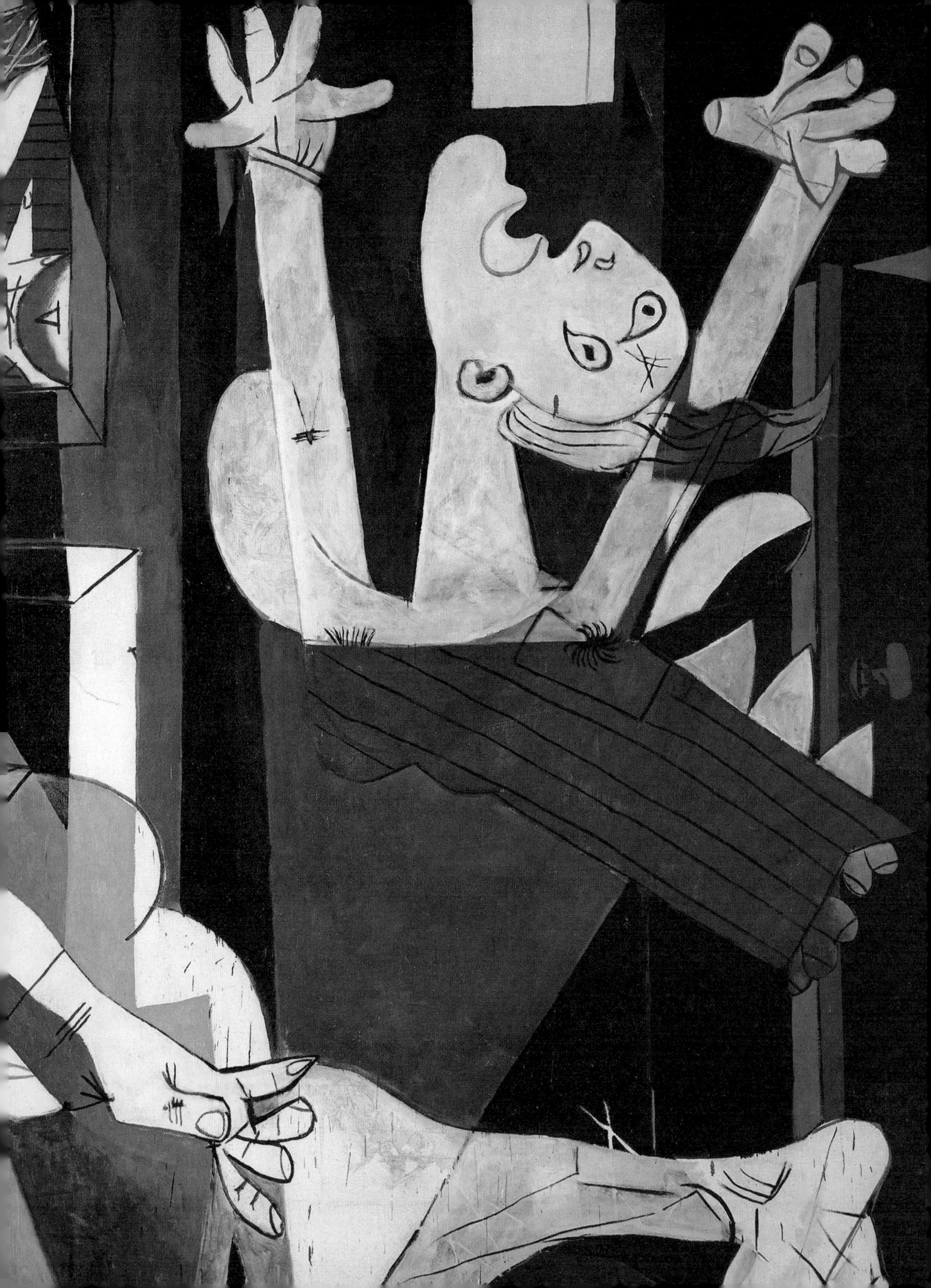

Guernica
Pablo Picasso

Not only Guernica, but Spain; not only Spain but Europe, is symbolized in this allegory. It is the modern Calvary, the agony in the bomb-shattered ruins of human tenderness and faith.

Herbert Read, October 1938

From his first years in Paris, Pablo Picasso pursued an intense engagement with the essential elements of traditional art. During his Blue Period (1901–04) and his Rose Period (1904–06) he explored the potential of limited colour and taut line. His austere *Portrait of Gertrude Stein* (1905–06) elevated the sitter's presence over her likeness, while the radical

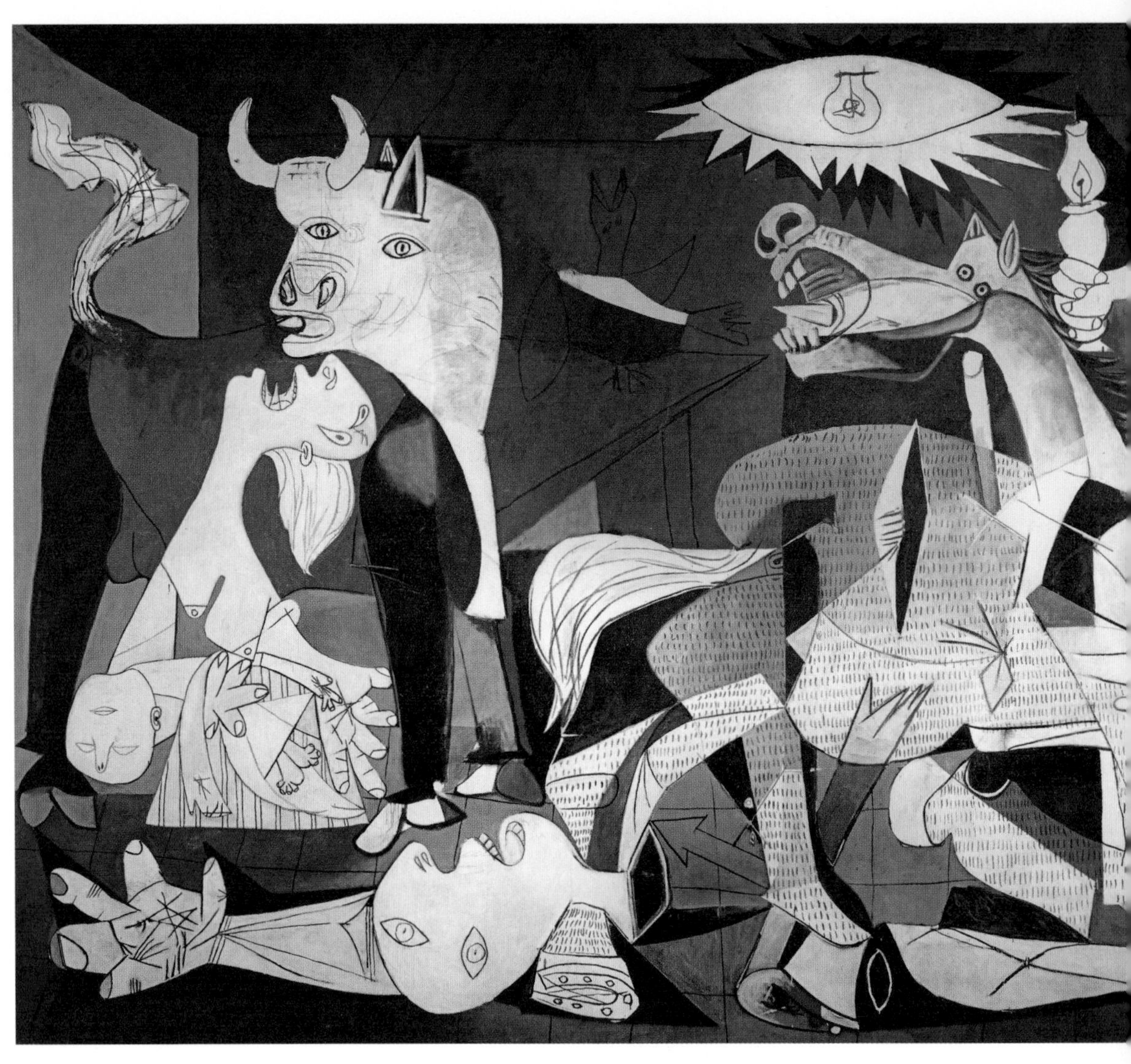

Guernica 1937
Pablo Picasso (1881–1973)
Oil on canvas
349.5 x 777.5 cm (137.5 x 306 in)
Museo Nacional Centro de Arte Reina
Sofía, Madrid

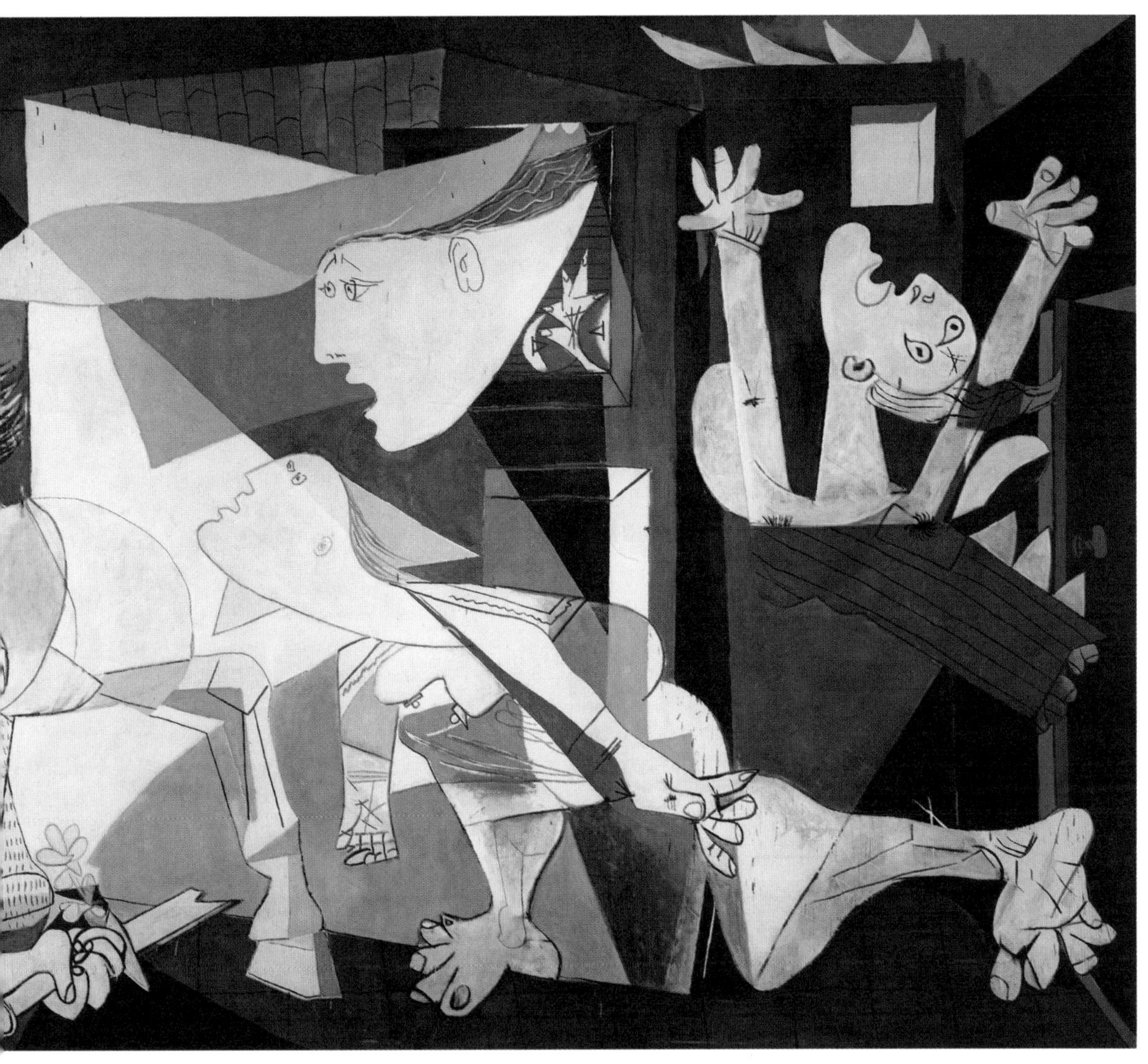

fragmentation of *Les Demoiselles d'Avignon* (1907) reimagined the role of figuration. Through Cubism (c. 1907–14) Picasso challenged the very concept and techniques of representational art, experimenting with set notions of dimensional space, plane and volume, illusion and perception, all the while never fully abandoning the depiction of objects in some recognizable form. Every stage of his relentless pictorial development questioned artistic conventions, but as he tested traditions, he never renounced them, realizing that more power resided in transformation than overt rejection. Nowhere is this more evident than in *Guernica*, his deeply personal response to the heinous reality of contemporary warfare.

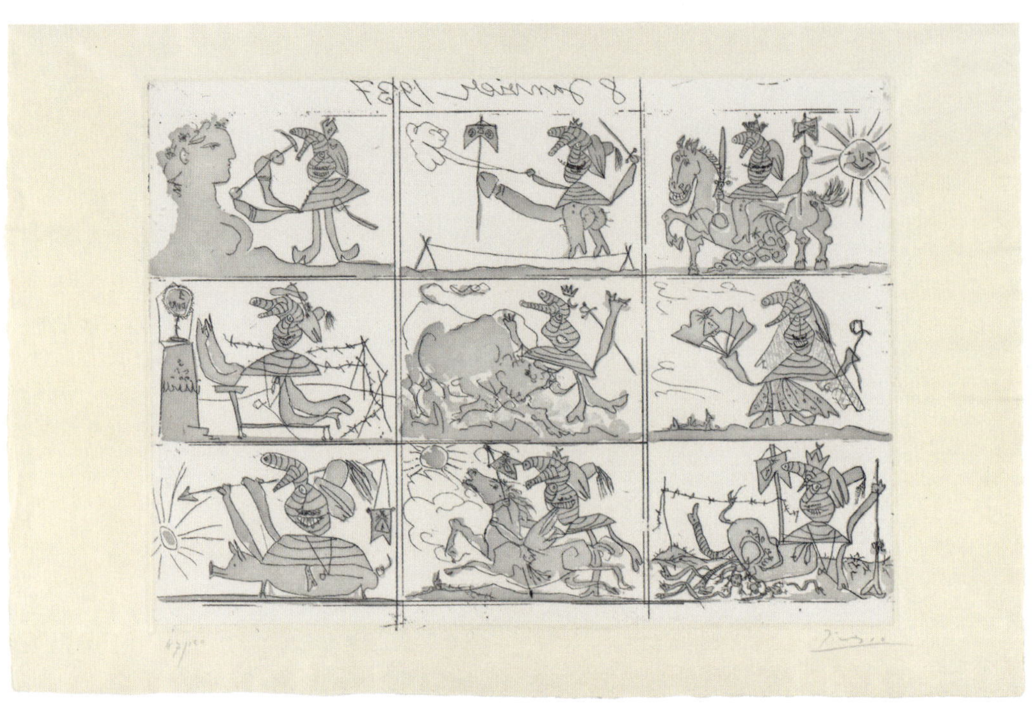

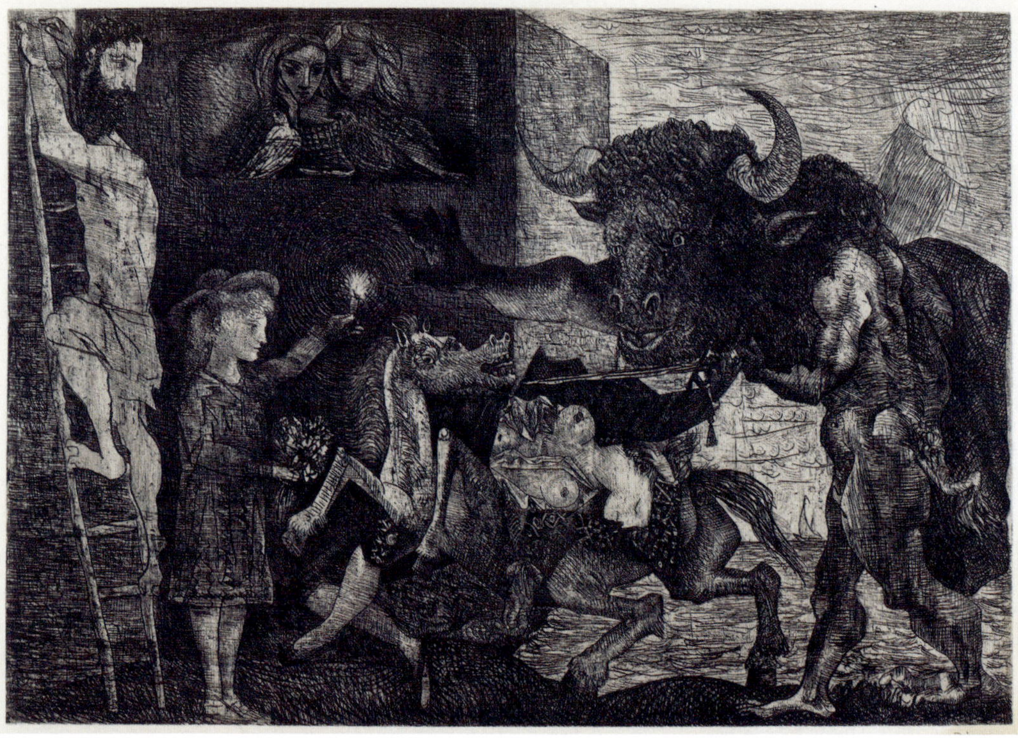

Guernica, inspired by the brutal bombing of the Basque city during the escalation of the Spanish Civil War (1936–39), stands as Picasso's most monumental public work of art. Months before the attack on Guernica, Picasso had accepted a commission for a grand-scale mural to be displayed in the Spanish Pavilion at the 1937 International Exposition in Paris, but he had been struggling to find a suitable subject. Now his response was immediate, and he completed the enormous painting in six weeks. When the pavilion opened, some critics found the explosive composition daunting; the lack of clarity and the cryptic symbolism seemed to defy Picasso's presumed intention to memorialize the victims of the recent attack. But others recognized that Picasso's objective transcended the commemoration of a single, yet singularly horrific event. By forcing viewers to see and feel beyond the safe, cerebral boundaries of conventional narrative and allegory, Picasso made *Guernica* a universal masterpiece.

In 1931, the Spanish electorate brought into power left-leaning candidates who favoured the dissolution of the Bourbon monarchy. The founding of the Second Spanish Republic – a socialist democracy – met with immediate resistance from right-wing nationalists. Within a few years, an aggressive, far-right, populist movement coalesced under the leadership of General Francisco Franco and by July 1936, with the

OPPOSITE TOP *Sueño y mentira de Franco (The Dream and Lie of Franco)* 1937
Etching and sugar-lift aquatint
38.5 x 57 cm (15¼ x 22½ in) (sheet)
Metropolitan Museum of Art, New York

Picasso's suite of prints – two sheets with nine scenes each – portray Franco as a monstrous agent of death and destruction. He began the series early in 1937 and finished around the time he completed *Guernica*.

OPPOSITE BOTTOM *La Minotauromachie (Minotauromachy)* 1935
Etching and engraving
49.5 x 69.5 cm (19½ x 27½ in)
Museum of Modern Art, New York

With a bull's head and a human body, the minotaur may represent bestial force. The presence of figures that suggest suffering (the fallen woman, the screaming horse) and peace (the women with the dove at the window) evoke unsettled feelings rather than articulate a narrative message. Like the man on the ladder, the viewer observes the scene in passive bewilderment.

backing of the military, their challenge to the legally elected Republican government erupted into civil war. Franco secured the support of the rising fascist states in Europe, and, on 26 April 1937, the Condor Legion, an elite division of the German Luftwaffe, carried out a campaign of saturation bombing and strafing on Guernica, a small city in the Basque region located near Bilbao. Within three hours the attack reduced the city to rubble and killed or wounded roughly one-third of the population.[1] Media coverage of this attack on a civilian target – an act of intimidation rather than strategic gain – exposed a terrifying new reality of twentieth-century warfare. No one was safe.

Although Picasso had lived in Paris since 1904, he maintained strong ties with his homeland and took pride in his Spanish identity. As the conflict accelerated in Spain, he openly endorsed the Republican cause. He made generous donations to the Spanish Aid Fund and encouraged others to do the same.[2] He officially allied himself with the standing government in September 1936 when he assumed the honorary position as director of the Museo del Prado in Madrid. The following January, he readily accepted the invitation to paint a mural for the entry hall to the Spanish Pavilion at the Exposition Internationale des Arts et Technique dans la Vie Moderne (International Exhibition), scheduled to open in Paris that May. The sheer scale of the work – unprecedented in Picasso's career – would make it the key feature of the nation's display. Yet a subject eluded him; he toyed with imagery of a mother and child but made little progress. During this time, Picasso worked on a suite of etchings he titled *Sueña y mentira de Franco* (*The Dream and Lie of Franco*) that ridiculed the populist leader as a brutal, clownish figure whose atrocities disgraced the nation. By 8 January 1937, he had completed fourteen etchings (the completed suite featured eighteen etchings and a prose poem) with the intent that the imagery be reproduced on postcards to raise revenue for the republican cause. But, despite his clear political commitment, he did not resolve the issue of his mural's subject until he received word of the destruction of Guernica. He made his position clear in a statement to the press, condemning the nationalists' cause as 'against the people, against freedom'. He declared that in his mural, which he now called *Guernica*, he would express 'abhorrence of the military caste which has sunk Spain into an ocean of pain and death'.[3]

Once Picasso settled on his subject, passion fuelled his speed. His initial sketches, dated to 1 May, reveal that he was drawing upon an enduring repertoire of imagery that had traditional associations in the history of art and long-standing significance in his work. The bull embodied masculinity and also represented Spain. The wounded horse,

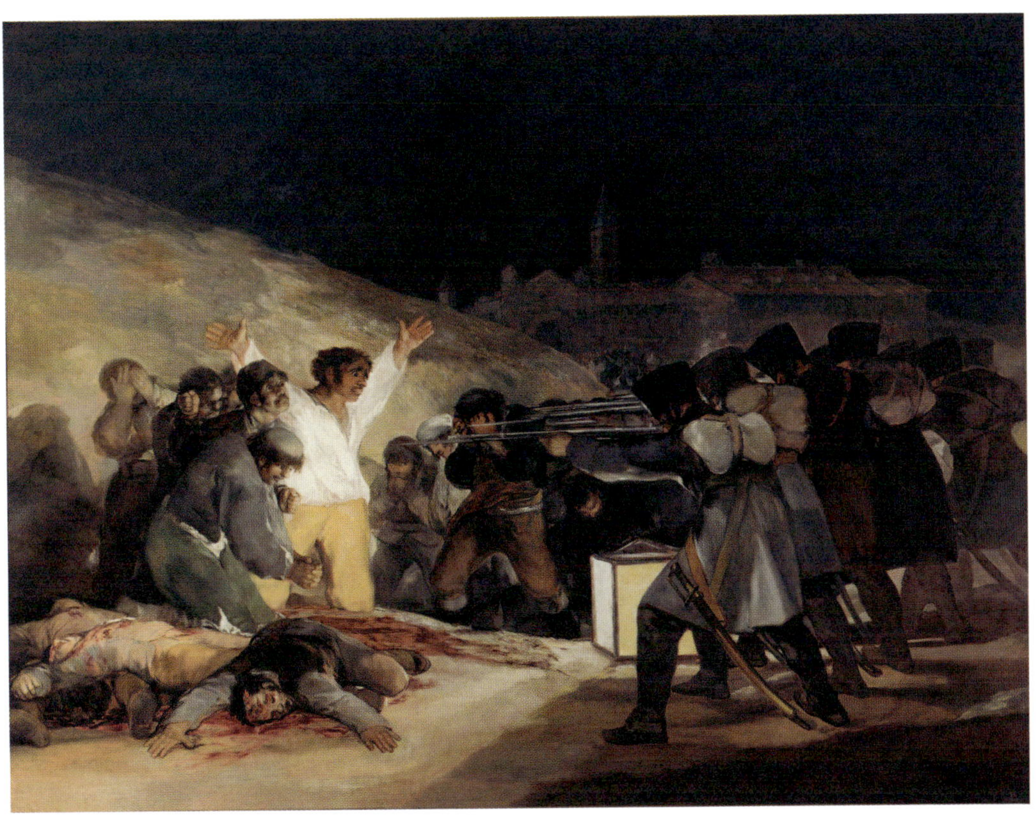

The Third of May in Madrid, 1808 1814
Francisco de Goya y Lucientes (1746–1828)
Oil on canvas
268 x 347 cm (105½ x 136½ in)
Museo del Prado, Madrid

When citizens of Madrid rose up against the French occupation of their
city, their efforts were brutally crushed. The next day, the resistance fighters
faced a firing squad. Goya conceived his depiction of the atrocity – still fresh
in memory – as a traditional scene of martyrdom, with the central figure
brightly illuminated and accepting his destiny in a position that
recalls Christ's crucifixion.

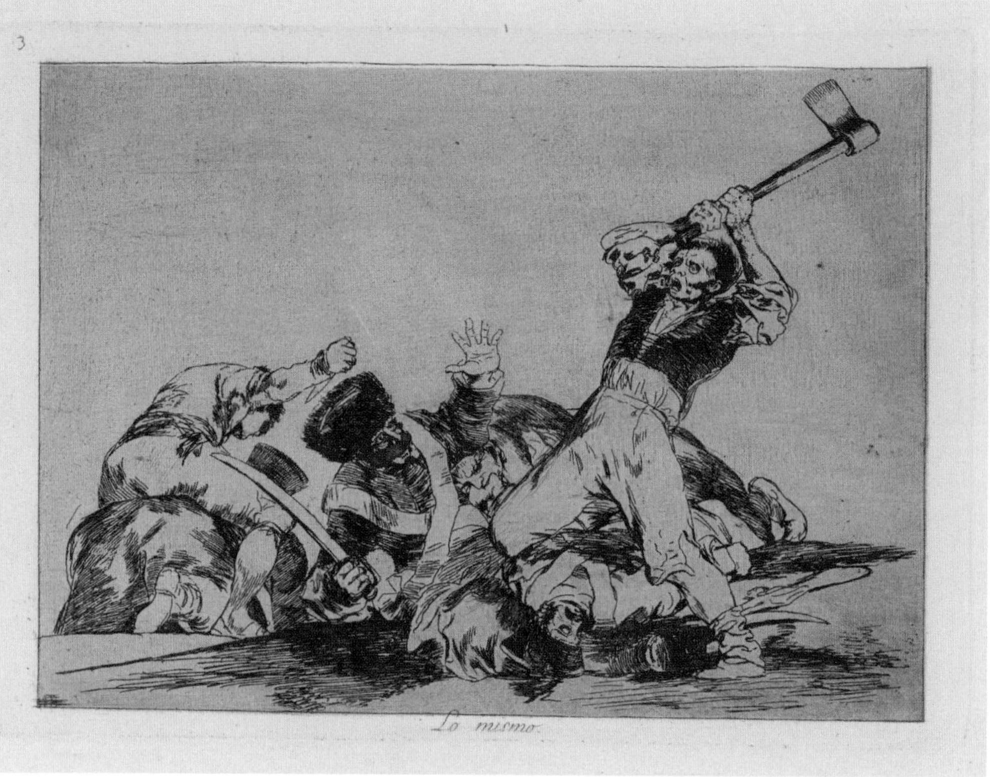

Lo Mismo, The Disasters of War, Plate 3 1810 (published 1863)
Francisco de Goya y Lucientes (1746–1828)
Etching and drypoint
25 x 34.5 cm (10 x 13½ in) (sheet)
Metropolitan Museum of Art, New York

Goya created his suite of eighty-two etchings between 1810 and 1812. Picasso
admired these prints; they share the unflinching honesty of *Guernica*, but
temper the horror through their intimate scale. Here, as a man swings an axe to
decapitate a soldier, the title, 'The Same', denounces the mindless cycle of war,
reprisal and death.

linked to the national blood sport of bullfighting, evoked suffering and sacrifice. The mother and child carried both religious and personal meaning as well as evoking the most essential and universal human relationship. While these symbols link Picasso's iconographic concept to traditional themes, his exploration of them in recent years had taken a more cryptic turn. The 1930s marked a time of introspection, a time when Picasso retreated into the studio to sketch and experiment with images that implied conventional meanings but resisted contextual interpretation. For example, the print *La Minotauromachie* (*Minotauromachy*, 1935) presents identifiable figures – the half man/ half bull of Greek myth, a young girl with a flower, a wounded horse, a man climbing a ladder – but rather than adding up to an intelligible allegory, these seemingly familiar images colliding in a cramped space stir feelings of confusion, trepidation and menace. Even though the viewer can recognize figures with established meanings, the subject itself eludes cohesive comprehension.

A pencil drawing dated 9 May records the full scope of Picasso's composition for *Guernica*, and within two days, he had transferred the preliminary outline to his vast canvas. From 11 May onwards, his partner Dora Maar documented his daily work in photographs. The sequence reveals continued yet subtle adjustments to figure size, placement and position, heightening the emotional force of his imagery through dynamic gesture, agonized expressions and the turmoil of writhing bodies tossed by the force of the blast. In what art historian T.J. Clark describes as 'an astounding feat of concentration', Picasso completed the mural in the early days of June.[4] Working solely in black, white and grey, he captured the horror of the attack. Every inch of the outwardly chaotic composition was calculated to force the viewer to endure the experience of the victims – pain, bewilderment, loss, terror – as death rained down from the sky.

The subject of warfare in Western culture can be followed back to ancient Mediterranean societies, seen in the portrayal of heavily armed troops, stalwart heroes, raging battles and the defeat of enemy forces, often facilitated by divine intervention. Along with the venerable celebrations of valour and victory are the less visible depictions of war's toll. In *Horrors of War* (c. 1637), Peter Paul Rubens drew motifs from classical mythology – including Venus attempting to restrain Mars – to depict what he described as 'whatever is built in peacetime' being 'ruined by the force of arms'.[5] Jacques-Louis David turned to the founding legend of Rome in *The Sabine Women* (1799), in which the Sabine women, kidnapped by the Romans three years earlier, enter the battlefield with their children to force the combatants to lay down

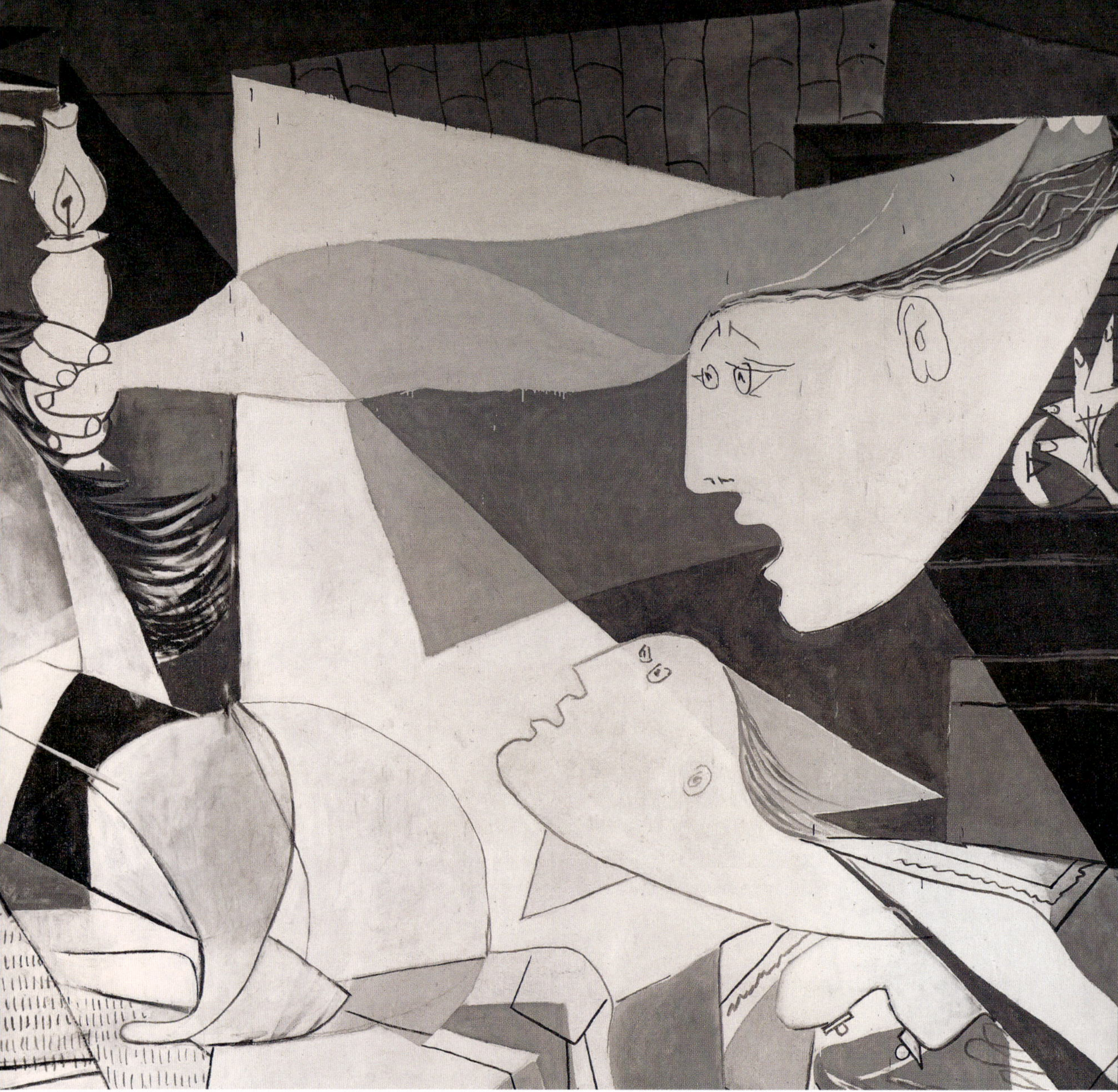

Guernica, detail

From the ancient myth of Prometheus giving light to humanity to the Statue of Liberty welcoming weary travellers to America's shores, the figure of a torchbearer in Western culture symbolizes enlightenment. But in *Guernica*, the intent is not clear. Does the torchbearer represent a glimmer of hope in the darkness or does she illuminate the harrowing truth that we would prefer not to see?

their arms. By the nineteenth century, artists were as likely to find their subjects in contemporary events as in myth or legend. Francisco de Goya y Lucientes painted *The Third of May, 1808* (1814), just six years after Napoleon's troops invaded Spain; Eugène Delacroix portrayed *The Massacre at Chios* (1824) two years after the Ottoman campaign against the Greeks resulted in catastrophic death and the enslavement of the survivors. Both present an unflinching vision of the hopeless despair of the conquered, as well as the heartless cruelty of the conquerors, but do so in the form of a narrative. It is a contained story that has an end. But the violence in *Guernica* appears to have no beginning and, even worse, no end; Picasso depicts everyday life exploding into a chaos of instantaneous destruction and death. The viewer has no reassurance that the event – whether derived from myth, legend or history – is distanced by time and the specificity of the event. Through its vast size and its compelling yet confusing imagery, *Guernica* plunges the defenseless viewer directly into the conflict. The observer becomes a participant forced to partake in the suffering wrought by the new reality of warfare.

The 1937 International Exposition had already been open for more than a month by the time the Spanish Pavilion was ready to welcome the public. The streamlined, elegant building, designed by Luis Lacasa and Josep Lluis Sert, embodied the fair's theme of art and technology in modern life. Modernist works, including Alexander Calder's *Mercury Fountain* and grand photomontages by Josep Renau, dominated the installation. But more than just Modernism, the display served to advocate for the threatened Republican state. No work in the ensemble made this point better than *Guernica*. With it hanging in the entranceway, visitors were immediately confronted by the barbarity of the recent attack.

Guernica, detail

OVERLEAF LEFT Picasso uses screaming, straining figures – the horse with its nostrils flaring, teeth exposed, tongue extended – to make the viewer feel the victim's terror. He heightens this by containing the composition in a single room. Although the bombs have dropped from the sky, the ceiling, with its single bulb casting a radiant pool of light, remains intact, trapping the viewer among the wailing women and shattered bodies.

OVERLEAF RIGHT If the bull represents Spain, it is in a state of paralysis. Frozen to the spot, it turns its massive head away from the centre of the composition where the figures writhe in agony. Its mouth hangs open – as if dumbfounded in despair – as a woman, cradling a dead baby, shrieks in sorrow.

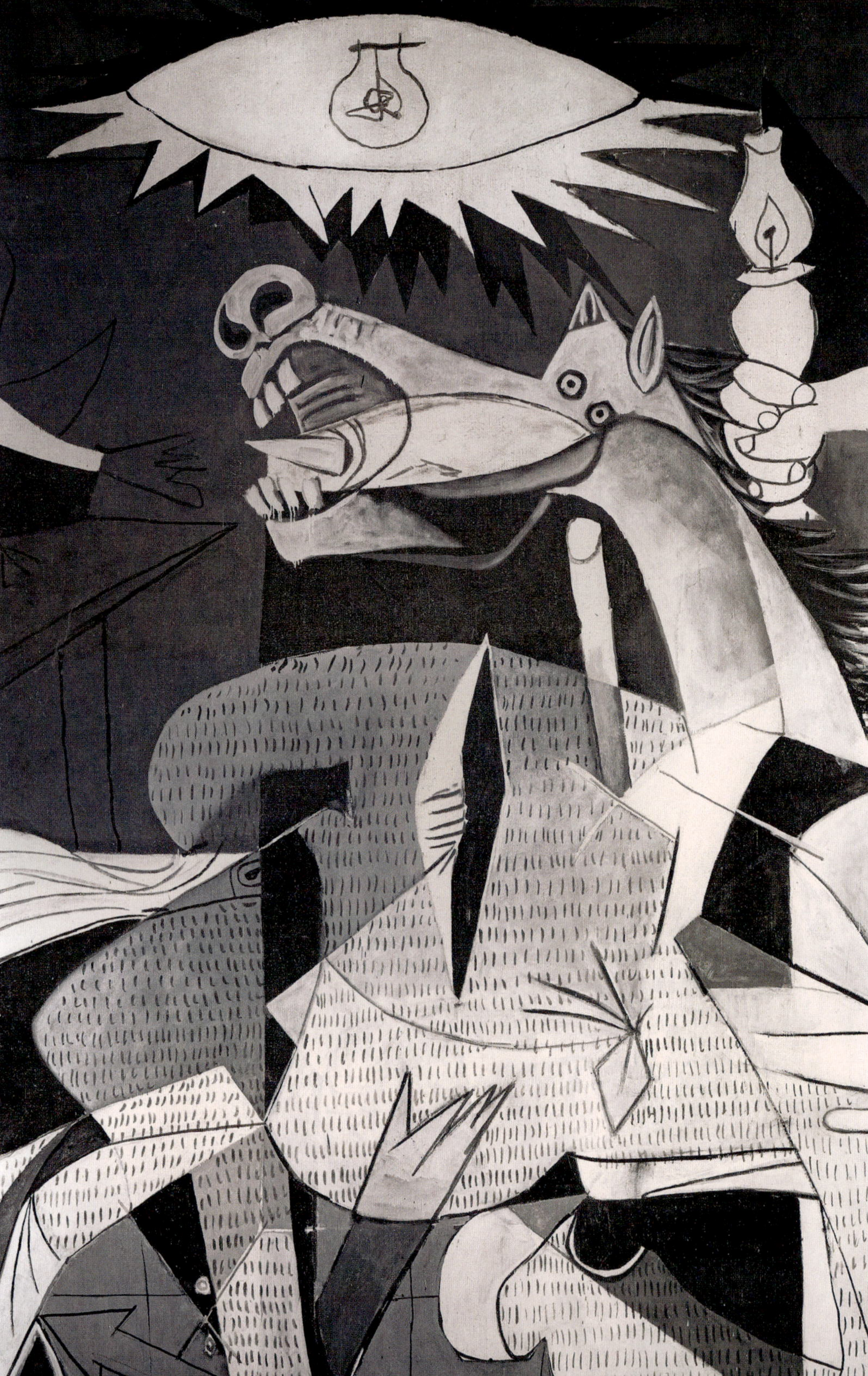

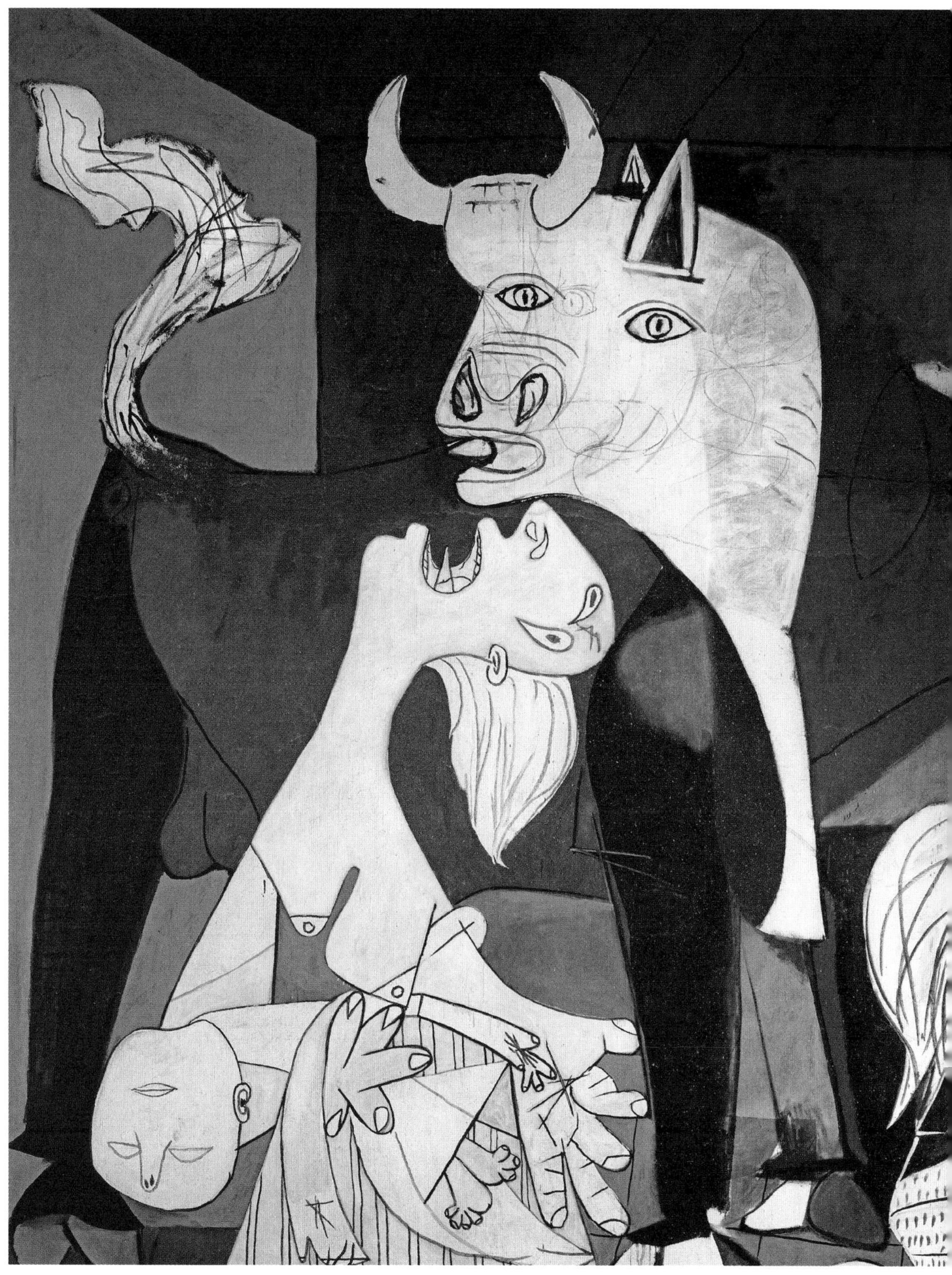

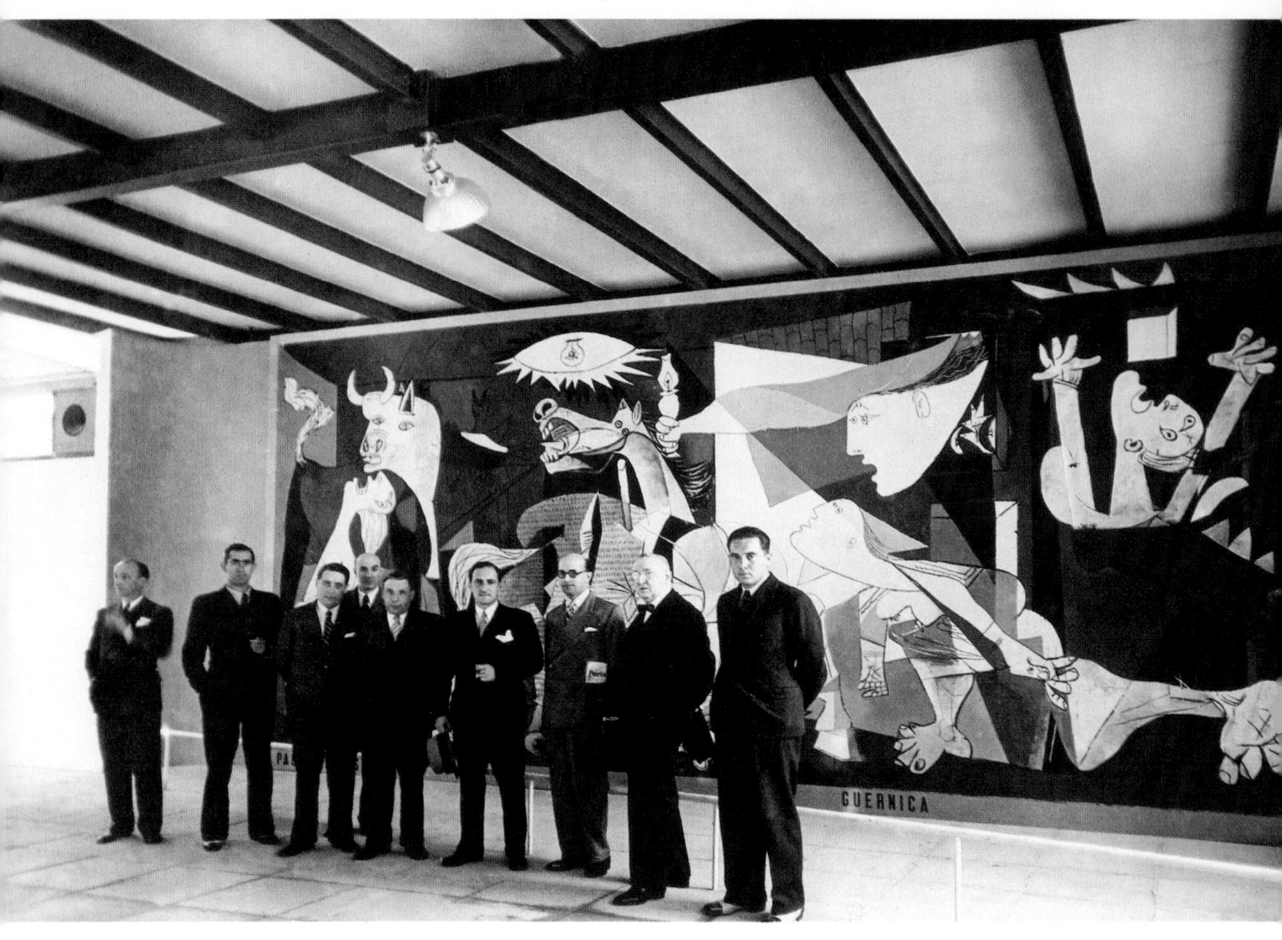

Spanish Pavilion
Exposition Internationale des Arts et Technique dans la Vie Moderne,
Paris, 1937

The organisers for the Spanish Pavilion deliberately showcased cultural
engagement with European Modernism as a counter to the ultra-
conservative, isolationist vision of the Fascists. The pavilion, designed by
Luis Lacasa and Josep Lluís Sert, housed works by contemporary artists
from Europe and the United States as well as Spain, including Josep
Renau, Joan Miró and Alexander Calder. *Guernica* dominated the ground
floor entryway; in this atmosphere of achievement, every visitor had to
confront the dire situation in present-day Spain.

But the deliberately unsettling imagery drew more criticism than praise, less for its raw honesty than its abstruse iconography. In a typical response, the prominent art critic Anthony Blunt described Picasso's art as 'a highly specialized product', deeply rooted in private expression and 'therefore not easily applied to public problems'.[6] If the mural sought to commemorate this atrocity – seared into the public's mind by reports in the media – it needed to retell that story in clear and certain terms. Only a few critics realized that it was precisely the chaotic and incomprehensible clash of symbols that gave *Guernica* its allegorical power. As writer Herbert Read observed, the mural transcended one single, horrific event – 'Not only Guernica, but Spain; not only Spain but Europe' – in its revelation of 'the bomb-shattered ruins of human tenderness and faith'.[7]

After the fair closed, Picasso arranged for *Guernica* to be exhibited in cities across Europe and North America to raise awareness of the perilous situation in Spain.[8] He gave permission for the work to be reproduced on posters and postcards to raise revenue for the resistance. After the populist forces decisively seized power and installed General Franco as '*El Caudillo*' (The Leader, in fact, the dictator) in April 1939, Picasso declared that the mural would not return to his homeland until democracy was restored. During the Second World War, with Spain now openly allied with the Axis powers, *Guernica* remained in North America for safe keeping, held primarily at the Museum of Modern Art in New York. It remained there after Picasso's death in 1973; he died intestate, but his desire for *Guernica's* destiny was well known and respected. Franco's government attempted to procure the painting but did not succeed. Only when the general died in 1975, and his dictatorship was replaced by a constitutional monarchy, did the process to return the painting begin. In 1981, as per Picasso's wish, the painting was sent to the Museo del Prado, where it was installed in the Casón del Buen Retiro, an annex of the main museum building. It was moved to its present location in the Museo Nacionale Centro de Arte Reina Sofía in 1992 and is no longer lent for exhibitions. But the jarring imagery – the horse screaming in agony, the mother with her dead child, the paralysed bull and the colossal figure extending her lamp – forged a new antiwar iconography, seen on placards at protests, in street art, inspiring other artists and even replicated in a tapestry displayed outside the Security Council Room at the United Nations.[9] As he had in so many aspects of his work, Picasso did not reject tradition; he transformed its conventions. In an allegory that appeals to the heart and soul of its viewers – rather than to their knowledge of cultural references – he created a masterpiece that transcended time and place.

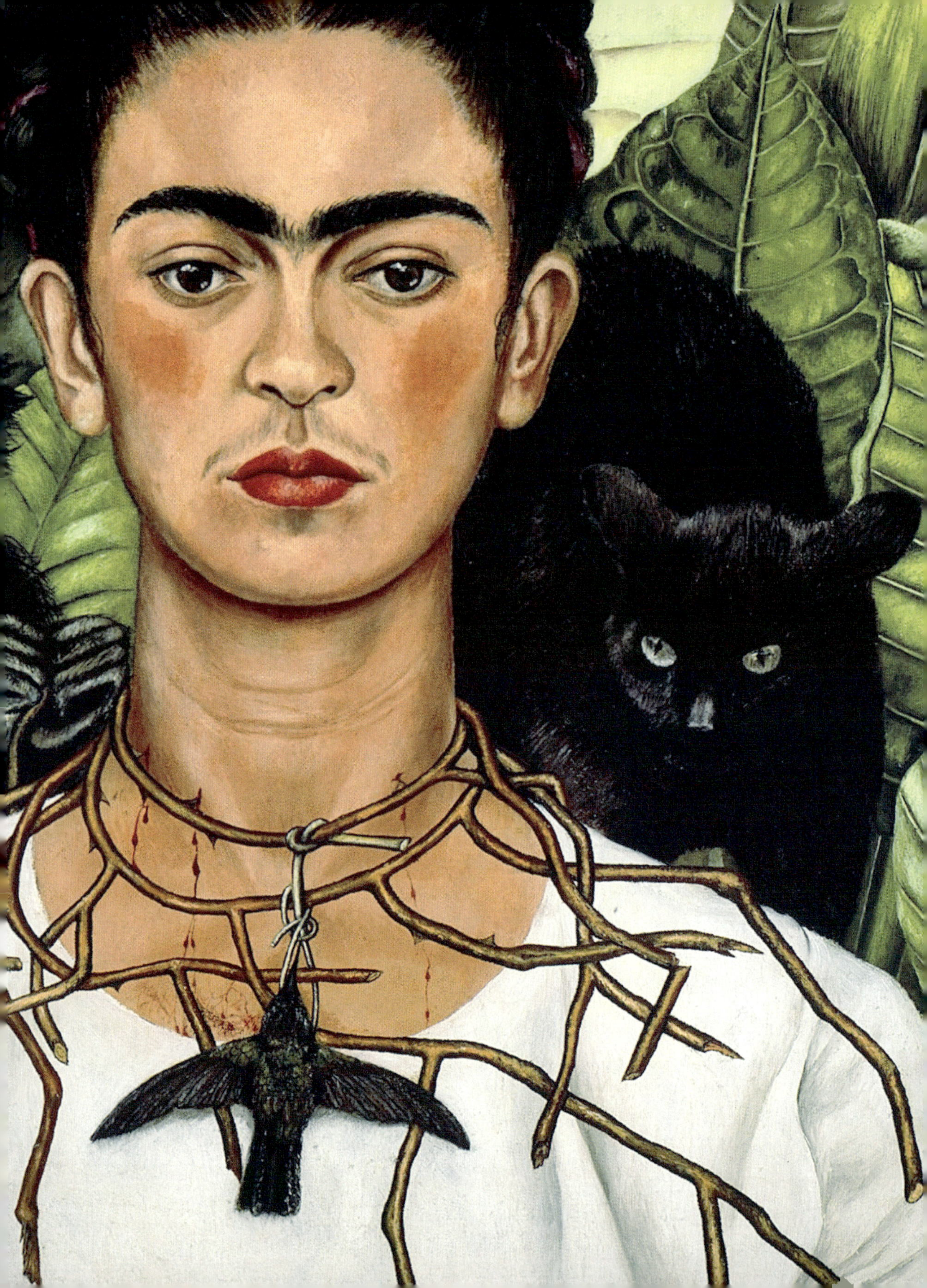

Self-Portrait with Thorn Necklace and Hummingbird

Frida Kahlo

Of my face, I like the eyebrows and the eyes. Aside from that, I like nothing.

Frida Kahlo

During his extended travels through Mexico in the late 1930s, American painter Addison Burbank stopped briefly in Coyoacán, a village outside Mexico City, to visit the famed muralist Diego Rivera. He looked forward as well to meeting Rivera's wife, Frida Kahlo, whose emotionally charged, confessional paintings were gaining international

recognition. Her work repeatedly featured her own image, so Burbank
was well aware of her striking appearance. But when he arrived at
her home for a midday meal, the sight of his hostess astonished him.
Dressed in colourful Tehuana garments, with her black hair tightly
braided and crowned with purple bougainvillea, she looked 'glowingly,
youthfully alive'. In his memoir Burbank dismissed conventional words
of praise – 'beautiful, charming, vivacious' – as 'simply too trite'.
Along with her natural beauty, Kahlo emanated 'originality', and
ultimately Burbank gave up the struggle to describe her: 'She was –
oh, hell! – breathtaking.'[1]

Frida Kahlo understood the power of her own image. She
portrayed herself in more than a third of her known works; this is
hardly surprising given that her art interrogates her life. In addition to
narrating her often shattering experiences, she painted self-portraits,
forthright likenesses that recall saints in holy pictures. Instead of
traditional iconography, Kahlo employed a repertoire of personal
symbols that she forged from her multicultural heritage and her
uncompromising assessment of her own appearance that she curated
as meticulously in life as she rendered it on canvas. Produced at the
height of her career – and within a year of Burbank's visit – *Self-Portrait
with Thorn Necklace and Hummingbird* offers a rich example of how
Kahlo drew meaning from her distinctive features and her performative
self-presentation. As one of more than fifty self-portraits that Kahlo
painted, it represents how she established her signature subject and
then made that subject her masterpiece.

Physical trauma bookended Frida Kahlo's childhood. In 1914, at
the age of six, she contracted poliomyelitis, which required months of
bed rest and permanently impaired her right leg and foot. A decade
later, in 1925, a horrific bus accident ended her student days. Once
again, she was confined to bed, this time to heal broken bones and the
damage to her spine and pelvis caused by a handrail that had impaled
her body. To pass the time and stimulate her spirits, her mother rigged
up a mirror on her bed so that Kahlo could draw her own image during
her convalescence. She had been studying the arts at the prestigious
Escuela Nacional Preparatoria in Mexico City, where she was one of
only thirty-five female enrollees in a student body of two thousand. Her
parents had raised her in a culturally diverse and artistic household.
Her father Guillermo Kahlo, a secular Jew from Germany, was a
photographer, and her mother Matilde Calderón, a devout Catholic,
took pride in her mixed indigenous and Spanish heritage. Prior to the
accident, Kahlo often accompanied her father as he photographed

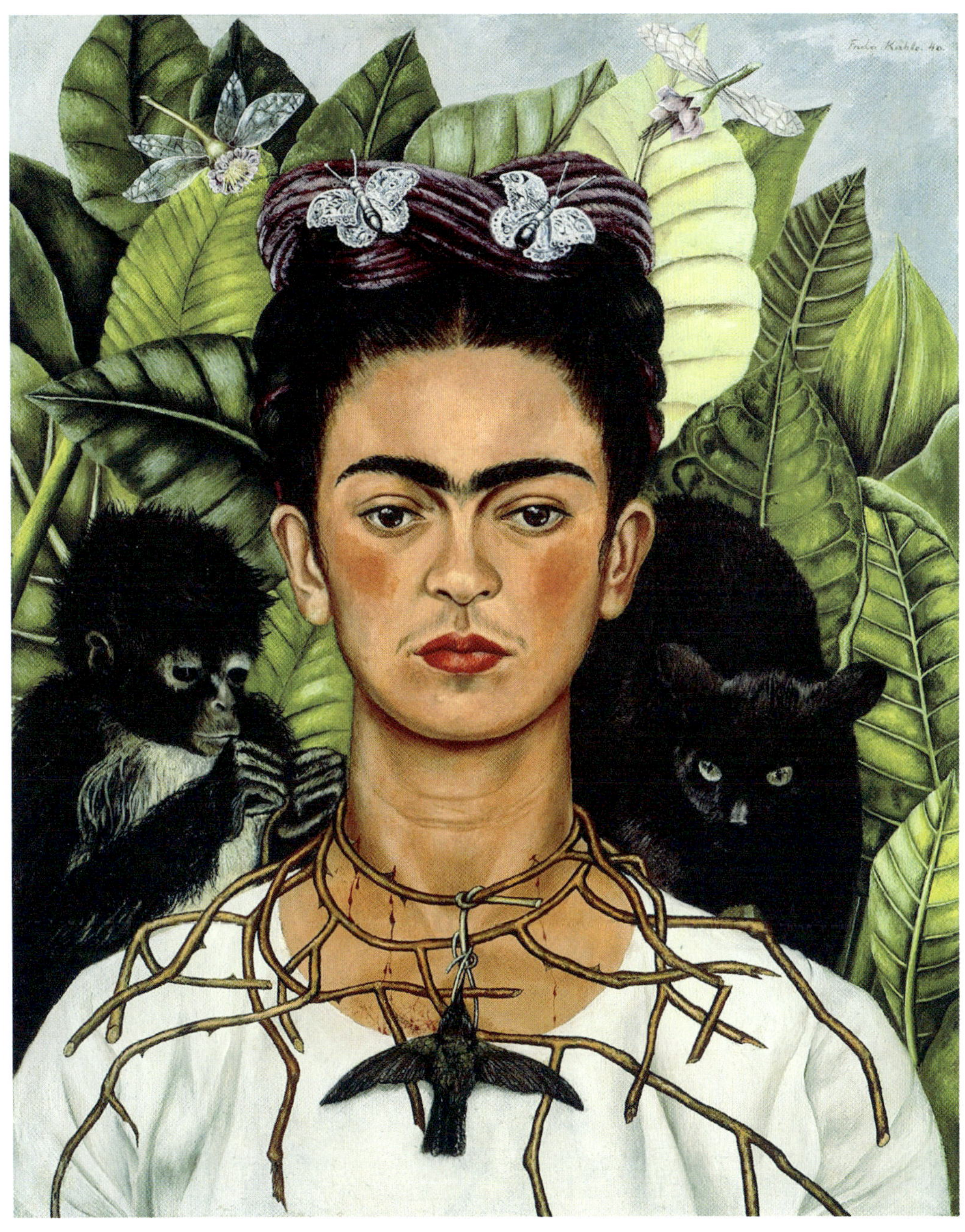

Self-Portrait with Thorn Necklace and Hummingbird 1940
Frida Kahlo (1907–54)
Oil on canvas
61.5 x 47 cm (25 x 18½ in)
Harry Ransom Center, Austin, TX

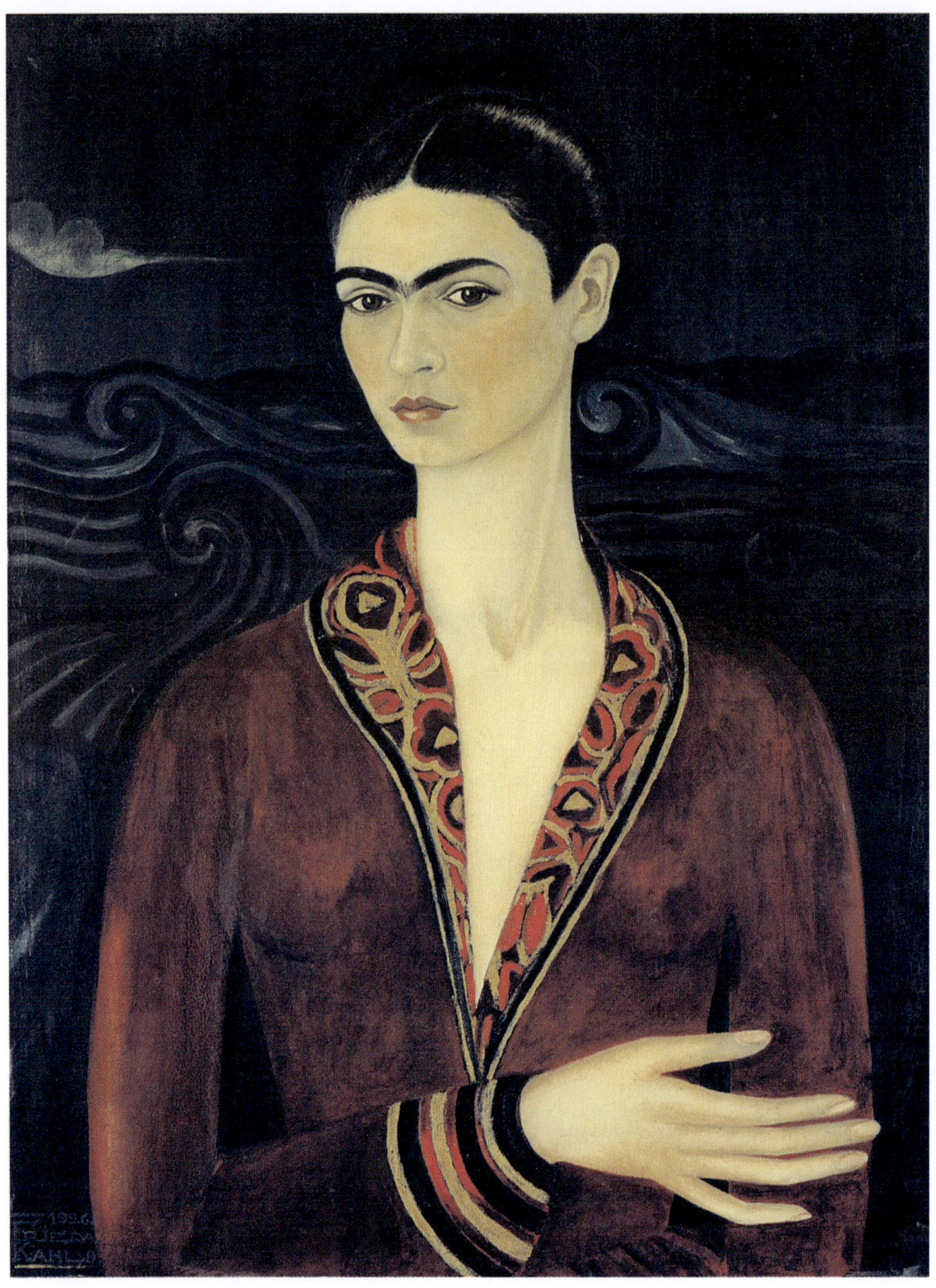

architectural sites, and she helped him in the darkroom. The accident and long recovery left her with severe chronic pain that restricted her activities; for the rest of her life, she wore a stiff corset and endured countless operations to relieve the stress on her spine.

In her first surviving self-portrait, painted in 1926, Kahlo appears half length, wearing an elegant velvet dress, against a background of stylized waves. She presents herself as a comely young woman of the time, her hair neatly parted in the centre and combed into a chignon that highlights her oval face and symmetrical features. Her compelling gaze – wide dark eyes under strongly defined brows that almost meet in the middle – expresses challenge and confidence, as if she is daring the viewer to look away. Even at this age, Kahlo regarded her image as a means to assert her identity. Her father had photographed her throughout her childhood; hardly camera shy, she presented herself expressively, even appearing in one family photograph with slicked-back hair and wearing her father's suit.

Her distinctive mode of dress is often attributed to Diego Rivera's influence, but several photographs document her mother wearing indigenous ensembles. Kahlo first met Rivera in 1922, during her first year as a student at the Escuela Nacional. She watched as he carried out a commission in the school's main lecture hall – he was already a prominent artist and leading advocate of Mexico's mural movement – and while they had a number of conversations, they did not become romantically involved until six years later. When they married on 21 August 1929, her wedding ensemble mixed contemporary style – a flowing, patterned dress with ruffled flounces – with such indigenous accessories as a multistring Aztec jade necklace (a gift from Rivera) and a *rebozo* (shawl), which some sources claim was borrowed from her family's housekeeper.[2] Within the year, she formulated what would

Self-Portrait in a Velvet Dress 1926
Oil on canvas
79 x 58.5 cm (31 x 23 in)
Private Collection, courtesy Galería Arvil, Mexico City

From her earliest known self-portrait, Kahlo carefully staged her appearance. Here, her severe centre-parted hair and sleek velvet gown evoke the type of serene beauty associated with Renaissance portraiture, which she admired at the time. The stylized waves behind her may well be a tribute to Botticelli's *Birth of Venus.*

 Frida Kahlo 1939
Nickolas Muray (1892–1965)
Carbro print
43 x 32 cm (17 x 13 in)
Metropolitan Museum of Art, New York

The Hungarian-born photographer met Kahlo in the United States in 1931.
Their affair began when Kahlo travelled to New York alone in 1938 and lasted
through the following year, when she divorced and then remarried Rivera.
Muray took more photographs of Kahlo than of any other sitter, aside from
his family members, and he kept *Self-Portrait with Thorn Necklace and
Hummingbird*, which he purchased straight out of her studio, until his death.

 Wedding Portrait of Frida Kahlo and Diego Rivera 19 August 1929
Victor Reyes
Gelatin silver print with hand-applied transparent watercolour
18 x 12.5 cm (7 x 5 in)
Museum of Fine Arts, Boston

Kahlo married Rivera on 21 August 1929. Despite the two-decade difference
in age, the couple shared a passion for leftist politics, activist art and Mexican
identity. Kahlo had yet to fully embrace Tehuantepec attire, but her wedding
ensemble included a *rebozo*, the traditional Mexican shawl, and a multistring,
jadeite necklace carved with Aztec symbols, which was a gift from her husband.

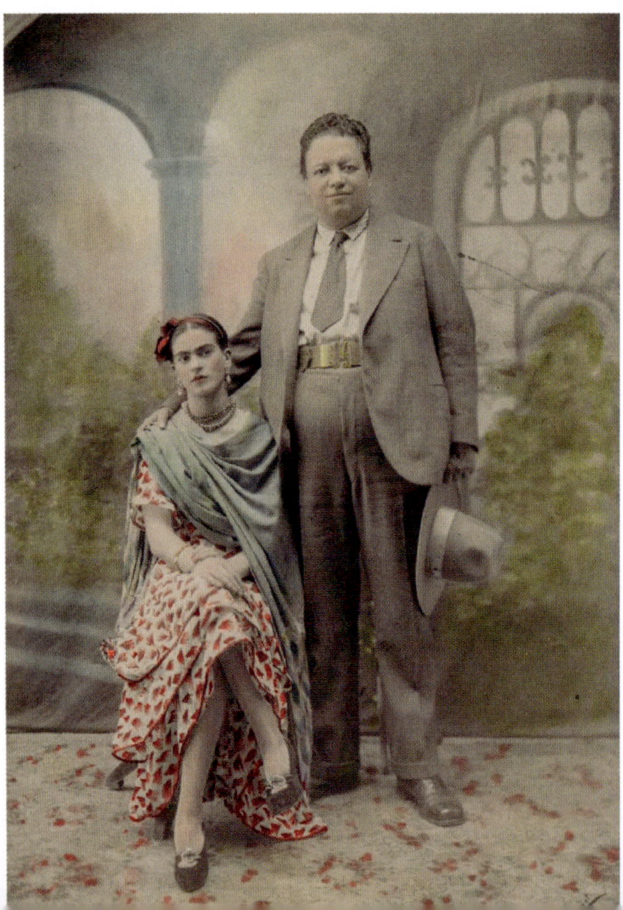

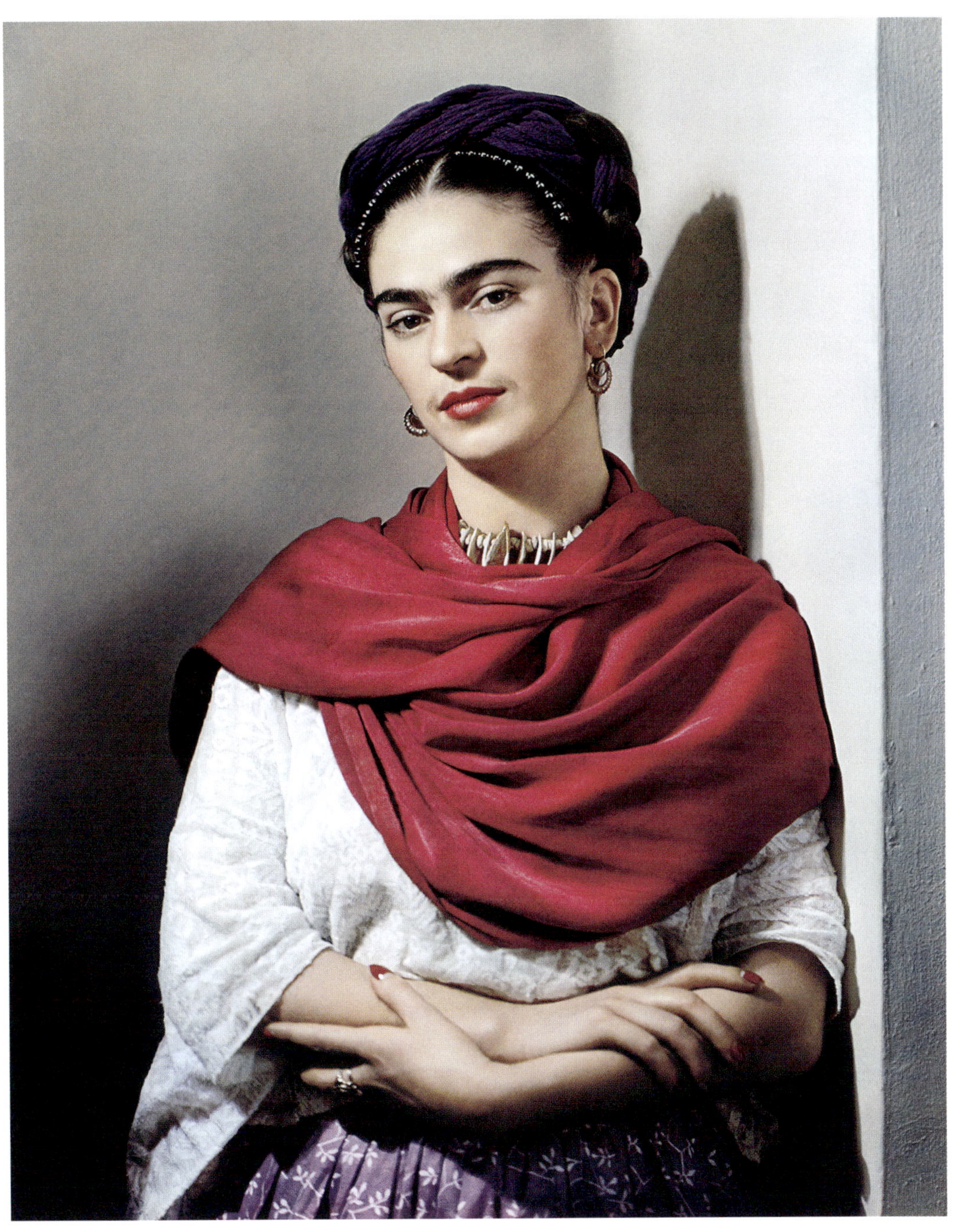

Self-Portrait with Thorn Necklace and Hummingbird   167

become her signature style based on the traditional attire of women from the Tehuantepec region on the west coast of southern Mexico: the *huipil*, a simple, square-cut cotton blouse, often embellished with embroidery or lace, and the *enagua*, a long, full skirt gathered into a wide waistband, often hemmed with embroidered bands, tucks or a pleated flounce. While these garments expressed her sense of *Mexicanidad* (Mexican identity), they also comfortably hid her orthopedic corset and disfigured leg. By the time she embarked with Rivera, in 1930, on a three-year sojourn to the United States to advance his international career, she dressed exclusively in her own version of Tehuana garments, and she revelled in the impression she made, writing to her mother: 'The *gringas* really like me a lot and pay close attention to all the dresses and *rebozos* that I brought with me … All the painters want me to pose for them.'[3]

During her stay in the United States, Kahlo did sit for a number of photographers, including Edward Weston and Imogen Cunningham, but she had little time to pose for painters. In defiance of press coverage that presented her as a charming novelty accompanying a great artist – 'Diego's beautiful young wife' in 'native costume' – Kahlo concentrated on her own work, painting a blunt and often brutal narrative of her physical and emotional experiences.[4] As the central character in her art, she employed her unmistakable appearance as both a weapon and a shield, developing three modes of self-imaging: as a figure in a larger narrative or allegory; in full length standing or seated in which her garments are prominently featured; and self-portraits in which her head and shoulders fill the frame. The composition of Kahlo's self-portraits echoes the traditional form of a small *retabolo* (devotional painting) that features a single saint.

The Two Fridas 1939
Oil on canvas
172 x 172 cm (67¾ x 67¾ in)
Museo Nacional de Arte Moderno, Mexico City

Holding hands, and joined by an artery that connects their hearts, Kahlo's 'Fridas' represent the duality of her heritage and identity. Her European self wears old-fashioned, Westernized garments and attempts to staunch the bleeding artery with surgical pinchers. Her Mexican self, in Tehuantepec *huipil* and *enagua*, holds a tiny portrait of Rivera.

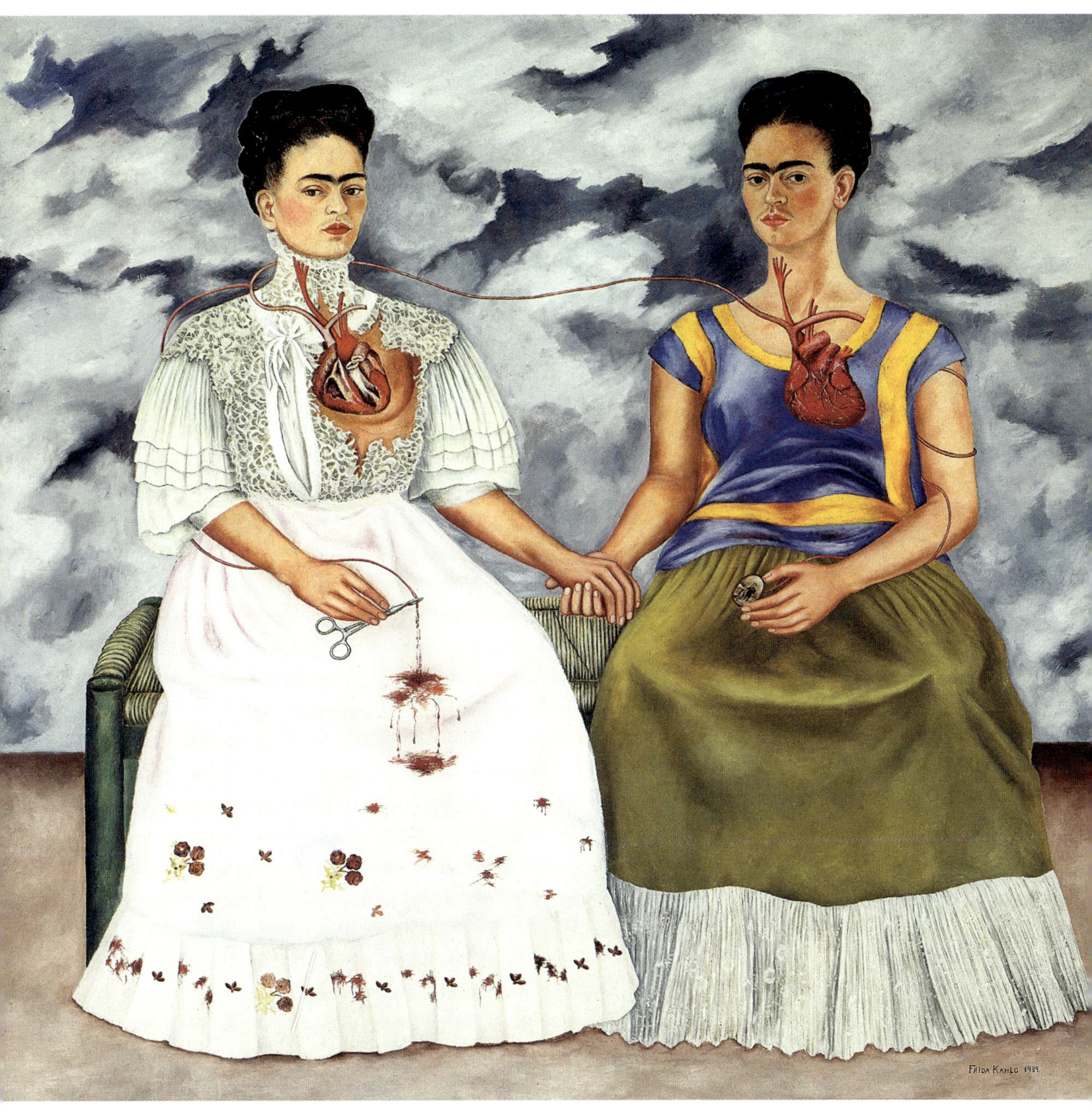

Self-Portrait with Thorn Necklace and Hummingbird   169

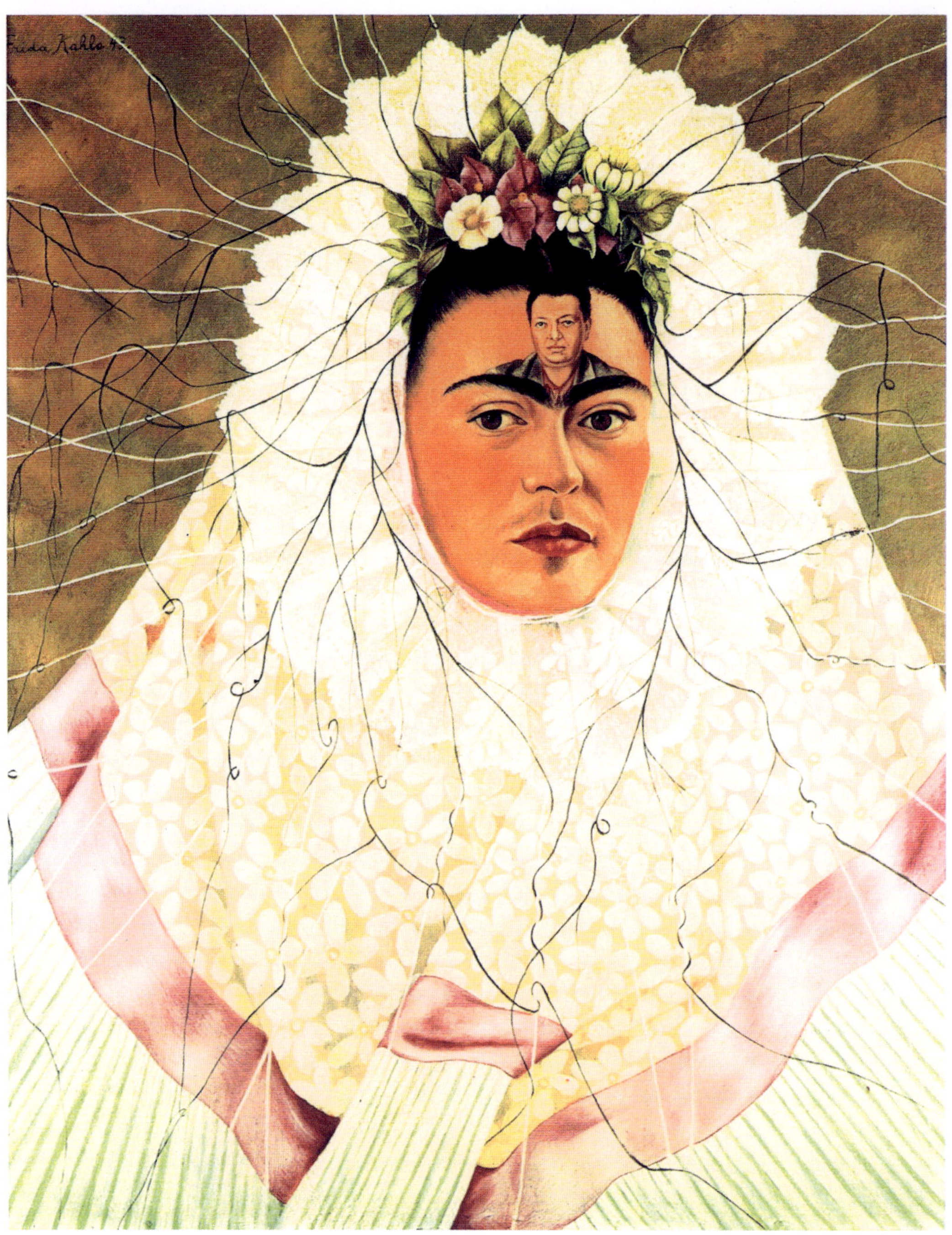

Throughout the 1930s, Kahlo repeated the same composition with subtle changes. Against either a plain background or one dense with foliage, she appears dressed in various *huipiles* and a wide range of jewellery. Her coiffure becomes more elaborate, evolving from the severe, centre-parted style of her youth into the now-iconic coronet of braids intertwined with ribbons or topped with flowers. She turns her head slightly to the left or right; at times she faces fully forward. Occasionally there is a hint of a smile, but in each, her facial features and unrelenting gaze project her identity through her unorthodox beauty and her inimitable flaws.

By 1940, when Kahlo painted *Self-Portrait with Thorn Necklace and Hummingbird*, she had succeeded in establishing a career independent from that of her husband. Her first solo exhibition, hosted two years earlier by the Julien Levy Gallery in New York, produced several major commissions, as well as substantial sales. Also in 1938, the Musée du Louvre in Paris purchased her self-portrait, *The Frame* (1937–38), marking the museum's first acquisition of a work by a Mexican artist. She travelled to New York and to Paris, where she was photographed for the French edition of *Vogue*. Her works were featured in an exhibition organized by the Surrealist pioneer André Breton, and her style inspired the couturiere Elsa Schiaparelli to design a 'robe Madame Rivera'. But it was also a time of personal strain. From the start of their marriage, Kahlo and Rivera had accommodated each other's infidelities. But by 1939, they lived separately in adjacent houses; they divorced on 6 November, only to remarry the following December. Kahlo's love affair with photographer Nickolas Muray was fraying, and her back pain became so severe that she travelled to San Francisco to consult Dr Leo Eloesser, an American physician who had

Self-Portrait as a Tehuana (Diego on my Mind) 1943
Oil on hardboard
76 x 61 cm (30 x 24 in)
The Jacques and Natasha Gelman Collection 20th-century Mexican Art
and the Vergel Foundation

This magnificent headdress, known as a *resplendor* (radiance), is actually a lace *huipil* worn so that the large collar surrounds the wearer's face, and the loose bodice and sleeves drape over her shoulders. Kahlo owned two, although she rarely wore them. Here, framing her face against the gold background, it evokes the aura of a secular saint whose thoughts literally turn to her husband.

treated her in 1930. She first used the thorn necklace motif in a self-portrait that she painted to thank him. In it she wears a pair of earrings in the shape of tiny hands; they were a gift from Pablo Picasso.

Both triumph and tragedy inform *Self-Portrait with Thorn Necklace and Hummingbird*. Kahlo faces the viewer and stares boldly out of the canvas. The glistening black cat on her left shoulder doubles her gaze. She renders her features in a series of strong arcs: her connected eyebrows, her flared nostrils, the hair above her compressed lips. A spider monkey – one of two that she owned – perches on her right shoulder and plays with the end of the branch of thorns that encircles and pierces her neck. This unorthodox ornament, causing rivulets of blood to flow from her punctured skin, recalls a key symbol of Christian martyrdom: the crown of thorns pressed upon Christ's head during his Passion. In contrast to the singular symbolism of the branch of thorns, the hummingbird tied to the necklace evokes layers of multicultural meaning. Many Western traditions associate the hummingbird with fleeting emotions and transience, based on the speed of its wings and the myth that it lives for only a day. But it was also the attribute of the immortal Aztec god Huitzilopochtli, overlord of war and the sun, and the resulting belief that hummingbirds embody the souls of dead warriors. The butterflies that hover above Kahlo's head repeat these dual and conflicting meanings: temporal life in European cultures and enduring spirit in Mesoamerican. In *Self-Portrait with Thorn Necklace and Hummingbird*, Kahlo draws upon her complex heritage to proclaim her individual yet dichotomous identity: martyr and warrior, fragile as well as resilient. She is a woman who proudly wears an ornament that causes her pain.

In a 1938 profile published in American *Vogue*, Bertram Wolfe observed that Kahlo 'seems herself a product of her art, and, like her work, one that is instinctively and calculatingly well composed'.[5] Throughout her life, as in her art, Kahlo subjected her appearance to relentless scrutiny. She readily admitted 'No part of my body is perfect', noting that her head was too small; one of her legs was too 'skinny' and one 'too fat'. Of her face, she only liked her eyes and eyebrows: 'Aside from that I like nothing . . . I have the moustache and in general the face of the opposite sex'.[6] Olga Campos, a close friend of Kahlo's in her later years – at a time when pain often confined Kahlo to bed – noted that she had rarely seen her friend without make-up. 'She was always made up and well dressed; even when she did not expect visitors.'[7] Just as her large and colourful wardrobe bore witness to her fascination with self-presentation, the contents of her cosmetic table reveals the

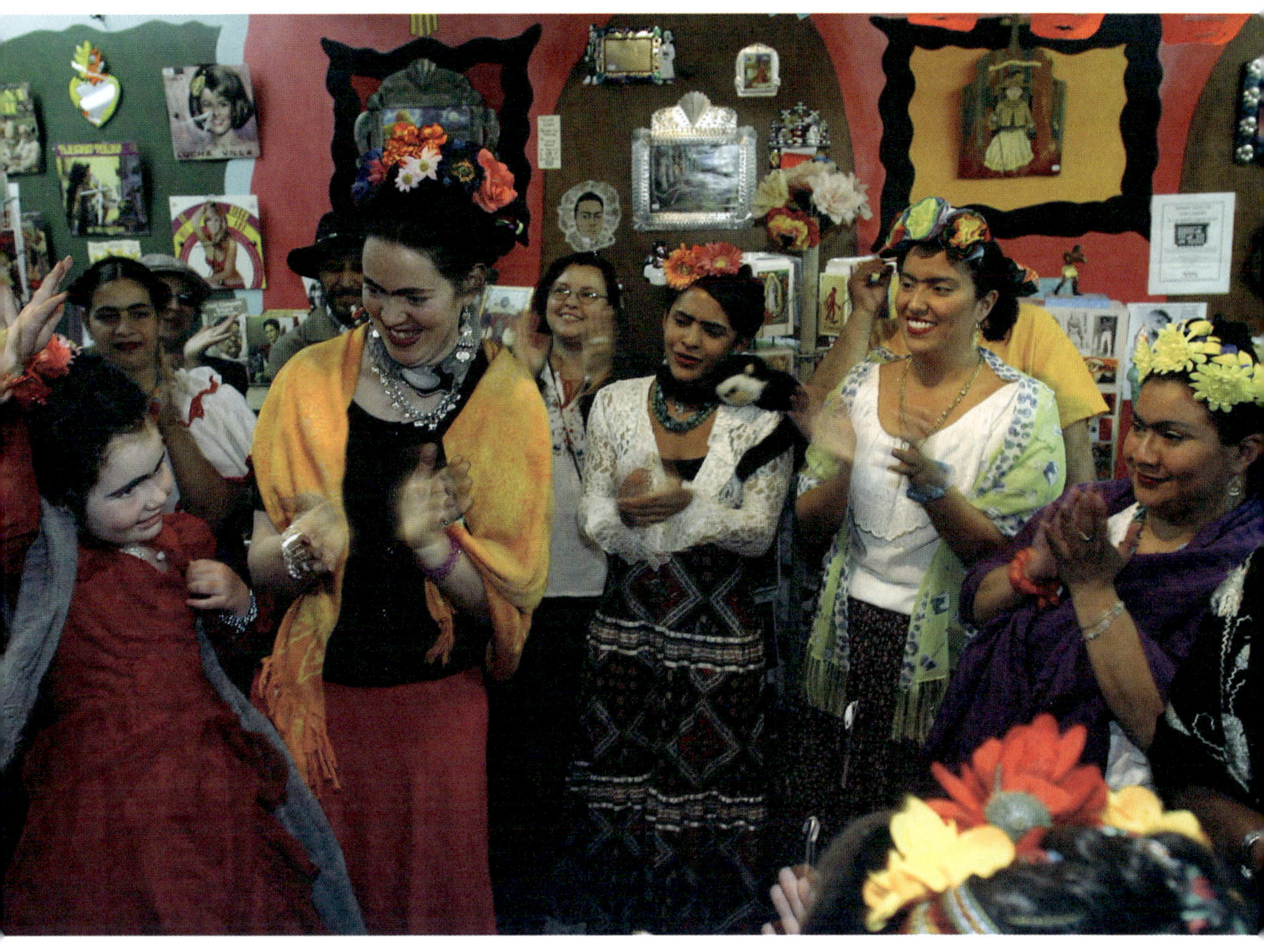

Women dressed as Frida Kahlo

In Mexico and elsewhere, festivals honour Kahlo through her signature style. At the largest known celebration, held at the Dallas Art Museum in July 2017, to mark what would have been her 110th birthday, more than one thousand people of diverse ages, genders and heritage gathered in colourful garments. Even the youngest participants – babies in their mother's arms – sported Kahlo's flower crowns and unibrow.

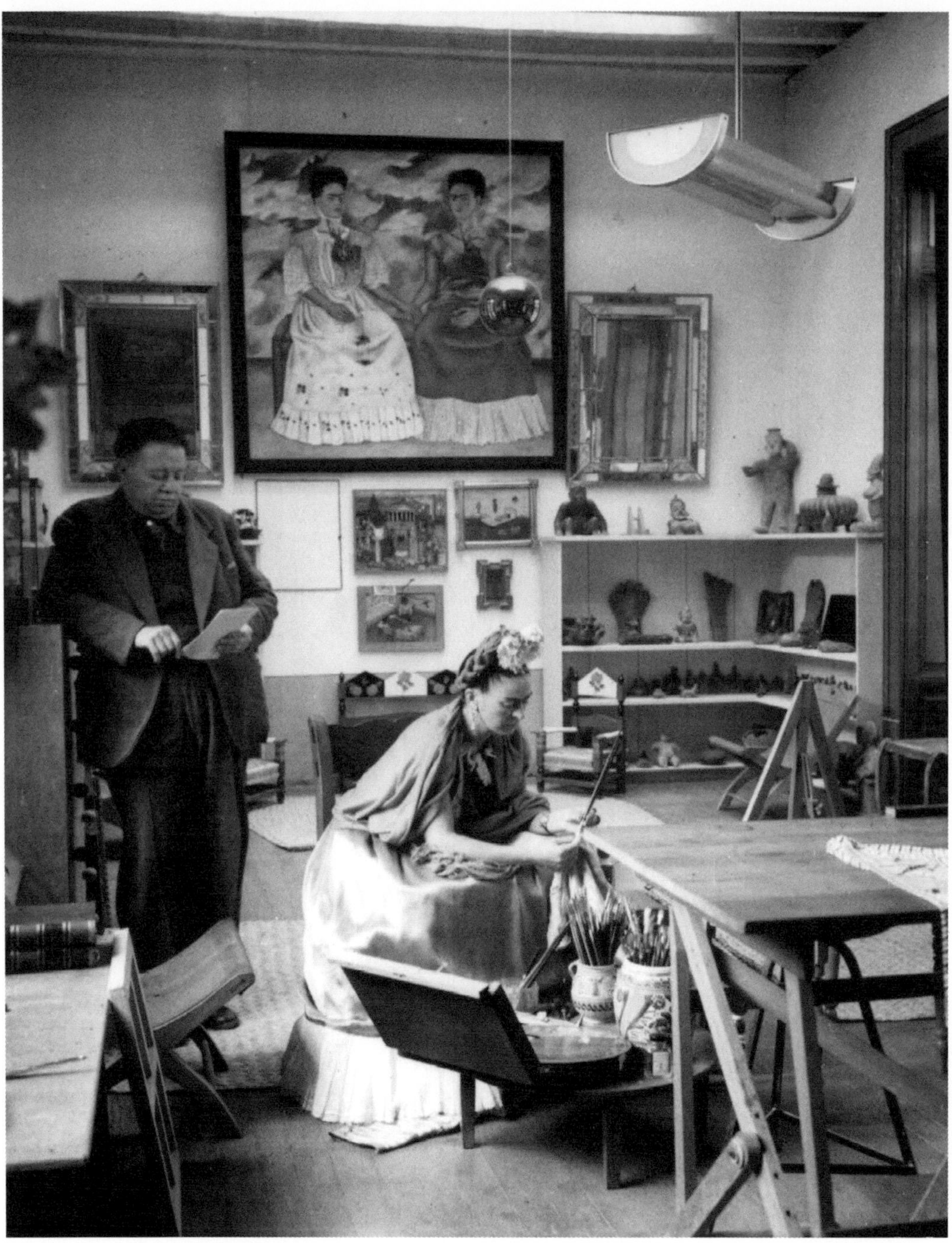

careful curation of her beauty. She enhanced her prominent eyebrows with a Revlon pencil in ebony and augmented them with black Talika powder, which encouraged hair growth. Her favourite shade of lipstick was Coty's Everything's Rosy, and she often closed letters to those she held dear with a kiss print.

Today, Kahlo's face is as familiar as it is remarkable. For the general public, her art and her appearance have converged to the extent that her biographer Hayden Herrera rightly describes her as an 'international cult figure'.[8] Kahlo's story – and her inimitable appearance – has been featured in film, fiction, ballet and opera. She is the subject of children's books and the model for dolls and other toys that inspire girls to embrace who they are and who they want to be. As well as a symbol of feminism, Kahlo's distinctive image marks the triumph of a type of beauty that disdains long-standing European conventions. Frida Kahlo 'lookalike' competitions are regularly held in Mexico as well as other parts of the world. But rather than an act of superficial masquerade, participants describe the experience as empowering. The young winner of the 2007 Frida Fascination festival, sponsored by the Mexican Fine Arts Museum in Chicago, to mark the artist's one-hundredth birthday, told the press that she valued the contest as instructive. Dressing as Kahlo gave her a greater appreciation for the woman's strength of character and a deeper understanding of Mexican art.[9] Kahlo's self-portraits represent many things: a quest for identity, a testament of her life, a demand for recognition, the vanity of self-absorption and unflinching self-examination. But above all they reveal how, in the right hands, a subject as well worn and long established as the self-portrait can be revitalized and transformed into a deeply personalized masterpiece.

The Three Fridas – Portrait of Frida in Studio (with 'Las Dos Fridas') 1943
Fritz Henle (1909–93)
Gelatin silver print (printed 1991)
Rago Arts and Auction Center

Whether receiving guests, working in the studio, appearing in public or resting in bed, Kahlo wore Tehuana attire, her ribbon-crowned braids and full make-up. She did, however, occasionally team her *huipil* with slacks. This photograph also presents her characteristic way of sitting – back supported by her corset and centring her torso above wide-spread legs – echoing the position of the figures in *The Two Fridas* on the studio wall.

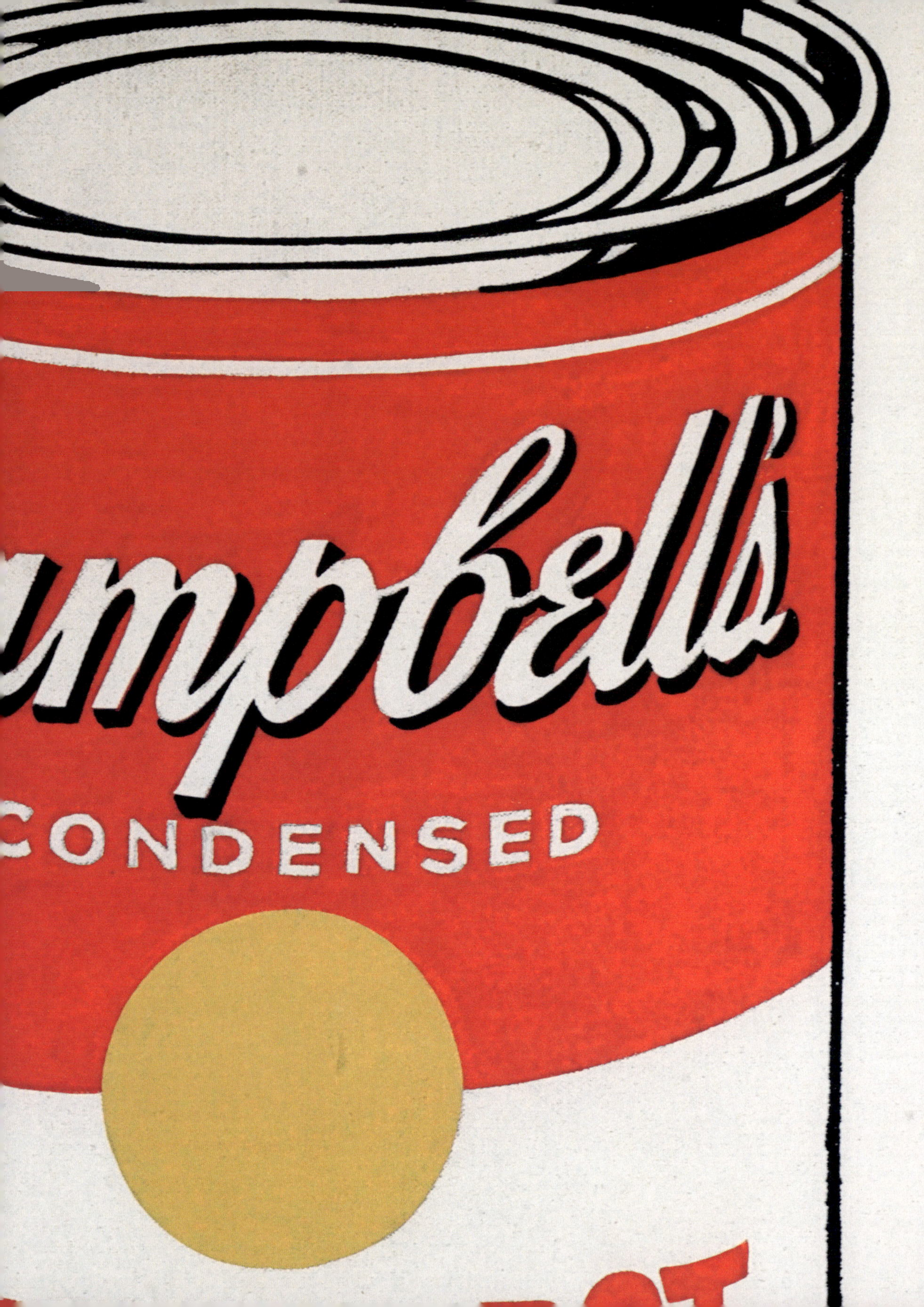
mpbells
CONDENSED

Campbell's Soup Cans

Andy Warhol

If you take a Campbell's Soup can and repeat it fifty times, you are not interested in the retinal image. What interests you is the concept that wants to put fifty Campbell's Soup cans on a canvas.

Marcel Duchamp, May 1964

Under Irving Blum's direction, the Ferus Gallery in Los Angeles became known for its daring, introducing such cutting-edge, New York-based artists as Jasper Johns, Roy Lichtenstein and Frank Stella to the West Coast art world. Late in 1961, on one of his scouting trips, Blum visited the studio of an aspiring artist whose 'cartoon paintings' struck him as too

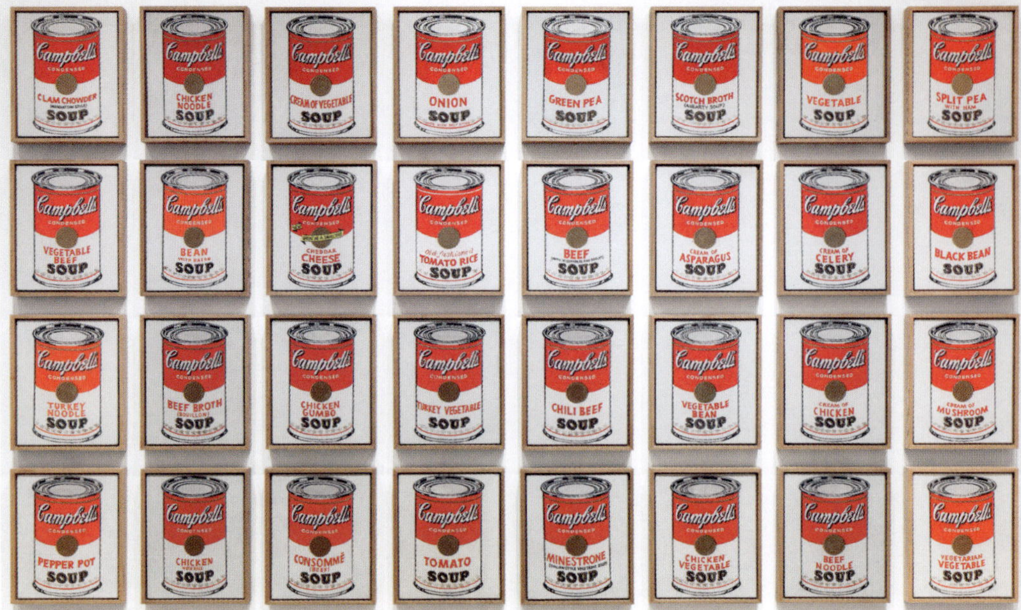

Campbell's Soup Cans (Thirty-Two Campbell's Soup Cans) 1962
Andy Warhol (1928–87)
Synthetic polymer paint on thirty-two canvases
51 x 40.5 cm (20 x 16 in) individual canvas
Museum of Modern Art, New York, NY

bizarre for even the Ferus: 'I couldn't make heads or tails of them.' But
when Blum returned a few months later, he saw new paintings leaning
against the wall and scattered across the floor. Identical in size and
composition; each featured a single can of Campbell's soup. The only
variance was the name of the flavour on the label. Blum enquired about
the intended scope of the series, and the artist replied with deadpan
earnestness that he planned to paint thirty-two, because: 'There are
thirty-two varieties.'[1] Blum took a chance and exhibited the series in
the gallery that summer. While sales were slim and the reviews ran the
gamut from bewildered to scathing, the exhibition attracted international
publicity and the little-known artist, Andy Warhol, became as much of a
household name as the brand of soup that he depicted.

More than any other artist of his generation, Andy Warhol transgressed
the conventional separation between fine art and popular culture. The

Photograph of Andy Warhol with Soup Cans 1962
Warhol Foundation, Pittsburgh, PA

Warhol's decision to paint soup cans baffled critics and collectors. With his refusal to explain his motives, commentators have offered their own interpretations ranging from a critique of consumerism to a prank on the art world. Artist Donald Judd, writing in *Arts Magazine* in 1963, probably came closest to Warhol's rationale for painting soup cans by asking a counter question: 'Why not?'

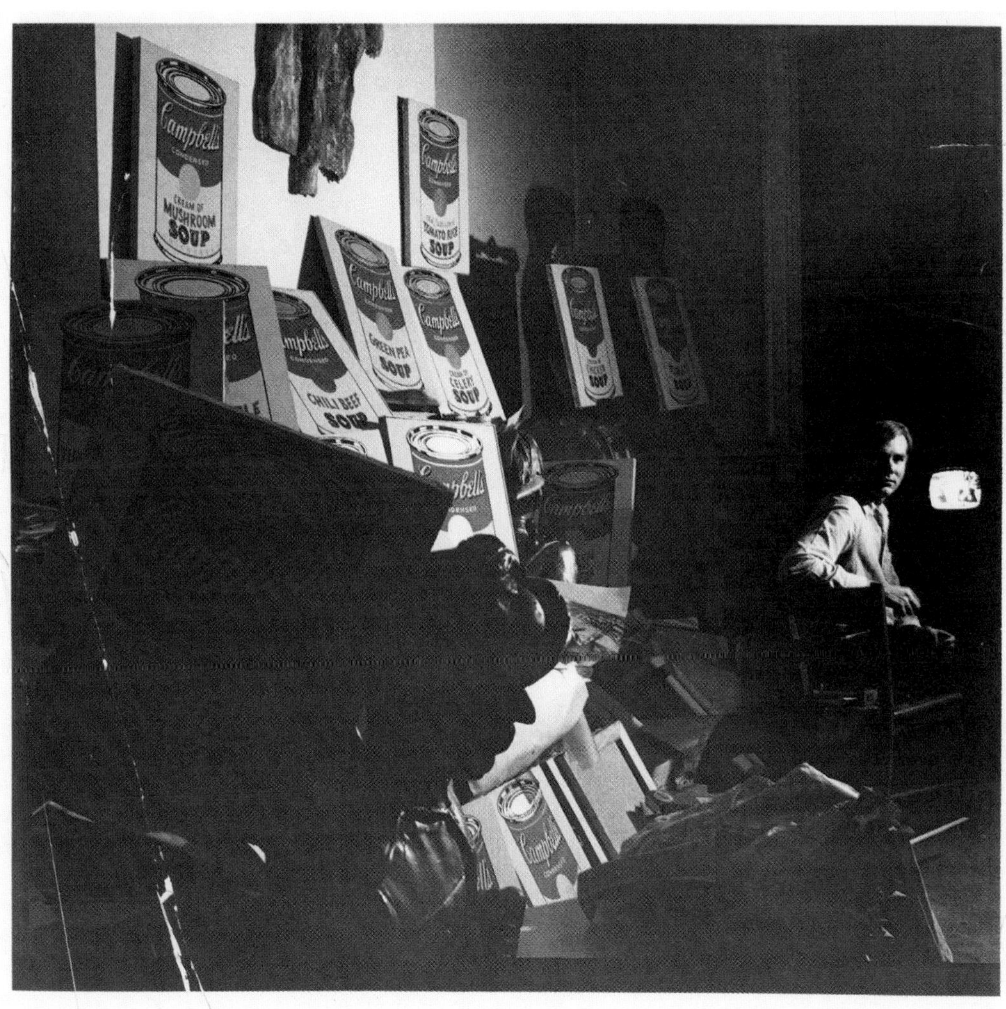

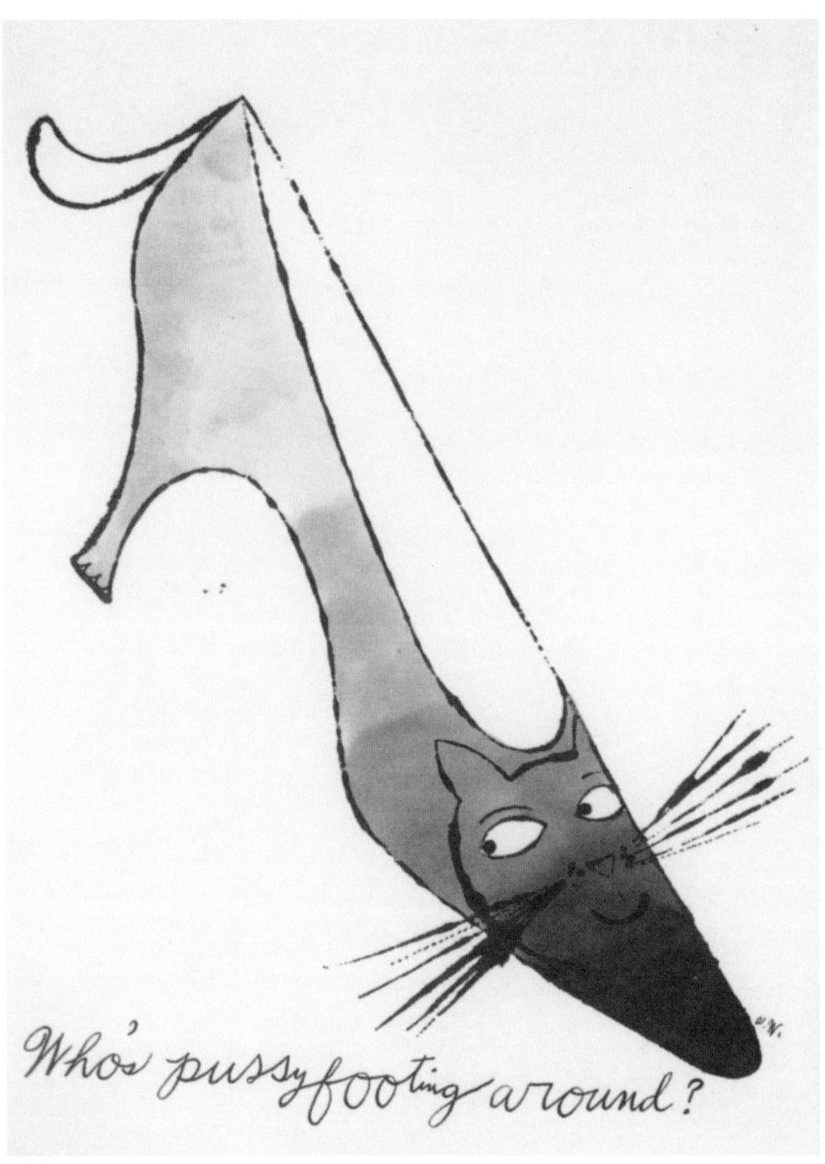

Who's pussy footing around? c. 1960
Watercolour on paper
48.5 x 36.5 cm (19 x 14½ in)
©1999 AWF
Andy Warhol Museum, Pittsburgh, PA

During the 1950s Warhol earned a reputation for his whimsical commercial
illustrations of fashion accessories. He was best known for sketches of shoes,
which he also featured in his non-commercial drawing, combining them with
playful inscriptions based on his mother Julia's looping handwriting.

sensational aspect of his first solo exhibition, Thirty-Two Cans of Campbell's Soup, gave him overnight celebrity, but, in fact, for more than a decade, Warhol had been pursuing a two-pronged path: as a highly innovative commercial illustrator and as a highly provocative, but little recognized artist. The soup cans marked a breakthrough for his career as well as for contemporary American art. Rather than as subject, satire or critique, Warhol used popular culture as his medium. He employed the technical tools of advertising and the formal language of consumer products to create work that was simultaneously strange and familiar, and his evasive explanations of his intentions generated as much attention as the works themselves. In *Thirty-Two Cans of Campbell's Soup*, Warhol elevated concept over contents to transform the ordinary into the iconic, calling into question the conventional idea of what makes a work a masterpiece.

Warhol, the youngest son of Ruthenian immigrants from eastern Slovakia, grew up in a working-class, ethnic neighbourhood in Pittsburgh.[2] After high school, he enrolled in the Pictorial Design Program at the Carnegie Institute of Technology (now the Carnegie Mellon University), where students had the opportunity to learn all the traditional studio practices – drawing, painting and sculpture – and enjoyed access to the institute's excellent art collection (known as the Department of Fine Arts, now the Carnegie Museum of Art). But the curriculum also emphasized training in design and media that prepared graduates for careers in commercial art. After completing the programme in 1949, Warhol moved to New York and over the next decade built an enviable clientele for his work as a commercial illustrator. His images of luxury goods and fashions – particularly shoes – were uncommonly whimsical, and he often teamed the unexpected – butterflies, cats, flowers – with the products he was hired to promote. At the same time, Warhol strove to gain a foothold in the contemporary art scene with playful and provocative works that echoed his primary trade in both media and imagery.

The relationship between the fine arts and the product market had been strengthening since the late nineteenth century when well-known works of art had been used to promote commercial goods; one of the most notable examples repurposed the image of a winsome boy blowing bubbles, painted by John Everett Millais (*Bubbles*, 1886) into an advertisement for Pear's Soap. The first half of the twentieth century saw a reversal of appropriation. The Cubists collaged headlines and phrases clipped from journals on to their canvases, while other artists, including Stuart Davis and Charles Green Shaw, occasionally incorporated consumer imagery into their compositions. In the 1950s, this trend took on new relevance. In the United States, Jasper Johns and Robert

Rauschenberg, both of whom worked in commercial art to support their studio practice, turned their attention to what Johns called ordinary things – flags, targets, beer cans – transforming the visually familiar through expressive rendition, while in the United Kingdom, artists such as Richard Hamilton and Eduardo Paolozzi embraced the visual vocabulary of consumer capitalism, often with satirical intent. The critic Lawrence Alloway attributed this trend to the growing circular pattern of influence between the high arts and popular culture in contemporary society. He coined the term 'mass popular art', which quickly evolved into the catchy 'Pop Art'. By the end of the decade, a group of American artists, including James Rosenquist, Claes Oldenburg and Roy Lichtenstein – like-minded but unaffiliated – created their own version of Pop Art featuring the everyday stuff of modern life – cars, hamburgers, comics – transformed in scale, material and format. The works that Blum saw during his first visit to Warhol's studio, featuring advertisements for nose jobs, diagrams for dance lessons and cartoon characters, reflected this new ethos, but in a manner so neutral and devoid of expressive aesthetics that Warhol's aim seemed to be simple replication.

The origin story of the soup can series – like much of Warhol's biography – derives from anecdote rather than evidence. After the work debuted, Warhol gave any number of explanations as to why he chose the subject, claiming that he liked soup or that everyone liked soup. In one interview he recalled that his mother served it for lunch throughout his childhood; in another he professed that he ate it every day for twenty years. He would deliver these statements with a deliberate naiveté, crafting a public persona as droll and enigmatic as his choice of subject. It is well documented that Warhol repeatedly turned to others for suggestions, giving a plausible weight to the anecdote told by his close friend Ted Carey. In the fall of 1961, Carey introduced Muriel Latow, an interior decorator and gallerist, to Warhol, who offered her fifty dollars for an idea that 'would be very personal' to set him apart from his perceived rivals Rosenquist and Lichtenstein. Latow suggested that he find 'Something you see every day that everybody would recognize. Something like a can of Campbell's Soup.'[3] This story is often further embellished with the claim that he sent his mother Julia, who had been living with him in New York since 1952, or an assistant, to the market to buy all thirty-two varieties for models. Whatever the case, he took up the subject, and the meticulous detail in the paintings themselves confirm that Warhol must have worked from those 'models'.

The soup can paintings are often described as 'portraits', but the element of portraiture in the series only extends to likeness. Warhol

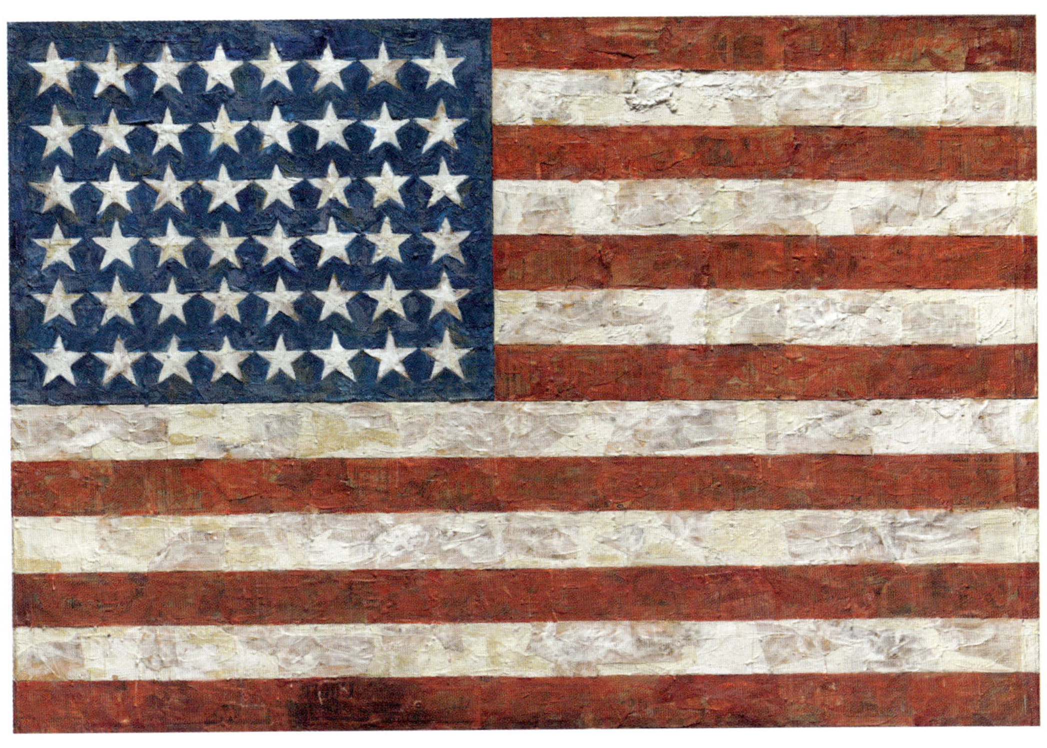

Flag 1954–55
Jasper Johns (born 1930)
Encaustic, oil collage on fabric mounted on plywood
107.5 x 154 cm (42¼ x 60½ in)
Museum of Modern Art, New York, NY

To paint the unmistakable image of the American flag, Johns used semi-translucent encaustic paint that revealed glimpses of the ground layers of newsprint. The result was a surface that was more engaging than the subject, in contrast to Warhol's treatment of the soup cans that neutralized both.

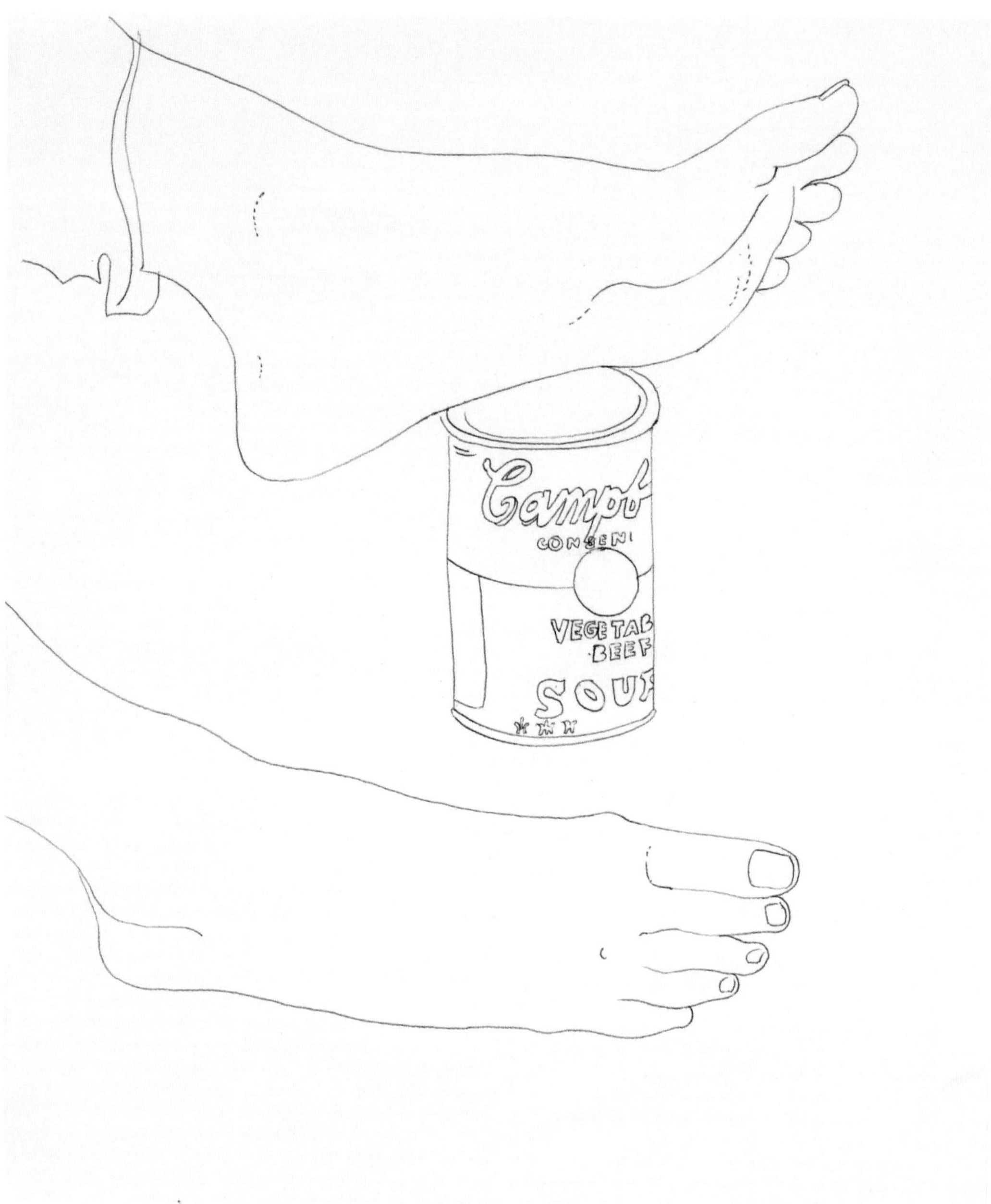
Campb
CONSENT
VEGETAB
BEEF
SOUP

made no attempt to give insight into his subject; his depiction of his 'sitters' focused on accurate surface representation rather than any deeper interpretation. To ensure accuracy, Warhol employed the tools of his commercial trade. He traced a label, projected the enlarged image on his canvas, and employed stencils and stamps for consistency in the typeface and design. The intended result was not the replication of cans but the creation of paintings, and Warhol played with the size, making each individual can roughly four times larger. On each canvas, the can is positioned in a white void; Warhol provides neither a spatial nor a contextual setting for his image. Working with synthetic polymer paint, he produced a smooth surface devoid of brushmarks, extinguishing any trace of an artist's hand. The can is rendered in three dimensions, but the image appears slightly flattened, resembling a mass-media reproduction. The distinctive red and white label – used since 1898 – is flawlessly rendered, as is the brand name and individual flavour of each soup. Warhol's sole departure from his model is the plain gold disc that replaces the pictorial medallion featuring a winged victory that became part of the label after 1900 when Campbell's Soup was awarded a medal of excellence at the Exposition Universelle in Paris.

For the 1962 summer exhibition at the Ferus Gallery, Warhol sent the completed series *Thirty-Two Campbell's Soup Cans* without any instruction for installing them. As he had no plans to visit the gallery prior to the opening, Irving Blum telephoned him for advice. Warhol claimed indifference as to how the works were hung, so Blum experimented, first trying to arrange them directly on the wall. The canvases would not hang straight, so Blum built a narrow shelf, about waist high, along the walls of the gallery and evenly spaced the paintings in the order that they came out of the box. Most art scholars compare Blum's installation

Feet with Campbell's Soup Can 1960
Black ballpoint pen on cream wove paper
43.5 x 35 cm (17¼ x 13¾ in)
Art Institute of Chicago, Chicago, IL

Throughout the 1950s, Warhol's personal drawings featured a repeated visual vocabulary, including cats, shoes, feet and good-looking young men. Like the Coke bottle, the soup can begins to appear at the end of the decade, generally in combination with other images. These drawings feature the signature elements of his commercial work: a deft line, spare representation and suggestive wit.

to shelves in a supermarket, but Warhol's biographer, Blake Gopnik, has rightly called this into question. The spatial rhythm of placement – one by one – prompts the viewer to take in each individual variation, 'like precious object d'art in an Old Master print room', rather than the closely crowded, serried shelves in actual store displays.[4] Whether or not it was his intention, Blum's presentation emphasized the idea of repetition as well as the choice of subject, likely enforcing the perception that Warhol was a trickster and his paintings were a blatant hoax. The exhibition drew critical ire, but it fuelled publicity for Warhol and his ability to baffle the viewer with such empty and ordinary imagery. During its brief run (9 July to 4 August), the installation inspired endless cartoons and parodies, including one in a nearby gallery's window featuring a pyramid of actual soup cans with the sign: Do not be Misled. Get the Original. Our Low Price 2- 33¢.[5]

What set *Thirty-Two Cans of Campbell's Soup* apart from Warhol's earlier forays into commercial imagery was the subtle simplicity of his artistic intervention. His rendition is so true to the original that the cans appear at first to be replicas, but the sheer number of renditions, as well as the rationale for the variety of flavours, inserts an imaginative step between the brand image and the artistic interpretation. Informed by the purposeful language of mass media, Warhol portrayed the can with its label as an infinitely repeatable matrix – able to accommodate slight variation – that triggers instant recognition. Warhol crystallizes the idea of the can as an icon, over its visual aesthetic or its practical function as a container in real life. As a successful ad man, Warhol understood, and then exploited, the essence of branding. His message was the media, rather than a commentary on consumer society, and, as Marcel Duchamp, the artist whose own transgressive appropriation of found objects challenged prevailing definitions of what could be considered 'art', astutely observed, Warhol's innovation came in his decision to repeat the

Big Torn Campbell's Soup Can (Pepper Pot) 1962
Casein and graphite on canvas
182 x 132 cm (71½ in x 52 in)
Andy Warhol Museum, Pittsburgh, PA

Along with the pristine rendering of the thirty-two varieties, Warhol painted battered cans with shredded labels, dents and opened lids. No matter the state of the can, it is clear that he was focused on the surface of the object rather than its context or its contents.

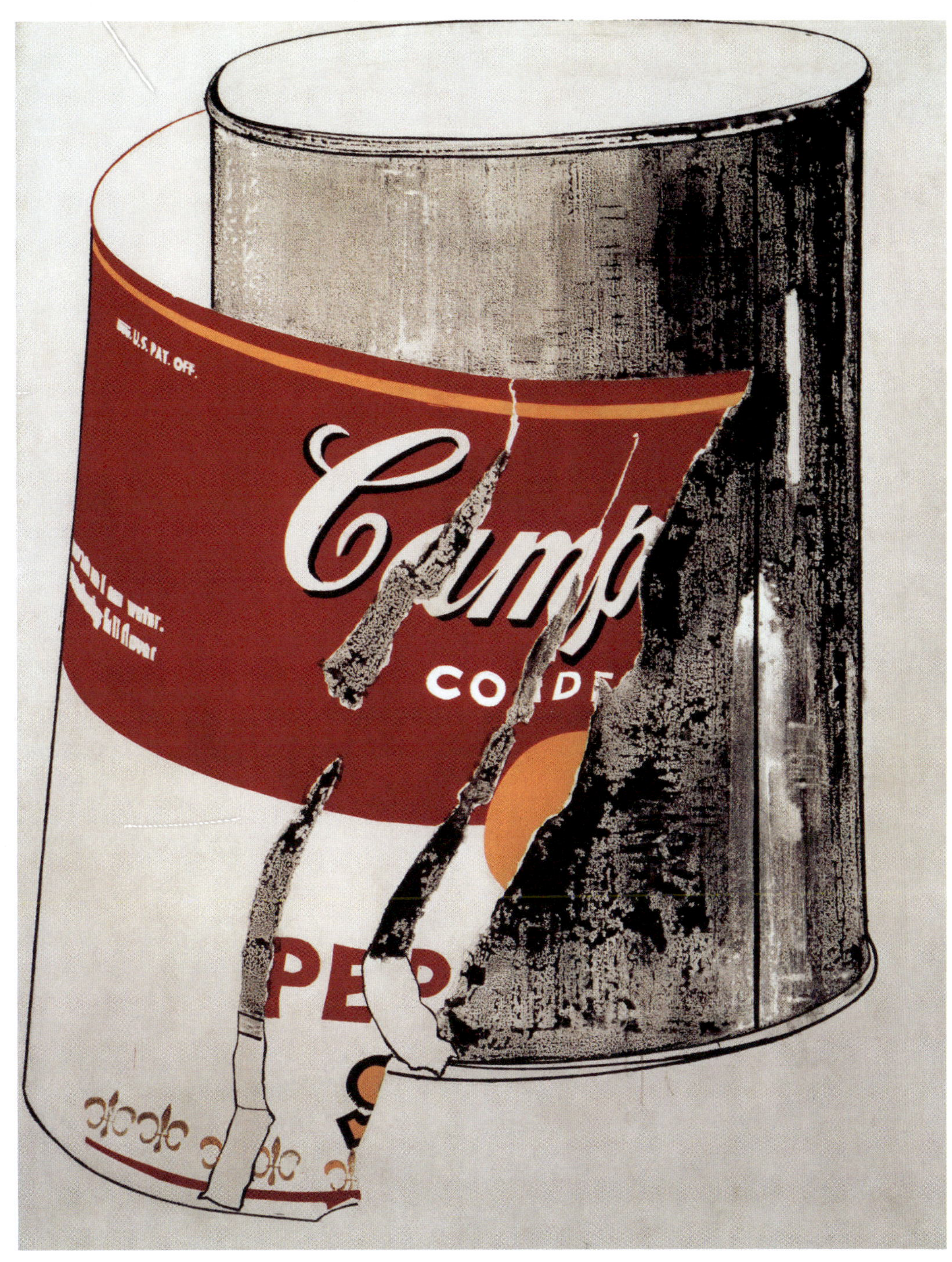

U.S. PAT. OFF.
Camp
COND
PE

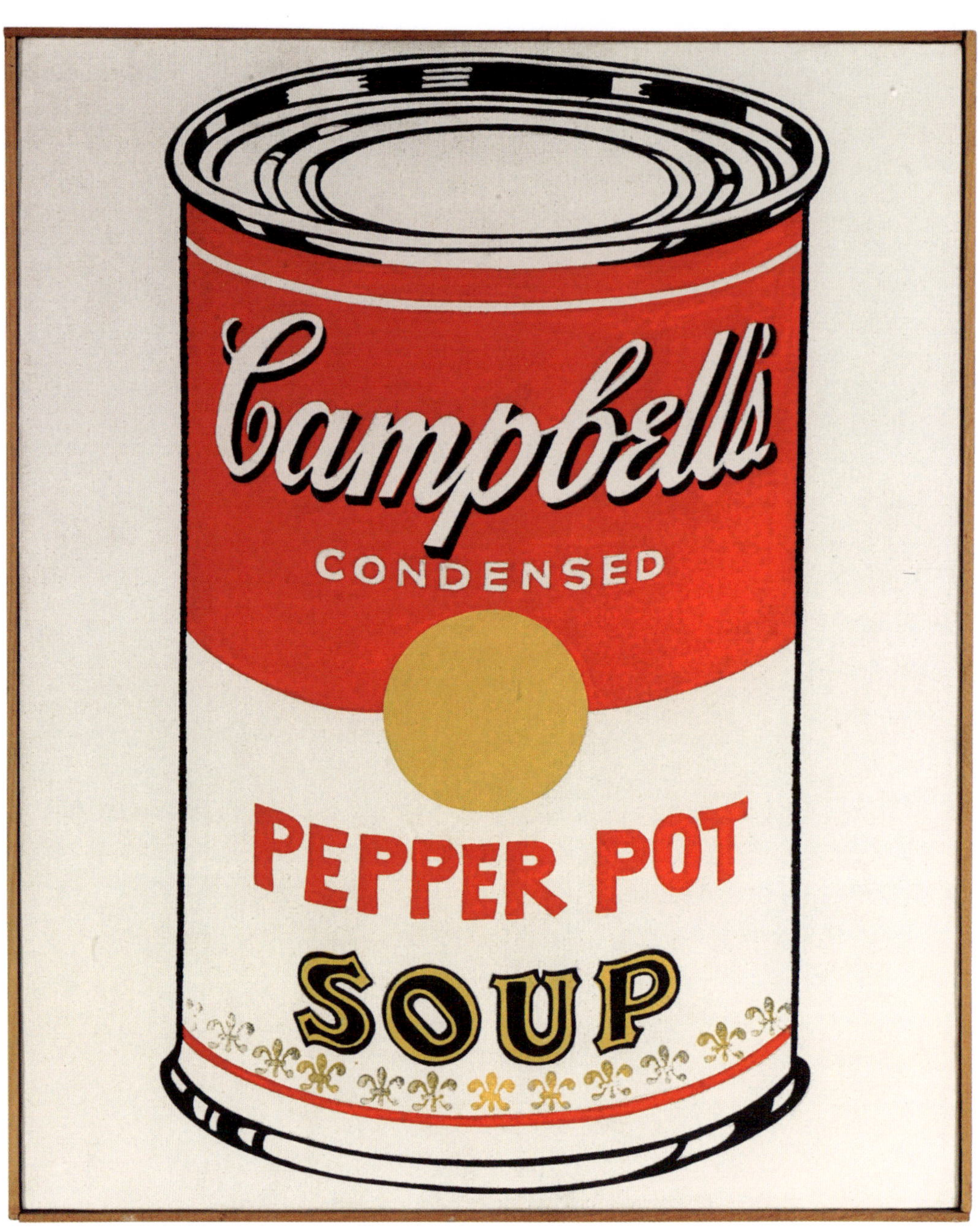

Campbell's
CONDENSED
PEPPER POT
SOUP

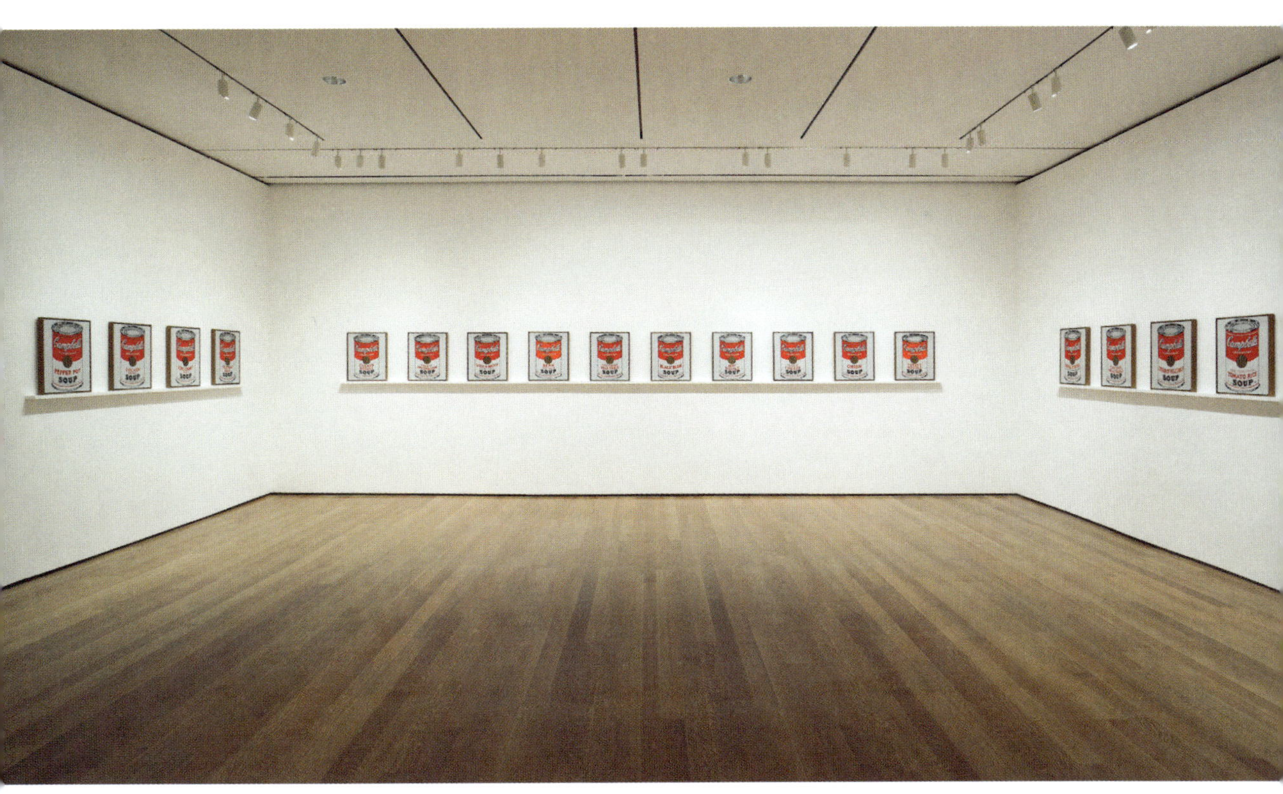

 Campbell's Soup Cans (Thirty-Two Campbell's Soup Cans), detail

Warhol used stencils and projected images as well as the flat application of paint to create a neutral surface. This lack of individual expression further suppressed the meaning of each can beyond its brand and its flavour. In this way he focused upon the visual repertoire of the commercial world as a mass media, instantly recognized but devoid of inflection.

 Installation View
Andy Warhol: 'Campbell's Soup Cans' and Other Works, 1953–67
25 April–12 October 2015
Museum of Modern Art, New York, NY

The distinctive installation at the Ferus Gallery was rarely repeated. Typically, the separate canvases have been grouped in a four-row grid. In 2015, the Museum of Modern Art in New York recreated the original display – removing the frames and protective Plexiglas and propping each of the canvases on a narrow shelf – for the exhibition Andy Warhol's Campbell's Soup Cans and Other Works, 1953–67.

image rather than the visual experience he created.[6] It was not the soup can or its contents that Warhol represented; his true subject was the form and content of mass media that was as egalitarian as it was artificial, an icon without iconography, available and intelligible to all.

Well before Warhol painted *Thirty-Two Campbell's Soup Cans*, he included the cans in his drawings. Placement is seemingly random and whimsical: set between a man's bare feet or empty and upturned on the neck of a Coke bottle. Other drawings, dating to 1962, reveal that he experimented with cans in every state: crushed; labels shredded or peeled; a lid bent back with a can opener hovering ominously above it. He tried different sizes, scaling up to as large as 1.8 m (6 ft). And, once he had painted them, the definitive thirty-two varieties lost their significance; he subsequently grouped *100 Cans* (1962) and then *200 Cans* (1963) with spray paint and stencils on a single canvas, arranged in serried rows just like well-stocked supermarket shelves. By this time, photographic silkscreen became Warhol's preferred medium; it guaranteed a more efficient and reliable means of repetition and amplified the role of assistants in his work. He also channelled his wily imagination into building his own brand as an eccentric, silver-wigged faux-naif, who answered complex questions with 'yes' or 'no', made such gnomic proclamations as the often quoted and dubiously attributed 'in the future everybody will be world famous for fifteen minutes' and was besotted with celebrities and stardom. His last invention on the soup can came in 1965, when he silkscreened cans in garish, contrasting colours.

In the years that followed, Warhol's restless creative drive played out in film, sculpture, installation, performance, music and silkscreen series that ranged from real-life disasters to celebrity portraiture. But the soup can prevailed as a defining image in his work, as seen in the sale of his 1962 painting *Big Campbell's Soup with Torn Label (Vegetable Beef)* at Parke-Bernet (today part of Sotheby's) in New York at $60,000 in 1970, a record-breaking price for a living artist. Just eight years earlier, when Blum took a risk on showing the *Thirty-Two Cans* in the Ferus Gallery, only five sold for $100 each. When the exhibition closed, Blum made a canny decision. He bought back the five canvases and paid Warhol $1,000 for the complete series. He stored them in his apartment where, due to space concerns, he hung them in a grid of four rows, eight canvases per row, uniting them as a single work in a practice that has become conventional. Blum resisted offers to buy them and rarely exhibited them, until 1996 when he transferred ownership to the Museum of Modern Art in New York as a partial gift with partial payment.[7] Just as Warhol knew how to turn mass media into a masterpiece, Blum knew how to recognize a masterpiece in the making.

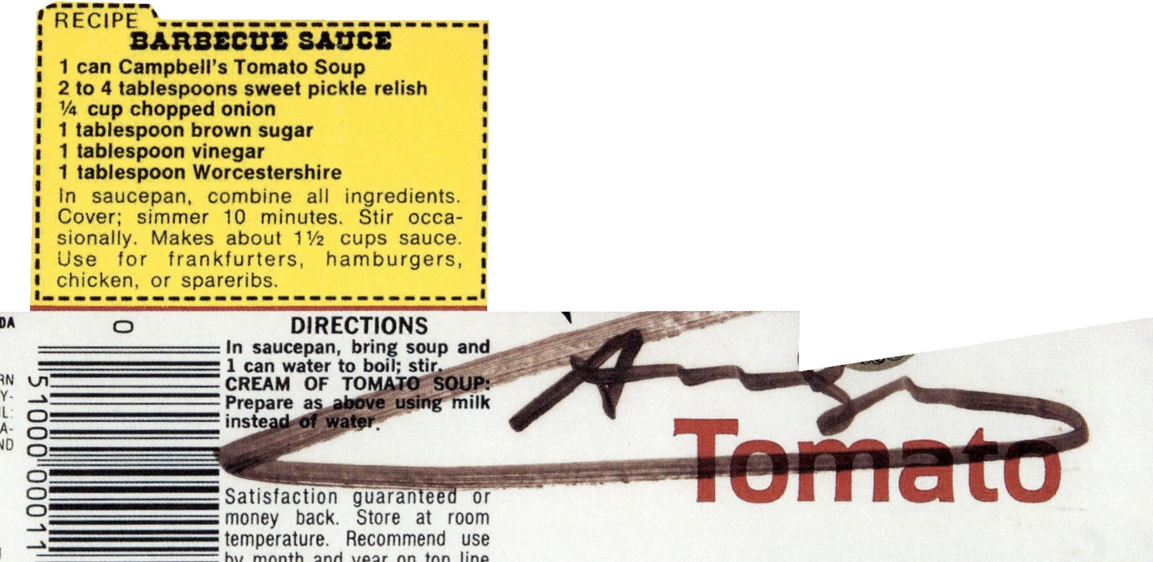

Campbell's Soup Label
Institute of Contemporary Art, University of Pennsylvania, Philadelphia, PA

Campbell's soup cans became Warhol's calling card. For his 1965 retrospective exhibition at the Institute of Contemporary Art, opening invitations were printed on the back of actual labels. And although he claimed that there was no commercial connection between his imagery and the soup company, he happily autographed soup cans for his fans.

Michelle Obama

Amy Sherald

I painted Michelle Obama from the south side of Chicago … and then I painted the First Lady.

Amy Sherald, June 2021

During the final weeks of President Barack Obama's administration (2009–16), Amy Sherald came to the White House for a potentially career-changing interview. For more than a decade she had been painting what she describes as 'American people' – mostly young, all anonymous, all Black – in a distinctive style that combines bold colour, flattened forms and an exacting realism. Although not known as a portraitist, Sherald had been chosen as a possible candidate to paint an official likeness for the collection of the National Portrait Gallery in Washington, DC, and like the others on the shortlist, she did not know whether her sitter might be the forty-fourth president or his wife, Michelle. But when she entered the Oval Office to speak with the president and the first lady, she felt an instant and specific connection, and near the end of the interview, Sherald turned to Mrs Obama to say, 'I really hope that you and I can work together.' Clearly the feeling was mutual, for Mrs Obama later recalled that 'within the first few sentences, I knew she was the one for me'.[1]

Sherald situates the concept of representation at the heart of her work. Through depicting the people that society has overlooked, and the historical record has neglected, she seeks to build a greater capacity for inclusion and empathy in the narrative of American painting. More often than not, her paintings begin when a stranger catches her eye, and she approaches them to ask if she can take a photograph for reference in her studio. The Obama commission set a very different challenge; not only was she asked to paint a portrait of a well-known – and much-admired – public figure, but she would be working within a defined, and admittedly old-fashioned tradition. Official portraits have a conservative history, and Sherald's approach is markedly contemporary. But the commission also involved an act of representation as reclamation: the first African American first lady seen through the artistic vision of another African American woman. In a remarkable fusion of likeness, presence and pride, Sherald seized the opportunity to transcend the conventional limits of the commission and envisioned a masterpiece.

Strictly speaking, the first lady is neither an official nor an executive position. The constitution does not define a role for her; she is neither elected nor paid. She is, and always has been, simply the president's spouse. Martha Washington, the wife of the first president, was called 'Lady Washington', and for decades her successors were similarly addressed with their husband's surname. Zachary Taylor, the twelfth president of the United States, is credited for the initial use of the term in the context of the presidency in his eulogy for Dolley Madison in 1849, declaring that she had been 'truly our First Lady for a half century'.[2] Dolley Madison, wife of the fourth president, James Madison (served 1809–19), was the first of the presidents' wives to embrace a public role. Before her husband took office, he served as secretary of state to the widowed Thomas Jefferson (served 1801–09), and, when

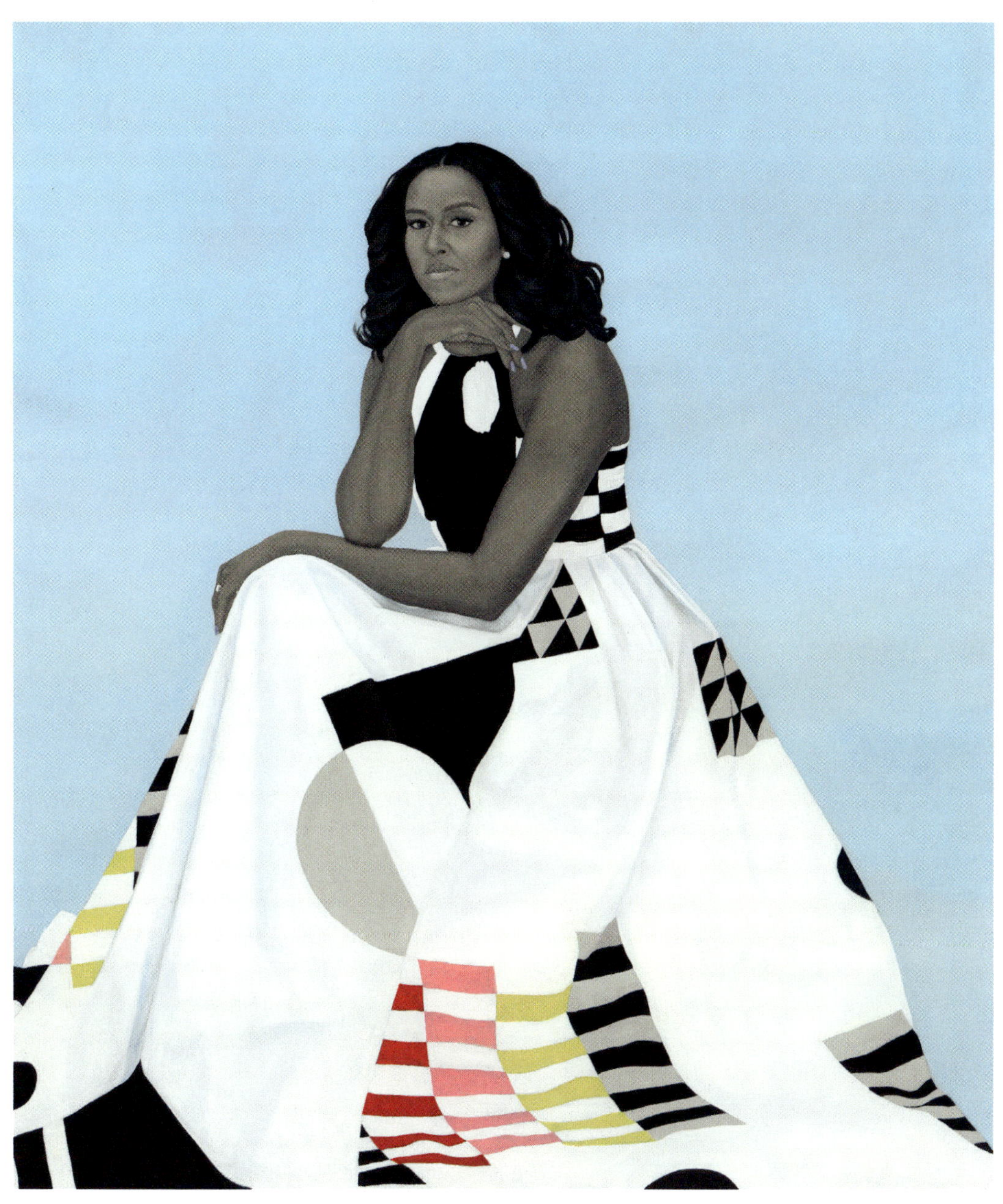

Michelle LaVaughn Robinson Obama 2018
Amy Sherald (born 1973)
Oil on linen
183 x 153 cm (72 x 60 in)
National Portrait Gallery, Smithsonian Institution, Washington, DC.

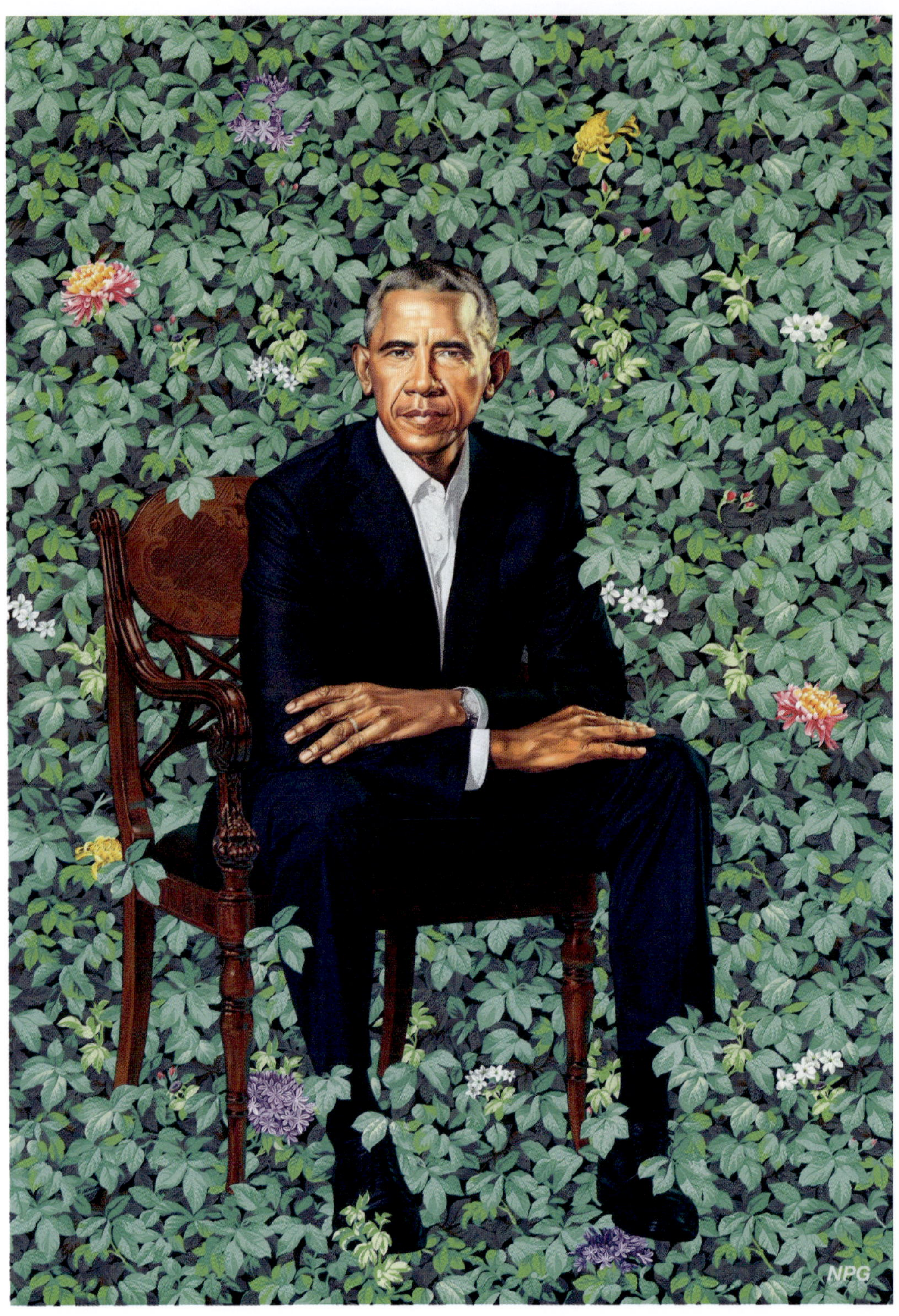

needed, Mrs Madison assisted Jefferson by organizing and presiding over social events. Even after her husband left office, she remained the most influential hostess in Washington, derided by some chroniclers as the 'presidentress'. The current use of the term as a title began in 1860. Over the years, the title has evolved – at least in public perception – into a position. After the activist example of Eleanor Roosevelt, most first ladies have used their prominence to advocate for a socially – but politically neutral – cause: Jacqueline Kennedy supported historic preservation; Laura Bush, a former librarian, promoted literacy; Michelle Obama encouraged childhood health and nutrition. Mrs Roosevelt set another precedent by using personal appearances, radio broadcasts and newspaper columns to champion her causes and, as a result, she created a very public presence for the first lady in American life.

From her husband's first run for public office in 1996, it was clear that Michelle Obama had little desire to share the political limelight. She was raised in Chicago in a middle-class home that valued family, education and excellence. After attending Princeton University and Harvard Law School, she worked as a lawyer, followed by service in the public sector, including city government and hospital administration. She met Barack Obama through work – she mentored him in intellectual property law – and they married in 1992. Her reluctance to join her husband on the campaign trail increased when their daughters were born; family and work were her priorities. When Obama secured the Democratic nomination for the 2008 presidential race, she had no choice but to embrace a more public role. She proved to be a captivating campaigner, developing a natural speaking style that was polished yet convincingly genuine, and many working women identified with her ability to navigate modern motherhood. Obama's

Barack Obama 2018
Kehinde Wiley (born 1977)
Oil on canvas
214 x 147 cm (84 x 58 in)
National Portrait Gallery, Smithsonian Institution, Washington, DC.

The flowers in the president's portrait symbolize his biography: African blue lilies for his paternal lineage, white jasmine for his childhood in Hawaii and colourful chrysanthemums, the official flower of Chicago, where he launched his career. Like Sherald, Wiley worked from a photograph of his sitter, but used hyperrealism for a natural rather than idealizing effect.

victory broke the colour line in the history of the American presidency, and Mrs Obama found herself in an unprecedented position. She has never lost sight of what she and her husband represented for the nation's history, as she compellingly stated in a reflection about her husband's years in office at the 2016 Democratic convention: 'I wake up every morning in a house built by slaves, and I watch my daughters – two beautiful, intelligent Black young women – playing with their dogs on the White House lawn.'[3]

Like the position of first lady, the concept of the 'official' presidential portrait has evolved over time. The collection assembled in the National Portrait Gallery is barely more than a half-century old, and it was not until 1994 that a portrait – of the forty-first president George H.W. Bush – was newly commissioned for the collection. Similarly, the first ladies are represented by a varied group of collected images – including prints and photographs – with the first commissioned portrait being that of Hillary Rodham Clinton painted by Ginny Stanford in 2006. In 2016, the last year of the Obama presidency, a committee at the National Portrait Gallery began the search for two artists to paint portraits of the president and his wife. After a broad review, they submitted fifteen portfolios to a panel that included a few of the gallery's curators as well as William G. Allman, the White House curator, and Thelma Golden, director of The Studio Museum in Harlem, to create a shortlist for the Obamas. Private sector donations were secured to fund the commissions. Each artist was interviewed in the Oval Office with the understanding that they were being considered for either portrait; the Obamas would make the final choice. The president chose Kehinde Wiley, whose work counters the

Miss Everything (Unsuppressed Deliverance) 2013
Oil on canvas
138 x 109.5 cm (54 x 43 in)
Collection of Frances and Burton Reifler

When Sherald encountered Krystal Mack on her bicycle in Baltimore, she was inspired by Mack's hopeful spirit and self-assured demeanour. Through dress, vibrant colour and a playful prop, Sherald spun Mack's natural poise into a compelling fictional character. In 2016, the National Portrait Gallery selected this work for the top prize in the Triennial Outwin Boochever Portrait Competition, making Sherald the first woman and the first African American to receive the award.

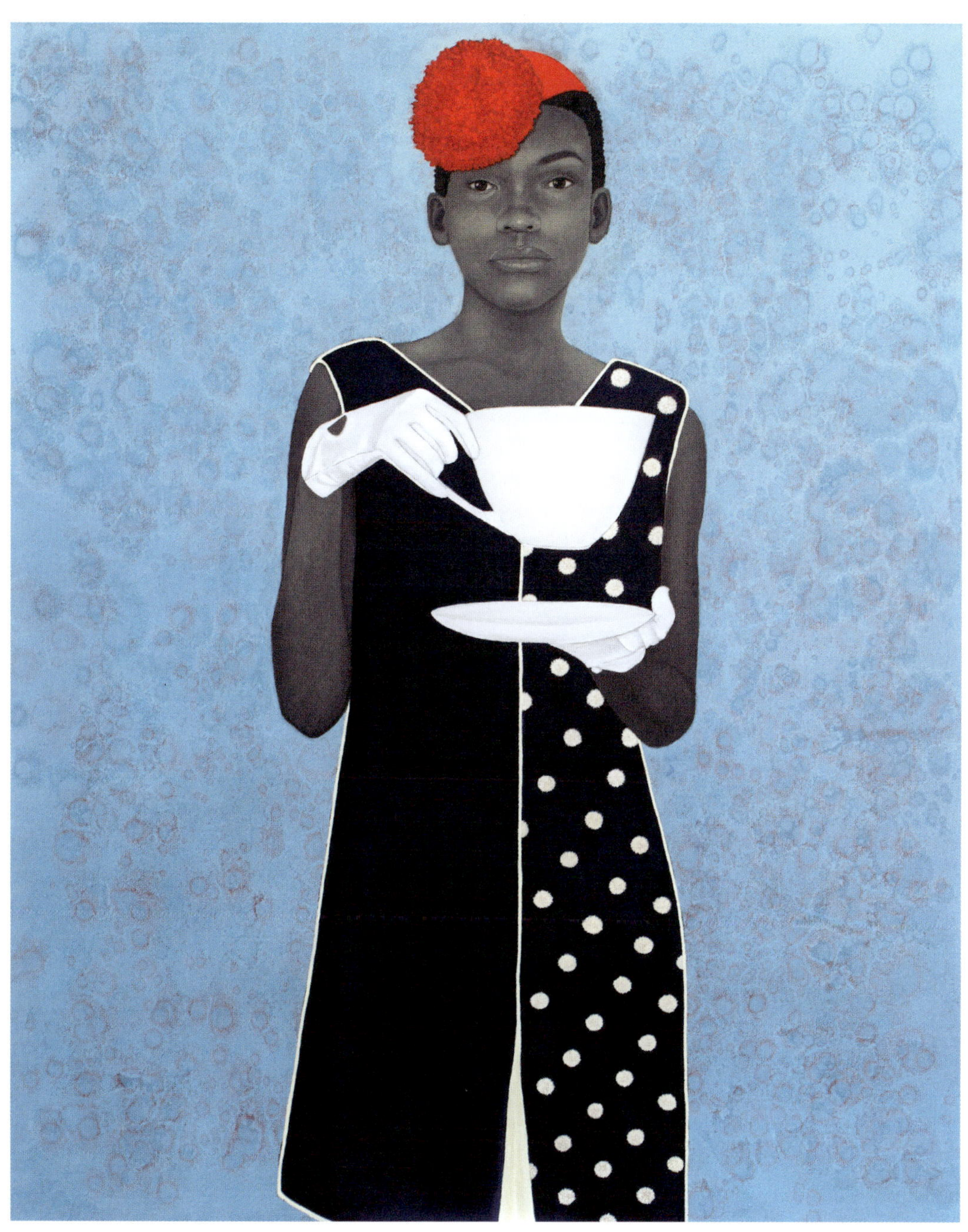

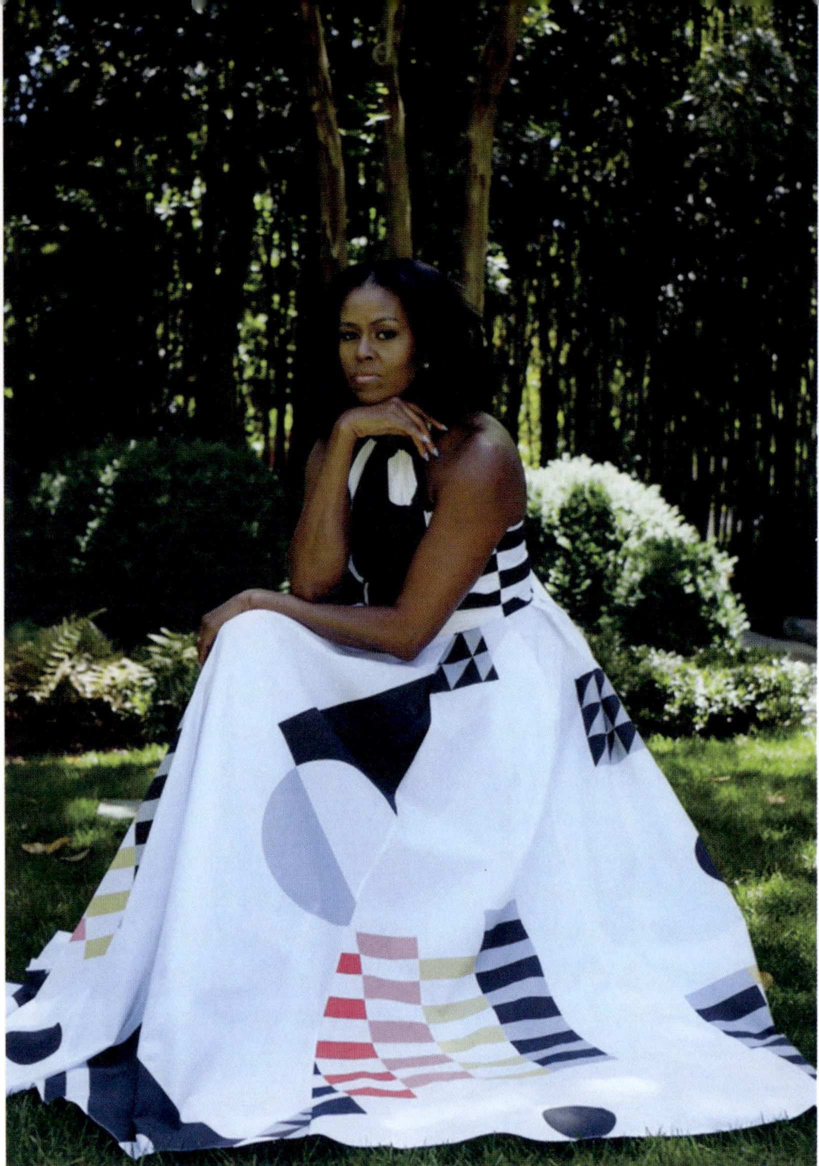

Photograph of First Lady Michelle Obama (posing for portrait)
Maryland, 2 October 2017
Courtesy Amy Sherald

Sherald's portraits begin with a photograph that captures a pose and records the sitter's appearance. In her paintings, Sherald strives to move beyond specific identity to what she calls an archetype – an essence larger and more universal than an individual's life – all the while rendering the face and figure with exacting naturalism.

absence of Black men and women in the history of grand portraiture through replacement and revision. Mrs Obama chose Amy Sherald, a rising artist gaining critical acclaim for her straightforward yet aesthetically distinctive depiction of 'American people' with the intent to 'tell American stories'.[4]

Although Sherald resists the label of portraitist, her paintings are rooted in her interest in a specific individual whose appearance sparks something in her imagination. She often discovers her subjects while walking around her neighbourhood in Baltimore, Maryland; they might be someone she knows or has seen in the area, or they might be a complete stranger. They all share the common element of being the type of people she sees every day, and in Sherald's experience those people are generally young and Black. She asks permission to take a photograph and once she returns to the studio, she transforms the image of the person from a sitter to a subject, turning their simple, often front-facing pose into a monumental stance through strong forms and flattened colour planes set against a single-toned background. As seen in *Miss Everything (Unsuppressed Deliverance)*, clothing plays an important role, defining the figure's silhouette and significance. Sherald often employs wit to confront the viewer and social expectations; in this case, the young woman – with her perfect posture, her exquisite manners and impeccable ensemble – holds an enormous teacup as if underscoring the absurdity of her own actions. But *Miss Everything*'s facial expression is serious, and she engages the viewer with a proud, and slightly wary demeanour. She is present before the viewer, not just ready to be seen, but meeting the viewer's gaze with equal power and privilege. Sherald has often talked about her conceptual intent to transform an individual's appearance into an archetype, and one element in that process is her use of *grisaille* (monotone grey) as a skin tone that detaches the figure from its natural appearance without eliminating the distinguishing factor of race.

Keeping to her practice, Sherald began her portrait of Michelle Obama with a photograph. Mrs Obama described the sitting as 'intimate' and based on trust, allowing Sherald to adjust her pose by physically shifting her shoulders, arranging her hair and even repositioning her fingers.[5] Seated crossed-legged, with her chin resting on her right hand, Mrs Obama regards the camera with a solemn expression, enlivened by a slightly raised eyebrow and parted lips, as if she is about to speak. The verdant tones of the garden highlights the burnished brown of her skin, an effect further emphasized by the bold black and white print of her gown. Throughout her husband's

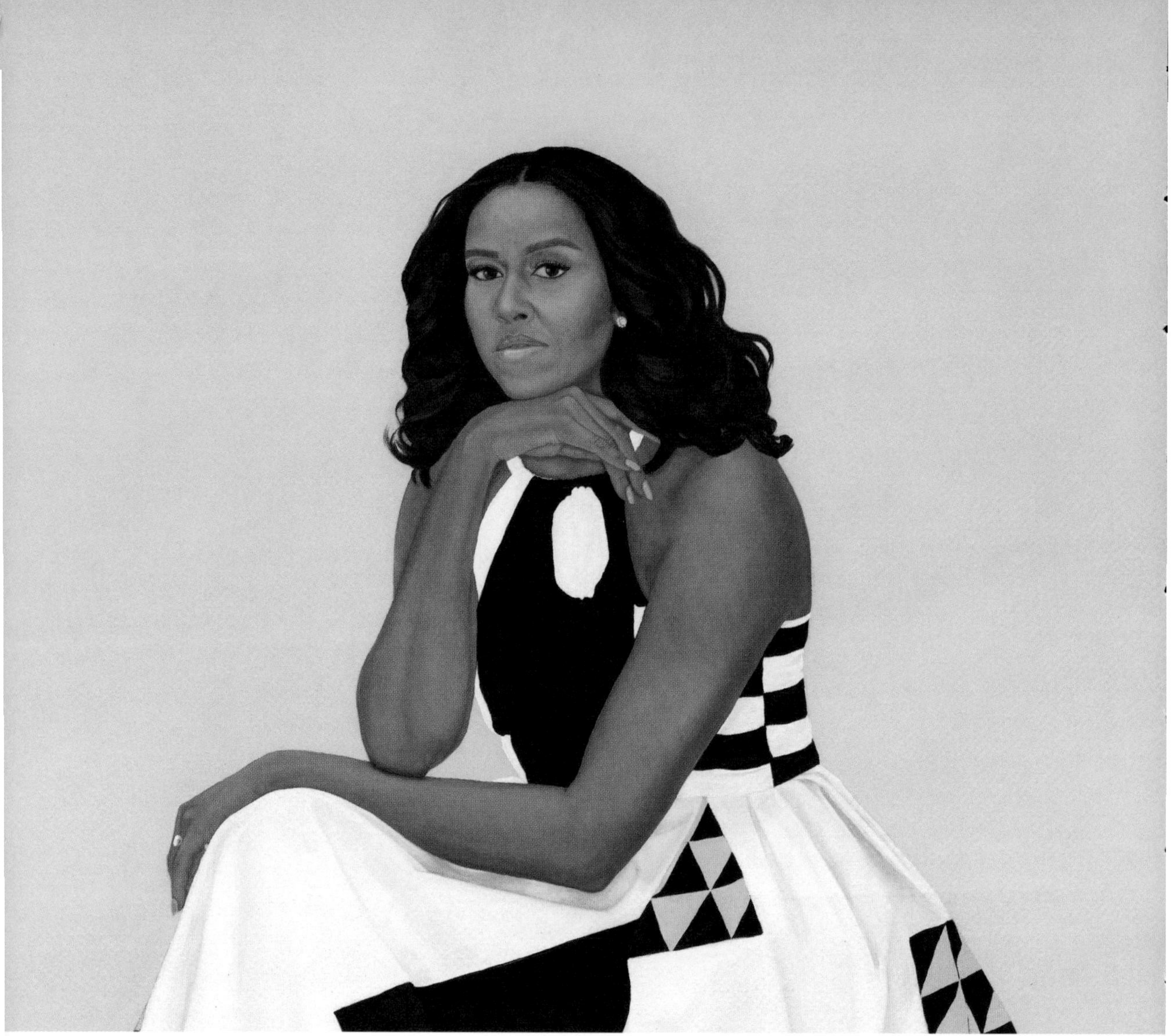

Michelle LaVaughn Robinson Obama, detail

Sherald cites nineteenth-century photographic portraits as one of the sources
for her inventive rendering of Black skin tones in shades of grey. Rather than
eliminating the issue of race, she seeks to assign colour a more neutral role in
the conversation about race, adding what she hopes to be an additional layer
of meaning in Black representation.

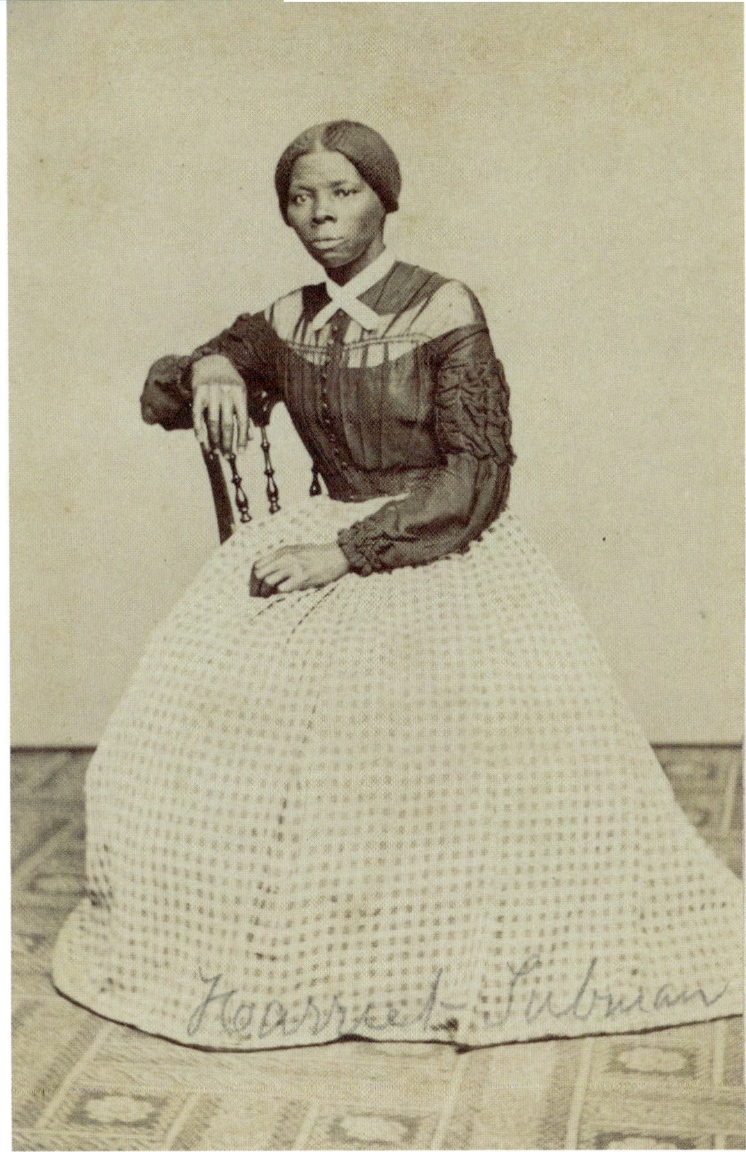

Portrait of Harriet Tubman 1868 or 1869
Benjamin F. Powelson (1823–85)
Albumen silver print
9.5 x 6 cm (4 x 2¼ in)
National Museum of African American History and Culture,
Smithsonian Institution shared with Library of Congress, Washington, DC.

This recently discovered photograph of the abolitionist Harriet Tubman presents
an intriguing parallel to Mrs Obama's portrait. There is no evidence that Sherald
knew of the photograph when she conceived the portrait, but the confident
pose and severe expression seem to mirror Tubman's dignified self-presentation.
During the nineteenth century this type of photograph would have been
produced in multiples and circulated to advance the sitter's reputation.

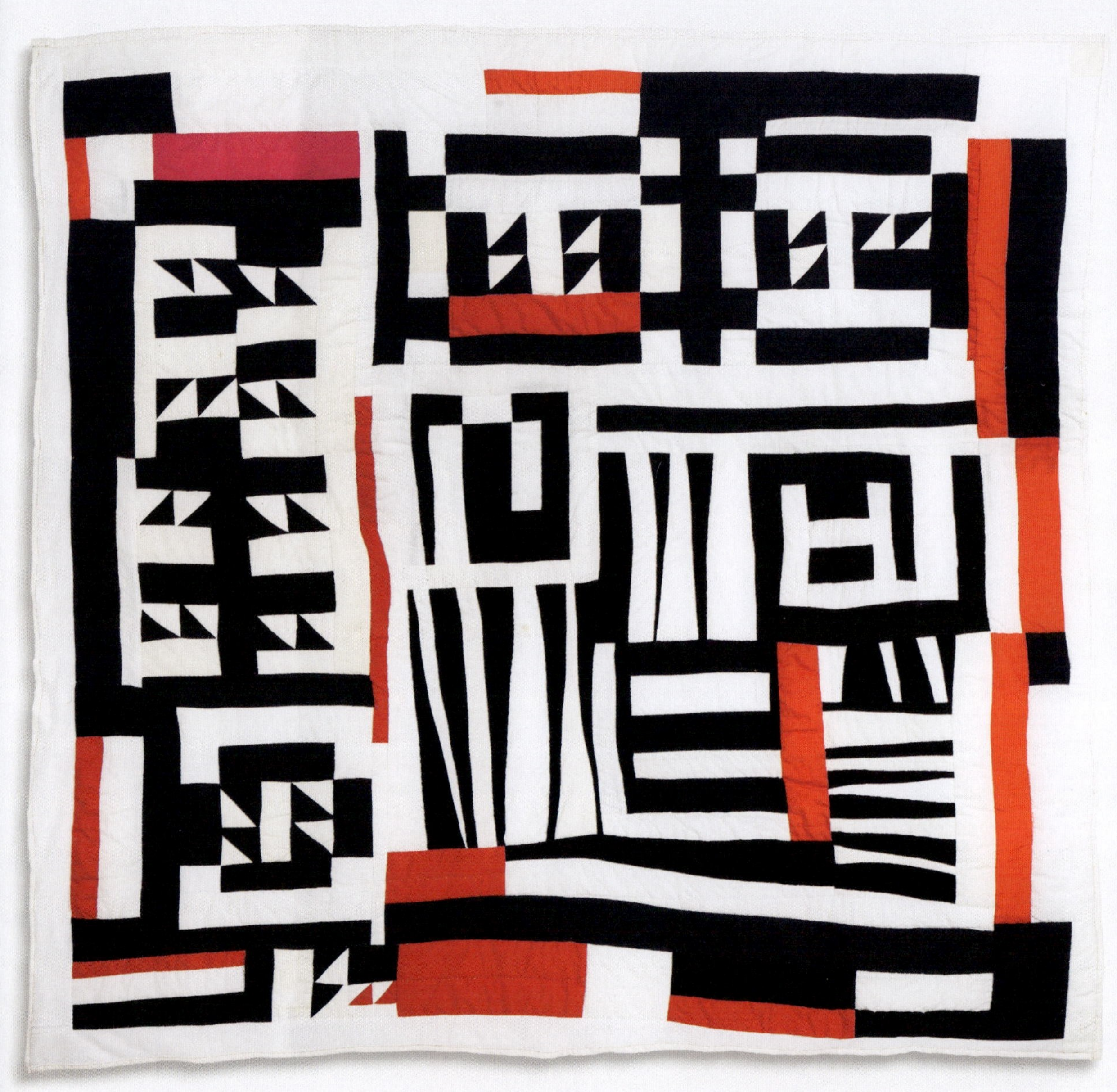

     Making a Masterpiece

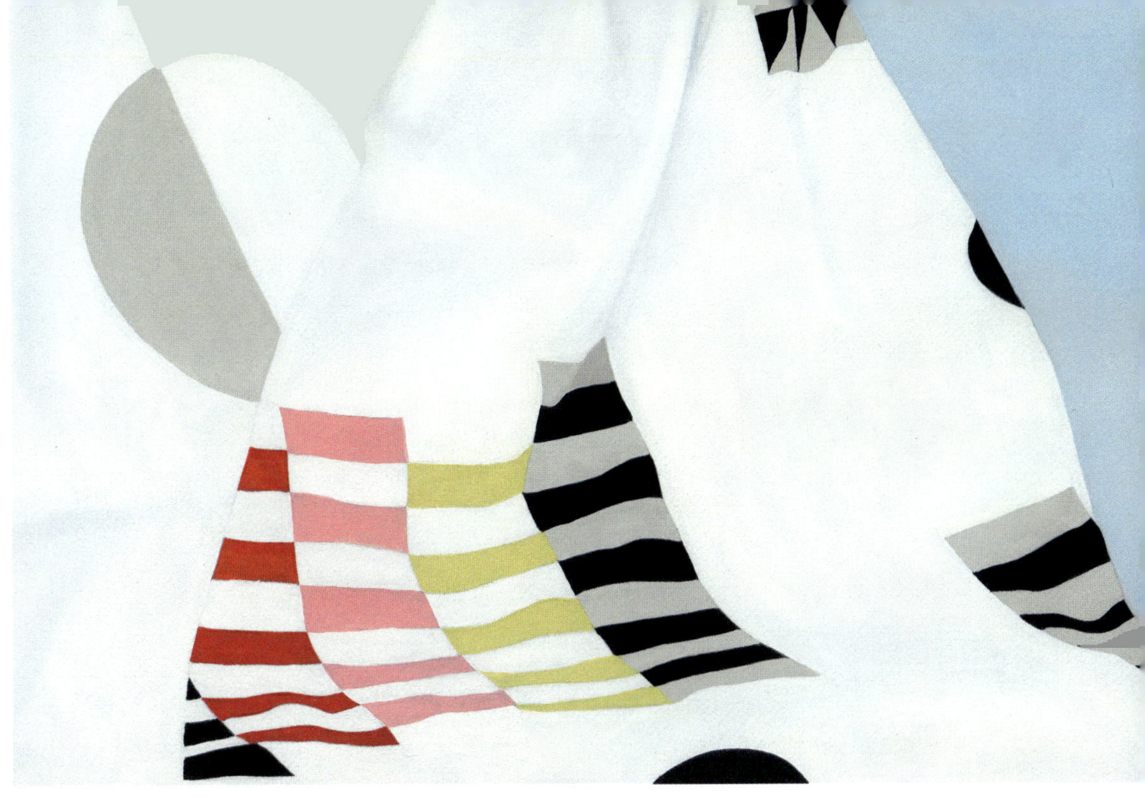

 Michelle LaVaughn Robinson Obama, detail

Sherald chose the Milly dress, in part, for its bold, graphic print. This block of chequered rectangles reminded her of the line-and-colour block paintings of the Dutch Modernist Piet Mondrian. But even more significant, the mix of geometric patterns forged a visual link with the distinctive, generations-old quilt-making traditions of Gee's Bend in Alabama.

 Blocks, Strips, Strings, and Half Squares 2005
Mary Lee Bendolph (born 1935)
Pieced cotton plain weave, twill, corduroy, nylon twill
and cellulose acetate knit
213.5 x 206 cm (84 x 81 in)
Philadelphia Museum of Art, Philadelphia, PA

The quilters of Gee's Bend honour their enslaved ancestors through their use of vibrant colour and repurposed fabric. But more than preserving a legacy, their inventive – even improvisational – patterning gives new life to a lasting tradition. Bendolph based this design on one of her own abstract, intaglio prints, while the terms in the title refer to conventional components of quilt making.

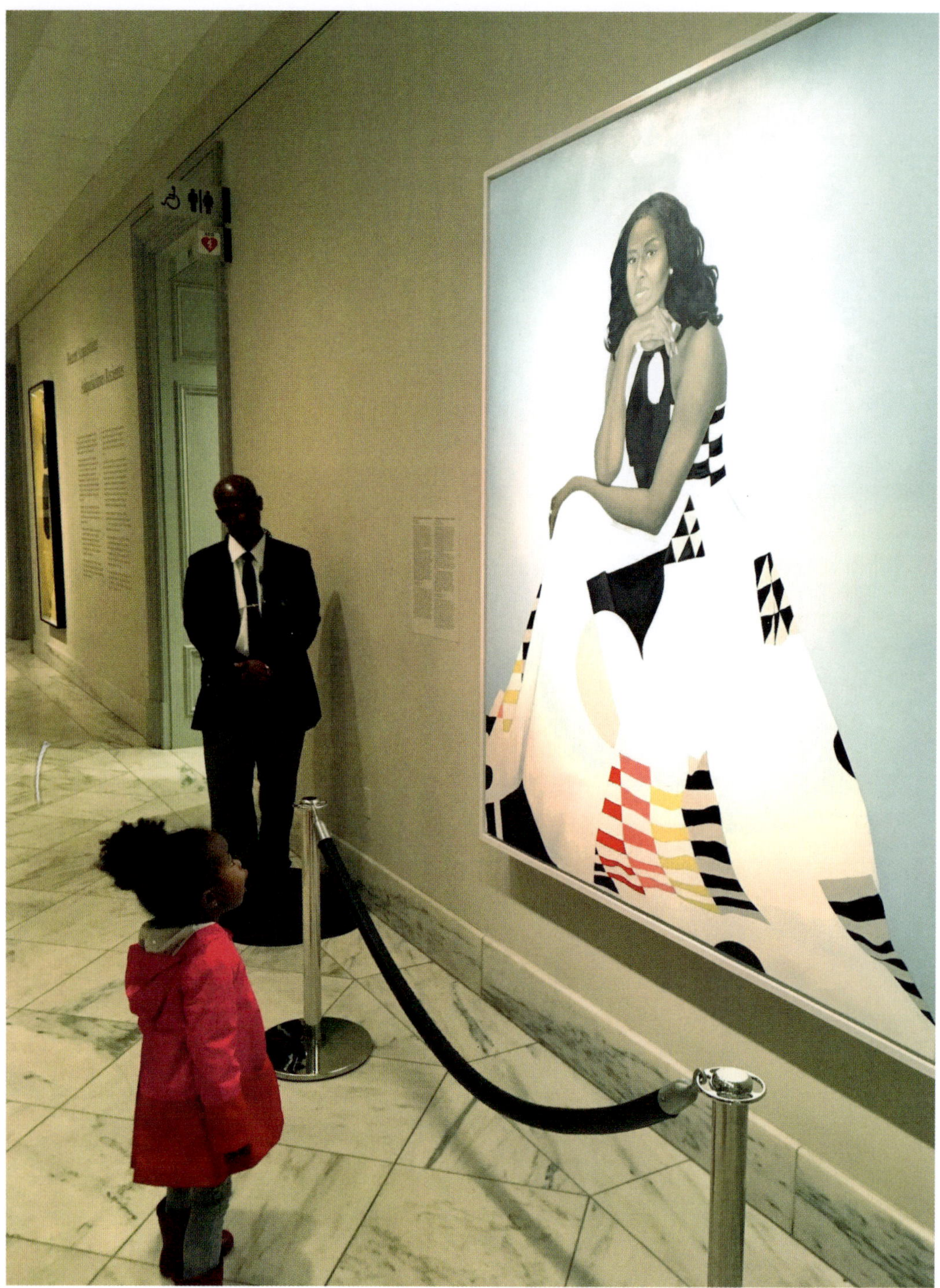

presidency, Mrs Obama was known for her comfortable sense of style; always at ease in her clothing, she was as likely to appear in purchases from such mid-priced retail shops as J. Crew or White House Black Market as in couture designs. To choose the dress for the portrait, Sherald enlisted the aid of Meredith Koop, a stylist who had worked with Mrs Obama since 2009. Koop presented a selection of dresses, and Sherald chose one based on a design from Michelle Smith's 2017 Spring Collection for her brand, Milly, that had been lightly altered to suit Mrs Obama's preferences. Although the dress features the elegant style lines of an occasion gown, it is made of stretch cotton poplin, a casual fabric more typically used for sportswear. The simple lines appealed to Sherald, as did the graphic, minimalist print. The high contrast of black, grey and white projected a strong, modern spirit, while the colourful patterning on the skirt reminded Sherald of the quilts made by the women of Gee's Bend, a multi-generational enclave of African American quilt makers, based in rural Alabama, southwest of Selma, who maintain the distinctive craft aesthetic of their enslaved ancestors by repurposing the fabric of worn clothing into bold geometric designs.

In an interview in June 2021, Sherald offered a succinct explanation of her process: 'I painted Michelle Obama from the south side of Chicago … and then I painted the first lady.'[6] Posing and photographing Mrs Obama built a relationship between the two women as real individuals based on trust, intent and collaboration. Alone in the studio, Sherald took this experience of 'painting' Michelle Obama as the foundation for portraying the first lady of the forty-fourth American presidency. She positioned the figure within the composition to emphasize monumentality. While Mrs Obama is, in fact, a tall woman, Sherald portrayed the first lady as a towering figure; although she is

Photograph of Parker Curry looking at the Obama Portrait in the National Portrait Gallery 2018
Ben Hines

Two-year-old Parker Curry was so entranced by Mrs Obama's portrait that she did not respond to her mother's request to turn around and pose for a photograph. Another visitor, Ben Hines, captured the child on his phone's camera, standing absolutely still, and looking up with eyes wide and mouth open at the inspiring woman she thought was a queen.

seated, the viewer must look up to meet her gaze. The format of the composition can barely contain her form; her voluminous skirts spill beyond the limits of the frame. Her upper body rises out of those skirts like a figure emerging from a mountain, and the background – a pale, still blue – replaces the lush garden in the photograph with a cool, limitless sky. The silvery tones of her complexion magnify the remote aura of the figure; no longer simply a woman exuding the warmth of her personality, the first lady becomes a presence to be observed, acknowledged and admired. Yet the face and the graceful lines of her arms and hands are unmistakable. Sherald has taken her deep impression of Michelle Obama – an accomplished, intelligent, yet highly approachable and compassionate woman – and created an archetype to represent an extraordinary moment in American history. In her portrait of Michelle Obama, Sherald balances the individual with the universal in a way that is essential to her art: 'She represents who I paint: American people. They are Black people doing things. And Black people become the first lady.'[7]

On 12 February 2018, in her remarks prior to the unveiling of the Obama portraits at the National Portrait Gallery, Sherald linked Mrs Obama's qualities of heart, mind and character with those that she aspires to express through her paintings. Sherald reflected on the way that Mrs Obama connected with the public as first lady, stating that her 'authentic self became a profound statement that engaged us all'. And although the portrait represents an ideal, it is the woman portrayed that connects with the public: 'You exist in our minds and our hearts in the way you do because we can see ourselves in you.'[8] The unprecedented number of visitors to the gallery during the first year that the portraits were on display – 2.3 million visitors, more than double the previous annual attendance figures – offered the proof. One visitor, in particular, caught the nation's imagination. A photograph of two-year-old Parker Curry, looking up in wonder at Mrs Obama's portrait, became a viral sensation; just as Sherald sought to embody an ideal in Mrs Obama's image, little Parker saw her own potential through that ideal.[9] Both Obama portraits mark a new direction in an old tradition, for as Chicago-based photographer Dawoud Bey observes, 'The historic weight of the first Black president *had* to culminate in portraits made by Black artists, and not any Black artists, but two younger artists whose works embody a forward-looking approach to painting and portraiture.'[10] Only time will tell whether Sherald's portrait of Michelle Obama will be regarded as a masterpiece, but in the present moment, it is a remarkable example of representation.

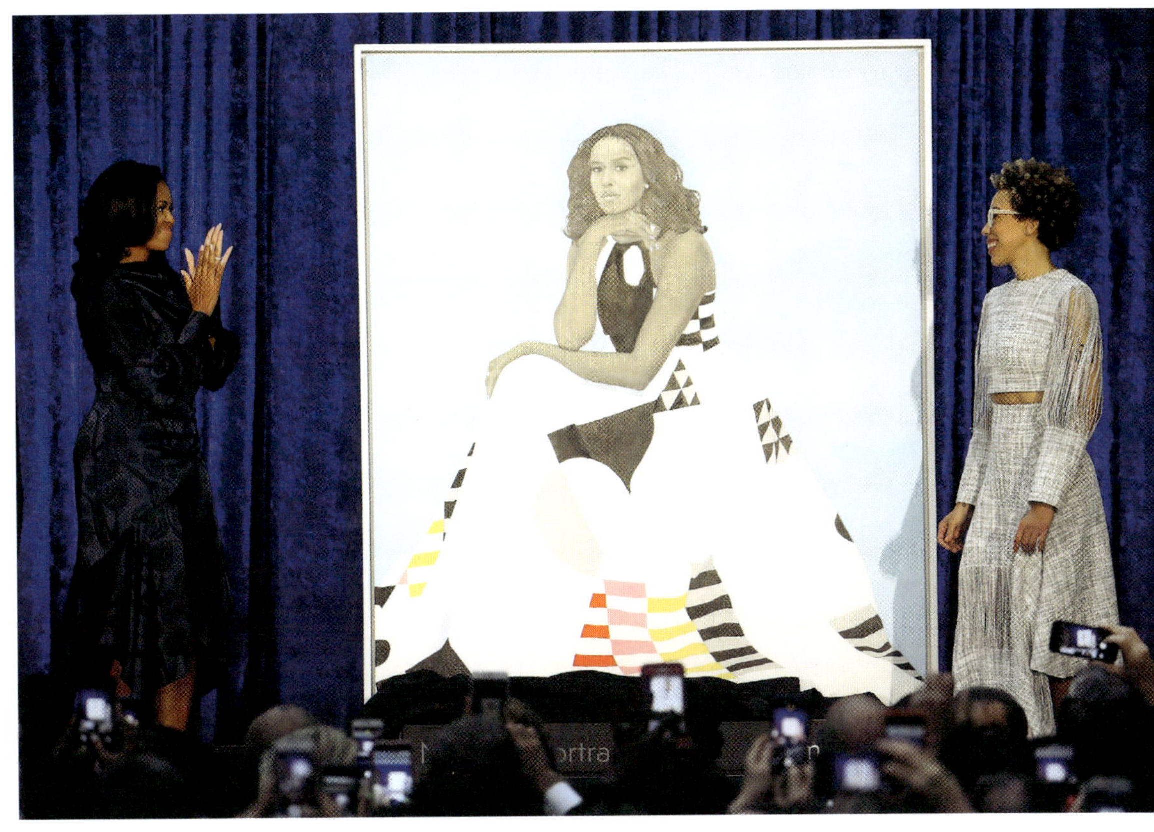

Photograph of Unveiling the Portrait Featuring Michelle Obama
and Amy Sherald

In their opening remarks at the unveiling, both Sherald and Mrs Obama
talked about their desire that children – and especially Black girls – see
themselves and their potential in the portrait. This is what Sherald means
by representation, to expand the cultural narrative to reflect a truer and
fuller account of American history.

Endnotes

BIRTH OF VENUS Sandro Botticelli
1. Ettore Modigliani, as quoted in Francis Haskell, *The Ephemeral Museum: Old Master Paintings and the Rise of the Art Exhibition* (New Haven and London: Yale University Press, 2000), p. 127. A high-standing arts official, Modigliani served as Director of the Pinacoteca di Brera and Superintendent of Monuments of Lombardy at the time of the exhibition. He was honoured as a Knight Commander of the Most Excellent Order of the British Empire (KBE) for his work in organizing the exhibition.
2. Hesiod, 'Theogony' ll. 194; 205–06, in *Hesiod, Works and Day and Theogony* (trans. Stanley Lombardo); Indianapolis/Cambridge: Hackett Publishing Company, Inc., 1993), pp. 66–67.
3. Agnolo Poliziano, *Stanze per la Giostra* (1475–78), as quoted in Frank Zöllner, *Botticelli* (Munich: Prestel Verlag, 2005), p. 136.
4. Poliziano, p. 136.
5. Giorgio Vasari, *The Lives of the Most Excellent Painters, Sculptors, and Architects* (trans. Gaston du C. de Vere); (New York: The Modern Library, 2006), p. 189.
6. Léon Lagrange (1862), as quoted in Ruben Rebmann, 'Botticelli Enters the Museum: The Rediscovery of a Painter and the Invention of the Public Art Museum', in Mark Evans and Stefan Weppelmann, *Botticelli Reimaged* (London: V&A Publishing, 2016), p. 54.
7. Walter Pater, *Studies in the History of the Renaissance* (London: Macmillan and Co., 1873), p. 48.

MONA LISA Leonardo da Vinci
1. Giorgio Vasari, *The Lives of the Most Excellent Painters, Sculptors, and Architects* (trans. Gaston du C. de Vere); (New York: The Modern Library, 2006), pp. 238–39.
2. Oscar Wilde, 'The Critic as Artist' (1890), in Richard Aldington and Stanley Weintraub (eds.), *The Portable Oscar Wilde* (New York: Penguin Books, 1981), p. 84. Wilde is quoting the words of Walter Pater from his essay on Leonardo da Vinci, included in *Studies in the History of the Renaissance* (1873).
3. Vasari, p. 238.

4. As quoted in Martin Kemp and Guiseppe Pallanti, *Mona Lisa: the People and the Painting* (Oxford University Press, 2017), p. 104. See Chapter VI, 'Renaissance Records' (pp. 101–18) for a full overview of documents that counter the so-called 'mystery' of the sitter's identity.
5. Père Pierre Dan, *Le trésor des merveilles de la maison royal de Fontainbleau* (1625), as quoted in Kemp, p. 115.
6. Vasari, p. 239.
7. As quoted in Kemp, p. 115.
8. As quoted in Donald Sassoon, *Becoming Mona Lisa: The Making of a Global Icon* (New York: Harcourt, Inc., 2001), p. 114.
9. For a thorough overview of this literature, see Sassoon, Chapter 5, 'Mona Lisa Becomes Mysterious', pp. 91–132.
10. Walter Pater, *Studies in the History of the Renaissance* (1873); (London: Macmillan and Co., 1912), pp. 125–27.
11. Wilde, p. 84.
12. As quoted in Sassoon, p.164.
13. Jason Farago, 'It's Time to Take Down the *Mona Lisa*', *New York Times*, 6 November 2019. Farago slyly calls the work the 'Kim Kardashian of 16th-century Italian portraiture' and suggests that the museum and visitors alike would be better served if the work was moved to its own venue.

JUDITH BEHEADING HOLOFERNES Artemisia Gentilechi
1. To differentiate between members of the Gentileschi family, they will be identified by their first names. This conforms to prevalent practice in current scholarship.
2. Artemisia Gentileschi to Antonio Ruffo (30 January 1649), as quoted in Letizia Treves, et al., *Artemisia* (London: National Gallery Company, 2020), p. 66.
3. Orazio Gentileschi to Christina of Lorraine, Dowager Grand Duchess of Tuscany (1612), as quoted in Treves, et al., *Artemisia*, pp. 108–109.
4. Elizabeth S. Cohen, 'The Trials of Artemisia Gentileschi: A Rape as History', *The Sixteenth Century Journal* 31:1 (Spring 2000), p. 59.
5. Letizia Treves, et al., *Artemisia* (London:

National Gallery Company, 2020), p. 129 and Jesse M. Locker, *Artemisia Gentileschi: The Language of Painting* (New Haven and London: Yale University Press, 2015), p. 173.
6. *Artemisia*, National Gallery, London, 4 April–20 July 2020.
7. Artemisia Gentileschi to Antonio Ruffo (7 August 1949), as quoted in Treves, et al., p. 66.

GIRL WITH A PEARL EARRING Johannes Vermeer
1. As quoted in Arthur K. Wheelock, Jr. (ed.), *Johannes Vermeer* (Washington DC: National Gallery of Art, 1995), p. 168.
2. *Frankfurter Zeitung* (23 March 1903), as quoted in Wheelock, p. 168; n. 15.
3. As quoted in Benjamin Binstock, *Vermeer's Family Secrets: Genius, Discovery, and the Unknown Apprentice* (New York: Routledge, 2009), p. 178.
4. Binstock, p. 307. In this context the term 'antique dress' refers to a general mode of fancy dress rather than historically accurate classical garments.
5. John Updike, 'Head of a Girl, at the Met', *Facing Nature* (New York: Alfred A. Knopf, 1985), p. 52.
6. As quoted in Jonathan Janson, 'Interview with Tracy Chevalier', *Essential Vermeer.com* (1 August 2003).

THE GREAT WAVE Katsushika Hokusai
1. Advertisement (1831), as quoted in Timothy Clark (ed.), *Hokusai: Beyond the Great Wave* (London: Thames & Hudson/British Museum, 2017), p. 108.
2. Asai Ryōi, *Ukiyo Monogatori (Tales of the Floating World*; 1691), as quoted in Gary Hickey, *Beauty and Desire in Edo Period Japan* (Canberra: National Gallery of Australia, 1998), p. 8.
3. This was not an uncommon practice, especially among artists, who often passed their 'art names' on to a favoured pupil, but the number of times is highly unusual.
4. A. Hyatt Mayor, 'Hokusai', *The Metropolitan Museum of Art Bulletin*, 43:1 (Summer 1985), p. 7. In discussing the work, Mayor notes that one translation of the word is 'curious'.
5. Timothy Clark explains that since the use of the Westernized title in the 2005 retrospective

Hokusai exhibition at the Tokyo National Museum 'ordinary Japanese people' use it 'affectionately and in recognition of its ever-growing iconic status'. Clark, *Hokusai's Great Wave* (London: The British Museum Press, 2011), p. 23. Christine M.E. Guth, using the transliteration *guerto uebu*, describes the title as an 'Anglophone characterization'. Guth, *Hokusai's Great Wave: Biography of a Global Icon* (Honolulu: University of Hawaii Press, 2015), p. 4.
6. Christie's New York, Japanese and Korean Art, Asian Art Week, Lot 144, 16 March 2021, accessed 8 April 2021.

FIFTEEN SUNFLOWERS Vincent van Gogh
1. Émile Bernard to Albert Aurier, 31 July 1890, as quoted in Robert Pickvance, *'A Great Artist is Dead': Letters of Condolence on Vincent van Gogh's Death* (Amsterdam: Van Gogh Museum, 1992), p. 34.
2. Vincent van Gogh to Horace Livens (September/October 1886), *Vincent van Gogh – The Letters: The complete illustrated and annotated edition* (2009), Letter 569. www.vangoghletters.org, accessed 10 December 2020.
3. Vincent van Gogh to Willemien van Gogh (October 1887), *Vincent van Gogh – The Letters: The complete illustrated and annotated edition* (2009), Letter 574. www.vangoghletters.org, accessed 10 December 2020.
4. Vincent van Gogh to Horace Livens (September/October 1886), *Vincent van Gogh – The Letters: The complete illustrated and annotated edition* 2009, Letter 569. www.vangoghletters.org, accessed 10 December 2020.
5. Vincent van Gogh to Willemien van Gogh (9 & 14 September 1888), *Vincent van Gogh – The Letters: The complete illustrated and annotated edition* 2009, Letter 678. www.vangoghletters.org, accessed 10 December 2020.
6. Vincent van Gogh to Theo van Gogh (9 September 1888), *Vincent van Gogh – The Letters: The complete illustrated and annotated edition* 2009, Letter 677. www.vangoghletters.org, accessed 14 December 2020.
7. Vincent van Gogh to Theo van Gogh (12 August 1888), *Vincent van Gogh – The Letters: The complete illustrated and annotated edition* 2009, Letter 659. www.vangoghletters.org, accessed 14 December 2020.

8. Vincent van Gogh to Theo van Gogh (21 or 22 August 1888), *Vincent van Gogh – The Letters: The complete illustrated and annotated edition* 2009, Letter 666. www.vangoghletters.org, accessed 14 December 2020.
9. See Martin Baily, *The Sunflowers are Mine: the Story of Van Gogh's Masterpiece* (London: Frances Lincoln Limited, 2013), pp. 51–52 ff. for the best documented and the most insightful account of the sunflower series.
10. Vincent van Gogh to Theo van Gogh (21 or 22 August 1888), *Vincent van Gogh – The Letters: The complete illustrated and annotated edition* 2009, Letter 666. www.vangoghletters.org, accessed 14 December 2020.
11. Vincent van Gogh to Theo van Gogh (on or about 29 October 1888), *Vincent van Gogh – The Letters: The complete illustrated and annotated edition* 2009, Letter 715. www.vangoghletters.org, accessed 18 December 2020.
12. Vincent van Gogh to Theo van Gogh (22 January 1889), *Vincent van Gogh – The Letters: The complete illustrated and annotated edition* 2009, Letter 741. www.vangoghletters.org, accessed 18 December 2020. The phrase, which he also shared in a letter to Gauguin with slightly different wording (21 January 1889, Letter 739), has been also translated, 'the sunflower is mine, in a way'.
13. Vincent van Gogh to Willemien van Gogh (19 February 1890), *Vincent van Gogh – The Letters: The complete illustrated and annotated edition* 2009, Letter 856. www.vangoghletters.org, accessed 18 December 2020.

WOMAN IN GOLD Gustav Klimt
1. Emil Pirchan (1942), as quoted in Anne-Marie O'Connor, *The Lady in Gold, The Extraordinary Tale of Gustav Klimt's Masterpiece, Portrait of Adele Block-Bauer* (New York: Vintage Books, Penguin Random House, 2012), p. 151.
2. Sophie Lillie and Georg Gaugusch, *Portrait of Adele-Bloch-Bauer* (New York: Neue Galerie, 2007), p. 15.
3. Adele Bloch Bauer to Julius Bauer (22 August 1903), as quoted in Tobias G. Natter (ed.), *Klimt and the Women of Vienna's Golden Age, 1900–1918* (Munich: Prestel, 2016), p. 128.
4. Adele had a deformed finger on her right hand. Her hand gestures are generally attributed to her desire to hide it.
5. Ludwig Hevesi, *Gustav Klimt und die Malmosaik* (1907), as quoted in O'Connor, pp. 58–9.
6. As quoted in Natter, p. 130.
7. Adele and Ferdinand's only children did not survive infancy.
8. For a summary of the seizure and dispersal of the Bloch-Bauer possessions, see Lillie and Gaugusch, pp. 68–72.
9. Ferdinand Bloch-Bauer to Oskar Kokoschka (1941), as quoted in Lillie and Gaugusch, p. 74.
10. The restitution case deserves more detail and analysis than possible in this brief essay. For an insightful and lively account see the documentary *Adele's Wish* (dir. Terrence Turner), Calendar Films, 2008.

AMERICAN GOTHIC Grant Wood
1. Grant Wood, interview in the *Chicago Leader* (25 December 1930), as quoted in Thomas Hoving, *American Gothic: The Biography of Grant Wood's American Masterpiece* (New York: Chamberlain Bros./Penguin Group, 2005), p. 64.
2. Although the word 'bronze' generally indicates third place, this was an award for second place. See Judith A. Barter, et al., *American Modernism at the Art Institute of Chicago, From World War I to 1955* (Chicago: Art Institute of Chicago/Yale University Press, 2009), cat. 79; p. 178. Along with the medal, Wood received a monetary award of $300 (equal to $4,700 in 2021). The purchase price for the painting brought an additional $300.
3. 'Wood, Hard-Bitten', *Art Digest* (1 February 1936), p. 18.
4. Nan Wood Graham, with John Zug and Julie Jensen McDonald, *My Brother, Grant Wood* (Iowa City: State Historical Society of Iowa, 1993), p. 69.
5. Grant Wood, in 'An Iowa Secret', *Art Digest*, 8:1 (1 October 1933), p. 6.
6. For a concise summary of this initial reaction and a selection of quotations from the letters, see, Steven Biel *American Gothic: A Life of America's Most Famous Painting* (New York and London: W. W. Norton & Company Limited, 2005), pp. 46–51.
7. As quoted in Nan Wood Graham, with John Zug and Julie Jensen McDonald, p. 75.
8. Gordon Parks, 'Half Past Autumn', interview with Phil Ponce *News Hour PBS.org* (6 January 1998.

GUERNICA Pablo Picasso
1. The exact number of dead and wounded remains a subject for debate, varying as widely as 150 to 1,650, depending upon the political affiliation of the source. The most commonly cited numbers confirm the high death toll, with at least 800 wounded. The population at the time was roughly 7,000.
2. His donations are estimated at 400,000 francs. Patricia Leighton, 'Artists in Times of War', *The Art Bulletin* 91:1 (March 2009), p. 41.
3. As quoted in Leighton, p. 41. He issued the statement in May or June 1937.
4. T.J. Clark, *Picasso and Truth: From Cubism to Guernica*. Princeton University Press/Washington, DC (National Gallery of Art, 2013, p. 243). Clark cites the finishing date as 4 June or 'very soon after' (p. 242).
5. As quoted in Eberhard Fisch, *Guernica by Picasso: A Study of the Picture and Its Context* (trans. James Hotchkiss); (London and Toronto: Associated University Presses, 1988), p. 56.
6. Anthony Blunt, *The Spectator*, 23 October 1937, p. 19.
7. Herbert Read, 'Picasso's Guernica', *London Bulletin*, October 1938, p. 6.
8. The details of legal ownership are not clear. Picasso received payment from the government – 150,000 francs – but retained rights of ownership and made the final decisions about when the painting would tour and where it would be exhibited. See Fisch, p. 19.
9. *Guernica* was replicated in tapestry, with Picasso's permission, in 1955 by the Atelier J. de la Baume-Dürrbach. Nelson Rockefeller purchased one of the three versions created and, in 1984, loaned it to the United Nations in New York to be displayed in the hallway outside the Security Council. It has recently been taken down and returned to the Rockefeller family without a reason for removal. See Kabir Jhala, 'Tapestry replica of Picasso's antiwar masterpiece *Guernica* removed from United Nations headquarters after 35 years', *The Art Newspaper*, 26 February 2021.

SELF-PORTRAIT WITH THORN NECKLACE AND HUMMINGBIRD Frida Kahlo
1. Addison Burbank, *Mexican Frieze* (New York: Coward-McCann, Inc., 1941), p. 27. I am grateful to Sarah Lea Burns for this reference. Burbank does not date this anecdote, but he mentions that Rivera and Kahlo were separated and that he saw *Two Fridas* in Kahlo's studio. That situates the visit in 1939 prior to the couple's divorce in November.
2. See, for example, Celia Stahr, *Frida in America: The Creative Awakening of a Great Artist* (New York: St. Martin's Press, 2020), p. 59. The source is never attributed, so it may be hearsay.
3. Frida Kahlo to Matilde Calderón (November 1930), as quoted in Claire Wilcox and Circe Henestrosa (eds.), *Frida Kahlo: Making Herself Up* (London: V&A Publishing, 2018), p. 146.
4. Helen Appleton Read, *Boston Evening Transcript*, 22 October 1930, p. 45.
5. Bertram Wolfe, 'The Rise of Madame Rivera', *Vogue*, 1 November 1938, p. 131. Wolfe was a friend of Diego Rivera as well as his biographer.
6. Frida Kahlo, as quoted, Salomon Grimberg, *Frida Kahlo: Song of Herself* (London: Merrell, 2008), p. 87.
7. Olga Campos (around 1949–1950), as quoted in Wilcox, p. 115, note 1.
8. Hayden Herrera, 'Frida Kahlo's Legacy: The Power of Self', in Elizabeth Carpenter (ed.), *Frida Kahlo* (Minneapolis: Walker Art Center, 2008), p. 56.
9. Gabriel Reno, as quoted in Amanda Mauer, 'Frida Fixation', *Chicago Tribune*, 'Q' Section (29 July 2007), p. 3. In addition to Tehuana dress and a crown of braids, fifteen-year-old Reno wore a stuffed monkey on her shoulder as part of her costume. Her prizes included books on Mexican art, passes to local museums, and a bottle of 'Frida Tequila'.

CAMPBELL'S SOUP CANS Andy Warhol
1. Irving Blum, in Peter M. Brandt, 'Irving Blum', *Interview Magazine*, 30 March 2012, accessed 13 April 2021, www.interviewmagazine.com/culture/irving-blum-1
2. Born Andrew Warhola, Warhol began to use the shorter version of his name in college; after his move to New York in 1949, he used 'Andy Warhol' both professionally and privately.
3. As quoted in Blake Gopnik, *Warhol* (New York: HarperCollins Publishers, 2020), p. 227. Gopnik states that Latow insisted on getting her check before she shared her idea.
4. Gopnik, p. 259.
5. As quoted in Gopnik, p. 260. Blum was selling

the works for $100 per canvas.
6. Marcel Duchamp, as quoted in Rosalind Constable, 'New York's Avant-Garde and How it It Got There', *New York Herald Tribune*, 17 May 1964, p. 10.
7. Blum told Peter Brandt that he received $15,000 from the museum. It is impossible to fix a price on the series today. See Brandt.

MICHELLE OBAMA Amy Sherald
1. Michelle Obama, remarks at the unveiling ceremony of the presentation of the Obama portraits, 12 February 2018, transcript in Taína Caragol, Dorothy Moss, Richard J. Powell and Kim Sajet, *The Obama Portraits* (Washington, DC: National Portrait Gallery, Smithsonian Institution/Princeton University Press, 2020), p. 108.
2. Carl Sferazza Anthony, *First Ladies: The Saga of the Presidents' Wives and Their Power* (New York: HarperCollins, 1990), p. 147.
3. Michelle Obama (25 July 2016), the 2016 Democratic National Convention. Accessed 3 August 2021, www.youtube.com/watch?v=zHnJ2sTlVUI
4. Amy Sherald, remarks at the unveiling ceremony of the presentation of the Obama portraits, 12 February 2018, transcript in Caragol, et al., p. 111.
5. Michelle Obama, as quoted in Caragol, et al., p. 38.
6. Amy Sherald, 17 June 2021, Art Institute of Chicago, 'Virtual Conversation: The Obama Portraits', 17 June 2021. Accessed 3 August 2021, www.youtube.com/watch?v=xgPETz1pLQ4
7. Amy Sherald, as quoted in wall text in the exhibition, The Obama Portraits, Art Institute of Chicago, 18 June–15 August 2021.
8. Amy Sherald, remarks at the unveiling ceremony of the presentation of the Obama portraits, 12 February 2018, transcript in Caragol, et al., p. 115.
9. With her mother's help, Parker Curry turned her experience of viewing the portrait into a storybook titled *Parker Looks Up* (New York: Aladdin, 2019). When Parker sees the portrait, which reminds her of her mother, her grandmother and herself, she wonders: 'How could someone look so real and so magical at the same time?'.
10. Dawoud Bey, as quoted in Christopher Borelli, 'A Chicago Story', *Chicago Tribune* Arts & Entertainment, Section 4, 13 June 2021, p. 2.

Select Bibliography

Sandro Botticelli
Mark Evans and Stefan Weppelmann, *Botticelli Reimaged*. London: V&A Publishing, 2016.
Francis Haskell, *The Ephemeral Museum: Old Master Paintings and the Rise of the Art Exhibition*. New Haven and London: Yale University Press, 2000.
Frank Zöllner, *Botticelli*. Munich: Prestel Verlag, 2005.

Leonardo da Vinci
Milton Esterow, *The Art Stealers*. New York: The Macmillan Company, 1966.
Martin Kemp and Guiseppe Pallanti, *Mona Lisa: the People and the Painting*. Oxford University Press, 2017.
Donald Sassoon, *Becoming Mona Lisa: The Making of a Global Icon*. New York: Harcourt, Inc., 2001.

Artemisia Gentileschi
Jesse M. Locker, *Artemisia Gentileschi: The Language of Painting*. New Haven and London: Yale University Press, 2015.
Eve Straussman-Pflanzer, *Violence & Virtue: Artemisia Gentileschi's Judith Slaying Holofernes*. New Haven and London: Yale University Press/The Art Institute of Chicago, 2013.
Letizia Treves, et al. *Artemisia*. London: National Gallery Company, 2020.

Johannes Vermeer
Lea van der Vinde, *Girl with a Pearl Earring: Dutch Paintings from the Mauritshuis*. Munich: Delmonico Books-Prestel, 2013.
Arthur K. Wheelock, Jr. (ed.), *Johannes Vermeer*. Washington DC: National Gallery of Art, 1995.

Katsushika Hokusai
Jocelyn Bouguillard, *Hokusai's Mount Fuji* (trans. Mark Getlein). New York: Abrams, 2007.
Timothy Clark (ed.), *Hokusai: Beyond the Great Wave*. London: Thames & Hudson/British Museum, 2017.
Timothy Clark, *Hokusai's Great Wave*. London: The British Museum Press, 2011.
Christine M.E. Guth, *Hokusai's Great Wave: Biography of a Global Icon*. Honolulu: University of Hawaii Press, 2015.

Vincent van Gogh
Martin Bailey, *The Sunflowers are Mine: the Story of Van Gogh's Masterpiece*. London: Frances Lincoln Limited, 2013.
Debra N. Mancoff, *Sunflowers*. London: Thames & Hudson, 2001.
Vincent van Gogh—The Letters: The complete illustrated and annotated edition 2009 www.vangoghletters.org

Gustav Klimt
Sophie Lillie and Georg Gaugusch, *Portrait of Adele Bloch-Bauer*. New York: Neue Galerie, 2007.
Tobias G. Natter (ed.), *Klimt and the Women of Vienna's Golden Age, 1900-1918*. Munich: Prestel, 2016.
Anne-Marie O'Connor, *The Lady in Gold, The Extraordinary Tale of Gustav Klimt's Masterpiece, Portrait of Adele Block-Bauer*. New York: Vintage Books, Penguin Random House, 2012.

Grant Wood
Judith A. Barter, et al., *American Modernism at the Art Institute of Chicago, From World War I to 1955*. Chicago: Art Institute of Chicago/Yale University Press, 2009, cat. 79.
Steven Biel, *American Gothic: A Life of America's Most Famous Painting*. New York and London: W. W. Norton & Company Limited, 2005.
Nan Wood Graham, with John Zug and Julie Jensen McDonald, *My Brother, Grant Wood*. Iowa City: State Historical Society of Iowa, 1993.

Pablo Picasso
Rudolf Arnheim, *Picasso's Guernica: The Genesis of a Painting*. Berkeley: University of California Press, 2006.
Eberhard Fisch, *Guernica by Picasso: A Study of the Picture and Its Context* (trans. James Hotchkiss). London and Toronto: Associated University Presses, 1988.
T.J. Clark, *Picasso and Truth: From Cubism to Guernica*. Princeton University Press/ Washington, DC, National Gallery of Art, 2013.
T.J. Clark, et al., *Pity and Terror: Picasso's Path to "Guernica"*. Madrid: Museo Nacional Centro de Arte Reina Sofía, 2017.

Frida Kahlo
Elizabeth Carpenter (ed.), *Frida Kahlo*. Minneapolis: Walker Art Center, 2007.
Celia Stahr, *Frida in America: The Creative Awakening of a Great Artist*. New York: St. Martin's Press, 2020.
Claire Wilcox and Circe Henestrosa (eds.), *Frida Kahlo: Making Herself Up*. London: V&A Publishing, 2018.

Andy Warhol
David Bourdon, *Warhol*. New York: Harry N. Abrams, Inc., 1989.
Blake Gopnik, *Warhol*. New York: HarperCollins Publishers, 2020.
Kynaston McShine, *Andy Warhol: A Retrospective*. ex. cat. New York: Museum of Modern Art, 1989.

Amy Sherald
Taína Caragol, Dorothy Moss, Richard J. Powell and Kim Sajet, *The Obama Portraits*. Washington, DC: National Portrait Gallery, Smithsonian Institution/Princeton University Press, 2020.
Lisa Melandri and Erin Christovale, *Amy Sherald*. St Louis: Contemporary Art Museum, 2018.
Gwendolyn DuBois Shaw, *First Ladies of the United States*. Washington, DC: Smithsonian Books, 2020.

Index

Picture Credits

The publishers would like to thank the institutions, picture libraries, artists, galleries and photographers for their kind permission to reproduce the works featured in this book. Every effort has been made to trace all copyright holders but if any have been inadvertently overlooked, the publishers would be pleased to make the necessary arrangements at the first opportunity.

Acknowledgements

The creation of a book involves talents and ideas beyond those of the author, and I would like to thank the people who helped bring *Making a Masterpiece* to publication. First and foremost, at Frances Lincoln, I thank Nicki Davis; for her ideas, guidance, and creative insights which ignited and sustained the project, along with her beautiful design. My sincere gratitude to Joe Hallsworth for his careful editing of the manuscript and illustrations. I would like to thank The Newberry Library for its ongoing support of my research, with special appreciation to Daniel Greene, President and Librarian, Keelin Burke, Director of Fellowships and Academic Programs, Madeline Crispell, Program Coordinator, and Margaret Cusick, General Collection Services Librarian. I am deeply grateful as well for the kind and helpful staff of the Popular Library at the Harold Washington Library Center in Chicago, most notably Leslie Patterson and Christina Cochard. For their response to my research queries, I thank Sarah Lea Burns, Professor Emeritus of Art History, Indiana University Bloomington; Wanda M. Corn, Robert and Ruth Halperin Professor Emerita in Art History, Stanford University; Annelise K. Madsen, Gilda and Henry Buchbinder Associate Curator, Arts of America, The Art Institute of Chicago; Greg Nosan, Associate Vice President, Publishing and Interpretation, The Art Institute of Chicago; Michal Raz-Russo, Programs Director, The Gordon Parks Foundation; and Brandon Ruud, Abert Family Curator of American Art, Milwaukee Art Museum. Thanks as well to Melvin L. Askew, Donald L. Hoffman, Kevin J. Harty, Richard Tempone, Patricia Wieber, Robert Wieber, Jeanne Steen, and, especially Paul B. Jaskot, for their generous interest and encouragement throughout the project.

This book is dedicated to my aunt, Fern Rothblatt, who makes every space that she graces a masterpiece.

Debra N. Mancoff
Scholar-in-Residence, The Newberry Library

About the Author

Debra N. Mancoff is an art historian and the author of more than twenty books on European and American art and culture. She lectures regularly at many of the major museums in the United States and United Kingdom. Based in Chicago, she is a Scholar-in-Residence at the Newberry Library.

FRANCES
LINCOLN

First published in 2022 by Frances Lincoln,
an imprint of The Quarto Group.
The Old Brewery, 6 Blundell Street
London, N7 9BH
United Kingdom
T (0)20 7700 6700
www.Quarto.com

Text © 2022 Debra N. Mancoff

Every effort has been made to trace the copyright holders of material quoted
in this book. If application is made in writing to the publisher, any omissions
will be included in future editions.

A catalogue record for this book is available from the British Library.

ISBN 978-0-7112-5707-8
Ebook ISBN 978-0-7112-5708-5

10 9 8 7 6 5 4 3 2 1

Design by Nicki Davis

Printed in China

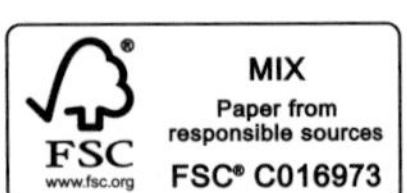